WORLD SOCCER RECORDS

This edition published in 2016

Copyright © Carlton Books Limited 2016

Carlton Books Limited
20 Mortimer Street
London W1T 3JW

A CIP catalogue record for this book is available from
the British Library

10 9 8 7 6 5 4 3 2 1

ISBN: 978-1-78097-864-2

Editor: Martin Corteel
Designers: Darren Jordan & Luke Griffin
Picture research: Paul Langan
Production: Lisa Cook

Printed in Dubai

Publisher's Note
Other than in its title, this book uses football
rather than soccer as the term for the game, as it
is predominately known around the world.

Right: Cristiano Ronaldo shows off the Henri Delaunay Trophy after
Portugal had won the 2016 UEFA European Football Championship
with a 1-0 extra-victory over hosts France in the final.

Next pages (left to right): Top: Gareth Bale (Wales), Clint Dempsey
(United States): **Middle:** Jerome Boateng (Germany), Antoine Griezmann
(France), Alexis Sanchez (Chile); **Bottom:** Leonardo Bonucci (Italy),
Cristiano Ronaldo (Portugal), Lionel Messi (Argentina).

WORLD SOCCER RECORDS

EIGHTH EDITION

KEIR RADNEDGE

CARLTON
BOOKS

CONTENTS

INTRODUCTION

FOOTBALL remains more than ever a global phenomenon. In another, former, era it was merely the most popular of a grand sweep of sports but the media and sponsorship explosion during the last three decades has fuelled the sport's rise to a different plane entirely.

The worldwide following for Euro 2016, the finals of the UEFA European Championship in France, proved the point. Television coverage took the 51 matches to homes in more than 215 countries, that is a tally beyond the registered memberships of world football federation FIFA, or the International Olympic Committee, or even the United Nations.

Simultaneously the riches of the modern game were doubled up with the staging in the United States of a tournament to mark the centenary of the South American championship, the Copa America. Portugal and Chile were the ultimately triumphant national teams in the two trans-continental football extravaganzas.

Football never stands still. Progress appears permanent. Thus Portugal won a major title for the first time at Euro 2016 and the Copa America Centenario brought unique co-operation between the two confederations of Central/North America and South America. At a time when the leadership of the international game had come under greater scrutiny than ever before these were positive signals.

The year ahead promises much more of the same, with a concentrated focus on the qualifying competition for the 2018 FIFA World Cup in Russia plus the 2017 Africa Cup of Nations finals in Gabon as well as a further edition of the CONCACAF Gold Cup.

A factor which mesmerizes fans is football's mixture of both team tradition with individual expertise. This has been represented in outstanding goalscoring fashion by the likes of Portugal's Cristiano Ronaldo and Argentina's Lionel Messi with both their countries and their clubs Real Madrid and Barcelona – respectively the 2016 European and Spanish champions.

All the many aspects of this grand football landscape feature in this latest, eighth edition of *World Soccer Records*. Here are the achievements and stars, old and new, from all of football's major international tournaments for men and women at senior and junior levels.

Keir Radnedge
London, July 2016

In what proved to be the tournament of the underdog, Iceland reached the Euro 2016 quarter-finals and the support from their fans will be one of the enduring memories of the competition.

PART 1:
THE COUNTRIES

SOME call it soccer, others say *futbol* or *calcio* or *futebol* – but go to virtually any country on earth and someone will be speaking about this game by whatever label. Association football knows no boundaries of race or politics or religion.

The structure is simple, helping ensure the sport's international success. At the head of the world football pyramid is FIFA, the world federation. Supporting FIFA's work are the six regional geographical confederations representing Africa, Asia, Europe, Oceania, South America, plus the Caribbean, Central and North America. Backing up the regions in turn are the national associations of 211 countries – and thus FIFA can boast more member countries than even the United Nations or the Olympic movement.

The countries are pivotal. They field the national teams who have built sporting history through their many and varied achievements in world-focused competitions such as the FIFA World Cup. But they also oversee the growth of football in their nation – from professional leagues to the game at grass-roots level.

Representative teams from England and Scotland played out the first formal internationals in the late 19th century, thus laying the foundation for the four British home nations' unique independent status within a world football family otherwise comprised of nation states. The original British Home Championships was the first competition for national teams but its demise, as a result of a congested fixture list, has left the Copa America in South America as the oldest survivor – apart from the Olympic Games.

The trend-setting example of the Olympic Games in the 1920s led directly to the creation of the FIFA World Cup and its launch in 1930. Already South America had its own national team championship and all the other five FIFA regions followed in due course. The winners meet once every four years in the FIFA Confederations Cup which is the rehearsal event for the extravaganza, one year later, which is the FIFA World Cup itself – the ultimate celebration of the planet's favourite sport.

The draw for the European section of the FIFA World Cup 2018 qualifying campaign took place in St Petersburg, Russia, in July 2015. Europe's qualifying competition began in earnest in September 2016.

EUROPE

As soon as modern association football's rules were written in England the game's growth was rapid – enthusiasm spreading swiftly across Europe, the cradle of the game. UEFA, the European football confederation, now boasts 55 member states, from tiny Andorra and Gibraltar to world giants, Spain, Germany, Italy, England, the Netherlands and France. The game is played and followed with a fervent passion across the continent, not only at club but also at national levels. Portugal are the reigning European champions after triumphing at Euro 2016.

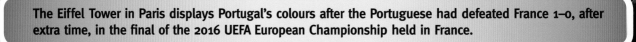

The Eiffel Tower in Paris displays Portugal's colours after the Portuguese had defeated France 1–0, after extra time, in the final of the 2016 UEFA European Championship held in France.

ENGLAND

England is where football began; the country where the game was first developed, which saw the creation of the game's first Football Association and the first organized league, and which now plays host to the richest domestic league in the world. But England have not had it all their own way on the international scene. Far from it. One solitary FIFA World Cup win apart, as hosts in 1966, the Three Lions have found it hard to shake off the "underachievers" tag when it comes to major tournaments.

IF THE CAP FITS

England's players in the historic first game against Scotland all wore **cricket-style caps** while the Scots wore hoods. England's "fashion statement" prompted the use of the term "cap" to refer to any international appearance. The tradition of awarding a cap to British international footballers still survives today.

HAVE A BASH, ASH

Left-back **Ashley Cole** is one of only nine England footballers to win 100 caps but is the only outfield player to reach the mark without ever having scored a goal – next on the list is Gary Neville (85 caps). He overtook Kenny Sansom as England's most-capped full-back when he represented his country for the 87th time, against Denmark in February 2011, and made his 100th appearance against Brazil at Wembley in February 2013. Cole's 98th international, against Italy in the Euro 2012 quarter-final, ended unhappily, as he missed England's final penalty in the shoot-out. But Cole did set another record that day: his 22nd finals match is the most by an England player. After 107 apperances, Cole announced his retirement from international football after being omitted from England's 2014 FIFA World Cup squad. In the club game he boasts more FA Cup winner's medals than any other player, three with Arsenal and four with Chelsea.

RUNAWAY SUCCESS

England have hit double figures five times: beating Ireland 13-0 and 13-2 in 1882 and 1899, thrashing Austria 11-1 in 1908, crushing Portugal 10-0 in Lisbon in 1947 and then the United States 10-0 in 1964 in New York. The ten goals were scored by Roger Hunt (four), Fred Pickering (three), Terry Paine (two) and **Bobby Charlton**.

IN THE BEGINNING

The day it all began ... 30 November 1872, when England played their first official international match, against Scotland, at Hamilton Crescent, Partick. The result was a 0-0 draw in front of a then massive crowd of 4,000, who each paid an admission fee of one shilling (5p). In fact, teams representing England and Scotland had played five times before, but most of the Scottish players had been based in England and the matches are considered unofficial. England's team for the first official game was selected by Charles Alcock, the secretary of the Football Association. His one regret was that, because of injury, he could not pick himself to play. In contrast, the first rugby union international between England and Scotland had been played in 1871, but England's first Test cricket match was not played until March 1877, against Australia in Melbourne.

FIRST DEFEAT

Hungary's 6-3 win at Wembley in 1953 was the first time England had lost at home to continental opposition. Their first home defeat by non-British opposition came against the Republic of Ireland, who beat them 2-0 at Goodison Park, Liverpool, in 1949.

FROZEN OUT

After overseeing England's worst performance at a FIFA World Cup finals in 2014, manager Roy Hodgson quit immediately after his side were eliminated from the 2016 UEFA European Championship in what many thought the country's most embarrassing defeat: a 2-1 second-round loss to Iceland. In Brazil, England had lost twice, to Italy and Uruguay, before drawing a meaningless game with group-winners Costa Rica. Despite then qualifying with a 100 per cent record for Euro 2016, another disappointing tournament left Hodgson with little option but to go, after winning just three tournament games out of ten since his appointment just before the 2012 UEFA European Championship.

ENGLAND'S BIGGEST WINS

1882	Ireland 0 England 13
1899	England 13 Ireland 2
1908	Austria 1 England 11
1964	United States 0 England 10
1947	Portugal 0 England 10
1982	England 9 Luxembourg 0
1960	Luxembourg 0 England 9
1895	England 9 Ireland 0
1927	Belgium 1 England 9
1896	Wales 1 England 9
1890	Ireland 1 England 9

ENGLAND'S BIGGEST DEFEATS

1954	Hungary 7 England 1
1878	Scotland 7 England 2
1881	England 1 Scotland 6
1958	Yugoslavia 5 England 0
1964	Brazil 5 England 1
1928	England 1 Scotland 5
1882	Scotland 5 England 1
1953	England 3 Hungary 6
1963	France 5 England 2
1931	France 5 England 2

NAUGHTY BOYS

Raheem Sterling's red card against Ecuador in June 2014 was the 15th for an England player in a full international. Alan Mullery was England's first player to be dismissed, against Yugoslavia in June 1968. David Beckham and Wayne Rooney have both been sent off twice. **Paul Scholes** was the only England player to be sent off at the old Wembley Stadium, against Sweden in June 1999.

SENIOR MOMENT

Goalkeeper David James became the oldest player ever to make his FIFA World Cup finals debut, aged 39 years and 321 days, when he appeared for England at the 2010 competition in South Africa. He kept a clean sheet in a goalless Group C draw against Algeria.

HEAD FOR GOAL

Robust and commanding centre-backs had the honour of scoring both the last England goal at the old Wembley stadium, closed down in 2000, and the first in the new version, which was finally opened in 2007. Tony Adams scored England's second in a 2-0 win over Ukraine in May 2000 – Germany's Dietmar Hamann hit the only goal of the final international at the old Wembley, four months later – and captain **John Terry** headed his side ahead in the new stadium's showpiece June 2007 friendly against Brazil, which ended 1-1. Terry shares the honour of scoring the most England goals (six) by a defender with 1966 FIFA World Cup winner Jack Charlton.

BLANKS OF ENGLAND

A goalless draw against Algeria in Cape Town in June 2010 made England the first country to finish 10 different FIFA World Cup matches 0-0. Their first was against Brazil in 1958, while the tally also includes both second-round group games in 1982 against eventual runners-up West Germany and hosts Spain. An 11th goalless draw followed against Costa Rica at Belo Horizonte in 2014.

FRANK'S A LOT, STEVIE G FORCE

A 15-year era encompassing what some dubbed England's "golden generation" ended in 2014 when midfield mainstays **Steven Gerrard** and Frank Lampard retired from international football. Gerrard bowed out as the country's third most-capped player, scoring 21 goals in 114 appearances. He was captain at the 2010 and 2014 tournaments, as well as the 2012 UEFA European Championship. The Liverpool legend, who joined LA Galaxy in summer 2015, is the only player to score in an FA Cup final, a League Cup final, a Uefa Cup final and a UEFA Champions League final. Lampard, who joined New York City FC in 2014, is England's most prolific penalty-scorer, amounting for nine of his 29 England goals in 106 appearances.

THE LONG AND THE SHORT OF IT

At 6ft 7in, centre-forward Peter Crouch is the tallest player ever to stretch above opposing defences for England – while Fanny Walden, the Tottenham winger who won two caps in 1914 and 1922, was the shortest at 5ft 2in. Sheffield United goalkeeper Billy "Fatty" Foulke became the heaviest England player at 18st when he played against Wales on 29 March 1897.

HURRICANE HARRY KANE

Tottenham Hotspur striker **Harry Kane** did not take long to get off the mark on his England debut, scoring just 79 seconds after coming on as a substitute in a 4-0 win over Lithuania in March 2015. Only two players scored sooner into their England careers: Bill Nicholson, also of Spurs, scored 19 seconds into his only England appearance, against Portugal in 1951; and John Cock, the first Cornishman to play for England, took 30 seconds to register against Ireland in 1919; he played only one more international. Kane's England debut crowned a stunning breakthrough season, during which he scored 37 goals for club and country. Remarkably, his first Premier League start did not come until November 2014, by which time – as a starter in cup ties or off the bench – he had scored 10 times for Spurs. He would prove he was no one-season wonder by winning the Golden Boot as the Premier League's top scorer for 2015–16.

WAITING FOR THE CALL

Four England internationals played at the 1966 FIFA World Cup yet missed out on the triumphant final against West Germany – Ian Callaghan, John Connelly, Jimmy Greaves and Terry Paine. Liverpool winger Callaghan would then endure the longest wait between England appearances, when he went 11 years and 49 days between his showing in a 2-0 win over France at that 1966 tournament and his return to international action in a goalless draw with Switzerland in September 1977. The game against the Swiss was his third – and penultimate – outing for England.

TEENAGE PROMISE

Manchester United rookie Marcus Rashford became, at 18 years and 209 days, the youngest England debutant to score, when he found the net just three minutes into his international bow, a friendly against Australia on 27 May 2016. England's youngest debutant is Theo Walcott, who was 17 years and 75 days when facing Hungary in May 2006. Michael Owen – at 18 years and 183 days – became the country's youngest player at a FIFA World Cup when coming on as a substitute against Tunisia in 1998.

BECKHAM'S RECORD

David Beckham played for England for the 109th time when he appeared as a second-half substitute in the 4-0 win over Slovakia in a friendly international on 28 March 2009. That overtook the record number of England games for an outfield player, which had been set by Bobby Moore, England's 1966 FIFA World Cup-winning captain. Beckham, born on 2 May 1975, in Leytonstone, London, made his first appearance for his country on 1 September 1996, in a FIFA World Cup qualifying match against Moldova. He was appointed full-time England captain in 2001 by the then manager Sven-Goran Eriksson – stepping down after England's quarter-final defeat by Portugal at the 2006 FIFA World Cup. He ended his England career on 115 caps and hung up his boots in May 2013, at the age of 38, having just won the league in a fourth different country with French club Paris Saint-Germain. His 68 competitive matches for England are also a national record. Also retiring from the game in summer 2013 was England's fourth highest scorer **Michael Owen**, who netted a stunning solo goal against Argentina at the 1998 FIFA World Cup – only for Beckham to be sent off in a 2-2 draw before England lost on penalties.

ALEXANDER THE LATE

The oldest player to make his debut for England remains Alexander Morten, who was 41 years and 114 days old when facing Scotland on 8 March 1873 in England's first home game, at The Oval in Kennington, London. He was also captain that day and is still the country's oldest-ever skipper.

THE GOOD SONS

Eighteen-year-old winger Alex Oxlade-Chamberlain became the fifth son of a former England international to earn a cap for his country when he made his debut against Norway in May 2012 – 28 years after the last of his father Mark Chamberlain's eight appearances. Oxlade-Chamberlain became England's youngest scorer in a FIFA World Cup qualifier with his strike against San Marino in October 2013. The earlier pairings were George Eastham Snr (one cap, 1935) and George Eastham Jnr (19, 1963–66); Brian Clough (two, 1959) and Nigel Clough (14, 1989–93); Frank Lampard Snr (two, 1972–80) and Frank Lampard Jnr (106, 1999–2014); and Ian Wright (33, 1991–98) and his adopted son Shaun Wright-Phillips (36, 2004– 10). The only grandfather and grandson to play for England are Bill Jones, who won two caps in 1950, and Rob Jones, who won eight between 1992 and 1995.

GRAND OLD MAN

Stanley Matthews became England's oldest-ever player when he lined up at outside-right against Denmark on 15 May 1957 at the age of 42 years 104 days. That was 22 years and 229 days after his first appearance. Matthews was also England's oldest marksman. He was 41 years eight months old when he scored against Northern Ireland on 10 October 1956.

CAPTAIN SOLO

Claude Ashton, the Corinthians centre-forward, set a record when he captained England on his only international appearance. This was a 0-0 draw against Northern Ireland in Belfast on 24 October 1925.

TOP SCORERS

1	Wayne Rooney	53
2	Bobby Charlton	49
3	Gary Lineker	48
4	Jimmy Greaves	44
5	Michael Owen	40
6	Tom Finney	30
=	Nat Lofthouse	30
=	Alan Shearer	30
9	Frank Lampard	29
=	Vivian Woodward	29

TOP CAPS

1	Peter Shilton	125
2	David Beckham	115
=	Wayne Rooney	115
4	Steven Gerrard	114
5	Bobby Moore	108
6	Ashley Cole	107
7	Bobby Charlton	106
=	Frank Lampard	106
9	Billy Wright	105
10	Bryan Robson	90

CAPTAINS COURAGEOUS

The international careers of Billy Wright and **Bobby Moore**, who both captained England a record 90 times, very nearly overlapped. Wright, from Wolves, played for England between 1946 and 1959 and Moore, from West Ham, between 1962 and 1973, including England's FIFA World Cup win in 1966.

SHARED RESPONSIBILITY

Substitutions meant the captain's armband passed between four different players during England's 2-1 friendly win over Serbia and Montenegro on 3 June 2003. Regular captain David Beckham was missing, so Michael Owen led the team out, but was substituted at half-time. England's second-half skippers were Owen's then-Liverpool team-mates Emile Heskey and Jamie Carragher and Manchester United's Philip Neville. The first time three different players have captained England in one FIFA World Cup finals match was against Morocco in 1986, when first-choice skipper Bryan Robson went off injured, his vice-captain Ray Wilkins was then sent off and goalkeeper Peter Shilton took over leadership duties.

CAMEO ROLE

Much-travelled striker **Jermain Defoe** has come on as substitute for England more often than any other player in history, 34 times since his debut in March 2004 – and his initial 17 starting appearances all ended in him being replaced before the end of 90 minutes.

SEVEN UP

Roy Hodgson's England equalled a national record when they trounced San Marino 8-0 in a March 2013 FIFA World Cup qualifier: the seven different goalscorers were as many who found the net when England defeated Luxembourg 9-0 in December 1982. This time, though, thanks to the opening own goal by Alessandro Della Valle, only six of the scorers were Englishmen. Adding to the tally were a Jermain Defoe brace and single strikes by Alex Oxlade-Chamberlain, Ashley Young, Frank Lampard, Wayne Rooney and **Daniel Sturridge**.

ROON AT THE TOP

When **Wayne Rooney** scored against Macedonia in September 2003, he became England's youngest goalscorer at the age of 17 years and 317 days – and it has long seemed only a matter of time before he broke Sir Bobby Charlton's England record of 49 strikes. He drew level thanks to a penalty against San Marino in September 2015, then reached his half-century with another spot-kick, against Switzerland, three days later. By this time Rooney was not only Manchester United but also England captain. His 100th cap against Slovenia in November 2014, aged 29 years and 22 days, made him the youngest man to reach a century of caps for England – three years younger than previous record-holder Bobby Moore. Rooney endured a more miserable ordeal when England lost to Iceland to be eliminated from Euro 2016 in the second round – but the game was his 115th international, equalling David Beckham's tally as England's most-capped outfield player.

COMING OVER HERE

Argentina were the first non-UK side to play at Wembley – England won 2-1 on 9 May 1951 – while Ferenc Puskas and the "Magical Magyars" of Hungary were the first "foreign", or "continental", side to beat England at home, with their famous 6-3 victory at Wembley in 1953. This humiliation marked Alf Ramsey's last game as an England player. England first tasted defeat to a "foreign" side when they lost 4-3 to Spain in Madrid on 15 May 1929. Two years later England gained their revenge with a 7-1 win at Highbury.

WRONG WAY!

Though the goal is sometimes credited to Scottish striker John Smith, it is believed that Edgar Field was the first England player to score an "own goal", which was his fate as Scotland crushed England 6-1 at The Oval on 12 March 1881. By the time Field put the ball in his own net, Scotland were already 4-1 up. The full-back, who was an FA Cup winner and loser with Clapham Rovers, is in good company. Manchester United's Gary Neville has scored two own goals "against" England.

ROLL UP, ROLL UP

The highest attendance for an England game came at Hampden Park on 17 April 1937, when 149,547 spectators crushed in to see Scotland's 3-1 victory in the British Home Championships. Only 2,378 turned up in Bologna, Italy, to see San Marino stun England after nine seconds in Graham Taylor's side's 7-1 victory that was not enough to secure qualification to the 1994 FIFA World Cup.

FIRST AND FOREMOST

England's first official international was a 0-0 draw against Scotland in Glasgow on 30 November 1872, though England and Scotland had already played a number of unofficial representative matches against each other prior to that. Given that England's only opponents for four decades were the home nations – and only Scotland for the first seven years, it is not surprising that England's first draw, win and defeat were all against their northern neighbours. After the goalless first game, the second fixture – played at The Oval on 8 March 1873 – proved a more exciting affair: England won 4-2 in a six-goal thriller. In their third game, back in Glasgow almost exactly a year later, Scotland evened things up with a 2-1 win. These fixtures completed the trio of first wins, defeats and draws for the oldest participants in international football. The Football Association's 150-year anniversary celebrations in 2013 included a 2013 Wembley friendly against Scotland, the first time the two sides were scheduled to meet since a two-leg play-off to qualify for Euro 2000 in October 1999. England won that tie 2-1 on aggregate, after a 2-0 victory at Hampden Park and a 1-0 defeat at home.

HOT SPURS

Defensive midfielder Eric Dier's free-kick goal against Russia in England's opening match at the 2016 UEFA European Championship made him the eighth Tottenham Hotspur player to score for England at a major tournament – more than any other club. He was following in the footsteps of such England and Spurs goalscoring legends as Jimmy Greaves and **Gary Lineker**. Greaves holds the England record for hat-tricks, with six, while Lineker has scored more FIFA World Cup goals than any of his compatriots – six in 1986, winning him the Golden Boot, before another four in 1990. Spurs have also provided England with more players than any other club, 75 so far.

YOUR COUNTRY NEEDS YOU

The first England teams were selected from open trials of Englishmen who responded to the FA's adverts for players. It was only when these proved too popular and unwieldy that, in 1887, the FA decided that it would be better to manage the process through an International Selection Committee, which continued to pick the team until Sir Alf Ramsey's appointment in 1962.

MANAGERIAL ROLL OF HONOUR

Walter Winterbottom	(1946–62)
Sir Alf Ramsey	(1962–74)
Joe Mercer	(1974)
Don Revie	(1974–77)
Ron Greenwood	(1977–82)
Bobby Robson	(1982–90)
Graham Taylor	(1990–93)
Terry Venables	(1994–96)
Glenn Hoddle	(1996–98)
Howard Wilkinson	(1999–2000)
Kevin Keegan	(1999–2000)
Peter Taylor	(November 2000)
Sven-Goran Eriksson	(2001–06)
Steve McClaren	(2006–07)
Fabio Capello	(2008–2012)
Stuart Pearce	(March 2012)
Roy Hodgson	(2012–2016)
Sam Allardyce	(2016–)

RARE COMEBACK

Liverpool striker Daniel Sturridge's injury-time winner against Wales in an all-British first-round clash in Lille at the 2016 UEFA European Championship, after 2015–16 Premier League Footballer of the Year Jamie Vardy's equalizer, meant it was the first time England had come from behind at half-time to win a match at a major tournament. Sturridge also became only the tenth Englishman to score at both a FIFA World Cup and a UEFA European Championship, having struck against Italy in Brazil two years earlier.

WONDERFUL WALTER

Walter Winterbottom was the England national team's first full-time manager – and remains both the longest-serving (with 138 games in charge) and the youngest-ever England manager, aged just 33 when he took the job in 1946 (initially as a coach and then, from 1947, as manager). The former teacher and Manchester United player led England to four FIFA World Cups.

FRANCE

France – nicknamed "Les Bleus" – are one of the most successful teams in the history of international football. They are one of only three countries to be World and European champions at the same time. They won the FIFA World Cup in 1998 as tournament hosts, routing Brazil 3-0 in the final. Two years later, they staged a sensational, last-gasp recovery to overhaul Italy in the Euro 2000 final. The French equalized in the fifth minute of stoppage time, then went on to win 2-1 on a golden goal. France had previously won the UEFA European Championship in 1984, beating Spain 2-0 in the final in Paris. They also won the 2001 and 2003 FIFA Confederations Cup and the 1984 Olympic Games football gold medal, but have lost their last two finals, the 2006 FIFA World Cup final to Italy on penalties then, as hosts, UEFA EURO 2016, to Portugal after extra time.

KOPA – FRANCE'S FIRST SUPERSTAR

Raymond Kopa (born on 13 October 1931) was France's first international superstar. Born into a family of Polish immigrants (the family name was Kopaszewski), he was instrumental in Reims's championship successes of the mid-1950s. He later joined Real Madrid and became the first French player to win a European Cup winner's medal. He was the playmaker of the France team that finished third in the 1958 FIFA World Cup finals. His performances for his country that year earned him the European Footballer of the Year award.

SINNER AND SAINT MICHEL

Michel Platini enjoyed a glittering career both on and off the pitch, rising from a youngster at Nancy to club glory with Saint-Etienne and Juventus and international triumph for France. He scored a tournament record nine goals as his country both hosted and won the 1984 UEFA European Championship before becoming national manager for the 1992 UEFA European Championship and then becoming joint organizing president (along with Ferdinand Sastre) as his nation staged the 1998 FIFA World Cup. He served as president of European football's governing body UEFA from January 2007 until his suspension for misconduct in December 2015.

BENZ MAKES AMENDS

Karim Benzema was the first French player to miss a penalty during a FIFA World Cup match – excluding shoot-outs. His effort, saved by Diego Benaglio, came in a Group E match against Switzerland at the 2014 tournament – the tenth FIFA World Cup spot-kick awarded to France. He did atone for the failure by scoring France's fourth in their 5-2 victory. Benzema had struck twice in France's first game, a 3-0 defeat of Honduras, and was denied a hat-trick after his shot struck the far post and trickled over the goal-line, but it crossed the line only after rebounding off goalkeeper Noel Valladares, so was ruled an own goal. This was the first time in FIFA World Cup history that a goal was given thanks to goal-line technology, introduced for the 2014 finals. And Benzema was denied another goal in the Swiss game when Dutch referee Bjorn Kuipers blew the final whistle as he was in the act of smashing a long-range shot which ended up in the Swiss net. Benzema's three goals at the 2014 finals lifted him up to ninth place in France's all-time scoring table, above Jean Vincent, who had died at the age of 82 the previous October.

GRIEZ LIGHTNING

Hosts France went through their first four games of the 2016 UEFA European Championship without scoring a first half goal. They then became, in their 5-2 quarter-final victory against Iceland, the first team in tournament history to register as many as four goals in the first half. Unlike when hosting the 1984 UEFA European Championship and the 1998 FIFA World Cup, they ended empty-handed thanks to a 1-0 defeat in the final to Portugal. Yet forward **Antoine Griezmann** claimed the prizes for both best player and top scorer, with six goals – double the tally of his closest challengers. Only Michel Platini has found the net more at a single UEFA European Championship.

KISSING COLLEAGUES

Marseille colleagues centre-back **Laurent Blanc** and goalkeeper **Fabien Barthez** had a special ritual during France's run to the 1998 FIFA World Cup crown. Before the game, Blanc would always kiss Barthez's shaven head, even when the veteran defender was suspended for the final. Blanc was on the winning side when France won the 2000 UEFA European Championship final, after which he announced his international retirement. He said at the time: "The French team has been my life and has led me to do things I shouldn't have. It has been my mistress – a beautiful mistress."

FRANCE AND FIFA

France were one of FIFA's founding members in 1904. Frenchman Robert Guerin became the first president of the governing body. Another Frenchman, Jules Rimet, was president from 1921 to 1954. He was the driving force behind the creation of the FIFA World Cup and the first version of football's most coveted trophy was named in his honour.

IT'S A SHAME ABOUT RAY

France's failure to win a match at the 2010 FIFA World Cup meant coach Raymond Domenech equalled but failed to exceed Michel Hidalgo's record of 41 victories in charge of the national side. Domenech did at least end his six-year reign having surpassed Euro 84-winning Hidalgo's tally of matches in the job. Domenech's final game, against South Africa, was his 79th as coach, four more than Hidalgo achieved. Domenech, a tough-tackling defender who was picked for France by Hidalgo, proved eccentric as national coach. He admitted partly judging players by their star signs and responded to being knocked out of the 2008 UEFA European Championship by proposing to his girlfriend on live television.

MICHEL PLATINI (league and national career)

Duration	Team	Appearances	Goals
1972–79	Nancy	181	98
1979–82	Saint-Etienne	104	58
1982–87	Juventus	147	68
1976–87	France	72	41

POGBA POWER

France's triumph at the 2013 FIFA U-20 World Cup in Turkey made them the first country to complete a grand slam of FIFA eleven-a-side international men's titles, having previously won the FIFA World Cup, the FIFA U-20 World Cup and Olympic Games gold medal. The star of the show in 2013 was dynamic midfielder and captain **Paul Pogba**, who was awarded the Golden Ball as the tournament's best player. He was among the French players who scored from the spot in a 4-1 penalty shoot-out victory against Uruguay in the final, the game having finished goalless after extra-time. Pogba had made his senior France debut in March 2013, in a 3-1 win over Georgia, but he was sent off against Spain in his next appearance, four days. Better was to come, in the summer of 2014, when Pogba was named Best Young Player at the FIFA World Cup. He has enjoyed success at club level too. Pogba joined Manchester United at the age of 16, and departed to Juventus three years later in 2012 and helped them to successive Serie A league titles as well as reach the 2015 UEFA Champions League final.

PRESIDENTIAL PARDON

Imperious centre-back Laurent Blanc was known as "Le President" during his playing days and went on to become national coach when he succeeded Raymond Domenech after the 2010 FIFA World Cup. He was unlucky to miss the 1998 FIFA World Cup final after being sent off in the semi-final for pushing Slaven Bilic in the face, though replays showed Bilic had over-reacted. Blanc did enjoy some redemption by being part of the French team that won the UEFA European Championship two years later. He became national coach 12 months after leading Bordeaux to the 2008–09 domestic championship, ending Olympique Lyonnais's run of seven league titles in a row.

BITTERSWEET FOR TREZEGUET

Striker David Trezeguet has bittersweet memories of France's clashes with Italy in major finals. He scored the "golden goal" that beat the Italians in extra-time in the Euro 2000 final but, six years later, he was the man who missed as France lost the FIFA World Cup final on penalties. Trezeguet's shot bounced off the bar and failed to cross the line.

TOP SCORERS

1	Thierry Henry	51
2	Michel Platini	41
3	David Trezeguet	34
4	Zinedine Zidane	31
5	Just Fontaine	30
=	Jean-Pierre Papin	30
7	Youri Djorkaeff	28
8	Karim Benzema	27
9	Sylvain Wiltord	26
10	Jean Vincent	22

UNITED FOR ABIDAL

Defender **Eric Abidal**, a key member of the French teams at the 2006 and 2010 FIFA World Cups, was enjoying his best form for Spanish club Barcelona when he was diagnosed with liver cancer in March 2011 – but managed to recover in time for a surprise return to action by the season's end. Club rivalries were put aside when players from rivals Real Madrid wore T-shirts bearing the supportive message "Animo Abidal" after their UEFA Champions League tie against Abidal's former club Olympique Lyonnais a few days later. Barcelona fans then clapped throughout the 22nd minute of their La Liga game against Getafe, in recognition of Abidal's shirt number. Remarkably, he was fit enough to return to action, as a substitute, in Barcelona's UEFA Champions League semi-final victory over Madrid in May 2011. Abidal started in the final and, although not the captain, was given the armband to lift the cup after their 3-1 win over Manchester United. Abidal came through further trauma in March 2012, when he was told he needed a liver transplant. Yet again Abidal returned to action with Barcelona towards the end of the 2012–13 season. He continued his club career until December 2014, playing for Monaco and Olympiacos, but then retired from all football.

TOP CAPS

1	Lilian Thuram	142
2	Thierry Henry	123
3	Marcel Desailly	116
4	Zinedine Zidane	108
5	Patrick Vieira	107
6	Didier Deschamps	103
7	Laurent Blanc	97
=	Bixente Lizarazu	97
9	Sylvain Wiltord	92
10	Fabien Barthez	87

DESCHAMPS THE LEADER

Compatriot Eric Cantona contemptuously dismissed him as a mere "water-carrier" in central midfield but Didier Deschamps provided his infamous critic with the perfect riposte in becoming the most successful captain in French football history. He lifted both the 1998 FIFA World Cup and 2000 UEFA European Championship trophies as skipper and wore the captain's armband 55 times – a record until 2016 when Hugo Lloris passed him – during his 103 internationals before retiring in July 2000. Deschamps succeeded Laurent Blanc as national coach after the 2012 UEFA European Championship and guided France to the final of the 2016 UEFA European Championship. Deschamps thus became only the third man – after Germany's Berti Vogts and Italy's Dino Zoff – to reach the UEFA EURO final both as a player and a manager.

PATRICK'S DAY

All six players to earn 100 caps for France were in the winning squads at the 1998 FIFA World Cup and 2000 UEFA European Championship: Lilian Thuram, Thierry Henry, Marcel Desailly, Zinedine Zidane, Patrick Vieira and Didier Deschamps. Only Vieira and Desailly added the 2001 FIFA Confederations Cup to their medals collection, and Vieira scored the only goal of the final against Japan, one of six the powerful midfielder netted for his country.

HENRY BENCHED

Thierry Henry missed out on an appearance in the 1998 FIFA World Cup final because of Marcel Desailly's red card. Henry, France's leading goalscorer in the finals with three, was a substitute and coach Aime Jacquet planned to use him late in the game. But Desailly's sending-off forced a re-think: Jacquet instead reinforced the midfield, with Arsenal team-mate Patrick Vieira going on instead, so Henry spent the full 90 minutes of the final on the bench. But Henry does have the distinction of being the only Frenchman to play at four different FIFA World Cups (1998, 2002, 2006 and 2010). He passed Michel Platini's all-time goal-scoring record for France with a brace against Lithuania in October 2007.

VICTOR HUGO

Hugo Lloris has worn the captain's armband more than any other Frenchman, after leading the host nation throughout the 2016 UEFA European Championship. The defeat in the final to Portugal was the goalkeeper's 58th appearance as France captain. Yet it took some time for him to be given the honour. After Patrice Evra lost the captaincy for his role in France's 2010 FIFA World Cup fiasco, when the players briefly went on strike and Nicolas Anelka was sent home for insulting manager Raymond Domenech, new coach Laurent Blanc tried three captains before turning to Lloris who was finally given the job permanently ahead of the 2012 UEFA European Championship.

THE FULL SET

Five France stars have a full set of top international medals as FIFA World Cup, UEFA European Championship and UEFA Champions League winners. Didier Deschamps, Marcel Desailly, Christian Karembeu, Bixente Lizarazu and Zinedine Zidane all played for France's winning teams in 1998 and 2000. Desailly won the European Cup with Marseille in 1993 and AC Milan the following year. Deschamps won with Marseille in 1993 and Juventus in 1996; Lizarazu did so with Bayern Munich in 2001, Karembeu with Real Madrid in 1998 and 2000, and Zidane with Real Madrid in 2002. While Karembeu ended the 1999–2000 season with UEFA Champions League and UEFA European Championship winners' medals, he was an unused substitute in both finals – making him the only player to have achieved that particular bittersweet double.

LILIAN IN THE PINK

Defender **Lilian Thuram** made his 142nd and final appearance for France in their defeat by Italy at Euro 2008. His international career had spanned nearly 14 years, since his debut against the Czech Republic on 17 August 1994. Thuram was born in Pointe a Pitre, Guadeloupe, on 1 January 1972. He played club football for Monaco, Parma, Juventus and Barcelona before retiring in the summer of 2008 because of a heart problem. He was one of the stars of France's 1998 FIFA World Cup-winning side and scored both goals in their semi-final victory over Croatia – the only international goals of his career. He gained another winner's medal at Euro 2000. He first retired from international football after Euro 2004, but was persuaded by coach Raymond Domenech to return for the 2006 FIFA World Cup campaign and made his second appearance in a FIFA World Cup final. He broke Marcel Desailly's record of 116 caps in the group game against Togo.

ALBERT THE FIRST

Albert Batteux was France's first national coach. Before his appointment in 1955, a selection committee picked the team. Batteux was also one of the most successful managers in French football history, even though he combined it with his club job at Reims. His biggest achievement was guiding France to third place at the 1958 FIFA World Cup finals. The team's two big stars, Raymond Kopa and Just Fontaine, had both played for him at Reims. The only non-Frenchman to be national coach was a Romanian, former Ajax Amsterdam boss, Stefan Kovacs. He was succeeded by Michel Hidalgo after failing to reach either the 1974 FIFA World Cup or the 1976 UEFA European Championship.

UMTITI BOOM

Barcelona-bound defender Samuel Umtiti was thrown in at the deep end at the 2016 UEFA European Championship, in France's 5-2 quarter-final victory against Iceland. He became the first outfield player to make his French international debut at a major tournament since Gabriel di Michele at the 1966 FIFA World Cup.

OVAL BALL

The father of France's most capped goalkeeper Fabien Barthez was also a French international. Alain Barthez was a fine rugby union player who won one cap for France.

JACQUET'S TRIUMPH

Aime Jacquet, who guided France to FIFA World Cup glory in 1998, was one of their most controversial national coaches. He had been attacked for alleged defensive tactics despite France's run to the semi-finals of Euro 96 and a record of only three defeats in four years. A month before the 1998 finals, the sports daily *L'Equipe* claimed he was not capable of building a successful team!

NO TIME FOR FONTAINE

Former striker **Just Fontaine** spent the shortest-ever spell in charge of the France team. He took over on 22 March 1967 and left on 3 June after two defeats in friendlies. More happily, he still holds the record for most goals at a single FIFA World Cup – 13 across all six games he played at the 1958 tournament, including four in France's 6-3 victory over West Germany to finish third. He remains the only Frenchman to score a FIFA World Cup hat-trick.

FRANCE MANAGERS

Albert Batteux	1955–62
Henri Guerin	1962–66
Jose Arribas/Jean Snella	1966
Just Fontaine	1967
Louis Dugauguez	1967–68
Georges Boulogne	1969–73
Stefan Kovacs	1973–75
Michel Hidalgo	1976–84
Henri Michel	1984–88
Michel Platini	1988–92
Gerard Houllier	1992–93
Aime Jacquet	1993–98
Roger Lemerre	1998–2002
Jacques Santini	2002–04
Raymond Domenech	2004–10
Laurent Blanc	2010–12
Didier Deschamps	2012–

JOLLY OLI DAY

France became the fifth country to reach 100 FIFA World Cup goals, when **Olivier Giroud** scored the 17th-minute opener during their 5-2 victory over Switzerland at Salvador in their 2014 first-round clash. The French thus joined Brazil, Germany (including West Germany), Argentina and Italy on three-figure tallies. By the end of the 2014 FIFA World Cup, France, with 106 in total, were more than 20 goals behind fourth-placed Italy – who had slipped behind Argentina after a second poor showing in a row – but a dozen clear of the sixth most prolific nation, Spain.

WINNING WITH YOUTH

In the early 1990s, France was the first European country to institute a national youth development programme. The best young players were picked to attend the national youth academy at Clairefontaine. They went on to the top clubs' academies across France. The scheme produced a rich harvest of stars. FIFA World Cup winners Didier Deschamps, Marcel Desailly and Christian Karembeu started at Nantes. Lilian Thuram, Thierry Henry, Manu Petit and David Trezeguet began with Monaco and **Zinedine Zidane** and Patrick Vieira graduated from Cannes. Zidane scored the only goal, against Spain, in the January 1998 inaugural match staged at the new national stadium, the 81,000-capacity Stade de France in St Denis, just north of Paris.

BLINK AND YOU'LL MISS HIM

Unfortunate defender Franck Jurietti's international debut proved bittersweet – it lasted just five seconds and he never won another cap. The Bordeaux full-back came on just before the final whistle of France's match against Cyprus in October 2005, amounting to an international career even shorter than fellow defender Bernard Boissier's two minutes against Portugal in April 1975.

HATS OFF

For all the goalscoring exploits of prolific forwards, such as Thierry Henry, David Trezeguet and Karim Benzema, no Frenchman has scored an international hat-trick since winger Dominique Rocheteau, against Luxembourg during a 6-0 win in October 1985. Just Fontaine hit a record five of France's 21 hat-tricks, though only Eugene Maes against Luxembourg in April 1913 and Thadee Cisowski versus Belgium in November 1956 have managed to score five times in a game.

EARNING THEIR STRIPES

France are the only country to play at a FIFA World Cup wearing another team's kit. In the 1978 tournament in Argentina, for a first-round match at Mar del Plata, *Les Bleus* were forced to wear the green and white stripes of a local club side, Atletico Kimberley, when they met Hungary. France brought their second, white, kit instead of their normal blue, while Hungary turned up in their second strip, white, too. The quick-change did not seem to affect France, who won the match 3-1.

COME ON, COMAN

Tricky winger **Kingsley Coman** became France's youngest player – aged 19 years and 363 days – at a major tournament when used as a substitute against Romania in the opening match of the 2016 UEFA European Championship. Five days later, he was in the starting line-up against Albania and, at 20 years and two days, he replaced Bruno Bellone – 20 years and 122 days in the 1982 FIFA World Cup third-place play-off – as France's youngest ever starter in a senior competition.

GERMANY

German footballers are almost ever-presents in the closing stages of major tournaments, but their well-deserved 2014 FIFA World Cup triumph provided much joy and relief back home as it ended an 18-year trophy drought. It was also the first FIFA World Cup triumph for the united Germany, having been West Germany when becoming champions in 1954, 1974 and 1990. The Germans are also three-time UEFA European champions (1972, 1980 and 1996) and in 1974 became the first country to hold the world and European titles simultaneously. Further glory always feels likely.

SHOOT-OUT SURE-SHOTS

Germany are renowned as penalty specialists, but they needed no shoot-outs when winning the 2014 FIFA World Cup, unlike their previous two titles, the 1990 FIFA World Cup and the 1996 UEFA European Championship. These both involved semi-final victories on penalties against England.

NO LOSS

Germany maintained their record of never losing their opening game at a UEFA European Championship by beating Ukraine 2-0 at Euro 2016, thanks to goals by **Shkodran Mustafi** and Bastian Schweinsteiger. They have now won more UEFA European Championship openers than any other country, seven, with the other five being draws, but Germany (including West Germany) is also the only country with 12 appearances in the finals.

BASTIAN THE BASTION

No man has played more games at FIFA World Cup and UEFA European Championship finals than Germany's **Bastian Schweinsteiger**, who took his tally to 38 at Euro 2016 – one ahead of compatriot Miroslav Klose. He reached the landmark in Germany's 2-0 semi-final defeat to France, during which he unfortunately handballed to give France a penalty and their opening goal. However it was not all gloom in July 2016 for Schweinsteiger – who took over the German captaincy from his fellow 2014 FIFA World Cup winner, the now retired Philipp Lahm. Later in the month he celebrated his marriage, two days after the final, to Serbian tennis star Ana Ivanovic.

BOTH SIDES NOW

Eight players appeared for both the old East Germany and then Germany after reunification in October 1990.

Player	East Germany	Germany
Ulf Kirsten	49	51
Matthias Sammer	23	51
Andreas Thom	51	10
Thomas Doll	29	18
Dariusz Wosz	7	17
Olaf Marschall	4	13
Heiko Scholz	7	1
Dirk Schuster	4	3

⚽ EAST GERMANY –
TOP APPEARANCES AND GOALS

Appearances

1	Joachim Streich	98
2	Hans-Jurgen Dorner	96
3	Jurgen Croy	86
4	Konrad Weise	78
5	Eberhard Vogel	69

Goals

1	Joachim Streich	53
2	Eberhard Vogel	24
3	Hans-Jurgen Kreische	22
4	Rainer Ernst	20
5	Henning Frenzel	19

⚽ SAMBA SILENCED

Germany's 1-0 win over Argentina in 2014 came in their record eighth FIFA World Cup Final, this coming after they were the first side to reach four consecutive semi-finals. But the 7-1 semi-final humiliation of Brazil may live longest in the memory – and the record books. Germany led 5-0 at half-time in what became the biggest FIFA World Cup semi-final win and the hosts' heaviest defeat. Other FIFA World Cup finals records include: Toni Kroos's two goals in 69 seconds were the fastest brace and Germany were the first team to score four goals in six minutes. Also Thomas Muller's opening goal was Germany's 2,000th.

⚽ TOP AND TAIL

Germany ended 2014 top of the FIFA world rankings – the first time they had occupied this position in December since 1993, when the rankings were originally introduced.

⚽ HOTTEST SHOTS

Germany's 7-1 defeat of Brazil in the 2014 FIFA World Cup semi-finals not only stunned the hosts, but also toppled them as the tournament's all-time top scorers. Germany's FIFA World Cup goals total is now 224, three more than Brazil. Stanislaus Kobierski scored Germany's first-ever FIFA World Cup goal, in a 5-2 victory over Belgium in 1934. Germany became the first team to enjoy three four-goal sprees at one tournament, beating Australia 4-0, England 4-1 and Argentina 4-0 in 2010. The 2014 vintage got off to a flying start by crushing Portugal 4-0 in their opening match.

⚽ GOLDEN WONDER

Germany became the first team to win a major title thanks to the now-discarded golden goal goal system when they beat the Czech Republic in the UEFA Euro 96 final at Wembley. **Oliver Bierhoff**'s equalizer forced extra-time after Patrik Berger scored a penalty for the Czechs. Bierhoff grabbed Germany's winner five minutes into extra-time to end the game and the championship.

⚽ HISTORY MAN

East and West Germany met only once at senior national team level. That was on 22 June 1974, in the FIFA World Cup finals. Drawn in the same group, East Germany produced a shock 1-0 win in Hamburg, but both teams advanced. Jurgen Sparwasser, scorer of East Germany's winning goal, defected to West Germany in 1988 – two years before the two countries reunited.

⚽ WE MEET AGAIN

Germany's first match after winning the 2014 FIFA World Cup final against Argentina in June was a friendly that September against ... Argentina in Dusseldorf. Mario Gotze scored yet again, but his late effort – plus one from Andre Schurrle, the creator of the FIFA World Cup winner – proved in vain as Argentina won 4-2. This was the Germany's first defeat in 18 matches across 13 months. But the team was missing veteran stars, such as Philipp Lahm, Per Mertesacker and Miroslav Klose, all of whom had retired from international football. Four of the Germans who started the FIFA World Cup final began the friendly, compared to seven Argentines.

MEIN BENDERS

You could have thought you were seeing double when manager Joachim Low made a double substitution with 12 minutes remaining during Germany's 5-3 defeat to Switzerland in May 2012. His two midfield substitutes were twin brothers Lars and Sven Bender. Born on 27 April 1989, they both began their careers with 1860 Munich before Lars (the elder by 12 minutes) moved to Bayer Leverkusen and Sven to Borussia Dortmund. Both were members of Germany's 2008 UEFA U-19 European Championship-winning side, but only Lars was selected for Euro 2012. They were were the second twins to play for Germany after Erwin and Helmut Kramers.

Striker Erwin scored three goals in 15 games between 1972 and 1974, while full-back Helmut played eight times without scoring. Erwin was part of the 1972 UEFA European Championship-winning squad, but was overlooked for the triumphant 1974 FIFA World Cup-winning squad, a set-up that included Helmut.

FINALLY BELITTLING ITALY

Germany went into the 2016 UEFA European Championship as reigning world champions and hoping to emulate holders Spain by uniting the two titles, only to lose 2-0 to hosts France in the semi-finals. Germany did, however, break two long-standing hoodoos against Italy in 2016. In a March friendly they beat the Italians 4-1 – Germany's first victory in the fixture for 21 years. They followed this up, in Bordeaux three months later, with a quarter-final victory over the same opponents on penalties – their first win against Italy in nine tournament clashes. Previous Italian glory included: 4-3 in the 1970 FIFA World Cup semi-final; 3-1 in the final 12 years later; and 2-0 in another semi-final in 2006. This time it took a 1-1 draw followed by an unusually long shoot-out for Germany to ultimately prevail 6-5 on spot-kicks, this despite three players, Thomas Muller, **Mesut Ozil** and Bastian Schweinsteiger missing for them. In the previous round's 3-0 win against Slovakia, Ozil had become the first German to miss a tournament penalty since Uli Hoeness in the 1976 UEFA European Championship final.

"DER BOMBER"

Gerd Muller was the most prolific scorer of the modern era. Neither tall nor graceful, he was quick, strong and had a predator's eye for the net. He also had the temperament to score decisive goals in big games, including the winner in the 1974 FIFA World Cup final, the winner in the semi-final against Poland and two goals in West Germany's 1972 UEFA European Championship final victory over the USSR. He netted 68 goals in 62 appearances for West Germany and remains the leading scorer in the Bundesliga and all-time record scorer for his club, Bayern Munich.

A LAHM CALL

Philipp Lahm surprised many when retiring from international football after the 2014 FIFA World Cup, at the age of only 30. He went out on a high, having just lifted the trophy as German captain at the end of his 113th appearance. Lahm had already made a mark in his two previous finals. He scored the opening goal of the 2006 FIFA World Cup, and played every minute of that tournament. Four years later, he became the youngest man to captain Germany at a FIFA World Cup – and the only action he missed was when given a well-earnest rest for the third-place play-off against Uruguay. In his youth, Lahm was a ballboy at Bayern Munich and he later captained them to 2013 UEFA Champions League glory.

DER KAISER

Franz Beckenbauer is widely regarded as the greatest player in German football history. He has also made a huge mark as a FIFA World Cup-winning coach, administrator and organizer. Beckenbauer (born on 11 September 1945) was a 20-year-old attacking wing-half when West Germany reached the 1966 FIFA World Cup final. He later defined the role of attacking sweeper, first in the 1970 FIFA World Cup finals, and then as West Germany won the 1972 UEFA European Championship and the 1974 FIFA World Cup. When West Germany needed a coach in the mid-1980s, they turned to Beckenbauer, despite his lack of experience. He delivered a FIFA World Cup final appearance in 1986, a Euro 88 semi-final and 1990 FIFA World Cup triumph in his final game in charge. He later became president of Bayern Munich, the club he captained to three consecutive European Cup victories between 1974 and 1976. He also led Germany's successful bid for the 2006 FIFA World Cup finals and headed the organizing committee. No wonder he is known as "Der Kaiser" ("the Emperor") for his enormous influence on German football.

MAGICAL MATTHAUS

Lothar Matthaus is Germany's most-capped player. He appeared in five FIFA World Cup finals – 1982, 1986, 1990, 1994 and 1998 – a record for an outfield player. Versatile Matthaus could operate as a defensive midfielder, an attacking midfielder, or as a sweeper. He was a FIFA World Cup winner in 1990, a finalist in 1982 and 1986 and a UEFA European Championship winner in 1980. His record 150 appearances – spread over a 20-year international career – were split 87 for West Germany and 63 for Germany. He also scored 23 goals and was voted top player at the 1990 FIFA World Cup.

TOP CAPS
(West Germany & Germany)

1	Lothar Matthaus	150
2	Miroslav Klose	137
3	Lukas Podolski	129
4	Bastian Schweinsteiger	120
5	Philipp Lahm	113
6	Jurgen Klinsmann	108
7	Jurgen Kohler	105
8	Per Mertesacker	104
9	Franz Beckenbauer	103
10	Thomas Hassler	101

TOP SCORERS
(West Germany & Germany)

1	Miroslav Klose	71
2	Gerd Muller	68
3	Lukas Podolski	48
3	Jurgen Klinsmann	47
=	Rudi Voller	47
6	Karl-Heinz Rummenigge	45
7	Uwe Seeler	43
8	Michael Ballack	42
9	Oliver Bierhoff	37
10	Fritz Walter	33

KLOSE ENCOUNTERS

Miroslav Klose became the third player, after Uwe Seeler and Pele to score in four FIFA World Cup finals. His first goal in Brazil, an equalizer against Ghana, put him alongside Ronaldo at the top of the all-time FIFA World Cup scoring charts. And it was against Ronaldo's Brazil that Klose pushed ahead on his own, his 16th finals goal being a typically-opportunistic finish to give Germany a 2-0 semi-final lead. All 16 of Klose's FIFA World Cup goals have come from inside the penalty area. He ended the 2014 FIFA World Cup not only with the scoring record and a winners' medal, but also on 24 appearances – behind only Italy's Paolo Maldini (25) – and 17 wins, one ahead of previous record-holder Cafu, of Brazil. Klose retired in 2014 as Germany's all-time leading scorer, with 71 goals in 137 matches – and his team-mates never lost an international in which he found the net.

KOPKE'S UP FOR CUPS

Andreas Kopke was involved – and celebrating – on the sidelines when West Germany won the FIFA World Cup in 1990 and when Germany won in 2014. He was one of Franz Beckenbauer's two back-ups to first-choice goalkeeper Bodo Illgner in 1990 and, 24 years later, he was Joachim Low's goalkeeping coach for No. 1 keeper Manuel Neuer, as well as reserves Ron-Robert Zieler and Roman Weidenfeller. Kopke did at least play throughout Germany's 1996 UEFA European Championship-winning campaign, contributing an especially crucial role in reaching the final when saving a spot-kick by England's Gareth Southgate in their semi-final shoot-out.

YOUNGEST CENTURION LUKAS

Lukas Podolski was briefly Europe's youngest footballer to reach 100 caps when, aged 27 years and 13 days old, he appeared in Germany's third first-round game of the 2012 UEFA European Championship, against Denmark. He marked the occasion by scoring the opener in a 2-1 win – his 44th goal for his country. Podolski was born in Gliwice in Poland, but opted to play for Germany – his family having emigrated there when he was two years old. He was voted best young player of the tournament when Germany hosted and finished third at the 2006 FIFA World Cup.

KROOS CONTROL

Attacking midfielder **Toni Kroos** became in 2014 the only man born in East Germany to win the FIFA World Cup. He was born in Greifswald in January 1990, nine months before Germany's reunification. His two goals in the 7-1 semi-final thrashing of hosts Brazil were scored in the 24th and 26th minutes, taking the score from 2-0 to an impregnable 4-0. He also played the full final against Argentina and ended the tournament on FIFA's ten-man Golden Ball shortlist. The World Cup medal came a year after he won the UEFA Champions League with Bayern Munich and the triumphs continued throughout 2014 – after a summer move to Real Madrid, he soon added triumphs in the UEFA Super Cup and the FIFA Club World Cup.

KEEPING A LOW PROFILE

Joachim Low was, in 2014, the 19th coach to win the FIFA World Cup, but the first German coach to do so without having played for his country. After a respectable career as a midfielder for a number of clubs, including Freiburg, and coaching spells in Germany, Austria and Turkey, Low was appointed as Jurgen Klinsmann's assistant in 2004, before taking the top job after the 2006 FIFA World Cup. He led Germany to the 2008 UEFA European Championship Final and the semi-finals of Euro 2012, as well as third-place at the 2010 FIFA World Cup. West Germany's 1954 FIFA World Cup-winning manager Sepp Herberger had won three caps as a player, 1974 boss Helmut Schon made 16 appearances and 1990 coach Franz Beckenbauer won 103 caps and lifted the trophy as captain in 1974.

GERMAN EFFICIENCY

Nineteen retired German or West Germany internationals have scored more than 20 goals while representing their country. Even more impressively, 12 of them ended their international careers with an average strike-rate of at least one goal every other game. Leading the way is Gerd Muller (his 68 goals in 62 appearances meant an average of 1.1 goals per game), and the other 11 hotshots are: Edmund Conen (0.96), Richard Hofmann (0.87), Max Morlock (0.81), Karl Hohmann (0.8), Klaus Fischer (0.71), Uwe Seeler (0.6), Fritz Walter (0.54), Oliver Bierhoff and Helmut Rahn (0.53), Miroslav Klose and Rudi Voller (0.52).

GERMANY'S MANAGERS

Otto Nerz	1928–36
Sepp Herberger	1936–64
Helmut Schon	1964–78
Jupp Derwall	1978–84
Franz Beckenbauer	1984–90
Berti Vogts	1990–98
Erich Ribbeck	1998–2000
Rudi Voller	2000–04
Jurgen Klinsmann	2004–06
Joachim Low	2006–

BONUS BATTLE

Helmut Schon's 1974 FIFA World Cup winners came close to walking out before the finals started. Schon was prepared to send his squad home in a row over bonuses. A last-minute deal was brokered between Franz Beckenbauer and federation vice-president Hermann Neuberger. The vote among the squad went 11-11, but Beckenbauer persuaded the players to accept the DFB's offer. It was a great decision: they beat Holland 2-1 in the final.

GOAL RUSH

Germany's biggest win was 16-0 against Russia in the 1912 Olympic Games in Stockholm. Karlsruhe's Gottfried Fuchs scored ten of the goals, still a national team record.

NEW BOYS REUNION

Bayern Munich's **Mario Gotze** was the hero when Germany finally overcame Argentina's resistance in the 2014 FIFA World Cup final. His 113th-minute volley was the first winner hit by a substitute. It seemed apt that Germany's first FIFA World Cup triumph since the reunification of East and West Germany in 1990 was secured by Gotze, set up by Andre Schurrle. They had jointly become the first German football internationals born post-reunification, when making their debuts as 79th-minute substitutes against Sweden in November 2010.

GERMANY'S BRONZE AGES

The 2010 FIFA World Cup third-place play-off between Germany and Uruguay was a rematch of the same tie at the 1970 tournament, when West Germany won 1-0. The German side again took third place 40 years later, thanks to a dramatic 3-2 victory in Port Elizabeth's Nelson Mandela Bay stadium. The result, secured by Sami Khedira's late goal, meant Germany had a record four third-place finishes at FIFA World Cups, having also come third in 1934 and 2006.

FRITZ WALTER BETTER

Fritz Walter was the inspirational inside-left and captain when West Germany won their first FIFA World Cup in 1954, coming from two goals down to defeat favourites Hungary 3-2 in the final in Switzerland – a triumph memorialized back home as "The Miracle of Berne". He and brother Ottmar became the first siblings to win a FIFA World Cup together. He played his entire club career for FC Kaiserslautern, whose home ground staged a FIFA World Cup tie between Italy and the USA on 17 June 2006, the fourth anniversary of his death at the age of 81 – and a minute's silence was held for him before kick-off. He was renowned for his ability to play well in the most inclement conditions, promoting talk of "Fritz-Walter-Wetter" or "Fritz Walter weather".

PRESSURE ON JULIAN

Julian Draxler became Germany's fifth-youngest player when he made his debut against Switzerland in May 2012, aged 18 years 248 days old. Team-mate Mario Gotze is third on that list, having been 18 years and 166 days old when he made his first appearance, against Sweden in November 2010, at the age of 18 years and 166 days. Germany's youngest-ever player remains Oskar Ritter, who was 17 years and 254 days old when he made his debut, also against Sweden, in June 1925. Uwe Seeler was 90 days older when he debuted against France in October 1954. Olaf Thon was 63 days older than Gotze when he made his first international appearance, against Malta, in December 1984.

SEPP'S SURPRISE

Sepp Herberger (1897–1977) was one of the most influential figures in Germany's football history. He was their longest-serving coach (28 years at the helm) and his legendary status was assured after West Germany surprised odds-on favourites Hungary to win the 1954 FIFA World Cup final – a result credited with dragging the country out of a post-war slump. Herberger took charge in 1936 and led the team into the 1938 FIFA World Cup finals. During the war years he used his influence to try to keep his best players away from the heavy fighting. When organized football resumed in 1949, the federation decided to advertise for a national coach, but Herberger persuaded DFB chief Peco Bauwens to give him back his old job. He had a clause in his contract guaranteeing him a totally free hand in organization and selection policy. Among Herberger's favourite sayings was: "The ball is round and the match lasts 90 minutes. Everything else is just theory."

ITALY

Only Brazil (with five victories) can claim to have won the FIFA World Cup more times than Italy. The *Azzurri* became the first nation to retain the trophy (through back-to-back successes in 1934 and 1938), snatched a surprise win in Spain in 1982, and collected football's most coveted trophy for a fourth time in 2006 following a dramatic penalty shoot-out win over France. Add the 1968 UEFA European Championship success to the mix and few nations can boast a better record. The success story does not end there. Italian clubs have won the European Cup or UEFA Champions League on 12 occasions and the country's domestic league, Serie A, is considered among the strongest in the game. Italy are a true powerhouse of world football.

ROTTEN RETURN

Italy were knocked out of the FIFA World Cup in the first round in both 2010 and 2014 – the first time they had done so in consecutive tournaments since 1962 and 1966. At least the modern players did not suffer the fate of those arriving home from England in 1966: they were pelted with rotten fruit after a dismal showing most notable for a 1-0 defeat to minnows North Korea.

OFF THE SPOT

Only England have lost as many FIFA World Cup penalty shoot-outs as Italy – three apiece. **Roberto Baggio**, nicknamed "The Divine Ponytail", was involved in all three of Italy's spot-kick defeats, in 1990, 1994 and 1998. Left-back Antonio Cabrini is the only man to have missed a penalty during normal time in a FIFA World Cup final – the score was 0-0 at the time but, fortunately for him, Italy still beat West Germany 3-1 in 1982.

SO NEAR, SO ZAZA

Italy were one of only four teams to qualify unbeaten for the 2016 UEFA European Championship – and while Austria and Romania went out in the first round and England the second, Antonio Conte's side reached the quarter-finals before losing to Germany on penalties. Simone Zaza, brought on as a substitute just in time for the shoot-out, apologized afterwards for his missed spot-kick that followed a bizarrely intricate run-up. Italy's opening game against Belgium saw them field a starting-eleven with an average age of 31 years and 169 days – the oldest side in UEFA European Championship history.

IN SAFE KEEPING

During World War Two, the Jules Rimet Trophy, the FIFA World Cup – won by Italy in 1938 – was hidden in a shoebox under the bed of football official Ottorino Barassi. He preferred to keep it there, rather than at its previous home – a bank in Rome. The trophy was handed back to FIFA, safe and untouched, only when the FIFA World Cup resumed in 1950.

BLUE BOYS

Internazionale full-back Davide Santon became Italy's second-youngest international of the post-war era when he played against Northern Ireland in a June 2009 friendly, aged just 18 years and 155 days and following just 20 first-team appearances for his club. Another Internazionale defender, the richly moustachioed Giuseppe Bergomi, was 42 days younger when he made his debut against East Germany in April 1982, just three months before helping Italy win the FIFA World Cup. Even more junior were Casale midfielder Luigi Barbesino, 18 years and 61 days old against Sweden in July 1912, and record-holder Renzo De Vecchi, an AC Milan defender who was aged just 16 years and 112 days when he lined up against Hungary in May 1910.

GLOVE CONQUERS ALL

Walter Zenga went 517 minutes without conceding a goal at the 1990 FIFA World Cup, an all-time tournament record only brought to an end by Argentina's Claudio Caniggia in the semi-finals.

BOSSI DE ROSSI

Central midfielder Daniele de Rossi was roundly condemned when he was sent off for elbowing Brian McBride of the USA in a 2006 FIFA World Cup group match. His suspension finished in time for him to be a substitute in the final, which Italy won against France. However, in March 2006, De Rossi had won widespread praise for his honesty. During a Serie A match his club AS Roma were awarded a goal against Messina when he diverted the ball into the net with his hand and he persuaded the referee to disallow the goal (Roma still won 2-1). De Rossi's international honours also include an Olympic bronze medal from 2004 and, in November 2014 he became only the sixth Italian to win 100 caps, in a 1-1 draw against Croatia in a UEFA European Championship 2016 qualifier.

TOP DRAW

No team has drawn more FIFA World Cup matches than Italy, who took their tally to 21 with 1-1 draws against both Paraguay and New Zealand in Group F at the 2010 competition in South Africa. Their first draw had also been 1-1, against Spain in a 1934 quarter-final tie. Italy's **Giuseppe Meazza** scored the only goal of a replay the following day, and Italy went on to lift the trophy for the first time that year.

TOURNAMENT SPECIALISTS

FIFA WORLD CUP: 18 appearances – winners 1934, 1938, 1982, 2006
UEFA EUROPEAN CHAMPIONSHIP: 9 appearances – winners 1968
FIRST INTERNATIONAL: Italy 6 France 2 (Milan, 15 May 1910)
BIGGEST WIN: Italy 9 USA 0 (Brentford, London, 17 August 1948 – Olympic Games)
BIGGEST DEFEAT: Hungary 7 Italy 1 (Budapest, 6 April 1924)

FLYING HIGH

Vittorio Pozzo is the only man to have won the FIFA World Cup twice as manager – both times with Italy, in 1934 and 1938 (only two players, Giuseppe Meazza and Giovanni Ferrari, were selected in both finals). Pozzo also led Italy to the 1936 Olympics title. Born in Turin on 2 March 1886, Pozzo learned to love football as a student in England, watching Manchester United. He returned home reluctantly when his family bought him a return ticket for his sister's wedding and then refused to let him leave Italy again. Pozzo fired up his Italian team ahead of their 1938 semi-final against Brazil by revealing their opponents had already booked their plane to Paris for the final – Italy won 2-1.

THE FULL CONTE

After Italy crashed out in the first round of a second successive FIFA World Cup in 2014, they turned to a man with experience of a FIFA World Cup final – even though midfielder **Antonio Conte** was an unused substitute when the Italians lost on penalties to Brazil in 1994. He had also been on the bench when Italy were beaten 2-1 by France in the final of the 2000 UEFA European Championship, and lost three UEFA Champions League finals with Juventus, in 1997, 1998 and 2003. His playing career did, however, bring 20 international caps as well as five league titles with Juve and the UEFA Champions League – and he later returned to the Turin club as coach where he won Serie A three seasons in a row before taking the national job. Conte announced, before taking Italy to the 2016 UEFA European Championship quarter-finals, he would subsequently be joining English club Chelsea. He was succeeded by Giampiero Ventura – just as he had been at Bari in 2009.

ITALY'S NATIONAL COACHES

Vittorio Pozzo	1912, 1924
Augusto Rangone	1925–28
Carlo Carcano	1928–29
Vittorio Pozzo	1929–48
Ferruccio Novo	1949–50
Carlino Beretta	1952–53
Giuseppe Viani	1960
Giovanni Ferrari	1960–61
Giovanni Ferrari/Paolo Mazza	1962
Edmondo Fabbri	1962–66
Helenio Herrera/Ferruccio Valcareggi	1966–67
Ferruccio Valcareggi	1967–74
Fulvio Bernardini	1974–75
Enzo Bearzot	1975–86
Azeglio Vicini	1986–91
Arrigo Sacchi	1991–96
Cesare Maldini	1997–98
Dino Zoff	1998–2000
Giovanni Trapattoni	2000–04
Marcello Lippi	2004–06
Roberto Donadoni	2006–08
Marcello Lippi	2008–10
Cesare Prandelli	2010–14
Antonio Conte	2014–16
Giampiero Ventura	2016-

COMEBACK KID

Paolo Rossi was the unlikely hero of Italy's 1982 FIFA World Cup triumph, winning the Golden Boot with six goals – including a memorable hat-trick against Brazil in the second round, and the first of Italy's three goals in their final win over West Germany. But he only just made it to the tournament at all, having completed a two-year ban for his alleged involvement in a betting scandal only six weeks before the start of the tournament.

GIO WHIZZ

Sebastian Giovinco is thought to have become the world's highest-paid Italian footballer in February 2015 – with a salary reported to be in the region of $7 million – after a surprise move from Juventus, his hometown club, to US Major League Soccer side Toronto FC.

ONCE BITTEN, TWICE SHY

Italy went out of the 2014 FIFA World Cup in Brazil in the first round despite beating England in their opening game. They then suffered a pair of 1-0 defeats, first to surprise group winners Costa Rica – Italy's first FIFA World Cup defeat to a Central American nation – then to Uruguay, for whom Diego Godin netted a late goal. Italy were incensed Uruguay striker Luis Suarez had not been sent off for biting Giorgio Chiellini on the shoulder. The defender pulled down his shirt to show Mexican referee Marco Rodriguez the toothmarks left in his skin, but to no avail. In October 2014, Chiellini scored all three goals in Italy's 2-1 victory against Azerbaijan in a 2016 UEFA European Championship qualifier in Palermo. He opened the scoring just before half-time, found his own net with 14 minutes to go, but went on to head the *Azzurri*'s 82nd-minute winner.

TOP CAPS

1	Gianluigi Buffon	161
2	Fabio Cannavaro	136
3	Paolo Maldini	126
4	Andrea Pirlo	116
5	Dino Zoff	112
6	Daniele De Rossi	106
7	Gianluca Zambrotta	98
8	Giacinto Facchetti	94
9	Alessandro Del Piero	91
10	Giorgio Chiellini	88

TOP SCORERS

1	Luigi Riva	35
2	Giuseppe Meazza	33
3	Silvio Piola	30
4	Roberto Baggio	27
=	Alessandro Del Piero	27
6	Alessandro Altobelli	25
=	Adolfo Baloncieri	25
=	Filippo Inzaghi	25
9	Francesco Graziani	23
=	Christian Vieri	23

MISTER INTER, GIACINTO

No Internazionale footballer will ever wear the No.3 shirt after it was retired in tribute to the legendary full-back **Giacinto Facchetti**, following his death in 2006 at the age of 64. He spent his entire senior career at Inter, between 1960 and 1978, and later served as the club's technical director and president. In his playing days he helped pioneer the role of a full-back as a stampeding, attacking presence – though favoured his right foot despite advancing on the left. He captained Italy 70 times, during his 94-cap international career and lifted the UEFA European Championship trophy in 1968.

ZOFF THE SCALE

Goalkeeper **Dino Zoff** set an international record by going 1,142 minutes without conceding a goal between September 1972 and June 1974. Zoff was Italy's captain when they won the 1982 FIFA World Cup – emulating the feat of another Juventus goalkeeper, Gianpiero Combi, who had been the victorious skipper in 1934. Zoff coached Italy to the final of the 2000 UEFA European Championship, which they lost 2-1 to France thanks to an extra-time "golden goal" – then quit a few days later, unhappy following the criticism levelled at him by Italy's then prime minister, Silvio Berlusconi.

SHARE AND SHARE ALIKE

Manager Marcelo Lippi used all of outfield squad members when winning Italy's fourth FIFA World Cup in Germany in 2006 – and all six of his named strikers found the net once apiece, apart from Luca Toni who scored twice. He might have had a third, but his 110th-minute header against France in the final was disallowed for a marginal offside. The other forwards to score were Alessandro Del Piero, Francesco Totti, Alberto Gilardino, Vincenzo Iaquinta and Filippo Inzaghi. Toni retired from football at the end of the 2015–16 season at the age of 39, having a year earlier become the oldest man to finish as Serie A's top scorer.

SUPER MARIO

Mario Balotelli was born in Palermo to Ghanaian parents, but health problems as a child prompted him to be adopted by an Italian couple when he was three. He was given clearance to play for Italy when given citizenship at the age of 18 and was one of the country's star players at the 2012 UEFA European Championship, when he scored his first three international goals – including a decisive double against Germany in the semi-finals.

RIGHT START

Torino defender Emiliano Moretti became Italy's oldest debutant when he made his international bow in November 2014, a friendly against Albania, at the age of 33 years and 160 days. His debut may yet pall compared to that of striker **Christian Vieri**, who not only marked his first appearance with a goal, the second in his side's 3-0 win over Moldova in March 1997 – it was also the 1,000th goal Italy had scored in all internationals.

ROLLING RIVA

Italy's all-time top scorer is **Luigi "Gigi" Riva**, who scored 35 goals in 42 appearances for his country. One of his most important strikes was the opening goal in the 1968 UEFA European Championship final win over Yugoslavia. Despite his prolific form after having switched from left-winger to striker, he never played for one of Italy's traditional club giants. Instead, Riva – born in Leggiuno on 7 November 1944 – spent his entire league career with unfashionable Sardinian club Cagliari, and at one point turned down a move to the mighty Juventus. His goals (21 of them) fired the club to their one and only league championship in 1970. Riva suffered his fair share of bad luck with injuries, breaking his left leg while playing for Italy in 1966, then his right leg in 1970, again when he was away on international duty.

HAPPY CENTENARY

After captaining Italy to the 2006 FIFA World Cup title, **Fabio Cannavaro** was named FIFA World Player of the Year – at 33, the oldest winner of the prize, as well as the first defender. Cannavaro, born in Naples in 1973, played every minute of the 2006 tournament and the final triumph against France was the ideal way to celebrate his 100th international appearance.

WHEN THE GOING GETS BUFF

Italy goalkeeper **Gianluigi Buffon** has not only been one of the finest modern-day goalkeepers in
the world but has also even surpassed some of the achievements of legendary Italian predecessor
Dino Zoff. Buffon emulated 1982 world champion Dino Zoff by being part of Italy's 2006 FIFA World
Cup-winning side – only conceding two goals during the tournament, one an own goal and the
other a penalty. Italy's progress to the 2012 UEFA European Championship final allowed him to
play his 25th game at a finals for Italy, one more than Zoff – and behind only defenders Paolo
Maldini (36) and Fabio Cannavaro (26). Italy's dismal first-round exit at the 2010 FIFA World Cup
could be blamed at least more than a little on Buffon's back injury in the first half of their first
match that ruled him out of the rest of the tournament. Unlike fellow veterans Cannavaro and
Gennaro Gattuso, who retired from internationals after the finals, Buffon insisted he would go on
and was rewarded with the captaincy by incoming coach Cesare Prandelli. Buffon became only the
third footballer selected for five different FIFA World Cups when he made two appearances in Brazil
in 2014, only missing the opening match against England due to a late ankle injury. He captained
Italy at the 2016 UEFA European Championship, pushing past 160 caps.

CLEAN SWEEP

Italian clubs won all three
UEFA trophies in the 1989–90
season, a unique treble. AC
Milan took the European
Cup (beating Benfica 1-0 in
the final), Juventus the UEFA
Cup (beating Fiorentina 3-1)
and Sampdoria the Cup-
Winners' Cup (beating
Anderlecht 2-0
in the
final).

KEEPING IT IN THE FAMILY

Cesare and **Paolo Maldini** are the only father and son to have
hoisted the European Cup as winning captains – both with
AC Milan and both for the first time in England. Cesare lifted
the trophy after his team beat Benfica at Wembley, London,
in 1963. Paolo repeated the feat 40 years later, when Milan
defeated Juventus at Old Trafford, Manchester. Cesare was Italy
coach and Paolo Italy captain at the 1998 FIFA World Cup, and
they both featured at the 2002 tournament – though by now
Cesare was in charge of Paraguay. The Maldini dynasty may
not end there – Paolo's son, Christian, is emerging through
the youth ranks at Milan. If he makes it into the first team,
Christian will be the only player allowed to wear Paolo's
famous No. 3 jersey. Although he retired as Italy's
second most-capped player, Paolo never managed
to win an international tournament – he played for
Italy sides that finished third and runners-up at the
FIFA World Cup and runners-up in the UEFA European
Championship. Cesare died on 3 April 2016, aged 84.

TRAVELLING TRAPATTONI

Italian **Giovanni Trapattoni** has won domestic
league titles as a coach in Italy, Germany,
Portugal and Austria – with Juventus,
Bayern Munich, Benfica and Salzburg.
Only Portugal's Jose Mourinho has
also coached teams in four different
top countries to league title success.
Trapattoni is the only manager to have
won all three UEFA club competitions as
well as the World Club Cup, all with the
great Juventus sides of the 1980s.

ITALY'S GREATEST PLAYERS

(as chosen by the Italian
football association)

1 Giuseppe Meazza
2 Luigi Riva
3 Roberto Baggio
4 Paolo Maldini
5 Giacinto Facchetti
6 Sandro Mazzola
7 Giuseppe Bergomi
8 Valentino Mazzola

PEERLESS PIRLO

Deep-lying playmaker **Andrea Pirlo** – Italy's fourth most-capped player with 116 – is one of the finest passers of a football in the modern era. He was one of the stand-out performers when Italy won the 2006 FIFA World Cup and the only player to win three man-of-the-match prizes at the 2012 UEFA European Championship. Perhaps his finest moment of Euro 2012 was the "Panenka" penalty he chipped down the centre of the goal in Italy's quarter-final shoot-out victory over England. Pirlo came to the tournament having gone through the Italian league season unbeaten, helping Juventus lift the Serie A title after joining them in 2011 from AC Milan on a free transfer.

MEDAL COLLECTORS

Giovanni Ferrari not only enjoys the status of having won both the 1934 and 1938 FIFA World Cups with Italy, he also shares the record for most Serie A titles, with eight triumphs. Five were with Juventus, two with Internazionale and one with Bologna. He shares the record of eight league championship medals with Virginio Rosetta, twice with Pro Vercelli and six times with Juventus, and Giuseppe Furino, all with Juventus.

ITALIAN LEAGUE TITLES

Juventus	32	Lazio	2
Internazionale	18	Napoli	2
AC Milan	18	Cagliari	1
Genoa	9	Casale	1
Bologna	7	Hellas Verona	1
Pro Vercelli	7	Novese	1
Torino	7	Sampdoria	1
Roma	3	Spezia	1
Fiorentina	2		

TRAGIC TORINO

Torino were Italy's most successful club side when their first-team squad was wiped out in an air crash at Superga, above Turin, on 4 May 1949. The club has only won the Serie A title once since then, in the 1976–77 season. Among the victims was star forward Valentino Mazzola, who had gone along on the trip despite being ill. His son **Sandro Mazzola**, only six at the time of the disaster, went on to star in the Italy teams that won the 1968 UEFA European Championship and finished as FIFA World Cup runners-up two years later.

AZZURRI SEEING RED

Three men have been sent off twice for Italy, and three others have been dismissed on their debut. Pietro Rava marked his international bow by being sent off 53 minutes in, against the USA in August 1936 at the Berlin Olympics. Gianfranco Leoncini of Juventus, against Argentina in June 1966, and Cagliari's Davide Astori against Ukraine in March 2011 were also sent for early baths in their first appearances for Italy. The trio to have unhappily suffered two red cards apiece are Giancarlo Antognoni, Franco Causio and **Daniele De Rossi.**

BEEFING UP

The stadium shared by AC Milan and Internazionale is popularly known as the San Siro, after the district in which it is located. Its official title, however, is Stadio Giuseppe Meazza, named after the star inside-forward on the pitch and dance enthusiast off it who played for both clubs as well as Italy's 1934 and 1938 FIFA World Cup-winning sides. Meazza, born in Milan on 23 August 1910, was first spotted by an Inter scout while playing keepy-uppy in the street with a ball made of rags – but he was so thin he had to be fattened up with plenty of steaks. His last goal for Italy was a penalty in the 1938 World Cup semi-final against Brazil – taken while trying to pull up his shorts, whose elastic had broken.

WELL IN, EMANUELE

Emanuele Giaccherini scored Italy's fastest goal, just 19 seconds into their June 2013 friendly against Haiti in June 2013 – one second quicker than Salvatore Bagni's strike against Mexico 29 years earlier. The Haiti game finished 2-2 and was played to raise funds for victims of that country's 2010 earthquake.

NETHERLANDS

The walled banks of orange-shirted Netherlands fans may have become a regular feature at the world's major football tournaments, but that has not always been the case. It wasn't until the 1970s, with Johan Cruyff and his team's spectacular brand of "Total Football", that the country possessed a side worthy of the modern legend. They won the UEFA European Championship in 1988 and have regularly challenged for the game's major honours.

NETHERLANDS MANAGERS
(Since 1980)

Jan Zwartkruis	1978–81
Rob Baan	1981
Kees Rijvers	1981–84
Rinus Michels	1984–85
Leo Beenhakker	1985–86
Rinus Michels	1986–88
Thijs Libregts	1988–90
Nol de Ruiter	1990
Leo Beenhakker	1990
Rinus Michels	1990–92
Dick Advocaat	1992–95
Guus Hiddink	1995–98
Frank Rijkaard	1998–2000
Louis van Gaal	2000–02
Dick Advocaat	2002–04
Marco van Basten	2004–08
Bert van Marwijk	2008–12
Louis van Gaal	2012–14
Guus Hiddink	2014–15
Danny Blind	2015–

MICHELS THE MASTER

Rinus Michels (1928–2005) was named FIFA's Coach of the Century in 1999 for his achievements with the Netherlands and Ajax. The former Ajax and Netherlands striker took over the manager's job at his old club in 1965 and began creating the side that would dominate European football in the early 1970s. Michels built the team around Johan Cruyff – as he later did with the national side – and introduced the concept known as "Total Football". He moved to Barcelona after Ajax's 1971 European Cup victory, but he was called back to mastermind the Netherlands' 1974 FIFA World Cup bid. Nicknamed "The General", he was known as a disciplinarian who could impose order on the many different factions within the Dutch dressing room. Michels used that skill to great effect after taking over the national team again for their 1988 UEFA European Championship campaign. In the finals, the Dutch beat England and the Republic of Ireland to reach the last four, then knocked out hosts West Germany before beating the Soviet Union 2-0 in the final. Michels took charge for a third spell as manager when the Netherlands reached the semi-finals of Euro 92. He retired straight after the tournament.

CRUYFF THE MAGICIAN

The football world united in tribute to one of the all-time legends and finest players ever when Johan Cruyff died aged 68 on 24 March 2016. Former Barcelona striker Gary Lineker said: "Cruyff did more to make the beautiful game beautiful than anyone in history," and Diego Maradona acclaimed the Dutch playmaker, captain and coach with the message: "We will never forget you, mate." Dutch prime minister Mark Rutte said: "The whole world knew him and, through him, the world knew the Netherlands." Cruyff, who was born in Amsterdam on 25 April 1947, was not only a genius with the ball at his feet but also an inspirational football philosopher, who spread the concept of "Total Football" not only with Ajax Amsterdam and the Netherlands in the 1970s but also in Spain where he played and managed Barcelona and acted as a mentor to those who followed him there, such as Pep Guardiola and Xavi Hernandez. He also gave the world the much-imitated "Cruyff turn", after managing to push the ball with the inside of his foot behind his standing leg before swivelling and surging past bemused Swedish defender Jan Olsson.

KLAASSEN OF THE AJAX CLASS

Midfielder **Davy Klaassen**'s first international appearance, a 2-0 defeat to France in March 2014, meant he was the 100th player to make his Netherlands debut as an Ajax Amsterdam player, having been brought up in the club's famed youth academy. Although he had to wait 12 months for his second appearance, he did manage to score his first international goal in a 2-0 victory over Spain in March 2015.

LOUIS LOUIS

Louis van Gaal returned for a second spell as Netherlands coach after the 2012 UEFA European Championship. He has enjoyed great success at clubs around Europe, winning the UEFA Champions League with Ajax, two La Liga titles with Barcelona and the Bundesliga with Bayern Munich. After the 2014 FIFA World Cup he took over as manager of Manchester United. The Dutch are no strangers to reappointing former coaches: Karel Kaufman, Friedrich Donenfeld, Leo Beenhakker, Dick Advocaat and Rinus Michels all had more than one spell – and Michels had four. Van Gaal was succeeded by Guus Hiddink, his second spell, too, having been national coach 1995–98.

GOALS GALORE

Only four players have scored five goals in a game for the Netherlands: Jan Vos, as Finland were crushed 9-0 in July 1912; Leen Vente, in a 9-3 defeat of Belgium in March 1934; John Bosman, in an 8-0 home trouncing of Cyprus in October 1987; and Marco van Basten, in an 8-0 win in Malta in December 1990. Bosman scored three separate hat-tricks for the Dutch, as did Mannes Francken, Beb Bakhuys and Faas Wilkes. Two of Wilkes' trebles were scored in 1946 – the third came a full 13 years later.

HERO HAPPEL

Ernst Happel is second only to Rinus Michels for his coaching achievements with Dutch teams. The former Austria defender made history by steering Feyenoord to the European Cup in 1970 – the first Dutch side to win the trophy. He was drafted in to coach the Netherlands at the 1978 FIFA World Cup finals after guiding Belgian side Brugge to the European Cup final. In Johan Cruyff's absence, Happel drew the best from Ruud Krol, Johan Neeskens and Arie Haan as the Netherlands reached the final before losing in extra-time to Argentina in Buenos Aires.

ALL CHANGE FOR THE ORANJE

Ten of the 11 men who started the 2010 FIFA World Cup final were in the Dutch squad for a disastrous UEFA European Championship in 2012. They lost all three first-round games and missed the knock-out stages of a major tournament for the first time since failing to qualify for Euro 2004. Things improved dramatically at the 2014 FIFA World Cup as the Netherlands finished third after losing the semi-final to Argentina in a penalty shoot-out. Only nine members of the 23-man Euro 2012 squad made it to Brazil 2014. The most memorable Dutch display in Brazil came in their opening match: avenging their 2010 FIFA World Cup final defeat by demolishing champions Spain 5-1 in Salvador. **Robin van Persie**'s fantastic diving header from the edge of the area that looped over goalkeeper Iker Casillas was the highlight. Van Persie thus became the first Dutchman to score at three separate FIFA World Cups. The 2014 FIFA World Cup was the first one which the Netherlands ended with a win: their 3-0 third-place play-off defeat of hosts Brazil. This set another record as the Netherlands became the first country to beat Brazil in FIFA World Cup finals three times.

VAN BASTEN'S TOURNAMENT

Marco van Basten was the hero of the Netherlands' 1988 UEFA European Championship success. He netted a hat-trick to see off England in the group games, scored a semi-final winner against West Germany, and then cracked a spectacular flying volley to clinch a 2-0 victory over the Soviet Union in the final. The Dutch forward also starred in Italy's Serie A with AC Milan, and was twice the league's top scorer before persistent ankle trouble ended his career prematurely. He was then Netherlands coach for their runs to the second round of the 2006 FIFA World Cup and quarter-finals of the UEFA European Championship two years later.

HANGING AROUND

Goalkeeper Sander Boschker waited a long time for his full introduction to international football, but he set two Dutch records when coming on as a second-half substitute against Ghana in a June 2010 friendly. At the age of 39 years and 256 days, he was not only the oldest Dutchman to win his first cap – but also the oldest Dutch international ever. He retired in 2014 and it proved to be his only cap.

FLYING FEAR DENIED BERGKAMP MORE CAPS

Dennis Bergkamp would have won many more than 79 caps, but for his fear of flying. Bergkamp refused to board aircraft after the Netherlands squad were involved in a bomb hoax incident during the 1994 FIFA World Cup in the United States. He missed every away game for the Netherlands and his clubs unless he could reach the venue by road, rail or boat. His intricately-skilful last-minute winner against Argentina in the quarter-finals of the 1998 FIFA World Cup is seen by many as one of the tournament's finest and most elegant goals.

DIFFERENT SIDES OF SNEIJDER

Wesley Sneijder was hoping to achieve an unprecedented quintuple when his Netherlands team took on Spain in the 2010 FIFA World Cup final. No footballer had ever before won the FIFA World Cup in the same season as a domestic league and cup double and the UEFA Champions League or European Cup – let alone adding the FIFA World Cup Golden Boot. Sneijder won the 2009–10 treble with his club side Internazionale before only just missing out on the FIFA World Cup and the Golden Boot. Despite his FIFA World Cup final heartbreak, Sneijder did enjoy some romantic solace six days after defeat to Spain, when he married Dutch actress and TV presenter Yolanthe Cabau van Kasbergen.

TOP CAPS

1	Edwin van der Sar	130
2	Wesley Sneijder	120
3	Frank de Boer	112
4	Rafael van der Vaart	109
5	Gio van Bronckhorst	106
6	Dirk Kuyt	104
7	Phillip Cocu	101
=	Robin van Persie	101
9	Arjen Robben	88
10	John Heitinga	87
=	Clarence Seedorf	87

NEESKENS'S EARLY GOAL

The Netherlands took a first-minute lead in the 1974 World Cup final without a West German player having touched the ball. The Dutch built a move of 14 passes from the kick-off and Johan Cruyff was tripped in the box by Uli Hoeness. **Johan Neeskens** converted the first penalty in a World Cup final history ... but they still went on to lose.

KRUL TO BE KIND

Louis van Gaal pulled a masterstoke when he replaced goalkeeper Jasper Cillessen with Tim Krul in the 119th minute of the Netherlands' quarter-final against Costa Rica in the 2014 FIFA World Cup. He reasoned that the Dutch stood a better chance of winning the resulting shoot-out with Krul between the sticks as he is two inches taller than Cillessen. Sure enough, Krul saved two penalties and the Dutch went through. Enforced substitutions during the semi-final against Argentina meant van Gaal could not repeat the trick and Cillessen was unable to emulate Krul's earlier heroics. Third-choice goalkeeper Michel Vorm replaced Cillessen during stoppage-time of the third-place play-off against Brazil, making the Netherlands the first country to field all 23 squad-members during a FIFA World Cup.

NETHERLANDS' DOUBLE LOSERS

Nine Netherlands players were on the losing side in both the 1974 (2-1 to West Germany) and 1978 (3-1 to Argentina) FIFA World Cup finals. Jan Jongbloed, Ruud Krol, Wim Jansen, Arie Haan, Johan Neeskens, Johnny Rep and Rob Rensenbrink started both games. Wim Suurbier started in 1974 and was a substitute in 1978. Rene van de Kerkhof was a sub in 1974 and started in 1978.

THE WINNING CAPTAIN

With his distinctive dreadlocks, **Ruud Gullit** cut a swathe through world football through the 1980s and '90s. Twice a European Cup winner with AC Milan and a former European Footballer of the Year, he will always be remembered fondly by the Dutch fans as being the first man in a Netherlands shirt to lift a major trophy – the 1988 UEFA European Championship.

TOP SCORERS

1	Robin van Persie	50
2	Klaas-Jan Huntelaar	42
3	Patrick Kluivert	40
4	Dennis Bergkamp	37
5	Ruud van Nistelrooy	35
=	Faas Wilkes	35
7	Johan Cruyff	33
=	Abe Lenstra	33
9	Arjen Robben	30
10	Wesley Sneijder	29

DE BOER BOYS SET RECORD

Twins **Frank** and **Ronald de Boer** hold the record for the most games played by brothers together for the Netherlands. Frank won 112 caps, while Ronald won 67. Ronald missed a crucial spot-kick as the Dutch lost to Brazil in the semi-finals of the 1998 FIFA World Cup, while Frank suffered a similar unfortunate fate at the same stage of the UEFA European Championship two years later. Frank took over as Ajax Amsterdam manager in December 2010, having earlier that year been assistant to Bert van Marwijk to help the Netherlands to the FIFA World Cup final.

TWO LOOK FAMILIAR

Twin brothers Arnold and Anton Horburger were called up to the Netherlands' 12-man squad for a game against Belgium in April 1910, but only Arnold was picked to play in an era when substitutes were not permitted. However, Arnold left the pitch with a knee injury after half an hour but returned, seemingly fully fit, for the second half. The Belgians were convinced that twin Anton had taken the field instead, suggestions both players laughingly dismissed. Arnold went on to make eight international appearances, but Anton never played for his country – officially, at least.

REP IT UP

Arjen Robben and Robin van Persie are the only Dutch footballers to score at three separate FIFA World Cups, both finding the net in 2006, 2010 and 2014. They have six FIFA World Cup goals apiece, as do Rob Rensenbrink (1974 and 1978), Dennis Bergkamp (1994 and 1998) and Wesley Sneijder (2010 and 2014). The Netherlands' leading FIFA World Cup scorer, however, remains Johnny Rep. He scored seven goals across the 1974 and 1978 tournaments.

WORK OF VAART

Rafael van der Vaart became the fifth player to make 100 appearances for the Netherlands, following Edwin van der Sar, Frank de Boer, Giovanni van Bronckhorst and Philip Cocu. Yet for a while it looked as if van der Vaart might just miss out on the milestone: he ended the 2012 UEFA European Championship on 99 caps and coach Bert van Marwijk said he may be left out of future squads. But Van Marwijk's departure after Euro 2012 was a boost for van der Vaart, who made his 100th appearance in a 4-2 friendly loss to Belgium in August 2012. Van der Vaart had marked his 99th cap with a stunning long-range goal against Portugal in the Netherlands' final first-round game at Euro 2012, and hit a post, in the 2-1 defeat that ended Dutch interest earlier than expected. Sadly, a calf injury ruled him out of the 2014 FIFA World Cup three days before Louis van Gaal announced his 23-man squad.

ALL-TIME LEADING SCORERS

Patrick Kluivert made his Netherlands debut in 1994 and, in the following ten years, won 79 caps and scored a then national record 40 goals. That mark was beaten by Robin van Persie, who was Netherlands captain at the 2014 FIFA World Cup, while Kluivert watched on as Louis van Gaal's assistant coach. Five goals in four games between November 2014 and June 2015 took Klaas-Jan Huntelaar to 41, one more than Kluivert, and in 72 appearances.

EARLY DAYS

The Netherlands played their first international against Belgium in Brussels on 30 April 1905. Eddy de Neve scored all the goals in the Netherlands' 4-1 win. The Dutch and their Belgian neighbours have been arch-rivals ever since.

BLIND LEADING THE BLIND

Dutch defender **Danny Blind** won 42 caps between 1986 and 1996, and appeared at the FIFA World Cups of 1990 and 1994. He was also involved at the 2014 final, this time as an assistant to coach Louis van Gaal. He thus got to see his son **Daley** – like Danny, a defender playing club football for Ajax Amsterdam – not only feature as a regular starter but score his first international goal, in the third-place play-off victory over Brazil. Danny Blind was appointed as Guus Hiddink's assistant for the 2016 UEFA European Championship qualifying campaign, with the promise of the top job at the end of that tournament but the chance came sooner, with Blind taking over in June 2015 as the Dutch failed to reach the finals.

SIXTH SENSE

Maarten Stekelenburg, Edwin van der Sar's successor as the Netherlands' first-choice goalkeeper, impressed many with his performances at the 2010 FIFA World Cup, conceding just six goals in seven games – two of them penalties. His rise is all the more startling because he is deaf in one ear. He also has the unenviable distinction of being the first Dutch international goalkeeper to be shown a red card. On 6 September 2008, in a 2-1 friendly defeat against Australia in Eindhoven, he was sent off for fouling Josh Kennedy.

KOEMAN PEOPLE

The only man to both play for and manage all of Dutch domestic football's "big three" of Ajax Amsterdam, PSV Eindhoven and Feyenoord is Ronald Koeman. He won the UEFA European Cup twice, with PSV Eindhoven in 1988, and with Barcelona four years later – a game in which he scored the winning goal, a ferocious long-range free-kick. Despite largely playing in defence, he scored 14 goals in 78 games for the Netherlands. Elder brother Erwin played 31 times for the Netherlands and their father Martin won one cap for his country in 1964. Both Ronald and Erwin were part of the Netherlands' 1988 UEFA European Championship-winning side.

MEMPHIS SWELL

Substitute Memphis Depay became the youngest FIFA World Cup goalscorer in Dutch history – aged 20 years and 125 days – by netting in the 3-2 Group B victory over Australia at Porto Alegre in 2014. He also scored against Chile five days later, again as a substitute. Depay was one of three nominees for the Best Young Player award, but lost out to France's Paul Pogba.

JETRO POWERED

Left-back **Jetro Willems** became the youngest player in UEFA European Championship tournament history when he started for the Netherlands against Denmark in their opening Group B game in the Ukrainian city of Kharkiv on 9 June 2012. He was 18 years and 71 days old, 44 days younger than Belgium's Enzo Scifo had been at the 1984 finals. Willems is the fourth-youngest player to be capped by the Netherlands, with the record held by Jan van Breda Kolff, who was 17 years and 74 days old when making his debut against Belgium on 2 April 1911. Van Breda Kolff's goal in a 3-1 win, the only one of his 11-cap career, means he remains his country's youngest scorer.

ABE AND WILLING

Abe Lenstra was, until 2010, the oldest Dutch player to appear in an international, but he does remain the nation's oldest goalscorer – something he achieved in his final international, a 2-2 draw with Belgium, on 19 April 1959, at the age of 38 years and 144 days. The country's second oldest goalscorer, and his regular strike partner, Faas Wilkes, found the net for the last time just over two years later – striking in a 1-1 draw against East Germany in May 1961, aged 37 years and 213 days. Lenstra scored 33 goals in 47 internationals while Wilkes – who endured a six-year hiatus from of the national side when playing his club football abroad for Internazionale, Torino and Valencia – managed 35 in 38. Lenstra is also thought to be the first Dutch sports star to record and release a single, "Geen, maar daden" ("No words but deeds"), in 1958.

PENALTY PLAGUE

Missed penalties have become a Dutch nightmare, causing their downfall in several tournaments. The jinx started in the 1992 UEFA European Championship semi-final, when Denmark's Peter Schmeichel won the shoot-out by saving from Marco van Basten. The Netherlands lost a Euro 96 quarter-final shoot-out to France and, two years later, went down on penalties to Brazil in a FIFA World Cup semi-final. And as co-hosts of Euro 2000, the Dutch missed two penalties in normal time in the semi-final against Italy and two more in the shoot-out. There was shoot-out joy at the 2014 FIFA World Cup when Costa Rica were beaten, but it turned to misery in the semi-final when they lost to Argentina on penalties.

VAN DER SAR TOPS THE LOT

Goalkeeper **Edwin van der Sar** (born in Voorhout on 29 October 1970) is the Netherlands' most-capped player, having made 130 appearances for the national side. He joined Ajax in 1990 and helped them win the European Cup five years later. He made his Netherlands debut on 7 June 1995, against Belarus, and was their first-choice keeper for 13 years. He quit international football after the Netherlands' elimination at Euro 2008, but new coach Bert van Marwijk persuaded him to return briefly after injuries to his successors, Maarten Stekelenburg and Henk Timmer. Van der Sar has also won the UEFA Champions League with Manchester United, as well as spending spells with Juventus and Fulham.

DUTCH CLOGS

The Netherlands became the first team to be shown as many as nine cards during a single FIFA World Cup match when they received eight yellows, including a lenient one for Nigel de Jong's chest-high challenge on Xabi Alonso, and a red during the 2010 final against Spain. The Netherlands were also involved in the FIFA World Cup game with the most cards: their second-round defeat to Portugal four years earlier, when 20 cards were shown in total – 16 yellows and four reds.

HIGH–SCORING "LOW COUNTRIES DERBY"

The Netherlands' first official international was against Belgium in April 1905, a 4-1 extra-time win and they have since met another 125 times – almost four times more than any other opponent, which is Switzerland with 33. Only Argentina and Uruguay (186) and Austria and Hungary (135), have met more often. The Netherlands' overall record against Belgium is 56 wins, 29 draws and 41 losses. One of the bitterest clashes was a goalless 1974 FIFA World Cup qualifier, which left the Netherlands top of the group, but Belgium had a last-minute "goal" controversially disallowed. Memorable scorelines include Dutch wins 9-3 in March 1934, 8-0 in March 1936 and 9-1 in November 1959, defeats 7-1 in March 1940 and 7-6 in November 1951, and a 5-5 draw in September 1999. The most recent meeting was a 4-2 Belgium win in August 2012.

SPAIN

Spain is home to some of Europe's strongest club sides (boasting 16 European Cup/UEFA Champions League wins between them) and has produced some of football's biggest names. For years, however, the national team was considered the world game's biggest underachievers (*La Roja's* only success had been the 1964 UEFA European Championship). Things changed in 2008, when Spain won the UEFA European Championship, its first international success for 44 years and a first-ever top position in the Coca-Cola/FIFA World Rankings. Even better came with victory in the 2010 FIFA World Cup, and an unprecedented third straight major trophy when the European crown was retained in 2012. But a disappointing first-round exit at the 2014 FIFA World Cup saw the run end.

FABREGAS 10

TRIPLE CROWN

Andres Iniesta was named man of the match in Barcelona's 2015 UEFA Champions League final victory over Juventus, making him the first man to win the prize in a UEFA Champions League final, a UEFA European Championship final (2012) and a FIFA World Cup final (2010). Spain were unable to claim a third successive UEFA European Championship in 2016, but their progress to the second round moved **Iniesta** and fellow midfielder **Cesc Fabregas** to a tournament record 11 victories apiece.

DOUBLING UP

Spain's 2010 FIFA World Cup triumph made them the first country since West Germany in 1974 to lift the trophy as the reigning European champions. When France combined the two titles, they did it the other way around, by winning the 1998 FIFA World Cup and then the UEFA European Championship two years later. Yet no country had won three major tournaments in a row until Spain won Euro 2012, trouncing Italy 4-0 in the final. This also made Spain the first team to make a successful defence of their UEFA European Championship title. That scoreline was also the largest victory in a FIFA World Cup or UEFA European Championship final. The clean sheet in the final also stretched their run without conceding a goal in knockout games at major tournaments to 990 minutes.

HARD TO BEAT

Spain share with Brazil the record for longest international unbeaten run – the Brazilians went 35 games without a defeat between 1993 and 1996, a tally matched by the Spanish from 2007 until losing 2-0 to the United States in a 2009 FIFA Confederations Cup semi-final. That vintage Spain side also became the only country to secure 30 points out of 30 points in a FIFA World Cup qualification campaign, and they went on to to lift the trophy in South Africa in 2010.

THREE AND EASY

David Villa and Fernando Torres share Spain's record for most hat-tricks, with three. They even managed one apiece in the same match, the 10-0 crushing of Tahiti at the 2013 FIFA Confederations Cup. It was Spain's third-largest victory, behind only a 13-0 win over Bulgaria in 1933 and a 12-1 rout of Malta in 1983. Torres set another record at the 2009 FIFA Confederations Cup: the fastest ever hat-trick for Spain, all coming in the first 17 minutes of a 5-0 victory over New Zealand.

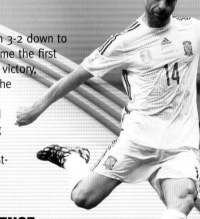

GROUNDS FOR APPEAL

No single country has provided more venues when hosting a FIFA World Cup finals than the 17 stadiums – in 14 cities – used by Spain in 1982. The 2002 tournament was played at 20 different venues but ten were in Japan and ten in South Korea. The 1982 competition was the first FIFA World Cup to be expanded from 16 to 24 teams. The final was played in Madrid's Estadio Santiago Bernabeu.

RIGHT SAID FRED

When Spain came back from 2-0 and then 3-2 down to win 4-3 in Madrid in May 1929, they became the first non-British team to beat England. Spain's victory, in the Estadio Metropolitano, came with the help of their English coach Fred Pentland, who had moved to Spain in 1920. He had most success with Athletic Bilbao, leading them to league and cup doubles in 1930 and 1931 – and inflicting Barcelona's worst-ever defeat, a 12-1 rout in 1931.

NOT TOO SHABBY XABI

Passmaster Xabi Alonso scored both goals as Spain beat France 2-0 in their 2012 UEFA European Championship quarter-final – an ideal way for him to celebrate a day in which he became the fifth Spaniard, after Iker Casillas, Raul, Xavi and Andoni Zubizarreta, to make 100 international appearances. The central midfielder's father Periko Alonso won 21 Spanish caps as well as three La Liga titles – two with Real Sociedad and one with Barcelona – though Xabi would later play for Barca's arch-rivals Real Madrid. Xabi's brother Mikel and half-brother Marcos are both professional footballers, while another brother Jon is a referee.

NO DEFENCE

Spain went into the 2014 FIFA World Cup in Brazil aiming not only to successfully retain their crown but also to clinch a historic fourth successive international title, having won the UEFA European Championship in 2008 and 2012. Yet their defence was a disaster – despite taking the lead against the Netherlands in their opening game through a **Xabi Alonso** penalty, they lost the match 5-1: the heaviest FIFA World Cup finals defeat any reigning champion have suffered. A 2-0 defeat to Chile made them the first defending champions to be eliminated with a game remaining, though they gained a token consolation with a 3-0 defeat of Australia. The competition brought to an end the otherwise-glorious international careers of players such as Xavi Hernandez and David Villa.

MAJOR TOURNAMENTS

FIFA WORLD CUP:
14 appearances – winners 2010

UEFA EUROPEAN CHAMPIONSHIP:
10 appearances – winners 1964, 2008, 2012

FIRST INTERNATIONAL:
Spain 1 Denmark 0 (Brussels, Belgium, 28 August 1920)

BIGGEST WIN:
Spain 13 Bulgaria 0 (Madrid, 21 May 1933)

BIGGEST DEFEAT:
Italy 7 Spain 1 (Amsterdam, Netherlands, 4 June 1928); England 7 Spain 1 (London, England, 9 December 1931)

RED ALERT

Spain refused to play in the first UEFA European Championship in 1960, in protest at having to travel to the Soviet Union, a Communist country. But they changed their minds four years later, not only hosting the tournament but also winning it – by beating the visiting Soviets 2-1 in the final. Spain were captained by Fernando Olivella and managed by Jose Villalonga, who had been the first coach to win the European Cup, with Real Madrid in 1956.

WISE HEAD, OLD SHOULDERS

In 2008, a month short of his 70th birthday, Spain's **Luis Aragones** – full name Luis Aragones Suarez – became the oldest coach to win the UEFA European Championship. A former centre-forward and known only as "Luis" during his playing days, he won 11 caps for Spain. As coach, the "Wise Man of Hortaleza" won 38 matches between 2004 and 2008 – a national record since beaten by his successor Vicente Del Bosque. Aragones died from leukaemia on 1 February 2014, aged 75. Tributes were paid across football, but especially at his former club Atletico Madrid who, that same weekend, went top of La Liga for the first time since 1995–96 – when Aragones was coach. Atletico later won their first title since 1996. The players also wore his name embroidered in gold inside the collars of their shirts during the 2014 UEFA Champions League final.

TORRES! TORRES!

As a child, **Fernando Torres** wanted to be a goalkeeper, but made the wise decision to become a striker instead. He has a penchant for scoring the only goal in the final of a tournament, doing so in the 2008 UEFA European Championship, for Spain against Germany in Vienna, having done the same in the Under-16 UEFA European Championship in 2001 and for the Under-19s the following year. Torres became the most expensive Spanish footballer ever when Chelsea paid €58.5million to sign him from fellow English club Liverpool in January 2011. In 2012, Torres became the first player to score in the final of two different UEFA European Championships, when he came on as a substitute and found the net against Italy. Torres's goal in Spain's 3-0 victory over Australia in June 2014 was his first at a FIFA World Cup finals since Germany 2006. He thus became the ninth Spanish player to have scored four FIFA World Cup goals.

TOP SCORERS

1	David Villa	59
2	Raul Gonzalez	44
3	Fernando Torres	38
4	Fernando Hierro	29
5	Fernando Morientes	27
6	Emilio Butragueno	26
7	David Silva	24
8	Alfredo Di Stefano	23
9	Julio Salinas	22
10	Michel	21

BEST CAS SCENARIO

Spain goalkeeper Iker Casillas has long been known to devotees back home as "Saint Iker" – an anointment richly supported by his haul of trophies and medals, both for team and individual. He is one of only three men to lift the FIFA World Cup, the UEFA European Championship and the UEFA Champions League trophies as captain, emulating Germany's Franz Beckenbauer and France's Didier Deschamps. As well as winning the 2008 and 2012 UEFA European Championships and the 2010 FIFA World Cup, he is also not only Spain's but Europe's most-capped player. He claimed the Spanish record in a rare defeat, 1-0 to England in November 2011, before passing Latvia's Vitalijs Astafjevs and winning his 167th cap in a 6-1 friendly victory over South Korea in June 2016 – only to be left on the bench, to his evident disappointment, throughout the 2016 UEFA European Championship.

SAVING FOR A REINA DAY

Jose 'Pepe' Reina finally saw action in the FIFA World Cup – at his third finals – when picked for Spain's 3-0 victory over Australia in June 2014. He had been an unused member at Germany 2006 and South Africa 2010. It was Reina's 34th appearance for Spain since making his debut in 2005. His father, Manuel Reina, also a goalkeeper, played in five internationals between 1969 and 1973.

HAPPY HERNANDEZ

When Spain's second most capped outfield player, with 133, retired from international football after the 2014 FIFA World Cup – and La Liga a year later – he was recognized as his country's most-decorated player. Curiously, both the first and final appearances of **Xavi Hernandez**'s international career were defeats to Netherlands sides coached by Louis van Gaal, 2-1 in 2000 and 5-1 in 2014. Triumph was far more familiar to the midfield playmaker, a mainstay of Spain's 2010 FIFA World Cup-winning side as well as the teams lifting the UEFA European Championship trophy in 2008 and 2012. The last match of his 24-year spell with Barcelona was, fittingly, their victory in the 2015 UEFA Champions League final, when he received the trophy from UEFA president Michel Platini, having come on as a late substitute for Andres Iniesta. Xavi collected a Spanish record 25 winners' medals with Barcelona, was named player of the tournament at the 2008 UEFA European Championship and his 82 competitive matches is second only to Latvia's Vitalijs Astafjevs in Europe.

TOP CAPS

1	Iker Casillas	167
2	Sergio Ramos	136
3	Xavi Hernandez	133
4	Andoni Zubizarreta	126
5	Xabi Alonso	114
6	Andres Iniesta	113
7	Cesc Fabregas	110
=	Fernando Torres	110
9	David Silva	103
10	Raul Gonzalez	102

VILLA FILLS HIS BOOTS

David Villa became Spain's all-time top scorer in FIFA World Cups with his first-round goal against Chile in 2010, his sixth overall across the 2006 and 2010 tournaments. Villa also became the first Spaniard to miss a penalty in a FIFA World Cup match, when he wasted the chance of a hat-trick against Honduras, also in 2010, by putting his spot-kick wide. Spain had scored their previous 14 FIFA World Cup penalties, not counting shoot-outs. Villa became Spain's all-time leading scorer with a brace against the Czech Republic in March 2011, but a broken leg ruled him out of the 2012 UEFA European Championship, thus missing out on adding to his Euro 2008 and 2010 FIFA World Cup winners' medals. Villa retired from international football as Spain departed the 2014 FIFA World Cup, signing off with a neat backheel goal against Australia – his 59th international strike in 97 appearances and the first backheeled goal at a FIFA World Cup since Austria's Bruno Pezzey against Northern Ireland in 1982.

SERGING SERGIO

Sergio Ramos became the youngest-ever European player to reach 100 international caps, in March 2013, at the age of 26 years and 358 days – and marked the occasion by scoring Spain's goal in a 1-1 draw with Finland. Germany's Lukas Podolski, had been 21 days older when he won his 100th cap. South Korea's Cha Bum-Kun, who was 24 years and 139 days old when he achieved the landmark, holds the global record. Ramos, who can play both at right-back or in central defence, played in Spain's team that won the 2008 and 2012 UEFA European Championships, as well as the 2010 FIFA World Cup. He held those trophies in safer hands than he had done when he raised the Spanish Copa del Rey, won by his club Real Madrid, during an open-top bus tour in April 2011: on that occasion, he dropped the cup from the upper deck and saw it crushed beneath the bus's wheels. He passed Xavi Hernandez to become Spain's second most capped player during the 2016 UEFA European Championship.

FIT FOR PURPOSE

Luis Suarez played through injury for Spain in the 1964 UEFA European Championship final – luckily for his team-mates, since he set up both goals in a 2-1 triumph. He was named European Footballer of the Year in 1960 – the only Spanish-born player to have taken the prize.

TRI-NATIONS

Ladislav Kubala played for not one, not two, but three different countries – though he never appeared in the finals of a major international tournament. Despite being born in Budapest on 10 June 1927, he made his international debut for Czechoslovakia in 1946 – winning five more caps for the country of his parents' birth. He then appeared three times for birthplace Hungary after moving back to the country in 1948, before playing 19 games for Spain after leaving Hungary as a refugee and securing a transfer to Barcelona in 1951.

VICTORY MARCH

Centre-back Carlos Marchena became the first footballer to go 50 internationals in a row unbeaten, when he played in Spain's 3-2 victory over Saudi Arabia in May 2009 – one more than Brazil's 1950s and 1960s winger Garrincha. Marchena was a member of Spain's successful 2010 FIFA World Cup squad, ending the tournament on 54 consecutive internationals without defeat. Marchena's 57-game unbeaten run came to an end when Argentina beat Spain 4-1 in September 2010.

TREASURE CHEST

The Spanish first division goalkeeper who concedes the fewest goals per game each season is awarded the Zamora Trophy. This is named after legendary keeper **Ricardo Zamora**, who played 46 times for Spain between 1920 and 1936 – including the legendary 4-3 win over England in Madrid in 1929. Zamora was the first Spanish star to play for both Barcelona and Real Madrid. Later he was league title-winning coach of ... Atletico Madrid.

LUCKY JUAN

Only one player has failed to score in a FIFA World Cup penalty shoot-out with a spot-kick that would have won the game had it gone in: Spain's Juan Carlos Valeron, whose effort went wide against the Republic of Ireland in 2002. The shoot-out score was 2-1 in Spain's favour, with just an Irish attempt to follow, when he missed – but his team went on to win anyway.

FAMILIAR FACES, UNFAMILIAR OUTCOME

Sixteen players from Spain's triumphant 2010 FIFA World Cup squad were picked for the 2014 tournament and seven who played in the final started against the Netherlands in their opening game four years later – the Dutch had four. It was the first time that the two countries to meet in a FIFA World Cup final played each other in the first-round of the next tournament. Spain's 5-1 defeat at the hands of the Dutch in Salvador was their heaviest FIFA World Cup defeat since losing 6-1 to Brazil in 1950.

SPANISH LEAGUE CHAMPIONSHIPS

Real Madrid	32
Barcelona	24
Atletico Madrid	10
Athletic Bilbao	8
Valencia	6
Real Sociedad	2
Deportivo de la Coruna	1
Sevilla	1
Betis	1

THE RAUL THING

Raul Gonzalez Blanco – known as Raul – remains a Spain and Real Madrid icon, despite his record goal tallies being passed, respectively, by David Villa and Cristiano Ronaldo. He was an Atletico Madrid youth-teamer before signing for city rivals Real, where he scored 228 goals in 550 games and captained them from 2003 to 2010. But despite playing at five tournaments between the 1998 and 2006 FIFA World Cups, he was left out of Spain's UEFA Euro 2008 squad – and they won the trophy. After leaving Real, Raul enjoyed further success at Schalke in Germany, Al Sadd in Qatar and New York Cosmos in the United States.

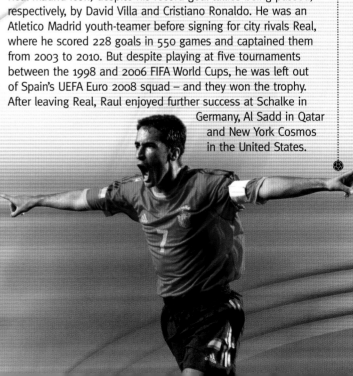

SUPER PED

Spanish winger **Pedro** is the only player to have scored in six separate official club tournaments in one calendar year, managing to hit the net for Barcelona in Spain's Primera Liga, Copa del Rey and Super Cup in 2009, as well as the UEFA Champions League, UEFA European Super Cup and FIFA Club World Cup. He was also in the starting line-up for the 2010 FIFA World Cup final – less than two years after being a member of the Barcelona reserve team in Spain's third division and needing new club manager Pep Guardiola's intervention to prevent him being sent home to Tenerife.

PERFECT PICHICHI

The annual award for top scorer in La Liga is called the "Pichichi" – the nickname of Rafael Moreno, a striker for Athletic Bilbao between 1911 and 1921. He scored 200 goals in 170 games for the club, and once in five matches for Spain. Pichichi, who often took the field wearing a large white cap, died suddenly in 1922 aged just 29.

WAITING FOR BUS

Barcelona midfielder **Sergio Busquets** won the FIFA World Cup, UEFA European Championship and two UEFA Champions Leagues before turning 24 in July 2012, but he only broke his scoring duck for Spain in September 2014 – his 68th cap – in a 5-1 win over Macedonia. Since then, he has claimed a third UEFA Champions League, and second international goal. His father, Carles Busquets, was a Barcelona goalkeeper in the 1990s, part of Johan Cruyff's 1992 UEFA European Cup-winning squad, though he was mainly understudy to Andoni Zubizarreta.

SEMI PRECIOUS

Centre-back Carles Puyol's thumping header not only gave Spain victory in their 2010 FIFA World Cup semi-final – it was also the country's first win over Germany in four FIFA World Cup matches. West Germany had won 2-1 in both 1966 and 1982, before a 1-1 draw at the 1994 tournament. But Spain's 1-0 win in 2010 was a repeat of their triumph over Germany in the UEFA European Championship final two years earlier. Puyol played his 100th and final international against Uruguay in February 2013, and retired from all forms of the game aged 36 in May 2014.

FIFA FIRST

Real Madrid were the only Spanish club formally represented at FIFA's first meeting in Paris in 1904 – though the club was then known simply as Madrid FC. Spanish clubs, such as Real Madrid and Real Betis, dropped the word "Real" – meaning "Royal" – from their names during the Second Spanish Republic, between 1931 and 1939.

SPAIN'S PLAYERS IN EURO 2008/FIFA WORLD CUP 2010/ EURO 2012 SQUADS

Iker Casillas*
Sergio Ramos*
Andres Iniesta*
Xabi Alonso*
Xavi Hernandez*
Cesc Fabregas*
Fernando Torres*
David Silva
Alvaro Arbeloa
Raul Albiol
Pepe Reina

* = appeared in all three finals.

TOP BOSS DEL BOSQUE

Vicente Del Bosque was an unused substitute during Ladislao Kubala's 68th and final match in charge of Spain in 1980. He was on Spain bench again when *La Roja* played Denmark in March 2013, but this time as manager, and for the 69th time, enabling him to surpass Kubala's record. Del Bosque won the 2010 FIFA World Cup and the 2012 UEFA European Championship as Spain manager, adding to the two UEFA Champions League titles he claimed as Real Madrid boss. He and Italy's Marcelo Lippi are the only men to have won both the UEFA Champions League or European Cup and the FIFA World Cup – but Del Bosque's Euro 2012 triumph gave him an unprecedented hat-trick. Another unmatched feat was his 13 victories in his first 13 matches as Spain manager after he succeeded Luis Aragones in 2008. His 100th game in charge of Spain was a 2016 UEFA European Championship qualifier – a 1-0 win in Belarus in June 2015. Del Bosque stepped down as manager after Spain's second-round departure from the 2016 UEFA European Championship but was promised an ongoing role within the Spanish football association.

BELGIUM

Belgium embarked on a golden period in the Eighties after eight decades spent on the fringes of international competition: first a runners-up finish at the 1980 UEFA European Championship, followed by a run to the semi-finals of the 1986 FIFA World Cup. A new crop of elite European stars did, however, help Belgium to reach the 2014 FIFA World Cup quarter-finals – in their first finals appearance since 2002. The improvement in form was recognized in the FIFA World Rankings as "the Red Devils" rose to an all-time high of No.1 in November 2015.

TOP SCORERS

1	Bernard Voorhoof	30
=	Paul van Himst	30
3	Joseph Mermans	28
=	Marc Wilmots	28
5	Robert De Veen	26
6	Wesley Sonck	24
7	Raymond Braine	23
=	Marc Degryse	23
9	Jan Ceulemans	22
10	Henri Coppens	21

SIXTH SENSE

By qualifying for the 2002 FIFA World Cup, Belgium became the first country to reach six successive tournaments without benefiting once from being either hosts or defending holders.

HE'S OUR GUY

Unquestionably Belgium's greatest manager – as well as their longest-serving – was **Guy Thys**. He led them to the final of the 1980 UEFA European Championship and – with a team featuring the likes of Enzo Scifo and Nico Claesen – the semi-finals of the FIFA World Cup six years later. He spent 13 years in the job from 1976 to 1989, then returned for a second spell just eight months after quitting. He stepped down again after managing Belgium at the 1990 FIFA World Cup. During his playing days in the 1940s and 1950s, he was a striker and won two caps for Belgium. He died at the age of 80 in August 2003.

SWINE FEVER

Nicknamed "The Fighting Pig" and "The Bull from Dongelberg", **Marc Wilmots** hogged more goals for Belgium than all but Paul van Himst and Bernard Voorhoof. His 28 goals in 70 internationals between 1990 and 2002 included a Belgian record five at FIFA World Cups. After retiring, he spent a short spell as an elected Belgian senator before becoming assistant coach for the national team 2009. And, when Georges Leekens suddenly resigned as Belgium coach in 2012, Wilmots was promoted to the top job. He not only successfully qualified Belgium for the 2014 FIFA World Cup in Brazil, but also oversaw record runs of seven wins in a row and 14 consecutive games unbeaten. Wilmots led Belgium to the 2016 UEFA European Championship but lost the job after his highly touted side were knocked out in the quarter-finals, losing 3-1 to Wales.

DIVOCK'S DIVIDEND

Divock Origi was a late choice for Belgium's 2014 FIFA World Cup squad, picked by manager Marc Wilmots to replace the injured Christian Benteke. He justified that faith with the only goal of Belgium's second game, in the 88th minute, against Russia, half an hour after coming on as a substitute. Aged 19 years and 65 days, he became Belgium's youngest FIFA World Cup goalscorer. Divock's father, Mike Origi, was an international for his native Kenya, but spent most of his career in Belgium, where Divock was born and raised. Belgium's oldest FIFA World Cup scorer remains centre-back Leo Clijsters, aged 33 years and 250 days. He headed the opener in a 3-1 win over Uruguay at Italia 90.

FIVE STAR

Croatian-born Joseph Weber scored once in three games in 1992 for the country where he was born, before family connections allowed him to switch allegiance to Belgium for whom he scored six times in eight appearances in 1994 – although five of these goals came in one match, his debut, a 9-0 triumph over Zambia.

CLUB MATES

Belgium ended a 1964 match against neighbours and rivals the Netherlands with a team entirely comprised of Anderlecht players, after Liege goalkeeper Guy Delhasse was substituted by the Brussels club's Jean Trappeniers.

TRIUMPHS AND TRAGEDY

The largest football venue in Belgium is the 50,000-capacity King Baudouin Stadium in Brussels, which opened under its first name, the Jubilee Stadium, on 23 August 1930 and was renamed Heysel in 1946. It was the scene of tragedy in 1985 when a wall collapsed and 39 fans died in disturbances while attending the European Cup final between Liverpool and Juventus. The stadium was rebuilt and given its current name in 1995. When Belgium and the Netherlands co-hosted the 2000 UEFA European Championship, it staged the opening ceremony and first match, Belgium's 2-1 victory over Sweden. Now used for Belgium's home internationals, the King Baudouin Stadium was chosen to stage four games, as one of 13 host cities, at the 2020 UEFA European Championship.

TOP CAPS

1	Jan Ceulemans	96
2	Timmy Simons	93
3	Eric Gerets	86
=	Franky van der Elst	86
5	Enzo Scifo	84
=	Daniel van Buyten	84
7	Paul van Himst	81
=	Jan Vertonghen	81
9	Bart Goor	78
10	Georges Grun	77

MOTHER'S BOY

Belgium's most-capped player, Jan Ceulemans, is unusual in having turned down a move to Italian giants AC Milan – and he did so on the advice of his mother. He opted to stay loyal to Club Brugge, where he spent most of his playing career, and became a national hero with his linchpin displays at three consecutive FIFA World Cups in 1982, 1986 and 1990. He scored three goals and was captain at Mexico 1986 as Belgium finished fourth. The Lier-born midfielder retired from international football after Belgium's second-round exit at the 1990 FIFA World Cup. Yet the longest-lasting Belgian international career belongs to Hector Goetinck, who made his debut in 1906 and the last of his 17 appearances 16 years, six months and ten days later in 1923.

THE FOUR-MOST

Belgium enjoyed their largest winning margin at a major tournament when they beat Hungary 4-0 in the second round at the 2018 UEFA European Championship. Until then, their most emphatic victories had been 3-0 victories over the Republic of Ireland in the previous round and against El Salvador at the 1970 FIFA World Cup. Striker **Romelu Lukaku**'s two goals in the Ireland game made him the first Belgian player to score a brace at a tournament since his international manager Marc Wilmots did similarly against Mexico at the 1998 FIFA World Cup.

BULGARIA

The glory days of the "golden generation" apart – when Bulgaria finished fourth at the 1994 FIFA World Cup in the United States, sensationally beating defending champions Germany 2-1 in the quarter-finals – a consistent pattern emerges with Bulgarian football. Regular qualifiers for the game's major competitions, and the birthplace of some of the sport's biggest names (such as Hristo Stoichkov and Dimitar Berbatov), the country has too often failed to deliver on the big occasions and make its mark on world football.

TOP SCORERS

1	Dimitar Berbatov	48
2	Hristo Bonev	47
3	Hristo Stoichkov	37
4	Emil Kostadinov	26
5	Ivan Kolev	25
=	Petar Zhekov	25
7	Atanas Mihaylov	23
=	Nasko Sirakov	23
9	Dimitar Milanov	20
=	Martin Petrov	20

TEETHING TROUBLES

Martin Petrov suffered a terrible start to his international career when he was sent off for two yellow cards just eight minutes into his debut as a substitute in a Euro 2000 qualifier against England. He broke down in tears when leaving the field, but recovered from the experience to become one of his country's most-capped players and enjoyed spells with top clubs such as Atletico Madrid in Spain and Manchester City in England. His 90 caps and 20 goals included Bulgaria's only strike at the 2004 UEFA European Championship, against Italy.

MAYOR WITH NO HAIR

Balding Yordan Letchkov headed the winning goal against holders and defending champions Germany in the 1994 FIFA World Cup quarter-final in the United States. At the time, he played for German club Hamburg. He later became mayor of Sliven, the Bulgarian town where he was born in July 1967.

A NATION MOURNS

Bulgaria lost two of its most popular footballing talents when a June 1971 car crash claimed the lives of strikers Georgi Asparukhov (28) and Nikola Kotkov (32). Asparukhov scored 19 goals in 50 internationals, including Bulgaria's only goal of the 1966 FIFA World Cup finals in a 3-1 defeat to Hungary.

MOB RULES

Much-travelled Bulgaria centre-forward **Dimitar Berbatov** claims to have learned English by watching the *Godfather* movies. Berbatov joined Manchester United from Tottenham in 2008 for a club and Bulgarian record fee of £30.75m. Before joining Spurs, he had been a member of the Bayer Leverkusen side who narrowly missed out on a treble in 2002. They lost in the final of both the UEFA Champions League and the German cup and finished runners-up in the German Bundesliga. Berbatov surprised and disappointed fans back home when he announced his international retirement aged just 29, in May 2010, having scored a national-record 48 goals in his 78 appearances for Bulgaria. He briefly considered a return to the national team in 2012, but ultimately opted against the idea, saying that he wanted to "give chances to younger players". After joining Fulham in the summer of that year, he raised eyebrows during one match by revealing a T-shirt with the slogan: "Keep calm and pass me the ball."

STAN THE BURGER VAN MAN

Stiliyan Petrov – nicknamed "Stan" by fans of his English club Aston Villa – was applauded onto the field when he became Bulgaria's first outfield player to reach 100 caps, against Switzerland in March 2011. The midfielder and Bulgaria captain has been playing in Britain since 1999, when he joined Scottish giants Celtic as a 20-year-old – but had to fight hard against a bout of homesickness. He later revealed that his English only improved when he started work behind the counter of a Scottish friend's burger van. Petrov said: "Some of the customers used to stare, thinking: 'That looks like Stiliyan Petrov, but it can't be.' But soon I started to understand things better." Tributes from across football and around the world poured in for Petrov when, in March 2012, he revealed he had been diagnosed with acute leukaemia. After 19 minutes of every home game for the rest of the season Villa fans stood and applauded for 60 seconds – 19 being his squad number.

STOY STORY

Goalkeeper Vladislav Stoyanov has denied Cristiano Ronaldo from the penalty spot not once, but twice. The first was at club level in October 2014, when Real Madrid beat Ludogorets Razgrad 2-1 in the UEFA Champions League; the second was in a March 2016 international friendly when Bulgaria beat Portugal 1-0 – Ronaldo's fourth failure from 12 yards that season. It was Bulgaria's first victory over Portugal since December 1981, and was clinched by a debut goal by Brazilian-born attacking midfielder Marcelinho, a 31-year-old who had come to Bulgaria five years earlier.

PLAYING LUBO

Bulgaria's last-but-one coach was Lubo Penev, nephew of Dimitar Penev who had coached the country to their best-ever FIFA World Cup finish of fourth in 1994. Lubo, a centre-forward, missed out on that tournament after being diagnosed with testicular cancer, but he recovered to play for his country at both the 1996 UEFA European Championship and 1998 FIFA World Cup.

ALL–ROUNDER ALEKSANDAR

Defender Aleksandar Shalamanov played for Bulgaria at the 1966 FIFA World Cup, six years after representing his country as an alpine skier at the Winter Olympics at Lake Placid. He also went to the 1964 Tokyo Summer Olympics as an unused member of the volleyball squad. Shalamanov was voted Bulgaria's best sportsman in both 1967 and 1973.

HRISTO'S HISTORY

Hristo Stoichkov, born in Plovdiv, Bulgaria, on 8 February 1968, shared the 1994 FIFA World Cup Golden Boot, awarded to the tournament's top scorer, with Russia's Oleg Salenko. Both scored six times, though Stoichkov became the sole winner of that year's European Footballer of the Year award. Earlier the same year, he had combined up-front with Brazilian Romario to help Barcelona reach the final of the UEFA Champions League. He was banned for a year after a brawl earlier in his career, during the 1985 Bulgarian cup final between CSKA Sofia and Levski Sofia. Stoichkov won trophies with clubs in Bulgaria, Spain, Saudi Arabia and the United States before retiring as a player in 2003.

TOP CAPS

1	Stiliyan Petrov	106
2	Borislav Mikhailov	102
3	Hristo Bonev	96
4	Krasimir Balakov	92
5	Dimitar Penev	90
=	Martin Petrov	90
7	Radostin Kishishev	83
=	Hristo Stoichkov	83
9	Zlatko Yankov	80
10	Ayan Sadkov	79
=	Nasko Sirakov	79

HEAD BOY

Bulgaria's second most-capped player is **Borislav Mikhailov**, born in Sofia on 12 February 1963, who sometimes wore a wig while playing and later had a hair transplant. After retiring in 2005, he was appointed president of the Bulgarian Football Union. His father Bisser was also a goalkeeper and Borislav's son, Nikolay, made his international debut in goal against Scotland in May 2006. All three have played for Levski Sofia.

CROATIA

Croatia's distinctive red-and-white chequered jersey has become one of the most recognized in world football – and their flamboyant attackers some of the most admired across the globe. Formerly part of Yugoslavia, they reached the quarter-finals in their very first senior competition (UEFA Euro 96) then finished third at the 1998 FIFA World Cup – and have remained regular qualifiers for both tournaments since.

TOP SCORERS

1	Davor Suker	45
2	Eduardo da Silva	29
3	Mario Mandzukic	24
4	Darijo Srna	22
5	Ivica Olic	20
6	Niko Kranjcar	16
7	Ivan Perisic	15
=	Goran Vlaovic	15
9	Niko Kovac	14
10	Mladen Petric	13

OLE, OLIC

Croatia's second game at the 2014 FIFA World Cup, a 4-0 trouncing of Cameroon, was doubly notable. It was the first time they had scored as many as four goals in a single FIFA World Cup finals match. It also saw striker **Ivica Olic** become the first player to score for Croatia at two separate FIFA World Cups, having previously found the net in 2002. His lengthy break between finals goals is matched only by Denmark's Michael Laudrup, who scored at the 1986 tournament and then had to wait until the 1998 finals to do so again.

LUKA LOOPY

Luka Modric became the first Croatian footballer to score at two different UEFA European Championships finals when his elegant long-range volley gave his side a 1-0 victory over Turkey in their opening game of the 2016 tournament. He had previously scored a fourth-minute penalty to defeat co-hosts Austria at Euro 2008 – though he did miss one of the spot-kicks when Croatia lost to Turkey in a quarter-final shoot-out. Modric spent four years with English club Tottenham Hotspur from 2008, before moving to Spanish giants Real Madrid and helping them win the UEFA Champions League in 2014 and 2016.

DOUBLE TREBLE

Croatia enjoyed their final warm-up friendly ahead of the 2016 UEFA European Championship – their 10-0 thrashing of San Marino was their biggest ever winning margin. Two players scored hat-tricks that day, both of them playing their club football in Italy: Mario Mandzukic of Juventus and Fiorentina's **Nikola Kalinic.** The latter would go on to score the opener in Croatia's 2-1 victory over reigning champions Spain in their last first-round game of Euro 2016, clinching top place in the group and inflicting Spain's first UEFA European Championship finals defeat since 2004. But despite impressing many with their attractive style in the group stage, Croatia were knocked out in the second round by Portugal.

CHECK MATES

Croatia are among the few nations who can claim an unbeaten overall record against Italy. In eight matches, Croatia have won three and drawn five, with all of the last three meetings ending 1-1, their two 2016 UEFA European Championship qualifiers coming after a Euro 2012 finals tie. The most recent encounter came in June 2015, and it saw a second meeting in six days for central midfielders Croatia's Ivan Rakitic and Italy's Andrea Pirlo. They had faced each other in the 2015 UEFA Champions League final, in which Rakitic struck Barcelona's first goal in a 3-1 defeat of Juventus.

DEER DARIJO

Darijo Srna is Croatia's fourth top scorer of all time, despite playing many games as a right-back or wing-back. He has a tattoo on his calf in the shape of a deer, the Croatian word for which is "srna". He also has a tattoo on his chest – the name of his brother Igor, who has Down's syndrome and to whom he dedicates each goal he scores. Now Croatia's most capped player, Srna was one of three players to reach 100 appearances for their country against South Korea in February 2013. The other two were goalkeeper Stipe Pletikosa and defender Josip Simunic.

THE KIDNEYS ARE ALL RIGHT

Striker Ivan Klasnic returned to international duty with Croatia despite suffering kidney failure in early 2007. A first attempt at a transplant failed when his body rejected a kidney donated by his mother, but follow-up surgery – using a kidney from his father – proved successful. He recovered enough to play for Croatia again in March 2008 and represented his country in that summer's UEFA European Championship, scoring twice – including a winning goal against Poland.

ROCK AND A HARD PLACE

Slaven Bilic and Igor Stimac were formidable central defensive partners as Croatia finished third at the 1998 FIFA World Cup. Bilic was more successful as national coach, taking Croatia to the 2008 and 2012 UEFA European Championships during his six-year reign. Stimac took over in 2012, but an underwhelming 2014 FIFA World Cup qualifying campaign saw him replaced by another former international, Niko Kovac, for the play-off tie against Iceland in November 2013, which they won 2-0 on aggregate. Croatia went out in the first round in Brazil – despite taking the lead in the opening game, which they ultimately lost 3-1 to the hosts.

TOP CAPS

1	Darijo Srna	134
2	Stipe Pletikosa	114
3	Josip Simunic	105
4	Ivica Olic	104
5	Dario Simic	100
6	Luka Modric	93
7	Vedran Corluka	92
8	Robert Kovac	84
9	Niko Kovac	83
10	Robert Jarni	81
=	Niko Kranjcar	81

DOUBLE IDENTITY

Robert Jarni and Robert Prosinecki both have the rare distinction of playing for two different countries at different FIFA World Cup tournaments. They both represented Yugoslavia in Italy in 1990, then newly independent Croatia eight years later in France. Full-back Jarni actually played for both Yugoslavia and Croatia in 1990, then only Yugoslavia in 1991, before switching back – and permanently – to Croat colours in 1992 after the country officially joined UEFA and FIFA. He retired with 81 caps for Croatia, seven for Yugoslavia.

SUPER SUKER

Striker **Davor Suker** won the Golden Boot for being top scorer at the FIFA World Cup in 1998, scoring six goals in seven games as Croatia finished third. His strikes included the opening goal in Croatia's 2-1 semi-final defeat to eventual champions France, and the winner in a 2-1 triumph over Holland in the third-place play-off. Suker, by far his country's leading scorer of all time, had hit three goals at the UEFA European Championship in 1996 – including an audacious long-distance lob over Denmark goalkeeper Peter Schmeichel. Suker was named president of the Croatian Football Federation in July 2012.

CZECH REPUBLIC

The most successful of the former Eastern Bloc countries, as Czechoslovakia they finished as runners-up in the 1934 and 1962 FIFA World Cups, and shocked West Germany in a penalty shoot-out to win the 1976 UEFA European Championship. Playing as the Czech Republic since 1994, they lost – on a golden goal – in the UEFA Euro 96 final, and in the semi-final eight years later. Recent times have been tougher, and although one of Europe's stronger nations, the Czechs failed to qualify for the 2010 or 2014 FIFA World Cups, but were UEFA Euro 2012 quarter-finalists.

PLASIL'S PLACE

Midfielder **Jaroslav Plasil** went into the 2016 UEFA European Championship having just become only the fourth Czech player to reach a century of caps, reaching the landmark in a 2-1 friendly defeat to South Korea. He had been part of the side which reached the semi-finals of the 2004 UEFA European Championship, scored against Turkey at the tournament four years later and also played every minute of his side's progress to the second round at Euro 2012. He was also a mainstay in helping reach the 2016 UEFA European Championship, although the 14 goals the Czechs conceded in qualifying were more than any other side to make the finals.

CHIP WITH EVERYTHING

One of the most famous penalties ever taken was Antonin Panenka's decisive spot-kick for Czechoslovakia against West Germany in the final of the 1976 UEFA European Championship, giving the Czechs victory in the shoot-out. Despite the tension, and the responsibility resting on him, Panenka cheekily chipped the ball into the middle of the goal – as goalkeeper Sepp Maier dived to the side. That style of spot-kick is now widely known as a "Panenka", and has been replicated by the likes of France's Zinedine Zidane, in the 2006 FIFA World Cup final.

POPULAR KAREL

UEFA Euro 96 gave **Karel Poborsky** the perfect platform to take his career to new heights as he helped the Czech Republic reach the final and then sealed a dream move to Manchester United. His lob against Portugal in the quarter-finals was rated as one of the finest opportunist goals in the tournament's history. His 118 appearances is a record for his country.

CECH CAP

Goalkeeper **Petr Cech** has worn a protective cap while playing ever since suffering a fractured skull during an English Premier League match in October 2006. He later added a chin protector after requiring a facial operation following a training accident. He was born as a triplet, along with sister Sarka and brother Michal, who died of an infection at the age of two. Cech served notice of his talents when he was beaten by only one penalty in a shoot-out against France in the 2002 UEFA U-21 European Championship final, helping the Czechs to win the trophy. He claimed winners' medals as Chelsea won the 2012 UEFA Champions League (he was named man of the match) and 2013 UEFA Europa League. Now the Czech Republic's most capped player, he marked his 100th international appearance in March 2013 with a clean sheet in a 3-0 defeat of Armenia. He played in all three games at the 2016 UEFA European Championship but the team went out in the first round.

PASSING THE PUC

The final of the 1934 FIFA World Cup was the first to go into extra-time, with Czechoslovakia ultimately losing 2-1 to hosts Italy despite taking a 76th-minute lead through Antonin Puc. Puc was Czechoslovakia/the Czech Republic's top international scorer with 34 goals when he retired in 1938 until he was passed, first by Jan Koller, 67 years later, and, latterly, by Milan Baros.

WALK-OUT

Belgium's 1920 victory in the Olympic Games was overshadowed when Czechoslovakia walked off the pitch after half an hour in protest following what they saw as biased refereeing. Czechoslovakia are the only team in the history of Olympic football to have been disqualified.

MOSTLY MOZART

The last Czech Republic player to score at a FIFA World Cup was **Tomas Rosicky**, a double in a 3-0 victory over the United States at the 2006 tournament. Despite an injury-plagued career, he became only the third Czech to reach a century of caps, in a 2-1 2016 European Championship qualifier defeat to Iceland in June 2015. The midfielder, nicknamed "The Little Mozart" for the way he orchestrates play, has performed with rock band Tri sestry after taking up the electric guitar during a spell on the sidelines. His father and his brother, both named Jiri, were professional but uncapped footballers. Rosicky retired from international football after the Czech Republic were eliminated from Euro 2016 in the first round, during which he became the oldest Czech player to appear in a UEFA EURO finals, aged 35. He had also been their youngest, aged 19, in 2000.

THE CANNON COLLECTS

Pavel Nedved's election as European Footballer of the Year in 2003 ended an impatient wait for fans in the Czech Republic who had seen a string of outstanding players overlooked since Josef Masopust had been honoured back in 1962. Masopust, a midfield general, had scored the opening goal in the FIFA World Cup final that year before Brazil hit back to win 3-1 in the Chilean capital of Santiago. Years later, Masopust was remembered by Pele and nominated as one of his 125 greatest living footballers. At club level, Masopust won eight Czechoslovak league titles with Dukla Prague, the army club. He was also the winner, in 1962, of the first Czech Golden Ball as domestic footballer of the year. It was another day and in another age. Masopust was presented with his award before the kick-off of a European Cup quarter-final with Benfica – with a minimum of fuss. Years later, Masopust said: "Eusebio just shook hands with me, I put the trophy in my sports bag and went home on the tram."

TOP SCORERS

1	Jan Koller	55
2	Milan Baros	41
3	Vladimir Smicer	27
4	Tomas Rosicky	23
5	Pavel Kuka	22
6	Patrick Berger	18
=	Pavel Nedved	18
8	Vratislav Lokvenc	14
9	Tomas Necid	12
10	Marek Jankulovski	11

TOP CAPS

1	Petr Cech	124
2	Karel Poborsky	118
3	Tomas Rosicky	105
4	Jaroslav Plasil	102
5	Milan Baros	93
6	Jan Koller	91
=	Pavel Nedved	91
8	Vladimir Smicer	81
9	Tomas Ujfalusi	78
10	Marek Jankulovski	77

TEN OUT OF TEN

Giant striker **Jan Koller** is Czech football's all-time leading marksman with 55 goals in 91 appearances. Koller scored on his senior debut against Belgium and struck ten goals in ten successive internationals. He scored six goals in each of the 2000, 2004 and 2008 UEFA European Championship qualifying campaigns. He began his career with Sparta Prague, who converted him from goalkeeper to goalscorer. Then, in Belgium, he was top scorer with Lokeren, before scoring 42 goals in two league title-winning campaigns with Anderlecht. Later, with Borussia Dortmund in Germany, he once went in goal after Jens Lehmann had been sent off and kept a clean sheet – having scored in the first half.

DENMARK

Denmark have been playing international football since 1908, but it was not until the mid-1980s that they became competitive at the game's major tournaments. The country's crowning moment came in 1992 when, after being called up as a replacement just ten days before the start of the tournament, they walked away with the UEFA European Championship crown, shocking defending world champions West Germany 2-0 in the final. They may not have been able to repeat that success, but remain a significant player in the world game.

TOP CAPS

1	Peter Schmeichel	129
2	Dennis Rommedahl	126
3	Jon Dahl Tomasson	112
4	Thomas Helveg	108
5	Michael Laudrup	104
6	Martin Jorgensen	102
=	Morten Olsen	102
8	Thomas Sorensen	101
9	Christian Poulsen	92
10	John Sivebaek	87

GOLDEN GLOVES

Peter Schmeichel was rated as the world's best goalkeeper in the early 1990s, winning many club honours with Manchester United and, famously, the UEFA European Championship with Denmark. His son Kasper Schmeichel was a member of Denmark's squad at the 2012 UEFA European Championship, but ended the tournament still uncapped. Kasper has since become Denamrk's first choice – and emulated his father by winning the English Premier League, with Leicester City in 2016.

LEADERSHIP STYLE

Morten Olsen captained Denmark at the 1986 FIFA World Cup and later became the first Dane to reach a century of caps, retiring in 1989 with four goals from 102 appearances. He then switched to coaching, first at club level with Brondby, FC Koln and Ajax Amsterdam, before taking on the job as Danish national coach in 2000 and leading them to the 2002 and 2010 FIFA World Cups. Denmark's 2-1 defeat to England in a February 2011 friendly was his 116th international in charge – taking him past the previous record set between 1979 and 1990 by his former national team boss Sepp Piontek. Olsen's 15-year reign as Denmark coach ended in November 2015, after a 4-3 aggregate defeat to Sweden in the 2016 UEFA European Championship qualifying play-offs. His 163 games in charge of his country comprised 79 victories, 42 draws and 42 defeats – an overall 48.47 win rate. His successor was Norwegian Age Hareide, who had been Norway boss between 2003 and 2008. His assistant was Denmark's joint record goalscorer Jon Dahl Tomasson.

PENALTY REDEMPTION

Midfielder Morten Wieghorst is the only player to be sent off twice while playing for Denmark – yet has also received a special award for fair play. His first international red card came just three minutes after entering the field as a substitute, against South Africa in the 1998 FIFA World Cup. He was again dismissed after coming on as a sub against Italy in the 2000 UEFA European Championship, though this time he managed a whole 28 minutes of action – and scored a goal in Denmark's 3-2 victory. But the other side of his character was shown during a Carlsberg Cup match against Iran in February 2003, when he deliberately missed a penalty. The spot-kick had been awarded after Iranian defender Jalal Kameli Mofrad had picked the ball up, thinking wrongly that a whistle from the crowd was actually the referee blowing for half-time. The International Olympic Committee later presented Wieghorst with a special fair play prize for deliberately striking his penalty wide – a gesture which looked all the more sporting since Denmark went on to lose the game 1-0.

DANISH DYNAMITE

Denmark's 6-1 defeat of Uruguay in the 1986 FIFA World Cup finals first-round group stage in Neza, Mexico, ranks among the country's finest performances. Sadly, Denmark's adventure was ended by Spain in the last 16, losing 5-1 after a horrendous back pass by Manchester United's Jesper Olsen allowed the Spanish to open the scoring. The Danes had already been hampered by the loss of playmaker Frank Arsesen through suspension, after he was sent off during their final group game, a victory over eventual runners-up West Germany. The side – popularly known as "Danish Dynamite" – was captained by future national coach Morten Olsen and managed by Sepp Piontek, a German who became the Danish national team's first professional coach when appointed in 1979. Michael Laudrup, a star member of the classic mid-1980s side, described them as "Europe's answer to Brazil".

CHRISTIAN AID

Nimble playmaker and free-kick specialist **Christian Eriksen** is merely among the most recent in a proud tradition of creative young Danish footballers – and another who has enjoyed a popular and successful association with Dutch giants Ajax Amsterdam. He followed the same career path as Danish stars, such as Soren Lerby and Frank Arnesen in the 1970s and 1980s and the Laudrup brothers, Michael and Brian, in the late 1990s. Eriksen helped inspire the Amsterdam club to a hat-trick of title triumphs before crossing the North Sea to join Tottenham Hotspur in the summer of 2013 – and ended his debut season being voted both player of the year and young player of the year by the London club's supporters. His Danish debut came in March 2010, having only turned 18 the previous month. This made him Denmark's fourth youngest debutant – and he was the youngest player at the 2010 FIFA World Cup. Eriksen's first international goal was scored in a win against Iceland in April 2011. Among his fans was Netherlands and Ajax legend Johan Cruyff, who said: "He's a player I really like with all my heart. You can compare him with Brian and Michael Laudrup."

TOP SCORERS

1	Poul Nielsen	52
=	Jon Dahl Tomasson	52
3	Pauli Jorgensen	44
4	Ole Madsen	42
5	Preben Elkjaer Larsen	38
6	Michael Laudrup	37
7	Nicklas Bendtner	29
=	Henning Enoksen	29
9	Michael Rohde	22
=	Ebbe Sand	22

QUICK DRAW

Ebbe Sand scored the fastest FIFA World Cup goal ever scored by a substitute, when he netted a mere 16 seconds after coming onto the pitch in Denmark's clash against Nigeria at the 1998 FIFA World Cup.

SAINT NICKLAS

Centre-forward Nicklas Bendtner has never lacked self-confidence, having repeatedly claimed he would be recognized among the world's best strikers, and yet he has been rising up the Danish all-time scoring charts despite a series of injuries and suspensions. He reached 29 goals with a hat-trick in a 3-2 win over the USA in March 2015. Some of his goals have come at a price, however: he celebrated his second goal at the 2012 UEFA European Championship by lowering his shorts and revealing the name of a betting firm on his underpants. Those antics resulted in a $100,000 fine and a one-game ban.

THE UNEXPECTED IN 1992

Few Danish football fans will forget June 1992, their national team's finest hour, when they won the UEFA European Championship, despite not qualifying for the finals in Sweden. Ten days before the tournament opened UEFA asked the Danes – who had finished second to Yugoslavia in their qualifying group – to take Yugoslavia's place, following their exclusion in the wake of international sanctions over the Balkan War. Expectations were minimal, but then the inconceivable happened. Relying heavily on goalkeeper Peter Schmeichel, his defence, and the creative spark of Brian Laudrup, Denmark crafted one of the biggest shocks in modern football history by winning the tournament, culminating in a 2-0 victory over world champions Germany. This victory was all the more remarkable in that Brian's brother Michael, their finest player, quit during the qualifying competition after falling out with coach **Richard Moller Nielsen**. Michael revived his international career in 1993, but Denmark failed to qualify for the 1994 FIFA World Cup in the United States. Among those paying their respects at Moller Nielsen's funeral after his death aged 76 in February 2014 were Schmeichel, Brian Laudrup and Euro 92 teammates Preben Elkjaer Larsen and John Jensen.

TAKING THE MICHAEL

One Danish player with unhappy memories of a spell with Ajax Amsterdam is Michael Krohn-Dehli, who made just four appearances for the club between 2006 and 2008. But if he felt any resentment for the Netherlands – and the injuries that hampered his progress there – then the 2012 UEFA European Championship brought some redemption. Krohn-Dehli scored the only goal in Denmark's surprise opening victory over the Netherlands.

BROTHERS IN ARMS

Brian (left) and Michael Laudrup are among the most successful footballing brothers of modern times. As well as making a combined 186 international appearances, they played across Europe at club level. Michael (104 caps, 37 goals) played in Italy with Lazio and Juventus and in Spain with Barcelona and Real Madrid. Brian (82 caps, 21 goals) starred in Germany with Bayer Uerdingen and Bayern Munich, Italy with Fiorentina and Milan, Scotland for Rangers and England for Chelsea.

GREECE

There is no argument about Greece's proudest footballing moment – their shock triumph at the 2004 UEFA European Championship, one of the game's greatest international upsets. Guided by German coach Otto Rehhagel, it was only the Greeks' second appearance at a UEFA Euro finals. Greece also made the last eight at Euro 2012 in Poland and Ukraine. In the FIFA World Cup, South Africa 2010 marked just their second qualification and they reached the second round of a FIFA World Cup for the first time in 2014.

TOP SCORERS

1	Nikos Anastopoulos	29
2	Angelos Charisteas	25
3	Theofanis Gekas	24
4	Dimitris Saravakos	22
5	Mimis Papaioannou	21
6	Nikos Machlas	18
7	Demis Nikolaidis	17
8	Panagiotis Tsalouchidis	16
9	Giorgos Sideris	14
10	Nikos Liberopoulos	13
=	Dimitris Salpingidis	13

SIMPLY THEO BEST

Theodoros "Theo" Zagorakis – born near Kavala on 27 October 1971 – was captain of Greece when they won the UEFA European Championship in 2004 and the defensive midfielder was also given the prize for the tournament's best player. He is the second most-capped Greek footballer of all time, with 120 caps. But it was not until his 101st international appearance – 10 years and five months after his Greek debut – that he scored his first goal for his country, in a FIFA World Cup qualifier against Denmark in February 2005. He retired from international football after making a 15-minute cameo appearance against Spain in August 2007.

PARTY CRASHERS

Shock UEFA Euro 2004 winners Greece became the first team to beat both the holders and the hosts on the way to winning either a UEFA European Championship or FIFA World Cup. In fact, they beat hosts Portugal twice – in both the tournament's opening game and the final, with a quarter-final victory over defending champions France in between.

GORGEOUS GEORGE

Georgios Samaras won and converted the last-minute penalty that sent Greece through to the knock-out stages of a FIFA World Cup for the first time, clinching a dramatic 2-1 victory over Group C opponents Ivory Coast at the 2014 tournament in Brazil. The goal, following a foul by Giovanni Sio, was former Celtic striker Samaras's ninth goal for his country – his first coming on his debut against Belarus in February 2006. Samaras could actually have played international football for Australia, because his father, Ioannis, was born in Melbourne and moved to Greece aged 13. Ioannis won 16 caps for Greece between 1986 and 1990, but he is a long way behind his son, who has made 81 appearances.

ALL WHITE NOW

The surprise triumph at UEFA Euro 2004 brought a major change to Greek international football – they switched the national team's kit from blue to white. The former colours had been used since the Hellenic Football Federation was formed in 1926, but the success of Otto Rehhagel's men in their second kit prompted the permanent change of colours.

TOP CAPS

1	Giorgos Karagounis	139
2	Theodoros Zagorakis	120
3	Kostas Katsouranis	116
4	Angelos Basinas	100
5	Stratos Apostolakis	96
6	Antonis Nikopolidis	90
7	Angelos Charisteas	88
8	Vasilis Torisidis	83
9	Dimitris Salpingidis	82
10	Georgios Samaras	81

WAITING GAME

In 2003, to mark Uefa's half-century, Greece's national football federation voted Uzbekistan-born midfielder Vasilis Hatzipanagis the country's "golden player" of the previous 50 years. However, he played just twice for the country of his parents' birth. They had moved to the Soviet Union as political refugees before Vasilis was born in 1954. Hatzipanagis made his Greek debut in May 1976, in a 1-0 victory over Poland, but had to wait 23 years and seven months, till December 1999, for his follow-up appearance, a 20 minute cameo – nine years after he retired from club football – in a 1-1 draw with Ghana. He been ruled ineligible to play for Greece having appeared for times for the USSR in qualifiers for the 1976 Olympics.

TOP KAP

Goalkeeper Stefanos Kapino became Greece's youngest international when he made his debut in November 2011 in a friendly against Romania, at the age of 17 years and 241 days – 80 days younger than previous record-holder, striker Thomas Mavros, had been when facing the Netherlands in February 1972. Greece's oldest player was another goalkeeper, Kostas Chalkias – 38 years and 13 days old – when playing his final international, against the Czech Republic in June 2012. He conceded twice in the first six minutes and was replaced by Michalis Sifakas midway through the first half.

DIMI MORE

Striker **Dimitrios Salpingidis** not only struck the only goal  of Greece's 2010 FIFA World Cup qualifying play-off victory against Ukraine, sealing their place in South Africa, he also then became the first Greek ever to score at a FIFA World Cup, with a 44th-minute deflected strike in the 2-1 Group B triumph over Nigeria. Yet another notable achievement was added with his equalizer against Poland in the opening game of UEFA Euro 2012: this made him the first Greek ever to score at a FIFA World Cup and a UEFA European Championship.

GEKAS SETBACK

With only two goals, Greece were the lowest scoring team to reach the second round at the 2014 FIFA World Cup. They then faced their first tournament penalty shoot-out, in the round-of-16, and lost to Costa Rica, 5-3 after a 1-1 draw. The only miss was by Theofanis Gekas, who at 34 years and 37 days, was the second-oldest man to miss in a FIFA World Cup shoot-out. Italy captain Franco Baresi was 33 days older when he missed in the 1994 FIFA World Cup final against Brazil.

GRIEF AND GLORY FOR GIORGOS

It was a bittersweet day for captain **Giorgos Karagounis** when he equalled the Greek record for international appearances, with his 120th cap against Russia in their final Group A game at the UEFA Euro 2012. The midfielder scored the only goal of the game, giving Greece a place in the quarter-finals at Russia's expense – but a second yellow card of the tournament ruled him out of the next match, in which the Greeks lost to Germany. Karagounis was one of three survivors from Greece's Euro 2004 success, along with fellow midfielder Kostas Katsouranis and goalkeeper Kostas Chalkias – though it was only in Poland that Chalkias made the first of his UEFA European Championship appearances, having been understudy in 2004 and 2008. Manager Fernando Santos also surprised many by leaving the winning goalscoring hero of Euro 2004, Angelos Charisteas, out of the squad. Chalkias was Euro 2012's oldest player, making his 32nd and final international appearance during the tournament.

KING OTTO

German coach Otto Rehhagel became the first foreigner to be voted "Greek of the Year" in 2004, after leading the country to glory at that year's UEFA European Championship. He was also offered honorary Greek citizenship. His nine years in charge, after being appointed in 2001, made him Greece's longest-serving international manager. The UEFA Euro 2004 triumph was the first time a country coached by a foreigner had triumphed at either the UEFA European Championship or FIFA World Cup. Rehhagel was aged 65 at UEFA Euro 2004, making him the oldest coach to win the UEFA European Championship – though that record was taken off him four years later, when 69-year-old Luis Aragones lifted the trophy with Spain.

HUNGARY

For a period in the early 1950s, Hungary possessed the most talented football team on the planet. They claimed Olympic gold at Helsinki in 1952, inflicted a crushing first-ever Wembley defeat on England the following year, and entered the 1954 FIFA World Cup, unbeaten in almost four years, as firm favourites to win the crown. They lost to West Germany in the final and Hungary's footballing fortunes on the world stage have never been the same again.

DZSUDZSAK'S NO DUD

Hungary have achieved an encouraging turnaround in the last few years, reaching the second round of the 2016 UEFA European Championship, less than three years after the nadir of an 8-1 defeat by the Netherlands in a 2014 FIFA World Cup qualifier. That equalled their heaviest ever losses, 7-0 to England in 1908 and to Germany in 1941. Under new German coach Bernd Storck, and captained by **Balazs Dzsudzsak**, they defeated Norway in a qualifying play-off to reach their first major tournament since the 1986 FIFA World Cup – and opened it perfectly by beating neighbours Austria 2-0. Dzsudzsak scored twice in a 3-3 draw with Portugal to clinch a place in the knock-out stages, where the Hungarians were unfortunate to lose quite so emphatically, 4-0, to Belgium.

TOP GERA

While no one can compare with Ferenc Puskas, elegant left-footed playmaker **Zoltan Gera** has been one of Hungary's finest footballers of recent times. He might have won even more international caps but for a brief retirement following a dispute with then-coach Erwin Koeman in 2009, after Gera had arrived late for a team meeting. The first three of his 25 international goals all came in a 3-0 victory over San Marino in October 2002, while his most recent was a stunning volley in a 3-3 draw with Portugal in the UEFA Euro 2016 first round. Aged 37 years and 62 days, he became the second oldest UEFA European Championship finals goalscorer – behind only Austria's Ivica Vastic, who was 38 years and 257 days old when he netted at Euro 2008.

TOP SCORERS

1	Ferenc Puskas	84
2	Sandor Kocsis	75
3	Imre Schlosser	59
4	Lajos Tichy	51
5	Gyorgy Sarosi	42
6	Nandor Hidegkuti	39
7	Ferenc Bene	36
8	Tibor Nyilasi	32
=	Gyula Zsengeller	32
10	Florian Albert	31

GOLDEN HEAD

Sandor Kocsis, top scorer in the 1954 FIFA World Cup finals with 11 goals, was so good in the air he was known as "The Man with the Golden Head". In 68 internationals he scored an incredible 75 goals, including a record seven hat-tricks. His tally included two decisive extra-time goals in the 1954 FIFA World Cup semi-final against Uruguay, when Hungary had appeared to be on the brink of defeat.

GALLOPING MAJOR

Ferenc Puskas was one of the greatest footballers of all time, scoring a remarkable 84 goals in 85 international matches for Hungary and 514 goals in 529 matches in the Hungarian and Spanish leagues. Possessing the most lethal left-foot shot in the history of football, he was known as the "Galloping Major" – by virtue of his playing for the army team Honved before joining Real Madrid and going on to play for Spain. During the 1950s he was top scorer and captain of the legendary "Mighty Magyars" (the nickname given to the Hungarian national team) as well as of the army club Honved.

EMPEROR ALBERT

The only Hungarian footballer to win the Ballon d'Or prize for footballer of the year was **Florian Albert** in 1967, when it was organized by the magazine *France Football* rather than FIFA. Albert – nicknamed "The Emperor" – finished joint top scorer at the 1962 FIFA World Cup with four goals and helped his country to third place at the 1960 Olympics and the 1964 UEFA European Championship. Hungary's 5-0 home friendly win against Liechtenstein in November 2011 was dedicated to his memory following his death the previous month at the age of 70. His son Florian Albert Jr won six caps for Hungary as a midfielder between 1993 and 1996.

HUNGARY FOR IT

Hungary's 6-3 win over England at Wembley in 1953 remains one of the most significant international results of all time. Hungary became the first team from outside the British Isles to beat England at home, a record that had stood since 1901. The Hungarians had been undefeated for three years and had won the Olympic tournament the year before, while England were the so-called "inventors" of football. The British press dubbed it "The Match of the Century". In the event, the match revolutionized the game in England, Hungary's unequivocal victory exposing the naivete of English football tactics. England captain Billy Wright later summed up the humiliation by saying: "We completely underestimated the advances that Hungary had made, and not only tactically. When we walked out at Wembley ... I looked down and noticed that the Hungarians had on these strangelightweight boots, cut away like slippers under the ankle bone. I turned to big Stan Mortensen and said: 'We should be all right here, Stan, they haven't got the proper kit.'"

EUROPEAN PIONEERS

While Argentina's match against Uruguay in July 1902 was the first international outside the British Isles, Hungary's 5-0 defeat to Austria in Vienna three months later was the first in Europe between two non-UK sides. Ten of Hungary's first 16 internationals were against Austria, with the Hungarians winning four, drawing one and losing five of them. In total, Hungary have won 68, drawn 30 and lost 40 against their Austrian neighbours.

GOODISON LESSON

In the 1966 FIFA World Cup, Hungary gave Brazil a footballing lesson at Goodison Park, running out 3-1 winners before their progress was stopped by the Soviet Union in the quarter-finals. It was Brazil's first defeat in the FIFA World Cup since the 1954 quarter-finals, when they had lost 4-2 to ... Hungary.

YEARS OF PLENTY

Hungary's dazzling line-up of the early 1950s was known as the "*Aranycsapat*" – or "Golden Team". They set a record for international matches unbeaten, going 31 consecutive games without defeat between May 1950 and their July 1954 FIFA World Cup final loss to West Germany – a run that included clinching Olympic gold at Helsinki in Finland in 1952. That 31-match tally has been overtaken since only by Brazil and Spain. Hungary in the 1950s also set a record for most consecutive games scoring at least one goal – 73 matches – while their average of 5.4 goals per game at the 1954 FIFA World Cup remains an all-time high for the tournament.

NERVES AND STEEL

Gabor Kiraly may now have won more caps, and earned more attention for his customary tracksuit bottoms – often compared to pyjama trousers – but **Gyula Grosics** is still recognised as Hungary's greatest goalkeeper. Unusual for a goalkeeper of his era, he was comfortable with the ball at his feet and was willing to rush out of his area. The on-field confidence was not always displayed off it, however – and he was thought to be a nervous character, a hypochondriac and a loner. He allegedly asked to be substituted before the end at Wembley in 1953. He suffered after Hungary's surprise loss to West Germany in the 1954 FIFA World Cup final, being blamed for the equalizer.

TOP CAPS

1	Gabor Kiraly	107
2	Jozsef Bozsik	101
3	Roland Juhasz	94
4	Zoltan Gera	93
5	Laszlo Fazekas	92
6	Gyula Grosics	89
7	Ferenc Puskas	85
8	Balazs Dzsudzsak	82
=	Imre Garaba	82
10	Sandor Matrai	81

NORTHERN IRELAND

Northern Ireland have played as a separate country since 1921 – before that there had been an all-Ireland side. They have qualified for the FIFA World Cup on three occasions: in 1958, 1982 and 1986, but it would be 30 years before they qualified for another major tournament, reaching the second round of the 2016 UEFA European Championship – their first appearance in the Euro finals.

GEORGE BEST

One of the greatest players never to grace a FIFA World Cup, **George Best** (capped 37 times by Northern Ireland) nevertheless won domestic and European honours with Manchester United – including both a European Champions Cup medal and the European Footballer of the Year award in 1968. He also played in the United States, Hong Kong and Australia before his "final" retirement in 1984.

GIANT JENNINGS

Pat Jennings's record 119 appearances for Northern Ireland also stood as an international record at one stage. The former Tottenham Hotspur and Arsenal goalkeeper made his international debut, aged just 18, against Wales on 15 April 1964, and played his final game in the 1986 FIFA World Cup, against Brazil, on his 41st birthday.

"PETER THE GREAT"

Former Manchester City and Derby County striker Peter Doherty, one of the most expensive players of his era, won the English league and FA Cup as a player, and earned 19 caps for Northern Ireland in a career interrupted by World War Two. His late goal to earn a 2-2 draw in 1947 ensured Northern Ireland avoided defeat against England for the first time. As manager, he led Northern Ireland to the quarter-finals of the 1958 FIFA World Cup – Northern Ireland remain the smallest country ever to reach that stage of the competition. They were defeated 4-0 by France, who went on to finish third.

OH DANNY BOY

Northern Ireland's captain at the 1958 FIFA World Cup was Tottenham Hotspur's cerebral **Danny Blanchflower** – the first twentieth-century captain of an English club to win both the league and FA Cup in the same season, in 1960–61. When asked the secret of his national team's success in 1958, he offered the explanation: "Our tactic is to equalize before the others have scored." More famously, he offered the philosophy: "The great fallacy is that the game is first and foremost about winning. It's nothing of the kind. The game is about glory. It's about doing things in style, with a flourish, about going out and beating the other lot, not waiting for them to die of boredom."

TOP SCORERS

1	David Healy	36
2	Kyle Lafferty	17
3	Colin Clarke	13
=	Billy Gillespie	13
5	Gerry Armstrong	12
=	Joe Bambrick	12
=	Iain Dowie	12
=	Jimmy Quinn	12
9	Olphie Stanfield	11
10	Billy Bingham	10
=	Johnny Crossan	10
=	Jimmy McIlroy	10
=	Peter McParland	10

THE BOY DAVIS

Midfielder **Steven Davis** became Northern Ireland's youngest post-war captain when he led out the side against Uruguay in May 2006, aged just 21 years, five months and 20 days. He has remained captain under current coach Michael O'Neill, who replaced Nigel Worthington in 2012 to become Northern Ireland's first Catholic manager for half a century.

McAULEY'S MIXED FORTUNES

Northern Ireland qualified for the 2016 UEFA European Championship as group-winners, and went into the finals on their longest ever unbeaten run – 12 games. A 2-0 victory over Ukraine in France was their first finals win since beating hosts Spain at the 1982 FIFA World Cup and **Gareth McAuley**'s opener their first major tournament goal since Colin Clarke, also against Spain, at the 1986 FIFA World Cup. However, McAuley scored at the "wrong" end to give Wales the only goal of a "Battle of Britain" second-round tie, the first Northern Ireland own goal since October 2011, against Italy – and he got that one too! Aaron Hughes played in the game against Ukraine at the age of 36, having become the country's first outfielder to reach 100 caps in a 2016 friendly against Slovakia.

TOP CAPS

1	Pat Jennings	119
2	Aaron Hughes	103
3	David Healy	95
4	Mal Donaghy	91
5	Sammy McIlroy	88
=	Maik Taylor	88
7	Steven Davis	87
8	Keith Gillespie	86
9	Chris Baird	79
10	Jimmy Nicholl	73

"PETER THE LATE"

Peter Watson is thought to have had the shortest Northern Ireland international career, spending two minutes on the pitch in a 5-0 UEFA European Championship qualifying win over Cyprus in April 1971. A Distillery club-mate of Watson that season was law student Martin O'Neill – who went on to win international 64 caps, including captaining his country at the 1982 FIFA World Cup.

HOSTILE HOSTS

Northern Ireland topped their first-round group at the 1982 FIFA World Cup, thanks to a 1-0 win over hosts Spain at a passionate Mestalla Stadium in Valencia. Watford striker Gerry Armstrong scored the goal and the Irish held on despite defender Mal Donaghy being sent off. A 4-1 second-round loss to France denied Northern Ireland a semi-finals place. Armstrong moved to Spain, joining Mallorca the following year and, predictably, was regularly booed by rival fans.

YOUNG GUN

Norman Whiteside became the then-youngest player at a FIFA World Cup finals (beating Pele's record) when he represented Northern Ireland in Spain in 1982 aged 17 years and 41 days. He won 38 caps, scoring nine goals, before injury forced his retirement aged just 26.

STRIFE OF BRIAN

Brian McLean's Northern Ireland career began and ended with a second-half appearance against Estonia in March 2006. The Scottish-born player had been thought eligible to play for Northern Ireland through family links, but he had played for Scotland Under-17s in a UEFA competition four years earlier and not officially changed his allegiance until after the official deadline of his 21st birthday.

HERO HEALY

Northern Ireland's record goalscorer **David Healy** has scored more than double the international goals – 36 – than the next highest player on the list, Kyle Lafferty on 17. Healy scored twice on his debut against Luxembourg in February 2000, and all three as Northern Ireland stunned Spain 3-2 in a qualifier for UEFA Euro 2008 on 6 September 2006. He also hit the winner against Sven-Goran Eriksson's England in September 2005, Northern Ireland's first victory over them since 1972. Healy would later endure a four-year, 24-game scoring drought between October 2008 and November 2012. His final Northern Ireland goal came in a 2-1 home loss to Israel in March 2013. He retired from all football later that year, aged 34.

NORWAY

Although they played their first international, against Sweden, in 1908 and qualified for the 1938 FIFA World Cup, it would take a further 56 years, and the introduction of a direct brand of football, before Norway reappeared at a major international tournament. Success in such competitions has been rare – they have never progressed beyond the second round – but Norway retains the distinction of being the only nation in history never to have lost to Brazil.

JUVE DONE IT ALL

Jorgen Juve netted his national record 33 international goals in 45 appearances between 1928 and 1937. He did not score as Norway claimed bronze at the Berlin 1936 Olympics, but was playing when Norway beat Germany 2-0 in the quarter-finals, prompting spectators Adolf Hitler and other Nazi leaders to storm out in fury. After retiring in 1938, he worked as a legal scholar, sports journalist and author of books about the Olympics and football.

GOALS FOR EITHER IVERSEN

Steffen Iversen scored the only goal of Norway's only win at a UEFA European Championship – against Spain at the 2000 tournament. Iversen's father Odd had previously been one of the country's leading strikers, hitting memorable strikes in unexpected victories over Yugoslavia in a 1966 FIFA World Cup qualifier and away to France ahead of the 1970 tournament. Odd scored a total of 19 times in 45 games for Norway between 1967 and 1979. Steffen equalled his father's international scoring tally with a hat-trick against Malta in November 2007 – then scored his next two goals against Iceland the following September. His 79th and final international cap came in 2011, aged 34, and he had 21 goals to his name.

YOUR BOYS TOOK A HELL OF A BEATING

Bjorge Lillelien's famous commentary after Norway beat England 2-1 in a qualifier for the 1982 FIFA World Cup remains one of the iconic moments of European football. A commentator from 1957 until just before his death from cancer in 1987, he concentrated on winter sports and football. Roughly translated, it sounded as follows: "Lord Nelson, Lord Beaverbrook, Sir Winston Churchill, Sir Anthony Eden, Clement Attlee, Henry Cooper, Lady Diana, Maggie Thatcher, can you hear me? Your boys took a hell of a beating." Although the commentary was for Norwegian radio, it soon made its way to an English audience and has achieved cliché status. In 2002, Lillelien's words were designated the greatest piece of sports commentary ever by the *Observer* newspaper's sports supplement. Such is its place in British sporting culture, parodies of the commentary have been written to celebrate a vast array of domestic sporting victories.

TOP SCORERS

1	Jorgen Juve	33
2	Einar Gundersen	26
3	Harald Hennum	25
4	John Carew	24
5	Tore Andre Flo	23
=	Ole Gunnar Solskjaer	23
7	Gunnar Thoresen	22
8	Steffen Iversen	21
9	Jan Age Fjortoft	20
10	Odd Iversen	19
=	Oyvind Leonhardsen	19
=	Olav Nilsen	19

LONG–DISTANCE RIISE

Fierce-shooting, ex-Liverpool, AS Monaco and AS Roma left-back Jon Arne Riise marked the game in which he matched Thorbjorn Svenssen's Norwegian appearances record, against Greece in August 2012, by getting onto the scoresheet, albeit in a 3-2 losing cause. He was also on the losing side when claiming the record for himself, a 2-0 loss in Iceland the following month, before scoring his 16th international goal in his 106th match four days later as Norway beat Slovenia 2-1. Midfielder Bjorn Helge Riise, Jon Arne's younger brother, joined him at English club Fulham, and has made more than 30 full international appearances.

BOOT CAMPER

Egil Olsen, one of Europe's most eccentric coaches, was signed up for a surprise second spell as national manager when Norway put their faith in the direct-football specialist trying to qualify for the 2010 FIFA World Cup – 15 years after he had led the unfancied Scandinavians to the 1994 finals. That had been Norway's first finals appearance since 1938 and they followed it up by beating Brazil in the first round in France in 1998, making a hero out of the man in Wellington boots who guided his country to No. 2 in FIFA's official rankings. Before answering his country's call for a second stint as manager, Olsen's last job had been as manager of Iraq, but he left after only three months in charge. Remarkably, in his first match back at the helm for Norway, he masterminded a 1-0 win away to Germany with his route-one tactics.

ERIK THE VIKING

Goalkeeper Erik Thorstvedt played at the 1984 Olympic Games in Los Angeles when Norway replaced the boycotting Poland and East Germany. He was also a key member of the team that qualified for the 1994 FIFA World Cup and played a Norwegian goalkeeping record of 97 internationals between 1982 and 1996.

NEW GAARD

Attacking midfielder **Martin Odegaard** became Norway's youngest international when he made his debut against the United Arab Emirates in August 2014, at the age of 15 years and 253 days. Forty-seven days later, he became the youngest player to feature in a UEFA European Championship qualifier, breaking a 31-year-old record held by Iceland's Siggi Jonsson. In March 2015, in a 5-1 loss to Croatia, Odegaard, at 16 years and 101 days, became the youngest European player to start in a competitive international. He was 164 days younger than Liechtenstein goalkeeper Peter Jehle, who played in a Euro 98 qualifier. Odegaard's rapid rise continued when he joined Real Madrid from Stromsgodset in January 2015 and made his Real debut four months later.

TOP CAPS

1	John Arne Riise	110
2	Thorbjorn Svenssen	104
3	Henning Berg	100
4	Erik Thorstvedt	97
5	John Carew	91
=	Brede Hangeland	91
7	Oyvind Leonhardsen	86
8	Morten Gamst Pedersen	83
=	Kjetil Rekdal	83
10	Steffen Iversen	79

LONG STAY TRAVELLERS

Norway's best finish at an international tournament was the bronze medal they clinched at the 1936 Summer Olympics in Berlin, having lost to Italy in the semi-finals but beaten Poland 3-2 in a medal play-off thanks to an Arne Brustad hat-trick. That year's side has gone down in Norwegian football history as the "*Bronselaget*", or "Bronze Team". However, they had entered the tournament with low expectations and were forced to alter their travel plans ahead of the semi-final against Italy on 10 August – Norwegian football authorities had originally booked their trip home for the previous day, not expecting their team to get so far. Italy beat Norway 2-1 in extra-time not only in that summer's Olympic semi-final, but also in the first round of the FIFA World Cup two years later – going on to win both tournaments.

GOLD TIMERS

Any Norway international who reaches 25 appearances for the country is traditionally awarded a gold watch by Norway's football association. This custom began with Gunnar Andersen after he reached his quarter-century on 29 June 1919. Andersen, Norway's football captain at the 1920 Summer Olympics in Antwerp, was also an accomplished ski-jumper.

ROCK STAR

He no longer holds Norway's record for international appearances but **Thorbjorn Svenssen** captained the country more than any other player – leading them out 93 times. The defender did not score a single goal in his 104 games for Norway between 1947 and 1962, but did become the first Norwegian to reach a century of caps and, at the time, only the second footballer ever, behind only England's Billy Wright. Svenssen – nicknamed "Klippen", or "The Rock" – made his last appearance in May 1962, aged 38 years and 24 days. He died, aged 86, in January 2011.

POLAND

The history of Polish football is littered with tremendous highs and depressing lows. Olympic gold-medal success in 1972, and third-place finishes in the 1974 and 1982 FIFA World Cup competitions were followed by failure to qualify for any tournament until 1992. Poland first qualified for the UEFA European Championship in 2008 and co-hosted the tournament with Ukraine in 2012, making first round exits both times. At Euro 2016, however, they were quarter-finalists.

TOP SCORERS

1	Wlodzimierz Lubanski	48
2	Grzegorz Lato	45
3	Kazimierz Deyna	41
4	Ernest Pol	39
5	Robert Lewandowski	35
6	Andrzej Szarmach	32
7	Gerard Cieslik	27
8	Zbigniew Boniek	24
9	Ernest Wilimowski	21
10	Darius Dziekanowski	20
=	Euzebiusz Smolarek	20

STAYING ON LATER THAN LATO

Record-breaking Polish stalwart **Michal Zewlakow** bowed out of international football on familiar turf, even though his country were playing an away game. The versatile defender's 102nd and final appearance for his country was a goalless friendly in Greece in March 2011, at the Karaiskakis stadium in Piraeus where he used to play club football for Olympiacos. Zewlakow had overtaken Grzegorz Lato's appearances record for Poland in his previous match, an October 2010 friendly against Ecuador. He had already helped make footballing history for his homeland when he and brother Marcin, a striker, became the first twins to line up together for Poland, against France in February 2000. Marcin would end his international career with 25 appearances and five goals.

LOVING LEWANDOWSKI

Striker **Robert Lewandowski**, fifth all-time on Poland's scoring list, is adept at proving people wrong. He was rejected by Legia Warsaw at the age of 16 and future Poland coach Franciszek Smuda saw nothing in him as a 20-year-old, chiding the man who had recommended him: "You owe me petrol money." His prolific form for Lech Poznan secured a big-money move to Germany's Borussia Dortmund in 2009, where he struggled in his first season. He soon became one of Europe's top goalscorers, inspiring Dortmund to two Bundesliga titles and the 2013 UEFA Champions League final. He was applauded by Dortmund's fans when he waved goodbye in spring 2014, having agreed a move to rivals Bayern Munich. Lewandowski scored on his international debut, as a substitute against San Marino in September 2008, and also struck the opening goal of the 2012 UEFA European Championship. But his sporting exploits should not be a surprise: his father Krzysztof was a footballer and judo champion; his mother Iwona and sister Milena played high-level volleyball; and his wife Anna is a karate champion.

MILIK DELIVERY

Arkadiusz Milik was the hero as Poland finally won a game at a UEFA European Championship in 2016, after three draws and three defeats in their two previous tournaments, in 2008 and 2012. The Ajax Amsterdam striker Milik struck in an opening win against Northern Ireland, kicking off what proved to be a run to the quarter-finals when only a penalty shoot-out defeat to Portugal ended Polish hopes. In fact, Poland did not trail for a single minute throughout the tournament until that 5-3 loss on spot-kicks.

TOP CAPS

1	Michael Zewlakow	102
2	Grzegorz Lato	100
3	Kazimierz Deyna	97
4	Jacek Bak	96
=	Jacek Krzynowek	96
6	Wladyslaw Zmuda	91
7	Jacub Blaszczykowski	84
8	Antoni Szymanowski	82
9	Robert Lewandowski	81
10	Zbigniew Boniek	80

LATO'S MISSION

Grzegorz Lato is not only second in both the tallies of Poland's most-capped and top-scoring players, the only Polish winner of the Golden Boot with his seven goals at the 1974 FIFA World Cup, and a member of the gold medal-winning team at the 1972 Summer Olympics. He was also a leading figure in Poland's co-hosting with Ukraine of the 2012 UEFA European Championship, having become president of the country's football federation in 2008. He vowed: "I am determined to change the image of Polish football, to make it transparent and pure." He was succeeded as federation president in 2012 by Zbigniew Boniek.

SUPER ERNEST

Ernest Wilimowski wrote his name into FIFA World Cup history in 1938 when he scored four goals but still finished on the losing side. Poland went down 6-5 after extra-time to Brazil in a first-round tie in Strasbourg, France.

PUNCTUALITY PUNISHMENT

Kazimierz Gorski was the coach – capped once as a player – who led Poland to third place at the 1974 FIFA World Cup, having won gold at the Olympics in Munich, Germany, two years earlier. While winning a reputation for closeness with his players, Gorski could also be ruthless – key player Adam Musial was dropped from the team for a second-round game against Sweden at the 1974 tournament as punishment for turning up 20 minutes late to training. Poland still won the game, 1-0.

TRAGEDY AND TRIUMPH

Jacub Blaszczykowski scored the winner against Ukraine in Poland's final group game at the 2016 UEFA European Championship to clinch a place in the knock-out stages for the first time. He scored again in the second-round draw against Switzerland – Poland won on penalties – making him the first Pole to score in successive games at a major tournament since Zbigniew Boniek at the 1982 FIFA World Cup. But Blaszczykowski's missed penalty meant Poland lost a quarter-final shoot-out to Portugal. He had been one of his country's few players to come out of Euro 2012 with credit, despite going into the tournament in testing circumstances. He joined the rest of the squad only after attending the funeral of his father. As a ten-year-old, Blaszczykowski had witnessed his mother Anna being stabbed to death by his father, who served 15 years in prison. Blaszczykowski was encouraged to pursue football as a teenager by his uncle Jerzy Brzeczek, a former Poland captain and 1992 Olympic Games silver medalist.

FIVE ASIDE

Poland had five different goalscorers when they beat Peru 5-1 at the 1982 FIFA World Cup: Wlodzimierz Smolarek, Grzegorz Lato, Zbigniew Boniek, Andrzej Buncol and Wlodzimierz Ciolek. The feat was not repeated until Phillip Cocu, Marc Overmars, Dennis Bergkamp, Pierre van Hooijdonk and Ronald de Boer gave Holland a 5-0 victory over South Korea at the 1998 FIFA World Cup.

GERMAN JINX JUNKED

At the 19th time of trying, Poland finally defeated neighbours Germany, surprising the newly-crowned world champions 2-0 in a 2016 UEFA European Championship qualifying match at Warsaw's National Stadium in October 2014. The goals were scored by Arkadiusz Milik – owned by German club Bayer Leverkusen – and Sebastian Mila, though goalkeeper Wojciech Szczesny also pulled off a string of crucial saves. It ended Germany's 33-match unbeaten run in competitive qualifying games, stretching back to October 2007.

A ZBIG IF

Zbigniew Boniek, arguably Poland's greatest ever player, earned a place among football's legends for his role in the country's progress to third place at the 1982 FIFA World Cup. However, his absence from the tournament's semi-final will go down as one of the great "what ifs" of the competition. Robbed of their star forward through suspension, could Poland have upset both Italy and the odds and reached the final? Instead they lost the match 2-0.

PORTUGAL

Portugal almost won their first international competition for which they qualified. Inspired by Eusebio, they reached the semi-finals of the 1966 FIFA World Cup, but lost to eventual champions England. A standout performance in the 1984 UEFA European Championship apart, more than 30 years would pass before Portugal enjoyed such giddy heights again. Two "golden" generations of players have made Portugal a consistent force on the world football stage for more than 20 years, but the 2016 UEFA European Championship was their first silverware.

TOP CAPS

1	Cristiano Ronaldo	133
2	Luis Figo	127
3	Fernando Couto	110
4	Nani	103
5	Rui Costa	94
6	Joao Moutinho	90
7	Ricardo Carvalho	89
8	Pauleta	88
9	Bruno Alves	86
10	Simao	85

TOP SCORERS

1	Cristiano Ronaldo	61
2	Pauleta	47
3	Eusebio	41
4	Luis Figo	32
5	Nuno Gomes	29
6	Helder Postiga	27
7	Rui Costa	26
8	Joao Pinto	24
9	Nene	22
=	Simao	22

HAPPY EDER AFTER

Substitute striker **Eder** was the unlikely hero when Portugal finally ended their long wait for an international trophy to triumph at the 2016 UEFA European Championship. The forward – who spent the 2015–16 season on loan at French club Lille – scored the only goal of the final in Paris, in the 109th minute, to defeat host nation France. It was the latest opening goal scored in any UEFA European Championship final. Portugal, coached by Fernando Santos, drew their three first-round games to qualify as one of the best third-place teams. They then defeated Croatia 1-0 after extra-time, with Ricardo Quaresma's 117th-minute winner the game's only shot on target, Poland on penalties after a 1-1 quarter-final draw, and Wales 2-0 in the semi-finals. The final victory was Portugal's first against France in 11 attempts, stretching back to 1975 – and meant former Greece manager Santos remained unbeaten in his first 14 competitive matches in charge of his homeland. The triumph came 12 years after Portugal lost, as hosts themselves, the 2004 UEFA European Championship final against Greece.

THE BLACK PANTHER

Born in Mozambique, **Eusebio** da Silva Ferreira was named Portugal's "Golden Player" to mark UEFA's 50th anniversary in 2004. Signed by Benfica in 1960 at the age of 18, he scored a hat-trick in his second game – against Santos in a friendly tournament in Paris – outshining their young star, Pele. He helped Benfica win a second European Cup in 1962, was named European Footballer of the Year in 1965 and led Portugal to third place in the 1966 FIFA World Cup, finishing as top scorer with nine goals. A phenomenal striker, he scored 320 goals in 313 Portuguese league matches, won the first European Golden Boot in 1968 (and earned a second in 1973). The world of football united in paying tribute to Eusebio after he died aged 71 in January 2014. Portugal declared three days of mourning, his statue at Benfica's Estadio da Luz home was transformed into a shrine, his coffin was carried around the pitch and the Benfica players wore his name on their backs during a 2-0 win over rivals Porto.

PRESIDENTIAL POWER

Cristiano Ronaldo dos Santos Aveiro got his second name because his father was a great fan of US President Ronald Reagan – and he has gone on to firmly establish himself as one of football's superstars. He grew up supporting Benfica but began his career with arch Lisbon rivals Sporting Clube do Portugal, before moving to Manchester United in 2003, then Real Madrid in 2009 for a then-world record fee of $93.9 million. The three-time FIFA World Player of the Year is the all-time leading scorer in the UEFA Champions League, a trophy he has lifted three times, and has also found the net for Real Madrid more than any other player. Already Portugal's top scorer, he became his country's most-capped player at the 2016 UEFA European Championship – and ended the competition lifting the trophy, despite going off injured 25 minutes into the final against France. He broke the appearances record in Portugal's first-round draw with Austria, but marred his 128th game by hitting a the post with a penalty. He did score three times in subsequent games, making him the first man to score at four different UEFA European Championships.

THE FAMOUS FIVE

Eusebio, Mario Coluna, Jose Augusto, Antonio Simoes, and Jose Torres were the "Fabulous Five" in Benfica's 1960s Dream Team, who made up the spine of the Portuguese national side at the 1966 FIFA World Cup. Coluna (the "Sacred Monster"), scored the vital third goal in the 1961 European Cup final and captained the national side in 1966. Jose Augusto, who scored two goals in the opening game against Hungary, went on to manage the national side and later the Portuguese women's team. Antonio Simoes (the "Giant Gnome" – just 1.58 metres/5ft 3in tall) made his debut for Portugal and Benfica in 1962, aged just 18. Jose Torres – the only one of the five not to win the European Cup (though he played in the defeats in both 1963 and 1968) – scored the winner against Russia in the 1966 third-place match, and went on to manage the national side to their next appearance at the FIFA World Cup finals in 1986.

THREE AND IN

After suffering a 4-0 trouncing against Germany in their opening game of the 2014 finals – their heaviest FIFA World Cup defeat – Portugal manager Paulo Bento replaced goalkeeper Rui Patricio with Beto for the next match, a 2-2 draw with the USA. Portugal ended their campaign by replacing the injured Beto with Eduardo for the final moments of a 2-1 victory over Ghana. They thus became only the fifth team to use all their goalkeepers in one FIFA World Cup finals and the first since Greece had done so 20 years earlier. The Netherlands became the sixth later in the tournament.

NICE ONE, SAN

Renato Sanches is Portugal's youngest player at an international tournament, he was 18 years and 301 days for their 2016 UEFA European Championship opener against Iceland. He was one of the stars of the tournament, and was voted UEFA Euro 2016's best young player. His superb long-range strike against Poland in the quarter-finals made him the youngest scorer at any UEFA European Championship knock-out round, aged 18 years and 316 days. Ten days later, he was the youngest man to play in a UEFA European Championship final.

REP. OF IRELAND

It took a combination of astute management and endless searching through ancestral records before the Republic of Ireland finally qualified for the finals of a major tournament, at the 20th time of asking. But ever since Jack Charlton took the team to UEFA Euro 88, Ireland have remained one of Europe's most dangerous opponents.

ROBBIE KEEN

The Republic of Ireland's all-time scoring record was taken by much-travelled striker **Robbie Keane** in October 2004 and he has been adding to it ever since – not least with last-minute equalizers against Germany and Spain at the 2006 FIFA World Cup. He marked the final game at the old Lansdowne Road with a hat-trick against San Marino in November 2006 and, four years later, won his 100th cap in the inaugural game at its replacement, the Aviva Stadium. Ireland's 2-1 win over Macedonia in March 2011 was Keane's 41st match as captain – equalling Andy Townsend's record. In the three-team Carling Nations Cup, with Northern Ireland and Scotland, Keane – still wearing the captain's armband – scored three goals in the two games, taking his overall tally to 49. A double against Macedonia in June 2011 took him to 51, making him the first player from the British Isles to score a half-century of international goals. Keane's third international hat-trick, in a 7-0 win over Gibraltar in October 2014, took him to 65 goals and, with 21, he passed Turkey's Hakan Sukur for the most in UEFA European Championship qualifiers. He ended Euro 2016 on 67 goals.

KILBANE KEEPS ON AND ON

Only England's Billy Wright, with 70, has played more consecutive internationals than **Kevin Kilbane**, whose 109th Republic of Ireland cap against Macedonia in March 2011 was also his 65th in a row, covering 11 years and five months. The versatile left-sider – nicknamed "Zinedine Kilbane" by fans – was given a rest for Ireland's next game three days later, though, a friendly against Uruguay.

KEANE CARRY–ON

Few star players have walked out on their country with quite the dramatic impact as Republic of Ireland captain **Roy Keane** in 2002 at their FIFA World Cup training camp in Saipan, Japan. The fiercely intense Manchester United skipper quit before a competitive ball had been kicked, complaining about a perceived lack of professionalism in the Irish preparations – and his loss of faith in manager Mick McCarthy. Ireland reached the second round without him, losing on penalties to Spain, but his behaviour divided a nation. When McCarthy stepped down Keane and the Irish football federation brokered a truce, and he returned to international duty in April 2004 under new boss Brian Kerr. Few expected his second comeback, however, when he was appointed assistant to new manager Martin O'Neill in November 2013. O'Neill, who played 64 times for Northern Ireland between 1971 and 1984 succeeded Italian veteran Giovanni Trapattoni, who resigned after failing to qualify for the 2014 FIFA World Cup finals.

CHAMPION CHARLTON

Jack Charlton became a hero after he took Ireland to their first major finals in 1988, defeating England 1-0 in their first game at the UEFA European Championship. Things got even better at their first FIFA World Cup finals two years later, where the unfancied Irish lost out only to hosts Italy in the quarter-finals.

BRADY BUNCH

Irish eyes were smiling again at Italy's expense in their final first-round group game at the 2016 UEFA European Championship, when **Robbie Brady** headed a late winning goal. It gave Martin O'Neill's team a place in the second round, where they took the lead through a Brady penalty against France, but succumbed 2-1. The spot-kick, after 118 seconds, was the earliest in the UEFA European Championship finals. Brady was the first Republic of Ireland player to score in consecutive UEFA European Championship games; Robbie Keane achieved the feat in the 2002 FIFA World Cup.

OLE, O'SHEA

Veteran versatile defender **John O'Shea** marked his century of caps – the sixth Irish player to reach the landmark – by scoring a rare goal, this one with the last kick of the game to secure a 1-1 draw away to world champions Germany in an October 2014 qualifier for the 2016 UEFA European Championship. It was only the third goal of his international career.

MORE FOR MOORE

Paddy Moore was the first player ever to score four goals in a FIFA World Cup qualifier when Ireland came from behind to draw 4-4 with Belgium on 25 February 1934. Don Givens became the only Irishman to equal Moore's feat when he scored all four as Ireland beat Turkey 4-0 in October 1975.

CAPTAIN ALL-ROUND

Johnny Carey not only captained Matt Busby's Manchester United to the English league title in 1952, he also captained both Northern Ireland (nine caps) and later the Republic of Ireland (27 caps). He went on to manage the Republic of Ireland between 1955 and 1967.

HOORAY FOR RAY

Ray Houghton may have been born in Glasgow and spoke with a Scottish accent, but he scored two of Ireland's most famous goals. A header gave the Republic a shock 1-0 win over England at UEFA Euro 88 in West Germany and, six years later, his long-range strike was the only goal of the game against eventual finalists Italy, in the first round of the 1994 FIFA World Cup in the USA. It was exactly 18 years to the day from that 1994 shock that Ireland – now managed by Italian Giovanni Trapattoni – lost 2-0 to Italy in their third and final Group C match of the 2012 UEFA European Championship. Playing for Ireland that day was defender John O'Shea, who had previously been part of the Irish team that beat Italy 2-1 in the final of the 1998 UEFA European U-16s Championship final in Scotland. The Republic's only other continental title was the UEFA European U-19s Championship trophy they lifted by beating Germany, also in 1998.

TOP CAPS

1	Robbie Keane	145
2	Shay Given	134
3	John O'Shea	114
4	Kevin Kilbane	110
5	Steve Staunton	102
6	Damien Duff	101
7	Niall Quinn	92
8	Tony Cascarino	88
9	Aiden McGeady	85
10	Paul McGrath	83

CROSSING THE CODES

Cornelius "Con" Martin was a Gaelic footballer whose passion for soccer resulted in his expulsion from the Gaelic Athletic Association. His versatility meant he was as good at centre-half as he was in goal, both for club (Aston Villa) and country. He played both in goal and outfield for the fledgling Irish national team, scoring a penalty in the 2-0 victory over England at Goodison Park in 1949 – in what was England's first home defeat to a non-British opponent.

TOP SCORERS

1	Robbie Keane	67
2	Niall Quinn	21
3	Frank Stapleton	20
4	John Aldridge	19
=	Tony Cascarino	19
=	Don Givens	19
7	Shane Long	16
8	Noel Cantwell	14
=	Kevin Doyle	14
10	Gerry Daly	13
=	Jimmy Dunne	13

ROMANIA

The history of Romanian football is littered with a series of bright moments – they were one of four countries (with Brazil, France and Belgium) to appear in the first three editions of the FIFA World Cup – followed by significant spells in the doldrums – since 1938 they have qualified for the finals of the tournament only four times in 14 attempts. The country's football highlight came in 1994 when, inspired by Gheorghe Hagi, they reached the quarter-finals of the FIFA World Cup.

TOP CAPS

1	Dorinel Munteanu	134
2	Gheorghe Hagi	124
3	Gheorghe Popescu	115
4	Razvan Rat	103
5	Ladislau Boloni	102
6	Dan Petrescu	95
7	Bogdan Stelea	91
8	Michael Klein	89
9	Bogdan Lobont	85
10	Marius Lacatus	83
=	Mircea Rednic	83

FAMOUS FOURSOME

Gheorghe Hagi, Florin Raducioiu, Ilie Dumitrescu and **Gheorghe "Gica" Popescu** helped Romania light up the FIFA World Cup in the USA in 1994. Raducioiu (four), Dumitrescu (three) and Hagi (two) scored nine of their country's ten goals that summer and also the trio converted their penalties in a quarter-final shoot-out against Sweden, only for misses by Dan Petrescu and Miodrag Belodedici to send the Romanians home. As well as being team-mates, Popescu and Hagi are also brothers-in-law – their wives, Luminiya Popescu and Marlilena Hagi, are sisters.

STANCU VERY MUCH

Romania conceded just two goals throughout the qualifying competition for the 2016 UEFA European Championship (the fewest of any team) – but then let in that same number in the tournament's opening match, a 2-1 defeat to hosts France. They exited the tournament in the first round after a 1-1 draw with Switzerland and 1-0 defeat against Albania. The two Romania goals in the finals were from the penalty spot, both being scored by striker Bogdan Stancu.

BORDER CROSSING

Some 14 footballers played for both Romania, during the 1930s, and Hungary, during the 1940s – the most prolific being striker Iuliu Bodola, who scored 31 goals in 48 games for Romania, including appearances at the 1934 and 1938 FIFA World Cups, and four in 13 matches for his adopted homeland Hungary.

YELLOW PERIL

Despite topping Group G ahead of England, Colombia and Tunisia at the 1998 FIFA World Cup, Romania's players of that tournament might perhaps be best remembered for their collective decision to dye their hair blond ahead of their final first-round game. The **newly bleached Romanians** struggled to a 1-1 draw against Tunisia, before being knocked out by Croatia in the second round, 1-0.

TOP SCORERS

1	Gheorghe Hagi	35
=	Adrian Mutu	35
3	Iuliu Bodola	31
4	Viorel Moldovan	25
=	Ciprian Marica	25
6	Ladislau Boloni	23
7	Rodion Camataru	21
=	Dudu Georgescu	21
=	Anghel Iordanescu	21
=	Florin Raducioiu	21

CEMETERY SENTRY

It was second time luckier for former international striker Victor Piturca when he coached Romania at the 2008 UEFA European Championship in Austria and Switzerland, even though they were eliminated in the first round. He had previously been manager when the country qualified for the 2000 UEFA European Championship, but was forced out of the job before the tournament started following arguments with big-name players such as Gheorghe Hagi. Piturca's cousin Florin Piturca was also a professional footballer but died aged only 27 in 1978. Florin's father and Victor's uncle Maximilian, a cobbler, not only built a mausoleum for Florin but also slept at night in the cemetery until his own death in 1994.

BACK TO THE FUTURE

Right-back Christian Manea became Romania's youngest international when making his debut against Albania in May 2014, aged 16 years, nine months and 22 days, having played only five senior matches for his club Vitoril Constanta. He broke the record set back in 1928 by Gratian Sepi, aged 17 years, three months and 15 days when facing Turkey. Romanian football chiefs showed another sense of history in October 2014, coaxing 64-year-old Anghel Iordanescu out of retirement for a third spell as national coach. The first spell included a run to the 1994 FIFA World Cup quarter-finals. One of Iordanescu's assistants was Viorel Moldovan, who had played for him at the 1996 UEFA European Championship and 1998 FIFA World Cup. Iordanescu retired again in June 2016.

CENTURY MAN

Gheorghe Hagi, Romania's "Player of the [twentieth] Century", scored three goals and was named in the Team of the Tournament at the 1994 FIFA World Cup in the United States, at which Romania lost out on penalties to Sweden after a 2-2 draw in the quarter-finals. Hagi made his international debut in 1983, aged just 18, scored his first goal aged 19 (in a 3-2 defeat to Northern Ireland) and remains Romania's joint-top goalscorer with 35 goals in 125 games. Despite retiring from international football after the 1998 FIFA World Cup, Hagi couldn't resist answering his country's call to play in UEFA Euro 2000. Sadly, two yellow-card offences in six minutes in the quarter-final against Italy meant Hagi's final bow on the international stage saw him receive a red card – and leave the field to take an early bath. Farul Constanta, in Hagi's hometown, named their stadium after him in 2000 – but fans stopped referring to it as such after he took the manager's job at rivals Timisoara.

ENDURING DORINEL

Dorinel Munteanu has played for Romania more times than any other although at one point his former team-mate Gheorghe Hagi's 125-cap record looked safe. Versatile defensive midfielder Munteanu was stuck on 119 appearances throughout an 18-month absence from the international scene before being surprisingly recalled at the age of 37 by manager Victor Piturca in February 2005. He ended his Romania career two years later, having scored 16 times in 134 games. Yet many Romanians believe he was wrongly denied a goal when a shot against Bulgaria at the 1996 UEFA European Championship appeared to bounce over the line, only to not be given. The match ended 1-0 to Bulgaria and Romania were eliminated in the first round following three straight defeats.

ADRIAN'S AID

Romania lost only once when **Adrian Mutu** scored – a fact made all the better for them since, with 35 goals, he is (with Gheorghe Hagi) his country's all-time leading goalscorer. Mutu matched Hagi with a FIFA World Cup qualifying game equalizer against Hungary in March 2013, though this was his first international goal in 21 months – and, it turned out, his final one, too. Unfortunately for Romania, controversy has followed their finest player of the 21st century: he has twice been banned for failed drugs tests. The first came when a test carried out by his club Chelsea, in September 2004, showed traces of cocaine and brought about his dismissal. After a seven-month ban he rehabilitated his career in Italy, first with Juventus and then Fiorentina, before receiving a nine-month suspension after he tested positive for a banned anti-obesity drug in January 2010.

RUSSIA

Before the break-up of the Soviet Union (USSR) in 1992, the team was a world football powerhouse, winning the first UEFA European Championship in 1960, gold at the 1956 and 1988 Olympic Games and qualifying for the FIFA World Cup on seven occasions. Playing as Russia since August 1992, the good times have eluded them – apart from being UEFA Euro 2008 semi-finalists. They did, however, reach the 2014 FIFA World Cup under Italian coach Fabio Capello but will be hoping to better their first-round exit when Russia gets to host the tournament for the first time in 2018.

KERZH LIFTS HIS CURSE

Only one man was in Russia's squads for the 2002 FIFA World Cup finals and the next time they qualified, in 2014: Aleksandr Kerzhakov. He made his international debut as a 19-year-old a teenager in March 2002, and he played just eight minutes of the finals three months later. With five goals, he was Russia's leading scorer in qualifying for the 2014 finals, and Kerzhakov scored his 26th international goal to earn a 1-1 draw in Russia's opener against South Korea in Cuiaba. This goal equalled Russia's all-time scoring record set by a team-mate in 2002, Vladimir Beschastnykh. Kerzhakov went on to claim the all-time scoring record for himself with a brace in Russia's 4-0 victory in a friendly against Azerbaijan in September 2014.

HOME RANGE

Russia were the only country at the 2014 FIFA World Cup whose entire 23-man squad played their club football domestically. Dynamo Moscow had six players and CSKA Moscow five, including defender **Sergei Ignashevich** who reached a century of caps in the final Group H game against Algeria. They may have had the highest-paid coach at the tournament, with Fabio Capello earning a reported £6.69million per year. But for the second FIFA World Cup running he was undone by a goalkeeping error in the opening game: in 2010 he watched England's Rob Green fumble in a shot from the USA's Clint Dempsey; in Russia's 2014 opener, keeper Igor Akinfeev did suffer similarly with a long-range effort by South Korea's Lee Keun-Ho. And, by coincidence, both lapses were equalizers in 1-1 draws.

TOP SCORERS
(Russia only)

1	Aleksandr Kerzhakov	30
2	Vladimir Beschastnykh	26
3	Roman Pavlyuchenko	21
4	Andrei Arshavin	17
=	Valeri Karpin	17
6	Dmitri Sychev	15
7	Roman Shirokov	13
8	Igor Kolyvanov	12
=	Aleksandr Kokorin	12
10	Sergei Kiryakov	10
=	Aleksandr Mostovoi	10

YOUNG PROMISE

Igor Akinfeev became post-Soviet Russia's youngest international footballer when he made his debut in a friendly against Norway on 28 April 2004. The CSKA Moscow goalkeeper was just 18 years and 20 days old. The following season would be perhaps just as memorable for him, clinching a domestic league and cup double with his club while also lifting the UEFA Cup as CSKA Moscow became post-Soviet Russia's first side to win a UEFA club trophy. The youngest Soviet-era debutant was Eduard Streltsov, who hit a hat-trick on his debut against Sweden in June 1956, at the age of 17 years and 340 days and then scored another treble in his second game, against India.

ARTEM'S TIME

Artem Dzyuba scored his first international goal for Russia on 8 September 2014, in a 4-0 victory over Liechtenstein – and he enjoyed a happy anniversary precisely a year later in a 7-0 thrashing of the same opponents, scoring four of his side's strikes. The win equalled the biggest in Russia's history, 7-0 against San Marino in June 1995. Dzyuba was Russia's top scorer, with eight, during qualification for the 2016 UEFA European Championship but could not find the net at the tournament itself as Russia finished bottom of their group behind Wales, England and Slovakia – costing manager Leonid Slutsky his job.

TOP CAPS
(Russia only)

1	Sergei Ignashevich	120
2	Viktor Onopko	109
3	Vasili Berezutskiy	98
4	Aleksandr Kerzhakov	91
5	Igor Akinfeev	90
6	Aleksandr Anyukov	77
7	Andrei Arshavin	75
8	Valeri Karpin	72
9	Vladimir Beschastnykh	71
10	Yuri Zhirkov	68

PAV A GO HERO

Roman Pavlyuchenko's thumping strike as a substitute to wrap up a 4-1 victory over the Czech Republic in Russia's opening game of the 2012 UEFA European Championship took him to within five goals of Vladimir Beschastnykh's post-Soviet scoring record. Pavlyuchenko also scored Russia's first goal of Euro 2008, this time in a 4-1 defeat at the hands of eventual champions Spain. Despite the loss, Russia still managed to reach the semi-finals that year, before failing to go beyond the group stages in 2012 and 2016. Pavlyuchenko remains Russia's top scorer in UEFA European Championships, with four overall – three in 2008 and one in 2012, although the latter one proved to be his last for his country.

SUPER STOPPER

FIFA declared **Lev Yashin** to be the finest goalkeeper of the 20th century – naturally, he made it into their Century XI team, too. In a career spanning 20 years, Yashin played 326 league games for Dynamo Moscow – the only club side he ever played for – and won 78 caps for the Soviet Union, conceding on average less than a goal a game (only 70 in total). With Dynamo, he won five Soviet championships and three Soviet cups, the last of which came in his final full season in 1970. He saved around 150 penalties in his long career, and kept four clean sheets in his 12 FIFA World Cup matches. Such was Yashin's worldwide reputation, Chilean international Eladio Rojas was so excited at scoring past the legendary Yashin in the 1962 FIFA World Cup that he gave the surprised keeper a big hug with the ball still sitting in the back of the net. Yashin was nicknamed the "Black Spider" for his distinctive black jersey and his uncanny ability to get a hand, arm, leg or foot in the way of shots and headers of all kinds. In 1963, Yashin became the first, and so far only, keeper to be named European Footballer of the Year, the same year in which he won his fifth Soviet championship and starred for the Rest of the World XI in the English FA's Centenary Match at Wembley.

CAPPING IT ALL

Viktor Onopko, despite being born in the Ukraine, played all his career for the CIS and Russian national football teams. The first of Onopko's 113 international caps (the first four for the CIS) came in a 2-2 draw against England in Moscow on 29 April 1992. He played in the 1994 and 1998 FIFA World Cups, as well as the UEFA European Championship in 1996. He was due to join the squad for the UEFA European Championship in 2004 but missed out through injury. Onopko's club career, spanning 19 years, took him to Shakhtar Donetsk, Spartak Moscow, Real Oviedo, Rayo Vallecano, Alania Vladikavkaz and FC Saturn. He was Russian footballer of the year in 1993 and 1994.

GOLDEN BOY

Igor Netto captained the USSR national side to their greatest successes: gold at the 1956 Olympics in Melbourne and victory in the first-ever UEFA European Championship in France in 1960. Born in Moscow in 1930, Netto was awarded the Order of Lenin in 1957 and became an ice hockey coach after retiring from football.

SCOTLAND

A country with a vibrant domestic league and a rich football tradition – it played host to the first-ever international football match, against England, in November 1872 – Scotland have never put in the performances on the international stage to match their lofty ambitions. There have been moments of triumph, such as the unexpected defeat of The Netherlands at the 1978 FIFA World Cup, but far too many moments of despair. Scotland have not qualified for the finals of a major tournament since 1998.

TOP SCORERS

1	Kenny Dalglish	30
=	Denis Law	30
3	Hughie Gallacher	23
4	Lawrie Reilly	22
5	Ally McCoist	19
6	Kenny Miller	18
7	Robert Hamilton	15
=	James McFadden	15
9	Maurice Johnston	14
10	Bob McColl	13
=	Andrew Wilson	13

KING KENNY

Kenny Dalglish is Scotland's joint-top international goalscorer (with Denis Law) and remains the only player to have won more than a century of caps for the national side, with 102 in total – 11 more than the next highest cap-winner, goalkeeper Jim Leighton. Despite growing up a Rangers fan (he was born in Glasgow on 4 March 1951), Dalglish made his name spearheading Celtic's domestic dominance in the 1970s, winning four league titles, four Scottish Cups and one League Cup. He then went on to become a legend at Liverpool, winning a hat-trick of European Cups (1978, 1981 and 1984) and leading the side as player-manager to their first-ever league and cup double in 1986. He later joined Herbert Chapman and Brian Clough as one of the few managers to lead two different sides to the league title – guiding Blackburn Rovers to the summit of English football in 1994–95. For Scotland, Dalglish scored at both the 1978 and 1982 FIFA World Cup finals, netting the first goal in the famous 3-2 victory over eventual runners-up Holland in the 1978 group stages. He played his last international in 1986.

THE LAWMAN

Denis Law is joint top scorer for Scotland with Kenny Dalglish, scoring 30 goals in only 55 games compared to the 102 it took Dalglish to do the same. Law twice scored four goals in a match for Scotland, the first against Northern Ireland on 7 November 1962 – helping the Scots to win the British Home Championships – and then against Norway in a friendly on 7 November 1963. Law clearly enjoyed playing against Norway, having grabbed a hat-trick in Bergen just five months earlier.

HOME FROM HOME

Hampden Park is Scotland's regular home for competitive matches, but alternatives were needed in 2013, as it was being refitted in preparation for the 2014 Commonwealth Games athletics events. Under coach **Gordon Strachan**, in 2016 UEFA European Championship qualifiers, Scotland stayed in the city and recorded 1-0 victories over both Georgia at Rangers' Ibrox Stadium in October and the Republic of Ireland at Celtic Park a month later.

RULE, BRIT ANYA

Winger Ikechi Anya had the choice of four countries to represent in international football: Scotland, where he was born, England where he lived from the age of seven, Nigeria where his research scientist father came from and Romania where his economist mother originated and met his father. He opted for Scotland, having spent his early childhood in Glasgow and made his debut in September 2013. He plays for English club Watford and has had spells in Spain, with Granada and Cadiz. Anya also attended the Glenn Hoddle Academy in Spain, set up by the ex-England player and manager for young footballers rejected elsewhere.

DIVIDED LOYALTIES

Scottish-born winger Jim Brown played and scored for the USA side which lost to Argentina in the first FIFA World Cup in 1930. He had moved to New Jersey three years earlier and qualified through his US citizen father. Two of his brothers also played professionally: younger brother John, a goalkeeper, was capped by Scotland, but Tom did not play at international level. Jim's son George appeared once for the USA, in 1957, while two of John's sons, Peter and Gordon, both played rugby for Scotland.

The first brothers to play for different countries, were John and Archie Goodall – members of Preston North End's 1888–89 league and FA Cup double-winning squad – and although their parents were both Scottish, London-born John played for England and Belfast-born Archie represented Ireland. Another pair of brothers with Scottish parents were Joe and Gerry Baker – though Joe chose to play for England in the 1960s and Gerry appeared for the USA.

I HAVEN'T FELT THIS GOOD SINCE ARCHIE GEMMILL SCORED AGAINST HOLLAND

Archie Gemmill scored Scotland's greatest goal on the world stage in the surprise 3-2 victory over Holland at the 1978 FIFA World Cup. He jinked past three defenders before chipping the ball neatly over Dutch goalkeeper Jan Jongbloed. Amazingly, in 2008, this magical moment was turned into a dance in the English National Ballet's "The Beautiful Game".

FLETCH LIVES

For Steven Fletcher, international goals are a bit like London buses: you wait ages for one and then three come along at once. He ended a six-year international goal drought with a hat-trick in Scotland's 6-1 victory over Gibraltar in March 2015 at Hampden Park. He thus became his country's first hat-trick scorer since Colin Stein struck four goals in a FIFA World Cup qualifier against Cyprus in 1969. His only previous goal – in 20 matches – was in a 2-1 win over Iceland in April 2009. Fletcher, born in Shrewsbury, England, moved to Scotland aged ten and qualified to play for them through his mother Mary.

TOP CAPS

1	Kenny Dalglish	102
2	Jim Leighton	91
3	Alex McLeish	77
4	Paul McStay	76
5	Tom Boyd	72
6	Darren Fletcher	71
7	Kenny Miller	69
=	David Weir	69
9	Christian Dailly	67
10	Willie Miller	65

WEIR ON THE BALL

Rugged Rangers centre-back **David Weir** became Scotland's oldest international footballer when he faced Lithuania in a 2012 UEFA European Championship qualifier on 3 September 2010, aged 40 years and 111 days, for his 66th appearance. He was still representing his country three caps and 39 days later, against reigning world and European champions Spain. The age record was previously held by ex-Aberdeen and Manchester United goalkeeper Jim Leighton, who was 40 years and 78 days old when he played his final international in 1998.

UNOFFICIAL WORLD CHAMPIONS

One of the victories most cherished by Scotland fans is the **3-2 triumph** over arch-rivals and reigning world champions England in April 1967 at Wembley – the first time Sir Alf Ramsey's team had lost since clinching the 1966 FIFA World Cup. Scotland's man of the match that day was ball-juggling left-half/midfielder Jim Baxter, while it was also the first game in charge for Scotland's first full-time manager, Bobby Brown. Less fondly recalled is Scotland's 9-3 trouncing by the same opposition at the same stadium in April 1961, which made unfortunate goalkeeper Frank Haffey the butt of a popular joke that did the rounds across the border in England: "What's the time? Nearly 10 past Haffey." The game was Haffey's second – and last – for Scotland.

⚽ SERBIA

The former Yugoslavia was one of the strongest football nations in eastern Europe. They reached the FIFA World Cup semi-finals in 1930 and 1962, they were also runners-up in the UEFA European Championships of 1960 and 1968. In addition, Yugoslavia's leading club, Red Star Belgrade, were only the second team from eastern Europe (after Romania's Steaua Bucharest in 1986) to win the European Cup, when they beat Marseille on penalties in the 1991 final.

⚽ STJEP UP

Yugoslavia/Serbia's all-time top goalscorer remains **Stjepan Bobek**, with 38 in 63 appearances. He also holds the record for most goals in a Yugoslavia/Serbia top-flight game – in June 1948 he got nine for Partizan Belgrade in a 10-1 rout of 14 Oktobar. Although Partizan won the title that season, his 24 goals were four fewer than Franjo Wolfl of second-placed Dinamo Zagreb. Wolfl scored six goals in 12 international appearances and the pair combined to help Yugoslavia win the silver medal at the London 1948 Olympic Games. Bobek also was in Yugoslavia's squad that again won silver at the 1952 Games.

⚽ MITIC'S PITCH

Serbia's national stadium, in the capital Belgrade, was long known as the Marakana – after the famous Maracana in Rio de Janeiro, Brazil – but was renamed in 2014 in honour of former Yugoslavia striker and manager Rajko Mitic. He scored 32 goals in 59 games for his country between 1946 and 1951 – helping win silver at the 1948 and 1952 Olympics – before becoming national coach between 1966 and 1970. Under his stewardship, Yugoslavia had another runners-up finish, this one at the 1968 UEFA European Championship.

⚽ TOP CAPS
([United] Yugoslavia and Serbia)

1	Dejan Stankovic	103
2	Savo Milosevic	102
3	Branislav Ivanovic	87
4	Dragan Dzajic	85
5	Dragan Stojkovic	84
6	Zoran Tosic	74
7	Predrag Mijatovic	73
8	Zlatko Vujovic	70
9	Vladimir Stojkovic	68
10	Branko Zebec	65

⚽ MAGIC DRAGAN

Yugoslavia's greatest player was Red Star left winger **Dragan Dzajic**, who later went on to become the club's president. He made his international debut at 18, won a national record 85 caps and scored 23 goals. The most important was his last-minute winner against world champions England in the 1968 UEFA European Championship semi-final in Florence, which took Yugoslavia to the final against Italy. Pele said of Dzajic: "He's a real wizard. I'm sorry he's not Brazilian."

TOP SCORERS

([United] Yugoslavia and Serbia)

1	Stjepan Bobek	38
2	Milan Galic	37
=	Savo Milosevic	37
4	Blagoje Marjanovic	36
5	Rajko Mitic	32
6	Dusan Bajevic	29
7	Todor Veselinovic	28
8	Borivoje Kostic	26
=	Predrag Mijatovic	26
10	Zlatko Vujovic	25

STAN'S THE MAN

Midfielder **Dejan Stankovic** is the only man to have represented three different countries at separate FIFA World Cups, playing for Yugoslavia in 2002, Serbia and Montenegro in 2006, and Serbia in 2010. His pragmatic comment on his achievement was: "I'm happy with the record, but I'd rather win. It's OK to have been in three World Cups, but I would have liked to have better results." Stankovic scored twice on his international debut for Yugoslavia in 1998. He has also twice scored memorable volleyed goals from virtually on the halfway line – once for Internazionale against Genoa in 2009–10, with a first-time shot from the opposing goalkeeper's clearance, and an almost identical finish against German club FC Schalke 04 in the UEFA Champions League the following season. Stankovic tied Savo Milosevic's Serbian appearances record with his final competitive international in October 2011, but went one better in October 2013, when playing the first ten minutes of a 2-0 friendly defeat of Japan at Novi Sad.

SAV A GO HERO

Savo Milosevic was the first Serbian player to reach a century of international appearances – and he can claim to have played for his country in four different guises, representing Yugoslavia before and after it broke up, Serbia & Montenegro and finally Serbia alone. Milosevic's 100th international appearance was memorable for the wrong reasons, coming in a 6-0 defeat to Argentina at the 2006 FIFA World Cup. He returned to the fold for a final, farewell match: a friendly against Bulgaria on 19 November 2008. Milosevic played only the first 34 minutes yet managed not only to score twice but also miss two penalties. He joked: "Maybe those 34 minutes sum up my career, in the best possible way, with good moments and bad times, when you are at the top and at the bottom. Believe me, I have never missed two penalties before – not even in training."

BRAN POWER

Versatile Chelsea defender and Serbia captain **Branislav Ivanovic** has enjoyed scoring significant late goals against Portuguese opposition. His first goal for his country was an 88th-minute equalizer in a UEFA European Championship qualifier away to Portugal in September 2007. His stoppage-time header gave Chelsea victory over Benfica in the final of the 2013 UEFA Europa League, a year after suspension ruled him out of the club's UEFA Champions League triumph over Bayern Munich. He was named Serb Footballer of the Year in 2012 and 2013, the first player to win the award in consecutive years since Serbia became independent – although this was then emulated by his Chelsea team-mate Nemanja Matic in 2014 and 2015.

MILORAD'S MILESTONE

The first man to captain and then coach his country at the FIFA World Cup was Milorad Arsenijevic, who captained Yugoslavia to the semi-finals at the inaugural tournament in Uruguay in 1930 and then managed their squad in Brazil 20 years later.

GOING IT ALONE

After Serbia and Montenegro competed at the 2006 FIFA World Cup, the 2010 tournament was the first featuring Serbia alone following Montenegro's independence. Topping their qualifying group ahead of France, Radomir Antic's Serbian side failed to make it through to the knockout stages in South Africa, despite a single-goal victory over Group D rivals Germany. A Serbian working for an opposing team was partly to blame – Milovan Rajevac was coach of the Ghana side that beat Serbia 1-0 in their opening first-round match. A mainstay in the Serbian defence was dominating centre-back **Nemanja Vidic**, a 2008 UEFA Champions League-winner and hero at Manchester United – but he announced his retirement from international football in October 2011.

SLOVAKIA

Slovakia have finally begun claiming bragging rights over their neighbours, the Czech Republic. A Slovak team did play games during the Second World War but then had to wait until post-war Czechoslovakia divided into Slovakia and the Czech Republic in 1993 before their next match. They returned to competitive action in qualifiers for the 1996 UEFA European Championship, finishing a promising third in their group. Continuing gradual progress culminated in qualification for their first FIFA World Cup, in 2010, at which they upset defending champions Italy 3-2 and reached the second round.

VLAD ALL OVER

Three relatives named Vladimir Weiss – different generations of the same family – have represented their country in international football, with two of them featuring at the 2010 FIFA World Cup. The first Vladimir won a footballing silver medal with Czechoslovakia at the 1964 Olympics, before his son Vladimir played for the same country at the 1990 FIFA World Cup. This second Vladimir then led Slovakia to the 2010 tournament as coach, picking his Manchester City winger son – yet another Vladimir – for three of the team's four matches. The first Vladimir made three appearances for Czechoslovakia, including the 1964 Olympics final in which he scored an own goal as Hungary triumped 2-1. The second Vladimir won 19 caps for Czechoslavakia and 12 for Slovakia, and the third, then aged only 20, ended the 2010 FIFA World Cup with 12. However, by the summer of 2015, the youngest Weiss had become the most-capped family member with 33. The coach described their 3-2 victory over holders Italy at the 2010 FIFA World Cup as the second happiest day of his life – only beaten by the day his son was born. He stepped down as boss after failing to qualify for the 2012 UEFA European Championship.

HOMEMADE MARIAN

Marian Masny holds the international appearances record for Slovak-born footballers who played for the united Czechoslovakia, earning 75 caps between 1974 and 1982. Masny, from Rybany, was also the second-highest-scoring Slovak during the united Czechoslovakia era. His 18 goals were only bettered by the 22 in 36 matches struck by Vrutky-born Adolf Scherer from 1958 to 1964. Scherer's tally included three at the 1962 FIFA World Cup, when Czechoslovakia finished runners-up. Scherer scored the winner against Hungary in the quarter-finals and Czechoslovakia's final goal in their 3-1 semi-final victory over Yugoslavia.

TOP SCORERS

1	Robert Vittek	23
2	Szilard Nemeth	22
3	Marek Hamsik	19
4	Miroslav Karhan	14
=	Marek Mintal	14
6	Stanislav Sestak	13
7	Peter Dubovsky	12
8	Martin Jakubko	9
=	Tibor Jancula	9
=	Lubomir Reita	9

MAREK OFF THE MARK

Slovakia's biggest win is 7-0, a result they have achieved three times – with wing-back Marek Cech the only man to play in all three games: against Liechtenstein in September 2004 and twice versus San Marino, in October 2007 and June 2009. He scored twice in the most recent match and in fact four of his five international goals since his 2004 debut came against San Marino – he also scored a brace in a 5-0 victory in November 2007.

TOP CAPS

1	Miroslav Karhan	107
2	Marek Hamsik	91
3	Martin Skrtel	85
4	Jan Durica	83
5	Robert Vittek	82
6	Peter Pekarik	71
7	Stanislav Sestak	66
8	Filip Holosko	65
9	Szilard Nemeth	58
10	Radoslav Zabavnik	57

CZECH EIGHT

Eight Slovakia players played in Czechoslovakia's triumphant 1976 UEFA European Championship final against West Germany, including captain Anton Ondrus and both their scorers in the 2-2 draw: Jan Svehlik and Karol Dobias. Three of the team's successful penalty-takers in their 5-3 shoot-out win were Slovak-born: Marian Masny, Ondrus and substitute Ladislav Jurkemik. The other Slovaks to feature were Jan Pivarnik, Jozef Capkovic and Jozef Moder. Defender Koloman Gogh was born in what is now the Czech Republic, but had Slovak family ties and played most of his club football for Slovan Bratislava in the Slovak capital.

COOL DUDA

Slovakia made it to the second round when reaching their first ever UEFA European Championship finals in 2016, only then going out 3-0 to reigning world champions Germany. **Ondrej Duda** became the first man to score for Slovakia at a UEFA European Championship, with an equalizer in their opening game against Wales just 52 seconds after coming on – the fastest Euros goal by a substitute since Spain's Juan Carlos Valeron needed just 36 seconds against Russia in 2004. Slovakia's qualification campaign for the 2016 tournament included a national record six straight victories, including a surprise 2-1 win against defending champions Spain in Zilina in October 2014.

ROBERT THE HERO

Slovakia's **Robert Vittek** became only the fourth player from a country making their FIFA World Cup debut to score as many as four goals in one tournament, at the 2010 event in South Africa. He hit one against New Zealand, two against defending champions Italy, and a late penalty in a second-round defeat to Holland. The previous three players to have done so were Portugal's Eusebio in 1966, Denmark's Preben Elkjaer Larsen in 1986 and Croatia's Davor Suker in 1998. Vittek's last-minute penalty against Holland made him Slovakia's all-time leading scorer with 23 goals, overtaking former Sparta Prague and Middlesbrough striker Szilard Nemeth. His 2010 FIFA World Cup form was all the more striking since he had failed to score at all in the qualifiers.

CUTTING EDGE HAMSIK

Playmaker Marek Hamsik was just 17 when he left Slovakia in 2004 – after only six games for Slovan Bratislava – and moved to Italy, joining Brescia, then Napoli. After helping Napoli to win the 2012 Coppa Italia, he fulfilled a promise to shave off his Mohawk hairstyle. Hamsik captained Slovakia at the 2010 FIFA World Cup, where he helped to eliminate Italy in the opening round. It was a less happy story for Hamsik and Slovakia when it came to qualifying for the 2014 FIFA World Cup. Slovakia finished a disappointing third behind Greece and group G winners Bosnia & Herzegovina. He scored twice in eight appearances, but missed the final two games. The Mohawk was back at the 2016 UEFA European Championship where Hamsik helped to inspire Slovakia to advance to the second round and he scored in a 2-1 group win over Russia.

BROKEN-DOWN KARHAN

Slovakia's defensive midfielder **Miroslav Karhan** helped his country qualify for the 2010 FIFA World Cup, taking his appearances tally to a national-record 95. But an Achilles tendon injury meant the team captain was ruled out of the tournament itself. After returning to action later in 2010, Karhan became the first Slovakia player to pass 100 caps.

SWEDEN

Eleven appearances at the FIFA World Cup finals (with a best result of second, as tournament hosts, in 1958) and three Olympic medals (including gold in London in 1948), bear testament to Sweden's rich history on the world football stage. Recent success has been harder to find, however, with semi-final appearances at the 1992 UEFA European Championship (again as hosts) and the 1994 FIFA World Cup the country's best performances in recent years.

GRE-NO-LI OLYMPIC AND ITALIAN GLORY

Having conquered the world by leading Sweden to gold in the 1948 Olympics in London, Gunnar Gren, Gunnar Nordahl and **Nils Liedholm** were snapped up by AC Milan. Their three-pronged "Gre-No-Li" forward line led the Italian giants to their 1951 scudetto win. Nordahl, who topped the Serie A scoring charts five times between 1950 and 1955, remains Milan's all-time top scorer with 221 goals in 268 games. Gren and Liedholm went on to appear for the Swedish national team in the 1958 FIFA World Cup – where they finished runners-up.

ONE MORE ENCORE, AGAIN!

One of the most famous and decorated Swedish footballers of modern times, **Henrik Larsson** (a star on the club scene with both Celtic and Barcelona) quit international football after the 2002 FIFA World Cup ... and again after the 2006 FIFA World Cup in Germany. He then made a further comeback in the 2010 FIFA World Cup qualifiers. With 37 goals in his 106 appearances, including five in his three FIFA World Cups, fans and officials clamoured for his return each time he tried to walk away. Sweden's failure to qualify for the tournament in 1998 meant a record-equalling 12 years elapsed between Larsson's first FIFA World Cup finals goal against Bulgaria in 1994 and his last, a dramatic late equalizer in a 2-2 group-stage draw with England in 2006. After finally retiring for good in 2009, he became manager of Swedish second-tier club Landskrona BoIS.

TOP CAPS

1	Anders Svensson	148
2	Thomas Ravelli	143
3	Andreas Isaksson	133
4	Kim Kallstrom	131
5	Olof Mellberg	117
6	Zlatan Ibrahimovic	116
=	Roland Nilsson	116
8	Bjorn Nordqvist	115
9	Niclas Alexandersson	109
10	Henrik Larsson	106

TOP-STOPPER RAVELLI

Thomas Ravelli kept goal for Sweden a record 143 times – conceding 143 goals. He saved two penalties in a shoot-out against Romania in the 1994 FIFA World Cup quarter-final to send Sweden into the last four, where they lost 1-0 to Brazil. Sweden went on to finish third, and were also the tournament's highest scorers with 15 goals in all – four more than eventual champions Brazil. Sweden's tally included five for Kennet Andersson, four for Martin Dahlin and three for Tomas Brolin.

IBRA–CADABRA

Few modern footballers can claim such consistent success – or boast such an unrepentant ego – as Swedish forward **Zlatan Ibrahimovic**. His proclamations have included "There's only one Zlatan", "I am like Muhammad Ali" and – in response to criticism from Norway's John Carew – "What Carew does with a football, I can do with an orange". He christened the newly built Friends Arena in Solna with all four goals as hosts Sweden beat England 4-2 in a November 2012 friendly – his final strike topping the lot, a 30-yard overhead kick which won the FIFA Ferenc Puskas goal of the year award. Despite also qualifying for Bosnia and Croatia through his family, Malmo-born Ibrahimovic made his Sweden debut in January and went on to score a national record 62 goals in 116 appearances before retiring from international football after Sweden's first-round departure from the 2016 UEFA European Championship. His clubs have included Ajax Amsterdam, Juventus, both Milan giants, Barcelona, Paris Saint-Germain and, from summer 2016 onwards, Manchester United.

ANDERS KEEPERS

Midfielder Anders Svensson celebrated equalling Thomas Ravelli's Sweden appearances record by scoring in both his 142nd and 143rd games for his country: a long-range strike as Norway were beaten 4-2 and then the winning goal against the Republic of Ireland in a qualifier for the 2014 FIFA World Cup. He then became his country's most-capped player in a 1-0 victory over Kazakhstan, but he didn't score. Svensson retired from international football in 2013, aged 37, after Sweden lost to Portugal in the qualifying play-off. He made 148 appearances, and scored 21 goals.

TOP SCORERS

1	Zlatan Ibrahimovic	62
2	Sven Rydell	49
3	Gunnar Nordahl	43
4	Henrik Larsson	37
5	Gunnar Gren	32
6	Kennet Andersson	31
7	Marcus Allback	30
8	Martin Dahlin	29
9	Tomas Brolin	27
=	Agne Simonsson	27

MANAGER SWAP

The most successful manager Sweden ever had was Englishman **George Raynor**, who led them to Olympic gold in London in 1948 and steered Sweden to third place and the runners-up spot in the 1950 and 1958 FIFA World Cups respectively. Raynor got one over on the country of his birth when Sweden became only the second foreign side to win at Wembley, with a 3-2 victory over England in 1959. Working in the opposite direction, in 2001 Sven-Goran Eriksson left Serie A side Lazio to become England's first foreign coach. He led the side to three consecutive quarter-finals – in the FIFA World Cups of 2002 and 2006 and, in between, the 2004 UEFA European Championship. Eriksson, however, failed to lead England to a win over his home country, recording three draws (1-1 in a 2001 friendly; 1-1 in a 2002 FIFA World Cup group game; 2-2 in a 2006 FIFA World Cup group game) and one defeat (0-1 in a 2004 friendly).

BJORN LEADER AND THERN'S TURN

No man has captained Sweden more often than defender Bjorn Nordqvist, who did so in 92 games – including six at the 1970, 1974 and 1978 FIFA World Cups. Next, numerically, is Zlatan Ibrahimovic, with 58 matches as captain, including six in the 2012 and 2016 UEFA European Championships. But **Jonas Thern**, with 55 appearances as captain among his 75 caps, has led out his team at major tournaments most – 10 times – once at the 1990 FIFA World Cup, four more when Sweden hosted the 1992 UEFA European Championship and another five in their run to third place at the 1994 FIFA World Cup.

MAGICAL MELL

Centre-back Olof Mellberg became one of only seven men to play at four different UEFA European Championship finals when he appeared at Euro 2012 – and the first Swedish player. The 34-year-old also became Sweden's oldest UEFA European Championship goalscorer, netting in a 3-2 defeat against England. Mellberg's six previous international goals had all come in qualifying matches for either the UEFA European Championship or the FIFA World Cup.

BEYOND THE KALL OF DUTY

Kim Kallstrom, Sweden's fourth-most capped footballer seemed extra-special to millions watching when he comforted his mascot, an eight-year-old named Max, before a 2014 FIFA World Cup qualifier against Germany in Solna in October 2013. Sweden's eleven mascots all had Williams syndrome, and when Kallstrom's escort became visibly distressed by the surrounding noise, Kallstrom crouched down and comforted him. "In a situation like this," he said, "I act more like a neighbour and parent than as the footballer I just happen to be."

SWITZERLAND

Switzerland set a record in 2006 when they became the first side in FIFA World Cup finals history to depart the tournament without conceding a goal. It sums up the country's football history: despite three FIFA World Cup quarter-final appearances (in 1934, 1938 and 1954 – the latter as tournament hosts) and the second round in 2006 and 2014, Switzerland have failed to establish themselves on the international football stage. The country co-hosted the 2008 UEFA European Championship, with Austria, and is better known as being the home of both FIFA and UEFA.

CLEAN SHEET WIPE-OUT

The Swiss national team made history in 2006 by becoming the first – and to date only – team to exit the FIFA World Cup without conceding a single goal in regulation time. However, in the shoot-out defeat to Ukraine in the second round, following a goalless 120 minutes, they failed to score a single penalty and lost 3-0. Despite being beaten three times in the shoot-out, goalkeeper **Pascal Zuberbuhler**'s performances in Germany earned him a Swiss record for consecutive clean sheets at an international tournament.

DERDIYOK AT THE DOZEN

Nineteen-year-old striker **Eren Derdiyok** scored with his very first kick of the ball in international football after coming on as a substitute against England at Wembley in a February 2009 friendly. But England won 2-1. He scored three of Switzerland's goals in a thrilling 5-3 friendly victory over Germany in May 2012 – making him the first player to score a hat-trick against the Germans since England's Michael Owen almost 11 years earlier. He was playing his club football at the time for German side Hoffenheim – and all three of his goals were set up by another Bundesliga-based player, Bayer Leverkusen's Tranquillo Barnetta.

TOP SCORERS

1	Alexander Frei	42
2	Max Abegglen	34
=	Kubilay Turkyilmaz	34
4	Andre Abegglen	29
=	Jacques Fatton	29
6	Adrian Knup	26
7	Josef Hugi	23
8	Charles Antenen	22
9	Lauro Amado	21
=	Stephane Chapuisat	21

LLAMA FARMER FREI-ING HIGH

After being compared to a llama by an angry Swiss sports press for spitting at Steven Gerrard at UEFA Euro 2004, **Alexander Frei**, Switzerland's all-time top scorer, adopted a llama at Basel zoo as part of his apology to the nation. Frei appeared to abandon all hope of adding to his record Swiss goal tally of 42 in 84 games when he announced his retirement from international football in April 2011, blaming abuse from his own fans during recent matches. These included a goalless draw against minnows Malta, when both Frei and team-mate Gokhan Inler missed penalties. Frei was joined in international retirement by strike partner Marco Streller, who had scored 12 goals in 37 games.

CHAMPION CHAPPI

Stephane "Chappi" Chapuisat – the third man to make 100 appearances for Switzerland – was the first Swiss player to win a UEFA Champions League medal when he led the line for Borussia Dortmund in their 3-1 victory over Juventus in 1997. But his most significant contribution in the final was to make way for Lars Ricken, whose goal with his first touch put the game beyond Juventus. Stephane's father, Pierre-Albert Chapuisat, was also a successful Swiss international – earning 34 caps for the national side in the 1970s and 1980s – but he failed to reach the heights of Stephane, who would later add both the Club World Cup and the Swiss super league (while playing for Grasshoppers) to his winners' medal collection.

ADMIR ADDS MORE

Switzerland reached the knock-out stages of the UEFA European Championship for the first time in 2016, and their 1-0 Group A victory over Romania – thanks to a goal by centre-back Fabian Schar – was the first time they had ever won their Euro tournament opener. In their next match they managed a 1-1 draw against Romania, courtesy of a second-half equalizer by Admir Mehmedi. That made the Bayer Leverkusen attacker the first Switzerland international to have scored at both a FIFA World Cup and a UEFA European Championship, after his strike against Ecuador in Brazil precisely two years earlier.

SEF ESTEEM

Switzerland not only set their 2014 FIFA World Cup campaign off to a dramatic and victorious beginning with a 2-1 triumph over Ecuador in Brasilia. They did so thanks to a strike three minutes into stoppage-time by substitute striker Haris Seferovic. This new mark for the latest winning goal recorded in the group stages of a FIFA World Cup lasted all of seven days – when Portugal equalized in the fifth minute of added time against the USA. Seferovic had previously scored the winning goal in the final of the 2009 FIFA U-17 World Cup, against hosts Nigeria, as Switzerland won their first FIFA title.

SHAQIRI SHAQIRI

Playmaker **Xerdan Shaqiri** scored one of the most spectacular goals of the 2016 UEFA European Championship, an overhead kick from outside the penalty area to give Switzerland a 1-1 draw in their second-round match with Poland – the Poles, however, prevailed on penalties. Two years earlier he had scored the 50th hat-trick in FIFA World Cup history during his side's 3-0 triumph over Honduras in Manaus. He was only the second Swiss footballer to hit a FIFA World Cup treble, following Josef Hugo in their 7-5 defeat to Austria in the 1954 quarter-finals.

"MERCI KOBI"

Former Swiss international player and manager, **Jakob "Kobi" Kuhn,** was left close to tears as his players unfurled a "thank you" banner at the end of his final game as Swiss national manager – the 2-0 victory over Portugal in the final group game of UEFA Euro 2008. How times have changed for Kuhn: while now a much-loved elder statesmen of the Swiss game, when he was just 22 years old, he was sent home from the 1966 FIFA World Cup for missing a curfew. He was then banned from the national side for a year. The shoe was on the other foot when Kuhn had to send Alexander Frei home from UEFA Euro 2004 after the centre-forward spat at England's Steven Gerrard. Kuhn spent most of his playing career, where he was described as playing "with honey in his boots", with FC Zurich, winning six league titles and five Swiss Cups. He played 63 times for the national side, scoring five goals. He then worked his way up through the ranks of the Swiss national team, leading first the Under-18s, then the Under-21s and finally the senior national team. He retired, aged 64, with a record of 32 victories, 18 draws and 23 defeats in 73 matches as Swiss coach.

TOP CAPS

1	Heinz Hermann	118
2	Alain Geiger	112
3	Stephane Chapuisat	103
4	Johann Vogel	94
5	Gokhan Inler	89
6	Hakan Yakin	87
7	Stephan Lichtsteiner	85
8	Alexander Frei	84
9	Patrick Muller	81
10	Severino Minelli	80

THE ORIGINAL BOLT

Karl Rappan did so much for Swiss football – including founding its first national football fan club – that it is often forgotten that he was Austrian. After a moderately successful career as a player and coach in Austria, Rappan achieved lasting fame as an innovative manager in Switzerland, leading the national side in the 1938 and 1954 FIFA World Cups, as well as securing league titles and cups as manager of Grasshopper Club, FC Servette and FC Zurich. He developed a flexible tactical system – which allowed players to switch positions depending on the situation and putting greater pressure on their opponents. This revolutionary new idea became known as the "Swiss bolt" and helped the unfancied hosts defeat Italy on the way to the quarter-finals of the 1954 FIFA World Cup, before losing out to Rappan's home country, Austria. An early advocate of a European league, Rappan eventually settled for the simpler knockout tournament, the Intertoto Cup, which he helped devise and launch in 1961. Rappan was, until Kobi Kuhn, Switzerland's longest-serving and statistically most successful manager, with 29 victories in 77 games in charge.

TURKEY

Galatasaray's penalty shoot-out success over Arsenal in the 2000 UEFA Cup final signalled a change in fortune for Turkish football. Prior to that night in Copenhagen, Turkey had qualified for the FIFA World Cup only twice (in 1950, when they withdrew, and 1954), and had consistently underachieved on the world stage. Since 2000, however, Turkish fans have had plenty to cheer about, including a third-place finish at the 2002 FIFA World Cup in Japan and South Korea, and a semi-final appearance at the 2008 UEFA European Championship.

SPOREL SPORTS

Zeki Riza Sporel scored Turkey's first goal in international football, against Romania on 26 October 1923. He actually hit a brace that day in a 2-2 draw, the first of 16 games for Turkey in which he hit 15 goals. Turkey's captain for their first international was his older brother Hasan Kamil Sporel.

SHOW ME MOR

Eighteen-year-old **Emre Mor** became Turkey's youngest player at a UEFA European Championship when he featured for them at the 2016 tournament in France, and the seventh youngest in the competition's history. But despite showing dazzling promise, Turkey were one of the two third-place finishers to miss out on a place in the knock-out stages. They lost 1-0 to Croatia and 3-0 Spain before beating the Czech Republic 1-0. Turkey have lost their opening match at every tournament finals they have reached.

QUICK OFF THE MARK

Hakan Sukur scored the fastest-ever FIFA World Cup finals goal  – taking only 11 seconds to score Turkey's first goal in their third-place play-off match against South Korea at the 2002 FIFA World Cup. Turkey went on to win the game 3-2 to claim third place, their finest-ever performance in the competition. His total of 51 goals (in 112 games) is more than double his nearest competitor in the national team ranking. His first goal came in only his second appearance, as Turkey beat Denmark 2-1 on 8 April 1992. He went on to score four goals in a single game twice – in the 6-4 win over Wales on 20 August 1997 and in the 5-0 crushing of Moldova on 11 October 2006.

RUSTU TO THE RESCUE

With his distinctive ponytail and charcoal-black warpaint, Turkey's most-capped international **Rustu Recber** has always stood out. But perhaps never more so than as a star mainstay in Turkey's third-place performance at the 2002 FIFA World Cup. He was elected into the Team of the Tournament before being named FIFA's Goalkeeper of the Year. He had been relegated to the bench by the time Turkey opened their campaign at the 2008 UEFA European Championship but played in the quarter-final after first-choice goalkeeper Volkan Demirel was sent off in the final group-game and suspended – and Recber became the hero again, saving from Croatia's Mladen Petric in a penalty shoot-out to send Turkey into their first UEFA European Championship semi-final, a narrow defeat to Germany.

OLD GOLD

The last FIFA World Cup "golden goal" was scored by Turkey substitute Ilhan Mansiz, in the 94th minute of their 2002 quarter-final against Senegal – giving his side a 1-0 win on their way to finishing third overall. The "golden goal" rule was abandoned ahead of the 2006 FIFA World Cup, which went back to two guaranteed 15-minute periods of extra-time if a knockout fixture ended level after 90 minutes.

TWIN TURKS

Hamit Altintop (right) was born 10 minutes before identical twin brother **Halil** (left) – and he has been just about leading the way throughout their parallel professional footballing careers since their birth in the city of Gelsenkirchen, Germany, on 8 December 1982. Both began playing for German amateur side Wattenscheid, before defender-cum-midfielder Hamit signed for FC Schalke 04 in the summer of 2006 and striker Halil followed suit shortly afterwards. Hamit would stay just a season there, though, before being bought by Bayern Munich. Both helped Turkey reach the semi-finals of the 2008 UEFA European Championship – losing to adopted homeland Germany – though only Hamit was voted among UEFA's 23 best players of the tournament.

TAKE FAT

Having coached Galatasaray to their UEFA Cup triumph in 2000, **Fatih Terim** led Turkey in their amazing run to the 2008 UEFA European Championship semi-finals. Defeat to Portugal in the opening game left the Turks with an uphill task, but stunning successive comebacks against Switzerland and the Czech Republic took them through to the quarter-finals. A 119th-minute goal seemed to have clinched the tie for Croatia, but, as the Croatian players celebrated, "Emperor" Fatih urged his players to get up, pick the ball out of the net and fight on to the very end. They did just that, and Semih Senturk's improbable equalizer took the match to penalties. The semi-final against Germany provided yet another rollercoaster ride, but this time there was no answer to the Germans' last-minute winner. Terim stepped down in 2009, returning to club football with Galatasaray, before beginning a third stint as Turkey coach in 2013. By the summer of 2016, Terim's record as Turkey's coach, in all three spells – the first was between 1993 and 1996 – stood at played 127, 66 wins, 30 draws and 31 defeats, a winning percentage of 51.97.

TOP SCORERS

1	Hakan Sukur	51
2	Tuncay Sanli	22
3	Lefter Kucukandonyadis	21
=	Burak Yilmaz	21
5	Nihat Kahveci	19
=	Metin Oktay	19
=	Cemil Turan	19
8	Arda Turan	17
9	Zeki Riza Sporel	15
10	Arif Erdem	11
=	Ertugrul Saglam	11

TOP CAPS

1	Rustu Recber	120
2	Hakan Sukur	112
3	Bulent Korkmaz	102
4	Tugay Kerimoglu	94
=	Arda Turan	94
6	Emre Belozoglu	93
7	Alpay Ozalan	90
8	Hamit Altintop	82
9	Tuncay Sanli	80
10	Ogun Temizkanoglu	76

SO NEAR, SO SAH

Playmaker **Nuri Sahin** became both Turkey's youngest international and youngest goalscorer, on the same day. Sahin was 17 years and 32 days old when he made his debut against Germany in Istanbul on 8 October 2005, and his goal, one minute from time, gave Turkey a 2-1 win. Ironically, Sahin was actually born in Germany, to Turkish parents, and he has played most of his club career there, for Borussia Dortmund though he has also had spells with Feyenoord, Real Madrid and Liverpool.

WORK HARD, PLAY ARDA

Wing wizard Arda Turan – Turkey's captain at the 2016 UEFA European Championship – has survived cardiac arrhythmia, swine flu and a car crash to emerge as one of Turkish football's leading lights. His international achievements include key goals at the 2008 UEFA European Championship, the first a stoppage-time winner against Switzerland, then Turkey's late opener when overturning a two-goal deficit against the Czech Republic in a first-round qualification decider. After leaving boyhood club Galatasaray for Spain's Atletico Madrid in 2011, he won the UEFA Europa League and UEFA Super Cup in 2013 and La Liga in 2014. A move to Barcelona in 2015, brought another La Liga title in 2016. Off the field, he mixes in prestigious circles – guests at his June 2013 wedding to TV presenter Sinem Kobal included Turkish prime minister Recep Tayyip Erdogan.

UKRAINE

Ukraine has been a stronghold of football in eastern Europe for many years. A steady flow of talent from Ukrainian clubs with a rich European pedigree, such as Dynamo Kiev, provided the Soviet national team with many standout players in the years before independence. Since separating from the Soviet Union in 1991, Ukraine has become a football force in its own right, qualifying for the FIFA World Cup for the first time in 2006, reaching the quarter-finals.

YARMED AND DANGEROUS

Midfielder Andriy Yarmolenko has scored more goals for Ukraine than any other player, except for Andriy Shevchenko. He also holds the record for the country's fastest goal in an international match, when he netted just 14 seconds into a home friendly against Uruguay in September 2011. It was not all good news, however, as the visitors hit back and went on to win 3-2. Yarmolenko, whose club team is Dynamo Kiev, has scored 19 goals for Ukraine and it includes his first international hat-trick, in a 2016 UEFA European Championship qualifying match. It came in a 3-0 win over Luxembourg in November 2014.

ROCKET MAN

Andriy Shevchenko beat team-mate **Anatoliy Tymoshchuk** to become the first Ukrainian footballer to reach a century of international appearances – but the defensive midfielder has since overtaken Shevchenko and is the country's most-capped player with 144 appearances. He also had the rare honour of seeing his name in space, when Ukrainian cosmonaut Yuri Malenchenko launched into orbit wearing a Zenit St Petersburg shirt with "Tymoshchuk" on the back in 2007.

YURI-KA MOMENT

Denys Harmash and Dmytro Korkishko scored the goals against England that gave Ukraine their first major international footballing title, in the final of the 2009 UEFA Under-19 European Championship. The coach was Yuri Kalitvintsev, later assistant to Oleg Blokhin with the senior international side.

HARD START

With the newly independent Ukraine unable to register with FIFA in time for the qualifying rounds for the 1994 FIFA World Cup, many of their stars opted to play for Russia and went to the finals in the United States representing that country. Andrei Kanchelskis, Viktor Onopko, Sergei Yuran and Oleg Salenko could all have played for the new Ukraine side, but decided not to. Ukraine then failed to qualify for an international tournament until the **2006 FIFA World Cup** in Germany, where they lost 3-0 in the quarter-finals to eventual winners Italy.

SUPER SHEVA

In 2004, **Andriy Shevchenko** became the third Ukrainian to win the Ballon D'Or. The first to do so, in 1975, was his 2006 FIFA World Cup coach Oleg Blokhin (second was Igor Belanov in 1986), but he was the first to win the award since Ukraine's independence from the Soviet Union. Born on 29 September 1976, Shevchenko was a promising boxer as a youngster, before deciding to focus on football full-time. He has won trophies at every club he's played for, including five titles in a row with Dynamo Kiev, the Serie A and the Champions League with AC Milan, and even two cups in his "disappointing" time at Chelsea. Shevchenko is Ukraine's second most-capped player and leading goalscorer, with 48 goals in 111 games. This includes two at the 2006 FIFA World Cup, where he captained his country in their first-ever major finals appearance, and a double to secure a 2-1 comeback win over Sweden in Ukraine's first match co-hosting the 2012 UEFA European Championship. Shevchenko was Ukraine's assistant coach at the 2016 UEFA European Championship and replaced Mykhailo Fomenko as manager after the tournament.

LEADING FROM THE FRONT

Oleg Blokhin, Ukraine's coach on their first appearance at a major tournament finals, made his name as a star striker with his hometown club Dynamo Kiev. Born on 5 November 1952, when Ukraine was part of the Soviet Union, Blokhin scored a record 211 goals in another record 432 appearances in the USSR national league. He also holds the goals and caps records for the USSR, with 42 in 112 games. He led Kiev to two victory in the European Cup-Winners' Cup in 1975 and 1986, scoring in both finals, and was named the 1975 European Footballer of the Year. Always an over-achiever, Blokhin managed Ukraine to the finals of the 2006 FIFA World Cup in Germany, where they lost out to eventual winners Italy 3-0 in the quarter-finals after knocking out Switzerland in the second round – also on penalties. Blokhin was renowned for his speed – when Olympic gold medallist Valeriy Borzov trained the Kiev squad in the 1970s, Blokhin recorded a 100 metres time of 11 seconds, just 0.46 seconds slower than Borzov's own 1972 medal-winning run. Blokhin quit as Ukraine manager in December 2007, but returned to the job in April 2011.

DEVASTATING DEVIC

Ukraine enjoyed their biggest win on 6 September 2013 thrashing San Marino 9-0 in a FIFA World Cup qualifier – then rubbed salt into the wounds by winning 8-0 away to the same opposition the following month, on 25 October 2013. There were eight different scorers in the first game, with the opening goal struck by striker **Marko Devic** – and he went on to hit a hat-trick in the rematch. Devic was actually born in Belgrade and brought up in Serbia but transferred to Ukrainian club Volyn Lutsk in 2005 and switched nationalities three years later.

TOP SCORERS

1	Andriy Shevchenko	48
2	Andriy Yarmolenko	25
3	Serhiy Rebrov	15
4	Oleh Husyev	13
=	Yevhen Konoplyanka	13
6	Serhiy Nazarenko	12
7	Yevhen Seleznyov	11
8	Andriy Husin	9
=	Andriy Vorobey	9
10	Tymerlan Huseynov	8
=	Artem Milevskyi	8
=	Andriy Voronin	8

GET ZIN IN

Ukraine performed disappointingly at the 2016 UEFA European Championship, failing to score and conceding five goals as they made a first-round exit. But hope for the future was provided by midfielder **Oleksandr Zinchenko**. He became Ukraine's youngest ever goalscorer two weeks before the tournament, in a 4-3 friendly win against Romania – then came on as a substitute in his country's tournament opener against Germany, aged 19 years and 179 days old, making him Ukraine's youngest player at an international finals. Also in the summer of 2016 Zinchenko left Russian club Ufa for England's Manchester City.

TOP CAPS

1	Anatoliy Tymoshchuk	144
2	Andriy Shevchenko	111
3	Oleh Husyev	98
4	Oleksandr Shovkovskyi	92
5	Ruslan Rotan	89
6	Serhiy Rebrov	75
7	Andriy Voronin	74
8	Andriy Husin	71
9	Andriy Vorobey	68
10	Andriy Nesmachnyi	67
=	Andriy Pyatov	67

WALES

In a land where rugby union has long been the main national obsession, Wales struggled for many years to impose themselves on the world of international football despite producing many hugely talented players. But recent progress – including a semi-finals appearance at the 2016 UEFA European Championship – has inspired unprecedented excitement and optimism.

GOOD ON RAMSEY

Arsenal midfielder **Aaron Ramsey** became Wales's youngest captain when appointed to the role in March 2011 by new manager Gary Speed. Ramsey was 20 years 90 days old when he led the side out for the first time at Cardiff's Millennium Stadium in a 2012 UEFA European Championship qualifier that ended in a 2-0 win for England. The record had previously been held by centre-back Mike England, who was 22 years 135 days old when skipper against Northern Ireland in April 1964.

FAMILY MISFORTUNES

Full-back Chris Gunter's parents had a dilemma when Wales made the semi-finals of the 2016 UEFA European Championship – they were meant to be attending his brother Marc's wedding in Mexico the day Wales faced Portugal. They opted to watch Chris in action instead, sadly seeing Wales bow out 2-0 in Lille.

WHERE'S OUR GOLDEN BOY?

One of the most skilful and successful players never to appear at the FIFA World Cup, **Ryan Giggs** somehow missed 18 consecutive friendlies for Wales. He made his Manchester United debut in 1990 and appeared in his 1,000th competitive match in a 2-1 UEFA Champions League defeat to Real Madrid. His tally by then included 932 club matches, 64 for Wales and four for Great Britain at the London 2012 Summer Olympics. Giggs finally hung up his boots aged 40 at the end of the 2013–14 season, the last four games of which he had spent as Manchester United's caretaker-manager following the dismissal of David Moyes.

BRICKS TO BRILLIANCE

Goalkeeper **Neville Southall** made the first of his record 92 appearances for Wales in a 3-2 win over Northern Ireland on 27 May 1982. The former hod-carrier and bin man kept 34 clean sheets in 15 years playing for Wales and won the English Football Writers' Player of the Year in 1985 thanks to his performances alongside Welsh captain Kevin Ratcliffe at Everton. In his final match for Wales, on 20 August 1997, he was substituted halfway through a 6-4 defeat against Turkey in Istanbul.

RUSH FOR GOAL

Ian Rush is Wales's leading goalscorer, with 28 goals in 73 games. His first came in a 3-0 win over Northern Ireland on 27 May 1982; he scored the 28th and final goal in a 2-1 win over Estonia in Tallinn in 1994.

CAUGHT ON CAMERA

Pioneer movie-makers Sagar Mitchell and James Kenyon captured Wales v Ireland in March 1906, making it the first filmed international football match.

TOP CAPS

1	Neville Southall	92
2	Gary Speed	85
3	Craig Bellamy	78
4	Dean Saunders	75
5	Chris Gunter	73
=	Peter Nicholas	73
=	Ian Rush	73
8	Mark Hughes	72
=	Joey Jones	72
10	Ivor Allchurch	68

TOP SCORERS

1	Ian Rush	28
2	Ivor Allchurch	23
=	Trevor Ford	23
4	Gareth Bale	22
=	Dean Saunders	22
6	Craig Bellamy	19
7	Robert Earnshaw	16
=	Mark Hughes	16
=	Cliff Jones	16
10	John Charles	10

KEEPING UP WITH THE JONESES

Cliff Jones, left-winger for Wales at the 1958 FIFA World Cup and for Tottenham Hotspur's league and cup "Double" winners in 1961, was part of a Welsh footballing dynasty. His father Ivor Jones had previously played for Wales, as did Ivor's brother Bryn. Cliff's cousin Ken, a goalkeeper, was another member of the 1958 FIFA World Cup squad, but never actually played for his country.

ALL HAIL BALE

It seemed fitting – and predictable – that Wales' first goalscorer at the 2016 UEFA European Championship, their first finals since the 1958 FIFA World Cup, would be their undoubted "Galatico" **Gareth Bale**. The Real Madrid star – whose $100 million (£86 million) move from Tottenham Hotspur in August 2013 made him the world's most expensive footballer – opened the scoring with a free-kick in their 2-1 first-round win over Slovakia, and repeated the trick in their next game, against England. That made him only the third man – after France's Michel Platini in 1984 and Germany's Thomas Hassler in 1992 – to score twice from direct free-kicks at one UEFA European Championship. A month earlier Cardiff-born Bale had won his second UEFA Champions League with Real Madrid. He was Wales' youngest international debutant against Trinidad and Tobago in May 2006 and scored his first goal for his country five months later – a sign of things to come – a free-kick against Slovakia.

HAT-TRICK HERO

Welsh striker Robert Earnshaw holds the remarkable record of scoring hat-tricks in all four divisions of English football, the FA Cup, the League Cup. He also grabbed a treble for Wales, against Scotland on 18 February 2004. In full internationals, Wales have registered 14 hat-tricks overall, each one by a different player, but no one has achieved the feat since Earnshaw.

SHOCK LOSS OF A MODEL PROFESSIONAL

Welsh and world football were united in shock and grief at the sudden death of Wales manager Gary Speed in November 2011. Former Leeds United, Everton, Newcastle United and Bolton Wanderers midfielder Speed, the country's most-capped outfield player, was found at his home in Cheshire, England. The 42-year-old had been manager for 11 months, overseeing a series of encouraging performances that saw a rise in the world rankings from 116th to 48th and a prize for FIFA's "Best Movers" of 2011. An official memorial game was played in Cardiff in February 2012 between Wales and Costa Rica – the country against whom he had made his international debut in May 1990.

RISE OF THE DRAGON

After reaching the quarter-finals of the 1958 FIFA World Cup, Wales had to wait another 58 years to play at another major tournament. They returned to the big time in style, reaching the semi-finals of the 2016 UEFA European Championship in France. Chris Coleman's men beat Slovakia 2-1 and Russia 3-0 in the first round, Northern Ireland 1-0 in a second-round clash and came from a goal down to defeat Belgium 3-1 in the quarter-finals. Their goals that day were all scored by English-born players: captain Ashley Williams, **Hal Robson-Kanu** and Sam Vokes. Robson-Kanu, who went into the tournament without a club after leaving English second-tier side Reading, was later awarded the prize for best goal of the tournament – his "Cruyff turn" solo effort against Belgium, rather than his winner against Slovakia. Coleman's side lost 2-0 to eventual champions Portugal in the semi-finals but did reach a record high of 11th in the July 2016 FIFA World Rankings and were welcomed home with an open-top bus parade in the capital Cardiff.

OTHER TEAMS EUROPE

For the major European football powers, a qualifying campaign for one of the game's major international tournaments would not be the same without an awkward trip to one of the former Eastern Bloc countries or the chance of a goal-fest against the likes of San Marino or Luxembourg. For these countries' players, the thrill of representing their nation is more important than harbouring dreams of world domination.

SELVA SERVICE

San Marino, with a population of under 30,000, remain near the bottom of FIFA's world rankings but they finally had something to celebrate in November 2014, thanks to a goalless draw with Estonia – their first ever point in a UEFA European Championship qualifier – and ending a run of 61 successive defeats. They have avoided defeat only five times and have never recorded a competitive victory. In fact, San Marino's only win was a 1-0 friendly triumph over Liechtenstein in April 2004. Striker and captain Andy Selva, still playing after making his debut in 1998, is top scorer with eight goals and for a long time was San Marino's only multiple goalscorer until midfielder Manuel Marani scored his second, against Malta, in August 2012. **Massimo Bonini,** San Marino manager between 1996 and 1998, previously lifted the UEFA European Cup with Italian giants Juventus in 1985.

UNDERDOGS HAVE THEIR DAY

Slovenia were the only unseeded team to win a UEFA qualifying play-off for the 2010 FIFA World Cup, beating Russia on away goals. Slovenia lost 2-1 in Moscow, thanks to substitute Nejc Pecnik's away goal late in the first leg and Ztlatko Dedic scored the only goal in Maribor for the victory. With two million inhabitants and 429 registered professional players, Slovenia was the finals' smallest nation.

LIT'S A KNOCK–OUT

Perhaps it's not be too surprising that **Jari Litmanen** should have become a football star – both his parents played for the Lahti-based club Reipas while Litmanen's father Olavi also won five caps for the national team. But Jari's skills and achievements far outstripped them both – and, arguably, any other player the country has produced. It was fitting that Litmanen became the first Finnish player to get his hands on the UEFA European Cup – or Champions League trophy – when his Ajax Amsterdam side beat AC Milan in 1995. Despite a series of injuries, he remained dedicated to his country, captaining the side between 1996 and 2008, and was still playing and scoring for Finland in 2010 at the age of 39 – having notched up more international goals and games than any other Finn, scoring 32 times in 137 appearances.

MOSQUITO STINGS

Malta ended a 20-year wait for an away win in a competitive international when they shocked Armenia 1-0 in a 2014 FIFA World Cup qualifier in June 2013. Appropriately enough, the vital strike came from veteran forward **Michael Mifsud,** his country's captain and all-time leading scorer, who made his international debut in February 2000. He made his name in Germany with Kaiserslautern and in England with Coventry City. Nicknamed "Mosquito", the 1.65m-tall player's international exploits include five goals in the 7-1 trouncing of Liechtenstein in March 2008 – including a hat-trick within the first 21 minutes. Before Armenia, the last time Malta won a UEFA European Championship or FIFA World Cup away qualifier had been a 1-0 success in Estonia in May 1993.

GIVING IT UP

Lithuania and Estonia did not bother playing their final group game against each other in the 1934 FIFA World Cup qualifying competition. Sweden had already guaranteed themselves top spot, and the sole finals place available, by beating Lithuania 2-0 and Estonia 6-2.

BEYOND THE IRON CURTAIN

The break-up of the Soviet Union in 1990 led to 15 new footballing nations, though initially Russia played on at the 1992 UEFA European Championship as CIS, or the Commonwealth of Independent States – without the involvement of Estonia, Latvia and Lithuania. In the coming years, UEFA and FIFA approved the creation of separate teams for Russia, Armenia, Azerbaijan, Belarus, Estonia, Georgia, Kazakhstan, Kyrgyzstan, Latvia, Lithuania, Moldova, Tajikstan, Turkmenistan, Ukraine and Uzbekistan. Upheavals in the early 1990s would also fragment the former Yugoslavia into Croatia, Serbia, Bosnia-Herzegovina, Macedonia, Slovenia and Montenegro, while Czechoslovakia split into Slovakia and the Czech Republic.

TRAVELLING MEN

Israel looked like qualifying for the 1958 FIFA World Cup without kicking a ball, because scheduled opponents Turkey, Indonesia and Sudan refused to play them. But FIFA ordered them into a two-legged play-off against a European side – which Israel lost 4-0 on aggregate to Wales. Israel were unfortunate again in the 2006 FIFA World Cup qualifiers, ending the campaign unbeaten – yet failing even to make the play-offs, finishing third in their group behind France and Switzerland. Their star midfielder that campaign was Israel's most-capped player Yossi Benayoun, whose clubs included Liverpool, Chelsea and Arsenal, while their coach at the time was Avram Grant who would later take Chelsea to the 2008 UEFA Champions League final. Israel hosted, and won, the 1964 Asian Nations Cup, and qualified for the 1970 FIFA World Cup through a combined Asia/Oceania qualifying competition, but are now members of the European Federation.

YEAR AFFILIATED TO FIFA

Albania	1932
Andorra	1996
Austria	1905
Belarus	1992
Bosnia-Herzegovina	1996
Cyprus	1948
Estonia	1923
Faroe Islands	1988
Finland	1908
Georgia	1992
Gibraltar	2016
Greece	1927
Iceland	1947
Israel	1929
Kazakhstan	1994
Kosovo	2016
Latvia	1922
Liechtenstein	1974
Luxembourg	1910
Macedonia	1994
Malta	1959
Moldova	1994
Montenegro	2007
San Marino	1988
Slovenia	1992

REBORN BOURG

A long and painful wait finally ended for traditional whipping-boys Luxembourg when they beat Northern Ireland 3-2 in September 2013. It was the "Red Lions" first home win in a FIFA World Cup qualifier for 41 years, since overcoming Turkey 2-0 in October 1972. It was also five years to the day since their last FIFA World Cup qualifying victory, a 2-1 triumph in Switzerland in 2008. Luxembourg's goals came from Aurelien Joachim, Stefano Bensi and **Mathias Janisch**. The winning goal, with three minutes remaining, was the first of Janisch's international career.

HAPPY AND SADIKU

Armando Sadiku scored Albania's first goal at an international tournament, his late effort beating Romania in their final group game at the 2016 UEFA European Championship. Coached by Italian Gianni De Biasi, they finished second in their qualifying group – ahead of Denmark, Serbia and Armenia – having beaten eventual UEFA Euro 2016 champions Portugal 1-0. Albania's captain and most-capped player Lorik Cana played a minor role in France – he saw yellow twice within 36 minutes of their opener against Switzerland and was sent off. Sadly, Albania were one of two third-place teams to miss the knockout stages.

HIT AND SWISS

When defender Elsad Zverotic made his 44th appearance, he passed Simon Vukcevic to become Montenegro's most-capped international. He was born in Behane, in what is now Serbia, but played for Switzerland U-18s, where he also played his club football from 2004. After a short spell in England with Fulham, 2013–15, Zverotic returned to Switzerland, signing with Sion.

MORE SIND AGAINST

Austria's star player **Matthias Sindelar** refused to play for a new, merged national team when Germany annexed Austria in 1938. Sindelar, born in modern-day Czech Republic in February 1903, was the inspirational leader of Austria's so-called Wunderteam of the 1930s. He scored 27 goals in 43 games for Austria, who went 14 internationals unbeaten between April 1931 and December 1932, won the 1932 Central European International Cup and silver at the 1936 Olympics. During a special reunification match between the Austrian and German teams in Vienna in April 1938, Sindelar disobeyed orders and scored a spectacular solo goal. Austria went on to win 2-0 in a game which might have been expected to end in a diplomatic draw. Sindelar was mysteriously found dead from carbon monoxide poisoning in his Vienna apartment in January 1939.

THE GUD SON

Iceland striker **Eidur Gudjohnsen** made history on his international debut away to Estonia in April 1996. He was a substitute for his father, Arnor Gudjohnsen. Eidur was 17 at the time, his father 34 – though both were disappointed they did not get to play on the pitch at the same time. The Icelandic Football Association thought they would get a chance to do so in Iceland's next home game, but Eidur had an ankle injury and the opportunity never arose again. Eidur's goal for Iceland in a 3-0 win over Kazakhstan in March 2014 made him the fourth oldest scorer in UEFA European Championship qualifiers, behind only Jari Jari Litmanen of Finland, thethe Republic of Ireland's John Aldridge and Krasimir Balakov from Bulgaria. At 37, Gudjohnsen came on twice as a substitute at the 2016 UEFA European Championship, Iceland's first major tournament.

THE GIB'S UP

The British Overseas Territory of Gibraltar became UEFA's 54th member state in time to take part in qualifiers for the 2016 UEFA European Championship, but they were deliberately kept apart from neighbours Spain in the draw. Their first official international ended goalless against Slovakia in November 2013. Gibraltar's competitive bow was a 7-0 defeat to Poland in September 2014, their first Euro 2016 qualifier. Kyle Casciaro was the hero with the only goal in their first victory, against Malta in June 2014, though near-namesake Lee Casciaro netted the first competitive goal, in a 6-1 defeat away to Scotland in March 2015. Kyle is a shipping agent, Lee a policeman and captain Roy Chipolina a customs officer.

GEORGIAN STYLE

Georgia became the lowest-ranked side ever to defeat Spain when they inflicted a shock 1-0 defeat in the reigning European champions' last friendly before competing in the 2016 UEFA European Championship finals. Georgia, for whom midfielder Tornike Okriashvili scored the only goal, stood 137th in the FIFA rankings – 131 places below their opponents. Missing that game was defender Zurab Khizanishvili, who, with 92 caps, is second in international appearances for Georgia, behind only 100-cap **Levan Kobiashvili**. The ex-Dinamo Tbilisi, Schalke and Hertha Berlin wing-back Kobiashvili, became president of the Georgian Football Federation in October 2015.

VETERAN VITALIJS

Estonia may have lost their June 2012 friendly against France 4-0 but they did make history that night, becoming the first country to play all 52 fellow UEFA nations. They also previously claimed the record for most-capped European footballer – holding midfielder Martin Reim scored 14 goals in 157 internationals between June 1992 and June 2009. He might have closed in on an unprecedented double century of caps but for missing 40 games between 2004 and 2007 following a dispute with Latvia's Dutch manager Jelle Goes. His European record was passed by Latvia midfielder Vitalijs Astafjevs, who played 167 internationals – including three at the 2004 UEFA European Championship – between his debut in 1992 and his final cap in November 2009 at the age of 38, in a friendly against Honduras. Spain goalkeeper Iker Casillas went one cap better in June 2016.

MOST INTERNATIONAL APPEARANCES

Albania	Lorik Cana	93
Andorra	Oscar Sonejee	106
Armenia	Sargis Hovsepyan	131
Austria	Andreas Herzog	103
Azerbaijan	Rashad Sadygov	103
Belarus	Alyaksandr Kulchy	102
Bosnia-Herz.	Emir Spahic	89
Cyprus	Ioannis Okkas	106
Estonia	Martin Reim	157
Faroe Islands	Frooi Benjaminsen	86
Finland	Jari Litmanen	137
Georgia	Levan Kobiashvili	100
Gibraltar	Joseph Chipolina	18
Iceland	Runar Kristinsson	104
Israel	Yossi Benayoun	97
Kazakhstan	Samat Smakov	74
Kosovo	F. Perdedaj/S. Hasani	6
Latvia	Vitalijs Astafjevs	167
Liechtenstein	Mario Frick	125
Lithuania	Andrius Skerla	84
Luxembourg	Jeff Strasser	98
Macedonia	Goce Sedloski	100
Malta	David Carabott	122
Moldova	Radu Rebeja	74
Montenegro	Elsad Zverotic	58
San Marino	Andy Selva	73
Slovenia	Bostjan Cesar	91

ED BOY

Edin Dzeko became Bosnia-Herzegovina's all-time leading scorer with a second-half hat-trick in an 8-1 2014 FIFA World Cup qualifier victory over Liechtenstein in September 2012. The goals not only took him past previous record-holder Elvir Bolic, but also ahead of Dzeko's international team-mate Zvejdan Misimovic whose brace earlier in the game had briefly put him in the lead. Midfielder Misimovic drew level again with Dzeko in the following game, scoring twice in a 4-1 win, before Dzeko's last-minute strike put him ahead again. Not bad for a forward sold by Bosnian club Zeljeznicar to the Czech Republic's FK Teplice for a cut-price €25,000 in 2005 – six years before English club Manchester City handed over €32million to sign him from Germany's VfL Wolfsburg. Dzeko's off-field activities include a role as a UNICEF ambassador – and he donated almost €25,000 in 2012 towards the care of a 17-year-old Bosnian boy fighting bone marrow disease.

SUPER PAN

Macedonia celebrated 100 years of football in the country with a friendly against world champions Spain in August 2009 – and striker **Goran Pandev** marked the occasion by becoming his country's all-time leading scorer. His first-half brace gave the hosts a 2-0 lead and although Spain came back to win 3-2, he replaced 16-goal Gorgi Hristov at the top of Macedonia's scoring charts. Pandev has played the majority of his club career in Italy, after signing for Internazionale from local team FK Belasica as an 18-year-old in 2001. Pandev helped Inter win a treble of the UEFA Champions League, Serie A and the Coppa Italia in 2009–10, before scoring in their 2010 FIFA Club World Cup victory. Pandev had a season in Turkey with Galatasaray before joining Genoa in 2015.

LAT'S ENTERTAINMENT

The 1938 FIFA World Cup went ahead with 15 instead of 16 teams after qualifiers Austria found themselves annexed by Germany – to the frustration of Latvia, who had finished runners-up in the Austrians' qualification group. Latvia was subsumed by the Soviet Union between 1940 and 1991, but qualified for their first major finals by beating Turkey in a play-off to reach the 2004 UEFA European Championship. Their team at that tournament featured all-time leading scorer 29-goal Maris Verpakovskis, who retired from international football in 2014, and their most-capped player Vitalijs Astafjevs, 167 caps.

BASKET CASE

Captain Rashad Sadygov not only secured Azerbaijan's biggest win in their history when he scored the only goal against Turkey in a UEFA Euro 2012 qualifier in October 2010 – he was also delivering a blow against the country in which he was making his living. Having previously played for Turkish top-flight side Kayserispor, he had since moved on to rivals Eskisehirspor. Not every transfer has worked out well for Sadygov: he missed the transfer deadline when signing for Azeri side PFC Neftchi in 2006, so he decided to play basketball for a season to keep himself fit until allowed to resume football.

MOST INTERNATIONAL GOALS

Albania	Erjon Bogdani	18
Andorra	Ildefons Lima	10
Armenia	Henrikh Mkhitaryan	19
Austria	Toni Polster	44
Azerbaijan	Gurban Gurbanov	14
Belarus	Maksim Romaschenko	20
Bosnia-Herz.	Edin Dzeko	46
Cyprus	Michalis Konstantinou	32
Estonia	Andres Oper	38
Faroe Islands	Rogvi Jacobsen	10
Finland	Jari Litmanen	32
Georgia	Shota Arveladze	26
Gibraltar	Jake Gosling	2
Iceland	Eidur Gudjohnsen	26
Israel	Mordechai Spiegler	33
Kazakhstan	Ruslan Baltiev	13
Kosovo	Albert Bunjaku	3
Latvia	Maris Verpakovskis	29
Liechtenstein	Mario Frick	16
Lithuania	Tomas Danilevicius	19
Luxembourg	Leon Mart	16
Macedonia	Goran Pandev	27
Malta	Michael Mifsud	40
Moldova	Serghei Clescenco	11
Montenegro	Mirko Vucinic	17
San Marino	Andy Selva	8
Slovenia	Zlatko Zahovic	35

LIVING HAND TO FOOT

The part-time international footballers of the Faroe Islands have a motley collection of day jobs – and other sporting achievements. Bobble hat-wearing goalkeeper Jens Martin Knudsen, man of the match in their shock 1-0 win over Austria in 1989, made his living as a forklift truck driver – while also winning a national gymnastics title and playing handball. Team-mates who have also played both football and handball include Uni Arge and John Petersen. A latter-day Faroes hero emerged in former Newcastle United striker Joan Edmundsson, the only goalscorer in a shock win away to former European champions Greece in a Euro 2016 qualifier in November 2014. The Faroes – under Danish coach Lars Olsen – were ranked 187th in the world; Greece were 18th.

TU-WHIT TWO-NIL

Finland's adopted lucky mascot is an eagle owl called "Bubi" that occasionally swoops down on the Helsinki Olympic Stadium during international matches – making his debut during a 2-0 UEFA European Championship qualifier win over Belgium in June 2007 and holding up the game for several minutes as he flew about the pitch and perched on goalposts. The eagle owl was later voted the Finnish capital's "Resident of the Year".

BOHEMIAN RHAPSODY

Striker **Josef "Pepi" Bican** is, for many Austrian fans, the most prolific goalscorer of all time. Some authorities put his total tally in officially recognized matches at 805 goals, higher in the rankings than Romario, Pele and Gerd Muller. Bican played for Austrian clubs Rapid Vienna and Admira in the 1930s, but the bulk of his strikes came for Czech-based Slavia Prague between 1937 and 1948. He also scored 19 goals in 19 games for Austria from 1933 to 1936, before switching citizenship and hitting 21 in 14 matches for Czechoslovakia between 1938 and 1949. Although he reached the semi-finals of the 1934 FIFA World Cup with Austria, an administrative error meant he was not registered with his new country in time for the 1938 tournament. He also played one international match for a representative Bohemia and Moravia side in 1939, scoring a hat-trick.

ICELAND ICE ENGLAND IN NICE

Iceland not only competed at their first major tournament at the 2016 UEFA European Championship – with a population of 330,000 only 182,000 Tahiti (2013 FIFA Confederations Cup) has been a smaller nation at an international finals – but they also made a major impression both on and off the pitch. Their fans popularized a much-imitated "thunderclap"-style celebration in the stands, as their side not only got out of their group but reached the quarter-finals before losing 5-2 to hosts France. Swedish coach Lars Lagerback, one of two joint managers, was leading a team at a record fourth UEFA European Championship while his colleague – who took sole control after the tournament – was former player and part-time dentist Heimir Hallgrimsson. The pair picked an unchanged starting eleven for all five of their games at the tournament, making Iceland the first team to do so in the UEFA European Championship. Experienced centre-back Ragnar Sigurdsson and striker Kolbeinn Sigthorsson scored the goals to clinch the greatest result in Iceland's history: a 2-1 second-round victory over England in Nice. FC Basel midfielder **Bikir Bjarnason** scored Iceland's first tournament goal, in their opening match, a 1-1 draw with Portugal.

A SEQUEL TO HAMLET

Striker Hamlet Mkhitaryan played twice for post-Soviet state Armenia in 1994, though died two years later from a brain tumour at the age of just 33. His son Henrikh, seven when his father died, has gone on to become the country's all-time leading scorer – and one who often dedicates his achievements to his late parent. The younger Mkhitaryan became Armenia's joint top scorer, alongside Artur Petrosyan, with a goal against Denmark in June 2013. While Petrosyan's goals came in 69 games, Mkhitaryan's 11 were scored in 39 – and he pulled away on his own, with a 12th international strike, in a 2-2 draw with Italy in October 2012. **Henrikh Mkhitaryan** made his Armenia debut in 2007, and his international career overlapped with an unrelated player also named Hamlet Mkhitaryan – a midfielder who won 56 caps between 1994 and 2008. Henrikh's hat-trick against Guatemala in May 2016 took him to 19 international goals and helped Armenia to a national record 7-1 win.

RECORD WINS

Albania	5-0	v Vietnam (Italy, February 2003);
	6-1	v Cyprus (H, August 2009)
Andorra	2-0	v Belarus (H, April 2000);
	2-0	v Albania (H, April 2002)
Armenia	7-1	v Guatemala (USA, May 2016)
Austria	9-0	v Malta (H, April 1977)
Azerbaijan	4-0	v Liechtenstein (H, June 1999)
Belarus	5-0	v Lithuania (H, June 1998);
	6-1	v Tajikstan (H, September 2014)
Bosnia-Herzegovina	7-0	v Estonia (H, September 2008);
	8-1	v Liechtenstein (A, September 2012)
Cyprus	5-0	v Andorra (H, November 2000);
	5-0	v Andorra (H, November 2014)
Estonia	6-0	v Lithuana (H, July 1928)
Faroe Islands	3-0	v San Marino (H, May 1995)
	4-1	v Gibraltar (A, March 2014)
Finland	10-2	v Estonia (H, August 1922)
	8-0	v San Marino (H, November 2010)
Georgia	7-0	v Armenia (H, March 1997)
Gibraltar	1-0	v Malta (H, June 2014)
Iceland	5-0	v Malta (H, July 2000)
Israel	9-0	v Chinese Taipei (A, March 1988)
Kazakhstan	7-0	v Pakistan (H, June 1997)
Kosovo	2-0	v Equatorial Guinea (H, October 2015)
	2-0	v Faroe Islands (H, June 2016)
Latvia	6-1	v Lithuania (H, May 1935);
	5-0	v Lithuania (Estonia, June 2012);
	5-0	v Gibraltar (A, March 2016)
Liechtenstein	4-0	v Luxembourg (A, October 2004)
Luxembourg	6-0	v Afghanistan (A, July 1948)
Macedonia	11-1	v Liechtenstein (A, November 1996)
Malta	7-1	v Liechtenstein (H, March 2008)
Moldova	5-0	v Pakistan (A, August 1992)
Montenegro	6-0	v San Marino (A, September 2012)
San Marino	1-0	v Liechtenstein (H, April 2004)
Slovenia	7-0	v Oman (A, February 1999)

RECORD DEFEATS

Albania	0-12	v Hungary (A, September 1950)
Andorra	1-8	v Czech Republic (A, June 2005);
	0-7	v Croatia (A, October 2006)
Armenia	0-7	v Chile (A, January 1997);
	0-7	v Georgia (A, March 1997)
Austria	1-11	v England (H, June 1908)
Azerbaijan	0-10	v France (A, September 1995)
Belarus	0-5	v Austria (A, June 2003)
Bosnia-Herzegovina	0-5	v Argentina (A, May 1998)
Cyprus	0-12	v West Germany (A, May 1969)
Estonia	2-10	v Finland (A, August 1922)
Faroe Islands	0-7	v Yugoslavia (A, May 1991);
	0-7	v Romania (A, May 1992);
	0-7	v Norway (H, August 1993);
	1-8	v Yugoslavia (H, October 1996)
Finland	0-13	v Germany (A, September 1940)
Georgia	0-5	v Romania (A, April 1996);
	1-6	v Denmark (A, September 2005)
Gibraltar	0-7	v Poland (H, September 2014);
	0-7	v Rep of Ireland (A, October 2014);
	0-7	v Germany (H, June 2015);
	1-8	v Poland (A, September 2015)
Iceland	2-14	v Denmark (A, August 1967)
Israel	1-7	v Germany (A, February 2002)
Kazakhstan	0-6	v Turkey (H, June 2006);
	0-6	v Russia (A, May 2008)
Kosovo	1-6	v Turkey (H, May 2014)
Latvia	0-12	v Sweden (A, May 1927)
Liechtenstein	1-11	v Macedonia (H, November 1996)
Luxembourg	0-9	v England (H, October 1960);
	0-9	v England (A, December 1982)
Macedonia	0-5	v Belgium (H, June 1995);
	0-5	v Slovakia (H, October 2001);
	0-5	v Hungary (A, November 2001);
	1-6	v Czech Republic (A, June 2005)
Malta	1-12	v Spain (A, December 1983)
Moldova	0-6	v Sweden (A, June 2001)
Montenegro	0-4	v Romania (A, May 2008);
	0-4	v Ukraine (H, June 2013)
San Marino	0-13	v Germany (H, September 2006)
Slovenia	0-5	v France (A, October 2002)

KULCHY COUP

Midfielder Alyaksandr Kulchy became the first player to win 100 caps for Belarus, skippering the side against Lithuania in a June 2012 friendly. He also ended ex-Arsenal and Barcelona playmaker Alexander Hleb's run of four successive Belarus footballer of the year awards by claiming the prize in 2009. Hleb, whose younger brother Vyacheslav has also played for Belarus, had previously won the accolade in 2002 and 2003 as well, only for Belarus's all-time top scorer Maksim Romashenko to take it in 2004.

NO-SCORE ANDORRA

Since playing their first international on New Year's Day 1996 – a 6-1 home defeat to Estonia – Andorra have won only three matches, two of them friendlies. Their only competitive triumph was a 1-0 success over Macedonia in an October 2004 FIFA World Cup qualifying match, when left-back Marc Bernaus struck the only goal of the game. Perhaps their lack of strength should come as no surprise – the principality is the sixth-smallest country in Europe, with a population of just 71,822 and they have played their most high-profile games, against England, across the Spanish border in Barcelona.

CAUGHT SHORT

If Montenegro are scoring, then fans can "put their shirt" on captain and all-time leading scorer **Mirko Vucinic** being among the goals. He celebrated scoring the winner against Switzerland in a UEFA Euro 2012 qualifier by removing not his top, but his shorts – and wearing them on his head, antics that earned him a yellow card. Vucinic had previously celebrated a goal for his Italian club side by taking off both his shorts and his shirt, revealing another AS Roma shirt underneath.

XHAKA CLAN

Granit and Taulant Xhaka, both born in Swiss city Basel to Kosovo Albanian parents, became the first brothers to face each other on opposing sides at a UEFA European Championship on 11 June 2016 – midfielder Granit, 23, for Switzerland, 25-year-old defender Taulant for Albania. Granit and Switzerland won 1-0.

SARG'S 20–YEAR SERVICE

Armenia's first international was a goalless draw at home to Moldova on 14 October 1992. In their starting line-up that day was centre-back **Sargis Hovsepyan**, who went on to win a record 131 caps for the country before his international retirement in November 2012. He was then appointed the Armenian national team's football director.

SOUTH AMERICA

Brazil hosted a spectacularly vivid and exciting FIFA World Cup in 2014 but the home fans' favourites finished "only" fourth. Argentina did reach the final, only to lose to Germany and thus failed to add to their previous two World Cup triumphs. South American fans were disappointed that football had nothing to celebrate. Colombia had gone out in the quarter-finals, while Chile and Uruguay fell in the second round. Consolation for Chile came when they recorded back-to-back Copa America triumphs in 2015 and 2016.

After 99 years of trying, Chile finally became continental champions for the first time in 2015, and they soon had more to cheer about with a repeat victory over Argentina in the final of Copa America Centenario in 2016.

ARGENTINA

Copa America champions on 14 occasions, FIFA Confederations Cup winners in 1992, Olympic gold medallists in 2004 and 2008 and, most treasured of all, FIFA World Cup winners in 1978 and 1986: few countries have won as many international titles as Argentina. The country has a long and rich football history (the first Argentine league was contested in 1891) and has produced some of the greatest footballers ever to have played the game.

LONGEST–SERVING MANAGERS

Guillermo Stabile	1939–60
Cesar Luis Menotti	1974–83
Carlos Bilardo	1983–90
Alfio Basile	1990–94
	2006–08
Marcelo Bielsa	1998–2004
Jose Maria Minella	1964–68
Daniel Passarella	1994–98
Manuel Seoane	1934–37
Juan Jose Pizzuti	1969–72
Alejandro Sabella	2011–14

MESSI ENDINGS

Argentina reached – and lost a final – for a third consecutive year when Chile won a penalty-shoot-out at the 2016 Copa America Centenario. This final – just as in 2015 when the then hosts Chile took the shoot-out 4-1 – in New Jersey's MetLife Stadium ended goalless after 120 minutes before Chile triumphed 4-2. Argentina had also fallen to Germany in the 2014 FIFA World Cup final. Earlier in the 2016 tournament, Lionel Messi's goal in the semi-final win over the United States was his 55th for Argentina and he passed Gabriel Batistuta to top the country's all-time list. But Messi ended the final in despair, after failing in the shoot-out – missing high and wide – then announced he was retiring from international football at the age of just 29. He had lost in three Copa America finals, in 2007, 2015 and 2006. Messi said after the 2016 final: "I tried so hard to be champion with Argentina. Now I am leaving without having managed it." Argentina's last won the Copa America in 1993 and the FIFA World Cup in 1986.

FRINGE PLAYERS

Daniel Passarella was a demanding captain when he led his country to glory at the 1978 FIFA World Cup. He was the same as coach. After taking over the national side in 1994, he refused to pick anyone unless they had their hair cut short – and ordered striker Claudio Caniggia to get rid of his "girl's hair".

GONZALO'S HIGHS AND LOWS

Striker **Gonzalo Higuain** ended the longest scoring drought of his international career – 528 minutes and six matches – when scoring against Belgium in the 2014 FIFA World Cup quarter-final. Higuain was born in Brest, where his ex-footballer father Jorge Higuain was playing, but left the country aged ten months. He holds dual French-Argentina nationality, but took up Argentine citizenship in 2007. His goal against Belgium was his only one in the 2014 FIFA World Cup, but he had one disallowed (for offside) in the final against Germany. Higuain, and midfielder Ever Banega, missed their spot-kicks in Argentina's penalty shoot-out loss to Chile 2015 Copa America final.

WORTH WAITING FOR

Argentina's national stadium, "El Monumental" in Buenos Aires, hosted its first game in 1938. But the original design was not completed until 20 years later – largely thanks to the £97,000 River Plate received for a transfer fee from Juventus for **Omar Sivori**. The stadium is a must-see stop on the itinerary of many global football tourists for the "Superclasico" derby between hosts River Plate and city rivals Boca Juniors.

NUMBERS GAME

Argentina's FIFA World Cup squads of 1978 and 1982 were given numbers based on alphabetical order rather than positions, which meant the No. 1 shirt was worn by midfielders Norberto Alonso in 1978 and Osvaldo Ardiles in 1982. The only member of the 1982 squad whose shirt number broke the alphabetical order was No. 10, Diego Maradona.

DO YOU COME HERE OFTEN?

Argentina and Uruguay have played each other more often than any other two nations. They first met in Montevideo in 1901 – the first international staged outside Great Britain – a 3-2 win for visitors Argentina. There have been 183 official internationals since then, with Argentina winning 85, Uruguay 56 and 42 being drawn. The most recent contest was settled by a solitary goal, from Argentina's Sergio Aguero, in the first round of the 2015 Copa America.

A ROUND DOZEN

Argentina were responsible for the biggest win in Copa America history, when five goals by Jose Manuel Moreno helped them thrash Ecuador 12-0 in 1942. The much-travelled Moreno won domestic league titles in Argentina, Mexico, Chile and Colombia.

CHINA IN YOUR HAND

In an unusual move, the two 2008 Olympics football finalists Argentina and Nigeria were allowed to take two drinks breaks during the match, which was watched by 89,102 spectators. The game was played in stifling heat in Chinese host city Beijing. Angel Di Maria scored the only goal for Argentina, allowing them to retain the title they won in Athens – for the first time – four years earlier.

THE KIDS ARE ALL RIGHT

Sergio Aguero struck in the final, and ended the tournament as six-goal top scorer, when Argentina won the FIFA World U-20 Championship for a record sixth time in 2007, in Canada, beating the Czech Republic 2-1. Two years later, Aguero married Giannina Maradona – the youngest daughter of Argentina legend Diego – and in February 2009 she gave birth to Diego's first grandchild, Benjamin. Sergio Aguero is widely known by his nickname of "Kun", after a cartoon character he was said to resemble as a child.

BEGINNER'S LUCK

Aged just 27 years and 267 days old, Juan Jose Tramutola became the FIFA World Cup's youngest-ever coach when Argentina opened their 1930 campaign by beating France 1-0. Argentina went on to reach the final, only to lose 4-2 to Uruguay. Top-scorer at the 1930 FIFA World Cup was Argentina's Guillermo Stabile, with eight goals in four games – the only internationals he played. He later won six Copa America titles as his country's longest-serving coach between 1939 and 1960.

TARNISHED GOLD

Despite winning the Olympic football tournament in 2004 and 2008 – with **Javier Mascherano** becoming the first male footballer since 1928 to collect two Olympic golds – Argentina did not qualify for London 2012. South America's two places went to Brazil and Uruguay, based on the 2011 South American Youth Championship staged in Peru. Argentina were third in the six-team final group, but they did qualify for the Rio 2016 Games.

MAJOR TOURNAMENTS

FIFA WORLD CUP Winners (2)	16 appearances – 1978, 1986
COPA AMERICA Winners (14)	40 appearances – 1921, 1925, 1927, 1929, 1937, 1941, 1945, 1946, 1947, 1955, 1957, 1959, 1991, 1993
CONFEDERATIONS CUP Winners (1)	Three appearances – 1992
FIRST INTERNATIONAL	Uruguay 2 Argentina 3 (Montevideo, Uruguay, 16 May 1901)
BIGGEST WIN	Argentina 12 Ecuador 0 (Montevideo, Uruguay, 22 January 1942)
BIGGEST DEFEATS	Czechoslovakia 6 Argentina 1 (Helsingborg, Sweden, 15 June 1958); Argentina 0, Colombia 5 (Buenos Aires, 5 September 1993) Bolivia 6 Argentina 1 (La Paz, Bolivia, 1 April 2009)

YELLOW GOODBYE

Some 20 years before France were forced to wear local Argentine club Atletico Kimberly's kit at the 1978 FIFA World Cup, Argentina themselves faced similar embarrassment for their first-round match against West Germany. The Argentines had neglected to bring along a second kit and a colour-clash with their opponents meant borrowing the yellow shirts of Swedish side IFK Malmo. Despite taking a third-minute lead, Argentina lost 3-1 and departed the tournament bottom of Group A.

PEOPLE'S FAVOURITE

Lionel Messi may be acclaimed as the finest footballer in the world – and one of the best of all-time – yet back home in Argentina the real hero for many fans is three-time South American Footballer of the Year **Carlos Tevez**. When Argentina staged the 2011 Copa America, team line-up announcements in stadia described Messi as "the best in the world" but Tevez as "the player of the people". Tevez grew up in poverty in Buenos Aires' tough "Fuerte Apache" neighbourhood and still bears scars on his neck from when boiling water was spilled on him as a child. Yet he ended the 2011 Copa America as a villain – his missed penalty gave Uruguay shoot-out victory in the quarter-final. Tevez failed even to make Argentina's squad for the 2014 FIFA World Cup, despite having scored 21 club goals the preceding season and been named Juventus's player of the year as they won their third consecutive Italian league title.

SPOT-KICK FLOP

If at first you don't succeed, try and try again – unfortunately Martin Palermo missed all three penalties he took during Argentina's 1999 Copa America clash with Colombia. The first hit the crossbar, the second flew over the bar and the third was saved. Colombia won the match 3-0.

WINNING TOUCH

Midfielder Marcelo Trobbiani played just two minutes of FIFA World Cup football – the last two minutes of the 1986 final, after replacing winning goalscorer Jorge Burruchaga. Trobbiani touched the ball once, a backheel. The former Boca star ended his international career with 15 caps and one goal to his name.

TOP SCORERS

1	Lionel Messi	55
2	Gabriel Batistuta	54
3	Hernan Crespo	35
4	Diego Maradona	34
5	Sergio Aguero	33
6	Gonzalo Higuain	30
7	Luis Artime	24
8	Daniel Passarella	23
9	Leopoldo Luque	22
=	Jose Sanfilippo	22

SECOND TIME LUCKY

Luisito Monti is the only man to play in the FIFA World Cup final for two different countries. The centre-half, born in Buenos Aires on 15 May 1901 but with Italian family origins, was highly influential in Argentina's run to the 1930 final. They lost the game 4-2 to Uruguay – after Monti allegedly received mysterious pre-match death threats. Following a transfer to Juventus the following year, he was allowed to play for Italy and was on the winning side when the *Azzurri* beat Czechoslovakia in the 1934 final. Another member of the 1934 team was Raimundo Orsi, who had also played for Argentina before switching countries in 1929.

DIVINE DIEGO

To many people **Diego Armando Maradona** is the greatest footballer the world has ever seen, better even than Pele. The Argentine legend, born in Lanus on 30 October 1960, first became famous as a ball-juggling child during half-time intervals at Argentinos Juniors matches. He was distraught to be left out of Argentina's 1978 FIFA World Cup squad and was then sent off for retaliation at the 1982 tournament. Maradona, as triumphant Argentina captain in Mexico in 1986, scored the notorious "Hand of God" goal and then a spectacular individual strike within five minutes of each other in a quarter-final win over England. He again captained Argentina to the final in 1990, in Italy – the country where he inspired Napoli to Serie A and UEFA Cup success. He was thrown out of the 1994 FIFA World Cup finals in disgrace after failing a drugs test. Maradona captained Argentina 16 times in FIFA World Cup matches, a record, and was surprisingly appointed national coach in 2008, despite scant previous experience as a manager.

FITTER, JAVIER

Javier Zanetti is Argentina's most-capped player, with 143 international appearances – despite being surprisingly left out of squads for both the 2006 and 2010 FIFA World Cups. Zanetti, who played at full-back or in midfield, also played more Serie A matches than any other non-Italian – and all for Internazionale of Milan, with whom he won the treble of Italian league, Italian Cup and UEFA Champions League in 2009–10. Despite those achievements, he and Inter team-mate Esteban Cambiasso failed to make Diego Maradona's squad for the 2010 FIFA World Cup – but Zanetti returned to the fold under Maradona's successor Sergio Batista and captained his country at the 2011 Copa America. Zanetti made his 600th appearance in Italy's Serie A in March 2013 and retired from club football, aged 40, in 2014.

SUPER MARIO

Mario Kempes, who scored twice in the 1978 FIFA World Cup final and won the Golden Boot, was the only member of Cesar Menotti's squad who played for a non-Argentine club. Playing for Valencia, he had been the Spanish league's top scorer for the previous two seasons.

THE ANGEL GABRIEL

Gabriel Batistuta, nicknamed "Batigol", is the only man to have scored hat-tricks in two separate FIFA World Cups. Argentina's former all-time leading goalscorer grabbed the first against Greece in 1994 and the second against Jamaica four years later. Hungary's Sandor Kocsis, France's Just Fontaine and Germany's Gerd Muller each scored two hat-tricks in the same FIFA World Cup. Batistuta, born in Reconquista on 1 February 1969, also set an Italian league record by scoring in 11 consecutive Serie A matches for his club Fiorentina at the start of the 1994–95 season.

LEO BRAVO

Lionel Messi became only the second substitute to hit a Copa America hat-trick when he came off the bench to score three times in 19 minutes in Argentina's 5-0 victory over Panama in the opening round of the 2016 Copa America Centenario. Before then, only Paulo Valentim had done so, for Brazil in 1959 as they beat Uruguay 3-1, before ultimately finishing runners-up to Argentina. This was just the latest in a long line of feats achieved by Messi, who – rather less gloriously – had been sent off just two minutes into his national debut, against Hungary in August 2005 after coming on as a substitute. He went on to become his Argentina's all-time record goalscorer with 55, youngest FIFA World Cup scorer (against Serbia and Montenegro in 2006, aged 19), their youngest captain (at 23 years old during the 2010 FIFA World Cup) and winner of the Golden Ball for best player at the 2014 FIFA World Cup, where his four Man of the Match awards were a record for one tournament.

TOP CAPS

1	Javier Zanetti	143
2	Javier Mascherano	129
3	Roberto Ayala	115
4	Lionel Messi	113
5	Diego Simeone	106
6	Oscar Ruggeri	97
7	Diego Maradona	91
8	Ariel Ortega	87
9	Sergio Romero	79
10	Gabriel Batistuta	78

HAIL AYALA

No one has captained Argentina more often than **Roberto Ayala**, who wore the armband for 63 international matches – having overtaken the record of 57 previously set by Diego Maradona. A powerful centre-back, Ayala was skipper when Argentina won football gold at the 2004 Summer Olympic Games in Athens, when Carlos Tevez scored the only goal of the final against Paraguay – adding to the silver medal Ayala and team-mates had won eight years earlier at the Atlanta Games, when Nigeria beat them 3-2 in the final. Angel Di Maria scored the only goal when Argentina retained Olympic gold at the 2008 Olympics in Beijing – this time with Ayala absent and Juan Roman Riquelme as captain.

BRAZIL

No country has captured the soul of the game to the same extent as Brazil. The country's distinctive yellow-shirted players have thrilled generations of football fans and produced some of the game's greatest moments. No FIFA World Cup tournament would be the same without Brazil – the nation that gave birth to Pele, Garrincha, Zico, Ronaldo and Kaka. The only nation to appear in every FIFA World Cup finals and competition winners a record five times, Brazil's widely-admired hosting of the 2014 tournament did not end with the sixth triumph they craved.

CONFED UP

The 2017 FIFA Confederations Cup in Russia will be the first in 20 years not to feature Brazil, after their quarter-final exit at the 2015 Copa America. The four-time winners took part in the previous seven editions either as reigning world or South American champions or, in 2013, as hosts.

CLOSE ENCOUNTERS

Brazil have been involved in many memorable games. Their 3-2 defeat to Italy in 1982 is regarded as one of the classic games in FIFA World Cup finals history. Paolo Rossi scored all three of Italy's goals with Brazil coach Tele Santana much criticized for going all out in attack when only a 2-2 draw was needed. Brazil's 1982 squad, with players such as **Socrates**, **Zico** and Falcao, is considered one of the greatest teams never to win the tournament. In 1994, a 3-2 win over the Netherlands in the quarter-finals – their first competitive meeting in 20 years – was just as thrilling, with all the goals coming in the second half. Socrates – a qualified medical doctor, as well as elder brother to 1994 FIFA World Cup-winner Rai – was mourned across the globe when he died at the age of 57 in December 2011.

TAKING AIM WITH NEYMAR

Brazil's triumph in the 2013 FIFA Confederations Cup, a record third in a row, was consolation for their failure in 2012 to break their Olympic hoodoo, Mexico beating them in the London Games final. This remains the only FIFA-approved prize to elude Brazil but they will be the hosts at Rio de Janeiro in 2016. **Neymar** was nine-goal top scorer at London 2012, voted South American Footballer of the Year for the second successive year and then, in 2013, was named player of the FIFA Confederations Cup. Those were his last matches as a Santos player before he joined Spanish giants Barcelona. He was Brazil's undoubted star man at the 2014 FIFA World Cup, with four goals in four games before suffering a tournament-ending broken bone in his back during the quarter-final win against Colombia. But he was sent off against Colombia at the 2015 Copa America Centenario and banned for four games, before missing the following year's Copa America Centenario so he could be saved for the 2016 Summer Olympics in Rio instead.

BRAZIL'S RECORD

FIFA WORLD CUP	20 appearances (every finals)	
Matches (104)	W70, D17, L17, GF221, GA102	
Winners (5)	1958, 1962, 1970, 1994, 2002	
Runners-up (2)	1950, 1998	
Third place (2)	1938, 1978	
Fourth place (1)	1974, 2014	
COPA AMERICA	35 appearances	
Winners (8)	1919, 1922, 1949, 1989,	
	1997, 1999, 2004, 2007	
CONFEDERATIONS CUP	Seven appearances	
Winners (4)	1997, 2005, 2009, 2013	
FIRST INTERNATIONAL	Argentina 3 Brazil 0	
	(Buenos Aires, 20 September 1914)	
BIGGEST WIN	Brazil 10 Bolivia 1 (Sao Paulo,	
	10 April 1949)	
HEAVIEST DEFEAT	Uruguay 6 Brazil 0 (Vina del	
	Mar, Chile, 18 September 1920)	
	Brazil 1 Germany 7	
	(Belo Horizonte, 8 July 2014)	

TOP OF THE FLOPS

Brazil's dreams of winning a sixth FIFA World Cup, but first on home soil, became a nightmare in 2014 – 64 years on from the trauma caused by Uruguay's surprise triumph at Rio de Janeiro's Maracana stadium. Luiz Felipe Scolari's 2014 vintage set a series of unenviable records as they crashed out, 7-1 to Germany, in the semi-final in Belo Horizonte. This was not only Brazil's heaviest FIFA World Cup defeat, but also the biggest any semi-finalist had ever suffered. It equalled the 6-0 trouncing by Uruguay at the 1920 Copa America as Brazil's worst defeat of all-time. Finally, it was Brazil's first home loss in a competitive international since Peru beat them 3-1 – also in Belo Horizonte – in a 1975 Copa America semi-final. A 3-0 setback against the Netherlands in the third-place play-off meant Brazil lost consecutive internationals at home for the first time since 1940, when Argentina, 3-0, and Uruguay 4-3, were victorious. The 14 goals Brazil conceded was their worst ever in a FIFA World Cup, three worse than in 1938, and they became the first FIFA World Cup hosts to concede the most goals in a tournament. Not only did Neymar miss the Germany game through injury, but centre-back and captain **Thiago Silva** was absent suspended.

LAND OF FOOTBALL

No country is more deeply identified with football success than Brazil, who have won the FIFA World Cup a record five times – in 1958, 1962, 1970, 1994 and 2002. They are also the only team never to have missed a FIFA World Cup finals and are favourites virtually every time the competition is staged. After winning the trophy for a third time in Mexico in 1970, Brazil kept the **Jules Rimet Trophy** permanently. Sadly, it was stolen from the federation's headquarters in 1983 and was never recovered. Brazilians often refer to their country as "o país do futebol" ("the country of football"). It is the favourite pastime of youngsters, while general elections are often held in the same year as the FIFA World Cup, with critics arguing that political parties try to take advantage of the nationalistic surge created by football and bring it into politics. Charles Miller, the son of a Scottish engineer, is credited with bringing football to Brazil in 1894. Yet the sport would only truly become Brazilian when blacks were able to play at the top level in 1933. At first, because of the game's European origin, it was the sport of Brazil's urban white elite. However, it quickly spread among the urban poor as Brazilians realized the only thing they needed to play was a ball, which could be substituted inexpensively with a bundle of socks, an orange, or even a cloth filled with paper.

CAPTAIN TO COACH

Brazil's 1994 FIFA World Cup-winning captain **Dunga** – real name Carlos Caetano Bledorn Verri – was appointed national coach in 2006, despite having no previous management experience, for the first of two separate spells in charge of his country. He led the team to 2007 Copa America and 2009 FIFA Confederations Cup successes before losing his job when Brazil departed the 2010 FIFA World Cup in the quarter-finals against the Netherlands. He returned four years later, but was sacked after Brazil failed to get past the first round for only the second time in Copa America history. Dunga had been on the bench both times as an unused substitute in 1987 and as manager in 2016. Replacing him as national coach after the embarrassing 2016 exit was former Corinthians manager Adenor Leonardo Bacchi, better known as Tite.

EYE FOR GOAL

Centre-forward **Tostao** – full name Eduardo Goncalves de Andrade – was one of the stars of Brazil's legendary 1970 FIFA World Cup-winning team but almost did not make the tournament. He had suffered a detached retina when hit in the face by a football the previous year, prompting some doctors' warnings that he should be left out. Tostao eventually retired at the age of 26 in 1973, after another eye injury, and went to work as a doctor instead. His 1970 team-mate Pele also experienced failing eyesight.

JOY OF THE PEOPLE

Garrincha, one of Brazil's greatest legends, was really Manuel Francisco dos Santos at birth but his nickname meant 'Little Bird' – inspired by his slender, bent legs. Despite the legacy of childhood illness, he was a star right-winger at Botafogo from 1953 to 1965. He and Pele were explosively decisive newcomers for Brazil at the 1958 FIFA World Cup finals. In 1962 Garrincha was voted player of the tournament four years later. He died in January 1983 at just 49. His epitaph was the title often bestowed on him in life: "The Joy of the People."

TOP CAPS

1	Cafu	142
2	Roberto Carlos	125
3	Lucio	105
4	Claudio Taffarel	101
5	Robinho	99
6	Djalma Santos	98
=	Ronaldo	98
8	Ronaldinho	97
9	Gilmar	94
10	Dani Alves	93
=	Gilberto Silva	93

TOP SCORERS

1	Pele	77
2	Ronaldo	62
3	Romario	55
4	Zico	48
5	Neymar	46
6	Bebeto	39
7	Rivaldo	35
8	Jairzinho	33
=	Ronaldinho	33
10	Ademir	32

THE KING

Pele is considered by many as the greatest player of all time, a sporting icon *par excellence* and not only for his exploits on the pitch. When, for instance, he scored his 1,000th goal, Pele dedicated it to the poor children of Brazil. He began playing for Santos at the age of 15 and won his first FIFA World Cup two years later, scoring twice in the final. Despite numerous offers from European clubs, the economic conditions and Brazilian football regulations at the time allowed Santos to keep hold of their prized asset for almost two decades, until 1974. All-time leading scorer of the Brazilian national team, he is the only footballer to be a member of three FIFA World Cup-winning teams. Despite being in the Brazilian squad at the start of the 1962 tournament, an injury suffered in the second match meant he was not able to play on and, initially, he missed out on a winner's medal. However, FIFA announced in November 2007 that he would be awarded a medal retrospectively. After the disastrous 1966 tournament, when Brazil fell in the first round, Pele said he did not wish to play in the FIFA World Cup again. He was finally talked round and ended up, in 1970, playing a key role in what is widely considered as one of the greatest sides ever. Since his retirement in 1977, Pele has been a worldwide ambassador for football, as well undertaking various acting roles and commercial ventures.

PARTY ANIMAL

Brazil's captain when they played Argentina (twice), Costa Rica and Mexico in autumn 2011 was a man many had not even expected to be in the international side again – former two-time FIFA World Footballer of the Year, Ronaldinho. Having amazed the world with his fancy footwork and prolific goalscoring for Paris Saint-Germain in France, Barcelona in Spain and AC Milan in Italy, he returned to his homeland with Flamengo in 2011 – but was widely accused of being more interested in partying than playing. But a return to form won him a recall under Mano Menezes. That appearance against Mexico took him to 33 goals, level with 1970 FIFA World Cup winner Jairzinho, then his next match – his 94th for Brazil – equalled the caps tally of 1958 and 1962 FIFA World Cup champion goalkeeper Gilmar. Ronaldinho himself became a FIFA World Cup winner in 2002, aged 22, when his long-range goal against England gave Brazil victory in the quarter-finals – though he was sent off seven minutes later and had to sit out the semi-final, before returning for the final.

WHITHER RONALDO?

Only one person knows exactly what happened to **Ronaldo** in the hours before the 1998 FIFA World Cup final – the man himself. He sparked one of the biggest mysteries in FIFA World Cup history when his name was left off the teamsheet before the game, only for it to reappear just in time for kick-off. It was initially reported that Ronaldo had an ankle injury, and then a upset stomach. Finally team doctor Lidio Toledo revealed the striker had been rushed to hospital after suffering a convulsion in his sleep, but that he had been cleared to play after neurological and cardiac tests. The most dramatic account came from Ronaldo's roommate Roberto Carlos. "Ronaldo was scared about what lay ahead. The pressure had got to him and he couldn't stop crying," said the legendary full-back. "At about four o'clock, he became ill. That's when I called the team doctor and told him to get over to our room as fast as he could."

PHIL YOUR BOOTS

Liverpool playmaker Philippe Coutinho scored Brazil's 54th international hat-trick in a 7-1 defeat of Haiti at the 2016 Copa America Centenario. Pele leads the way with seven trebles, followed by Zico on five, two of them four-timers. But only Evaristo – born Evaristo de Macedo Filho – against Colombia in March 1957, netted five goals in one game for Brazil. Evaristo scored a total of eight goals in 14 appearances for Brazil.

THAT'S MY BOY

When Bebeto scored for Brazil against the Netherlands in their 1994 FIFA World Cup quarter-final, he and strike partner Romario celebrated with a "cradling the baby" dance that would be much-imitated for years to come. Bebeto's wife had just given birth to their son Matheus – who would grow up to become a footballer himself, joining Flamengo's youth set-up in 2011. By this time, both **Bebeto** (middle) and **Romario** (right, Mazinho is left) were in tandem again – as elected politicians in Brazil.

INAUSPICIOUS START

Left-back/left-winger **Marcelo** achieved the dubious "honour" of being the first player to score the opening goal of a FIFA World Cup finals in his own net. He inadvertently gave Croatia the lead in the 2014 tournament's curtain-raiser in Sao Paulo, but Brazil did come back to win 3-1, thanks to a pair of goals from Neymar and one from Oscar. Marcelo, who a couple of weeks earlier had scored for his club, Real Madrid, as they won the UEFA Champions League final, also became the first Brazil player ever to score past his own goalkeeper in the FIFA World Cup finals.

BRAZIL'S YOUNGEST PLAYERS

1 Pele, 16 years and 257 days
    (v Argentina, 7 July 1958)
2 Ronaldo, 17 years and 182 days
    (v Argentina, 24 March 1994)
3 Adriano, 17 years and 272 days
    (v Australia, 17 November 1999)
4 Toninho, 17 years and 343 days
    (v Uruguay, 28 April 1976)
5 Carvalho Leite, 18 years and 26 days
    (v Bolivia, 22 July 1930)
6 Diego, 18 years and 60 days
    (v Mexico, 30 April 2003)
7 Marcelo, 18 years and 115 days
    (v Wales, 5 September 2006)
8 Philippe Coutinho, 18 years and 116 days
    (v Iran, 7 October 2010)
9 Doria, 18 years and 149 days
    (v Bolivia, 6 April 2013)
10 Neymar, 18 years and 186 days
    (v USA, 10 August 2010)

ROLLING RIVA

Brazilian legend **Rivaldo** played into his 40s – a decade after the highlight of his career,  helping Brazil win the 2002 FIFA World Cup. He scored 34 goals in 74 matches for his country between 1993 and 2003, including three goals at the 1998 FIFA World Cup and five more in Japan and South Korea four years later. His 2002 FIFA World Cup was marred only by blatant play-acting that helped get Turkey's Hakan Unsal sent off and earned Rivaldo a fine. Rivaldo – full name Rivaldo Vitor Borba Ferreira – became one of the world's finest footballers despite suffering malnourishment in a poverty-stricken childhood. His individual achievements including FIFA World Footballer of the Year and European Footballer of the Year prizes in 1999 while playing in Spain for Barcelona. His later clubs included AC Milan in Italy, Olympiacos and AEK Athens in Greece, Bunyodkor in Uzbekistan and Kabuscorp in Angola before he returned home to Brazil where he played for Sao Caetano in 2013 and Mogi Mirim in 2014–15 before retiring aged 43 in August 2015.

WORLD–BEATING SAINTS

 Right-back **Djalma Santos** is one of only two players to be voted into the official all-star team of a FIFA World Cup on three different occasions. He was honoured for his performances at the 1954, 1958 and 1962 finals – even though his only appearance in 1958 was in the final. West Germany's Franz Beckenbauer was the other, chosen in 1966, 1970 and 1974. On the opposite flank to Djalma Santos was the left-back Nilton Santos – no relation – who also played in 1954, 1958 and 1962 and had also been a member of Brazil's runners-up squad on home turf in 1950.

SILVA VALUE

Centre-back Thiago Silva scored Brazil's opener in the 2-1 win over Venezuela that gave them a place in the 2015 Copa America quarter-final – but it was his handball that allowed Paraguay to equalize with a penalty in the last eight, which Brazil then lost in a shoot-out. This was his sixth international tournament in six years and his seventh in eight. He won a bronze medal at the 2008 Beijing Olympics and silver at London 2012, and captain when Brazil won the FIFA Confederations Cup in 2013.

YELLOW FEVER

The world-renowned yellow and blue kit now worn by Brazil was not adopted until 1954, as a replacement for their former all-white strip. The *Correio da Manha* newspaper organised a design competition which was won by 19-year-old Aldyr Garcia Schlee and the new colours were worn for the first time in March 1954 against Chile. Schlee was from Pelotas, close to Brazil's border with Uruguay and actually supported Uruguayan sides against Brazil.

THE OLD RIVALS: BRAZIL V ARGENTINA

Matches played: 97
Brazil wins: 36
Argentina wins: 36
Draws: 25
Brazil goals: 148
Argentina goals: 152
First match: Argentina 3 Brazil 0 (20 September 1914)
Latest match: Brazil 1, Argentina 1 (13 November 2015)
Biggest Brazil win: Brazil 6 Argentina 2 (20 December 1945)
Biggest Argentina win: Argentina 6 Brazil 1 (5 March 1940)

GRAND ACHIEVEMENT

Brazil played their 1,000th match on 14 November 2012, with Neymar's second-half equaliser securing a 1-1 draw against Colombia in New Jersey, United States.  Brazil's first match is considered generally to have been a 2-0 victory over visiting English club Exeter City on 21 July 1914, at the Estadio das Laranjeiras in Rio – still used by Fluminense. Brazil won that day despite star striker **Arthur Friedenreich** losing two teeth in a collision. Brazil's first international against another country was a 3-0 defeat to Argentina on 20 September 1914.

BRAZIL'S 2014 WORLD CUP STADIA

1. Maracana, Rio de Janeiro (76,804)
2. Brasilia, Estadio Nacional Mane Garrincha (70,064)
3. Mineirao, Belo Horizonte (62,547, Atletico Mineiro and Cruzeiro)
4. Arena Corinthians, Sao Paulo (65,807)
5. Estadio Castelao, Fortaleza (64,846)
6. Estadio Beira-Rio, Porto Alegre (48,849)
7. Arena Fonte Neva, Salvador (48,747)
8. Arena Pernambuco, Recife (46,000)
9. Arena Pantanal, Cuiaba (42,968)
10. Arena da Amazonia, Manaus (42,374)
11. Arena das Dunas, Natal (42,086)
12. Arena da Baixaba, Curitiba (41,456)

BRAZIL HAVE HAD THEIR PHIL

The return of "Big Phil" **Luiz Felipe Scolari** as Brazil coach in November 2012 was meant to culminate, in 2014, with a repeat of his success spearheading the country to triumph at the 2002 FIFA World Cup. Yet although his second reign did bring glory at the 2013 FIFA Confederations Cup, the following year's FIFA World Cup on home turf will be remembered for the many unwanted records his team set and the embarrassment with which their efforts ended – most notably, the 7-1 defeat by Germany in their Belo Horizonte semi-final. Scolari was relieved of his role just days after a 3-0 defeat to the Netherlands in the third-place play-off. However, the tournament gave him a second fourth-place finish, achieving that mark as Portugal boss in 2006, and he became the first coach to be in charge in three different FIFA World Cup semi-finals.

WRY SMILE FOR RAI

Brazil Midfielder **Rai** could be forgiven for thinking "What if?" as he joined squad-members celebrating their 1994 FIFA World Cup triumph in the United States. Rai – a younger brother of legendary Brazilian international Socrates – had gone into the tournament as captain, but was replaced by Mazinho after three games, with the armband passing to Dunga, who lifted the trophy and then captained Brazil to another FIFA World Cup final four years later, where they lost to France. Rai had scored a penalty in Brazil's opening game in 1994, a 2-0 win against Russia, but in the knock-out stages he managed just ten minutes in the quarter-final against the Netherlands and 45 against Sweden in the semi. He later said: "Winning the 1994 World Cup is a great memory, despite being dropped. It wasn't my best moment, but the win was beautiful – Brazil's first for 24 years." After retiring, Rai founded two social justice charities to help under-privileged youngsters – one of them set up with 1994 FIFA World Cup team-mate, Leonardo.

LETTING LUCIO

Elegant centre-back **Lucio** set a FIFA World Cup record during the 2006 tournament by playing for 386 minutes without conceding a foul – only ending in Brazil's 1-0 quarter-final defeat to France. While mostly noted for leadership and control at the back, he also had an eye for goal – heading the late winner that gave Brazil a 3-2 triumph over the USA in the 2009 FIFA Confederations Cup final. The following year he was part of Italian club Internazionale's treble success, clinching the Italian league and cup as well as the UEFA Champions League.

SUPER-POWERS' POWER CUT

There was a new addition to the annual international calendar in 2011: the Superclasico de los Americas, a two-legged event between Brazil and Argentina. Brazil were the first winners, thanks to a goalless draw followed by a 2-0 win. They dramatically retained the crown in 2012. Brazil won the first leg at home, 2-1, but the return game in Chaco was postponed after a power cut – possibly because Brazil's team bus hit an electricity trailer. The rearranged game ended 2-1 to Argentina, but Brazil won 4-3 on penalties, their goal being scored by Fred, while strike partner Neymar netted the winning spot-kick. For Brazil's coach Mano Menezes, however, his "reward" was the sack. There was no Superclasico in 2013 before a one-off match played in the Chinese capital Beijing in October 2014 ended 2-0 to Brazil, thanks to a brace by Diego Tardelli. The only meeting of 2015 was a FIFA World Cup 2018 qualifier, which ended in a 1–1 draw in Buenos Aires.

CHILE

Chile were one of four founding members of CONMEBOL, South America's football confederation, in 1916. They played in the first match at a South American football championship – losing the opener of the unofficial 1910 tournament 3-0 to Uruguay – and they played in the first official Copa America, in 1916. Their greatest glories were hosting and finishing third at the 1962 FIFA World Cup and winning their first two Copa America titles in 2015 and 2016. Chile had been Copa runners-up in 1955, 1956, 1979 and 1987.

TOP SCORERS

1	Marcelo Salas	37
2	Alexis Sanchez	34
=	Ivan Zamorano	34
4	Eduardo Vargas	31
5	Carlos Caszely	29
6	Leonel Sanchez	24
7	Jorge Aravena	22
8	Humberto Suazo	21
9	Juan Carlos Letelier	18
10	Enrique Hormazabal	17
=	Arturo Vidal	17

VIDAL ESCAPES TO VICTORY

Hosts Chile's 2015 Copa America campaign nearly careered off the road, literally. Star midfielder **Arturo Vidal** crashed his red Ferrari after over-enjoying a night out, having scored twice in a 5-0 thrashing of Bolivia to confirm his side's quarter-final place. Coach Jorge Sampaoli resisted public pressure to drop him after Vidal promised to donate his tournament fee to charity. Despite this indiscretion, Vidal was named man of the match in the final and was named in the 2015 Copa America team of the tournament. The dynamic midfielder was crucial again in the 2016 Copa America Centenario, aside from missing the semi-final victory over Colombia, and was again named in the team of tournament – this time alongside seven team-mates from Chile and three players from Argentina.

CENTRE-BACK'S HAT-TRICK

The first player to be named South American Footballer of the Year three times was not Pele, Garrincha or Diego Maradona but Chilean centre-back **Elias Figueroa**, who took the prize in three consecutive years from 1974 to 1976 while playing for Brazilian club Internacional. The only players to emulate such a hat-trick were Brazil's Zico, in 1977, 1981 and 1982, and Argentina forward Carlos Tevez, in 2003, 2004 and 2005. Two more Chileans have won the award: Marcelo Salas in 1997 and Matias Fernandez in 2006. In all, the 45 annual awards have gone to players from Brazil and Argentina 13 times each, followed by Chile, Uruguay and Paraguay, five apiece, Colombia, three, and Peru, one. Although Figueroa started and ended his playing career in Chile, he also played for clubs in Brazil, Uruguay and the US, while also representing his country for 16 years from 1966 to 1982 – including FIFA World Cup appearances in 1966, 1974 and 1982.

ALL-GO IN SANTIAGO AT LAST

Having taken part in the first Copa America in 1916, Chile ended their 99-year wait to first lift the trophy by triumphing as hosts in summer 2015. They defeated Argentina 4-1 on penalties in the final following a goalless draw after extra-time in Santiago's Estadio Nacional. The winning spot-kick was struck by the well-travelled **Alexis Sanchez**, after a successful debut season with Arsenal in England following spells in Italy with Udinese and in Spain with Barcelona. Fellow Chile forward Eduardo Vargas shared the Golden Boot prize with Peru's Paolo Guerrero after scoring four goals – two of them in Chile's 2-1 defeat of Peru in the semi-finals – while captain Claudio Bravo was named best goalkeeper. Sanchez holds the record as Chile's youngest ever international, having made his debut against New Zealand in April 2006 at the age of 17 years and four months.

TOP CAPS

1	Claudio Bravo	106
2	Alexis Sanchez	101
3	Gonzalo Jara	95
=	Gary Medel	95
5	Leonel Sanchez	84
6	Jean Beausejour	82
7	Arturo Vidal	80
8	Mauricio Isla	79
9	Nelson Tapia	73
=	Jorge Valdivia	73

SALAS DAYS

Chile's all-time leading scorer **Marcelo Salas** formed a much-feared striking partnership with Ivan Zamorano during the late 1990s and early 21st century. Salas scored four goals as Chile reached the second round of the 1998 FIFA World Cup in France despite not winning a game. The striker spent two years in international retirement, from 2005 to 2007, but returned for the first four games of qualification for the 2010 FIFA World Cup. His scored twice in Chile's 2-2 draw with Uruguay on 18 November 2007, but his international career ended for good three days later, following a 3-0 defeat to Paraguay.

HAPPY SAMP

Chile had never reached the knock-out stages of consecutive FIFA World Cups until their 2014 vintage in Brazil matched the 2010 squad's achievement. And both times they had coaches from Argentina: Marcelo Bielsa was in charge in 2010 and Jorge Sampaoli four years later – and another compatriot, Claudio Borghi, served a spell in between. Sampaoli retired from playing aged 19, because of tibia and fibula injuries, and devoted himself to a coaching career that took in Peru and Ecuador before he took the Chilean hotseat in 2012.

BRAVO, BEAUSEJOUR

Chile went precisely 48 years between victories at a FIFA World Cup, from a 1-0 third-place play-off success against Yugoslavia on 16 June 1962 to a first-round victory by the same scoreline over Honduras on 16 June 2010. That long-awaited winner in South Africa came from Jean Beausejour, who then hit Chile's third in their opening-game 3-1 triumph over Australia in Brazil four years later. It meant he became the first Chilean player ever to score at more than one FIFA World Cup. Goalkeeper and captain at both tournaments was Claudio Bravo, Chile's second-most-capped player.

LUCKY LEO

For many years **Leonel Sanchez** held the Chilean record for international appearances, scoring 23 goals in 84 games. But he was lucky to remain on the pitch for one of them. Sanchez escaped an early bath despite punching Italy's Humberto Maschio in the face during their so-called "Battle of Santiago" clash at the 1962 FIFA World Cup, when English referee Ken Aston could have sent off more than just the two players he did dismiss. Sanchez, a left-winger born in Santiago on 25 April 1936, finished the tournament as one of its six four-goal leading scorers – along with Brazilians Garrincha and Vava, Russian Valentin Ivanov, Yugoslav Drazan Jerkovic and Hungarian Florian Albert.

URUGUAY

Uruguay was the first country to win a FIFA World Cup, in 1930, and with a population of under four million, they remain the smallest to do so. They claimed the game's greatest prize for a second time in 1950, having already won Olympic gold in 1924 and 1928. Recent years were less productive, until a fourth-place finish at the 2010 FIFA World Cup and a record-breaking 15th Copa America triumph the following year.

TOP SCORERS

1	Luis Suarez	45
2	Diego Forlan	36
3	Edinson Cavani	32
4	Hector Scarone	31
5	Angel Romano	28
6	Oscar Miguez	27
7	Sebastian Abreu	26
8	Pedro Petrone	24
9	Carlos Aguilera	22
=	Fernando Morena	22

FORLAN HERO

Diego Forlan was Uruguay's star man at the 2010 FIFA World Cup, scoring five goals – including three from outside the penalty area, the first player to achieve that feat at a FIFA World Cup since Germany's Lothar Matthaus in 1990. He also hit the crossbar with a free-kick, the final touch of his country's 3-2 defeat to Germany in the 2010 third-place play-off. Uruguay's fourth-place finish in South Africa meant Diego fared better than his father Pablo, who had played in the Uruguay team that was knocked out in the first round of the 1974 FIFA World Cup.

MAX POWER

Right-back **Maxi Pereira** became only the second Uruguayan to reach 100 caps, in a 1-0 friendly victory over Morocco in March 2015. He made his international debut in 2005 and played in the 2010 and 2014 FIFA World Cups and Uruguay's 2011 Copa America triumph. His FIFA World Cup fortunes have been mixed. In 2010 he became the first Uruguayan to miss a FIFA World Cup penalty, in their winning quarter-final shoot-out against Ghana before scoring his first international goal in a 3-2 defeat to Germany in the third-place play-off. Pereira opened the scoring in Uruguay's 5-0 play-off win over Jordan to reach the 2014 finals but became the first player of the tournament to be shown a red card, against Costa Rica. He entered the 2016 Copa America Centenario as Uruguay's second most-capped player, one behind Diego Forlan, and won his new record 114th cap in the Uruguay's final group game, at which point they were eliminated.

DIFFERENT BALL GAME

Uruguay were the inaugural hosts – and the first winners – of the FIFA World Cup in 1930, having won football gold at the Olympics of 1924 in Paris and 1928 in Amsterdam. Among the players who won all three of those titles was forward Hector Scarone, who remains Uruguay's second-highest scorer with 31 goals in 52 internationals. Uruguay beat arch-rivals Argentina 4-2 in the 1930 final, in a game which used two different footballs – Argentina's choice in the first half, in which they led 2-1, before Uruguay's was used for their second-half comeback.

HAPPY ANNIVERSARY

A so-called "Mundialito", or "Little World Cup", was staged in December 1980 and January 1981 to mark the 50th anniversary of the FIFA World Cup – and, as in 1930, Uruguay emerged triumphant. The tournament was meant to involve all six countries who had previously won the tournament, though 1966 champions England turned down the invitation and were replaced by 1978 runners-up Holland. Uruguay beat Brazil 2-1 in the final, a repeat of the scoreline from the two teams' final match of the 1950 FIFA World Cup. The Mundialito-winning Uruguay side was captained by goalkeeper Rodolfo Rodriguez and coached by Roque Maspoli, who had played in goal in that 1950 final.

TOP CAPS

1	Maxi Pereira	114
2	Diego Forlan	113
3	Diego Godin	101
4	Diego Lugano	95
5	Cristian Rodriguez	91
6	Diego Perez	89
7	Edinson Cavani	84
=	Luis Suarez	74
9	Fernando Muslera	82
10	Egidio Arevalo Rios	81

CAV FAITH

It took just three minutes for Edinson Cavani to score his first international goal, after coming on as a substitute for his Uruguay debut against Colombia in February 2008. He not only helped Uruguay finish fourth at the 2010 FIFA World Cup and win a record 15th Copa America in 2011, but his scoring exploits in club football for Italy's Napoli and Paris Saint-Germain in France have established him as one of the world's finest modern strikers. Cavani, a devout Christian, received high praise from the Archbishop of Naples, Crescenzio Sepe, who said: "God serves himself by having Cavani score goals." The forward was given his Uruguay debut by Oscar Tabarez, a former schoolteacher known as "The Maestro", whose second spell as international boss began in 2006. Cavani was aged just three when Tabarez led Uruguay at their most recent FIFA World Cup before 2010, reaching the second round in 1990.

BITE RETURN

Notoriety has cast many shadows over the career of **Luis Suarez** and the controversy he caused at the 2010 FIFA World Cup was mild compared to what followed in Brazil four years later. Uruguay's all-time leading scorer is one of the world's most talented strikers but is also a danger not only to others but to himself and team-mates. He earned infamy with a deliberate goal-line handball to concede a penalty when Uruguay and Ghana were level in their 2010 FIFA World Cup quarter-final – then celebrated wildly when Asamoah Gyan missed – and Uruguay won the resulting shoot-out. Worse followed, however, at the 2014 FIFA World Cup, when he bit into the shoulder of Italian defender Giorgio Chiellini, earning himself a nine-match international ban and a four-month suspension from all football. Astonishingly, this was the third time Suarez had bitten someone on the football field – having previously done so while playing for both Ajax Amsterdam and Liverpool. His scoring instincts, are much more admirable – his 45 international goals include four during Uruguay's triumphant 2011 Copa America campaign. Suarez does inspire loyalty among supporters and team-mates, who even pegged his shirt up in the dressing-room before their 2014 second-round clash with Colombia despite his enforced departure from Brazil the previous day.

GODIN WILLING

Uruguay went into the special 2016 Copa America Centenario hoping to emulate their 1916 performance and lift the trophy for a 16th time. Instead, they achieved an unwanted feat – a national-record five games in a row without a win in the Copa – by losing their first two fixtures, 3–1 against Mexico and 1–0 against Venezuela. Centre-back and captain **Diego Godin** scored his eighth goal for his country against Mexico, and against Venezuela became the third Uruguayan to win 100 caps.

TRAVEL SICKNESS

Despite winning the 1930 FIFA World Cup, Uruguay turned down the chance to defend their crown four years later, when the tournament was held in Italy. Uruguayan football authorities were unhappy that only four European countries had made the effort to travel to Uruguay and take part in 1930.

OLE, FRANCESCOLI

Until Diego Forlan passed him in 2011, no outfield player had represented Uruguay more often than **Enzo Francescoli** (73 caps) – and few can have taken the field quite so gracefully as the playmaker whose club career included stints with River Plate in Argentina, Racing and Marseille in France and Cagliari and Torino in Italy. His international swansong for Uruguay brought Copa America glory in 1995, when he starred as both midfielder and emergency striker and also scored one of Uruguay's spot-kicks in their penalty shoot-out final victory over Brazil. Among Francescoli's high-profile fans was Zinedine Zidane, who later named his first-born son Enzo, in honour of the Uruguayan maestro.

OTHER TEAMS SOUTH AMERICA

GOING CARACAS FOR FOOTBALL

Baseball and boxing may have held more sway with Venezuelans in recent decades but football fever has been on the rise in the twenty-first century – given a big boost by the country staging its first Copa America in 2007. This not only saw extravagant investment in new stadia but also Venezuela's first Copa America victory since 1967 – and unprecedented progress into the knock-out stages. **Juan Arango,** a popular success in Spain with La Liga club RCD Mallorca, scored Venezuela's goal in a 4-1 quarter-final loss to Uruguay. They followed this relative breakthrough by finishing eighth out of 10 in South America's qualification campaign for the 2010 FIFA World Cup, then sixth of nine for 2014 – above Peru, Bolivia and Paraguay.

NATIONAL STADIUMS

Bolivia:
Estadio Hernando Siles, La Paz (45,000 capacity)

Chile:
Estadio Nacional, Santiago (63,379)

Colombia:
Estadio El Campin, Bogota (48,600)

Ecuador:
Estadio Olimpico Atahualpa, Quito (40,948)

Paraguay:
Estadio Defensores del Chaco, Asuncion (36,000)

Peru:
Estadio Nacional, Lima (45,574)

Venezuela:
Estadio Polideportivo de Pueblo Nuevo, San Cristobal (38,755)

BOLIVIA LEAVE IT LATE

Bolivia have only ever won the Copa America once, but did so in dramatic and memorable style when playing host in 1963. They were the only team to finish the competition unbeaten in all six matches, topping the league table. But they almost threw away glory on the competition's final day, twice squandering two-goal leads against Brazil. Bolivia led 2-0 before being pegged back to 2-2, then saw a 4-2 advantage turn to 4-4, before Maximo Alcocer scored what proved to be Bolivia's winning goal with four minutes remaining.

ECUADOR'S EARTHQUAKE TRIBUTE

Ecuador reached the knock-out stages of the 2016 Copa America Centenario – the first time they had advanced from the opening round since 1987. They drew with Brazil (0-0) and Peru (2-2) and defeated Haiti 4-0. Head coach Gustavo Quinteros dedicated their progress to the more than 600 people killed by an earthquake in the country's Manabi region on 16 April 2016. Ecuador's opening goal against Haiti was scored by West Ham United striker **Enner Valencia**, who had netted three times at the 2014 FIFA World Cup, including a brace against Honduras in a 2-1 win – the first Ecuadorian to score more than once in a FIFA World Cup finals match.

YEP MAN

Two of Colombia's most-capped players are **Carlos Valderrama** (first, with 111 appearances) and Leonel Alvarez (third, with 101). Valderrama led the criticism when Alvarez was fired after just three games as national coach in 2011. But his successor, ex-Argentina boss Jose Pekerman, led Colombia to the 2014 FIFA World Cup quarter-finals – their best ever performance. Colombia defender Mario Yepes, at 38 one of the finals' oldest players, won four more caps to take him to 102. He had been worried about playing on, but right-back Camilo Zuniga said: "You have to be there – we'll do the running for you."

RE-ENTER THE MONDRAGON

Colombia goalkeeper Faryd Mondragon set a number of records at the 2014 FIFA World Cup. He became the oldest player to appear in the finals when he came on as a substitute with five minutes remaining of their first-round match against Japan, on 24 June, aged 43 years and three days, breaking the record formerly held by Cameroon's 42-year-old Roger Milla in 1994. Mondragon also set a new mark for the longest gap between FIFA World Cup appearances, two days short of 16 years. His last game had been in Colombia's final match at the 1998 tournament – a 2-0 defeat to England. This was actually Mondragon's third FIFA World Cup finals, spanning a record 20 years, but he did not appear in the 1994 tournament.

ABOVE-PAR PARAGUAY

In their eighth appearance at a FIFA World Cup, Paraguay topped their first-round group for the first time in 2010. Not only that, they went on to reach a later stage of the tournament than ever before, the quarter-finals, before narrowly losing 1-0 to Spain. Their penalty shoot-out victory over Japan in the second round (**Oscar Cardozo** converting the decisive kick) meant four South American countries made the quarter-finals – outnumbering the three European nations – for the first time. That said, there were no quarter-finals in 1930, 1950, 1974, 1978 or 1982. Paraguay followed up their impressive FIFA World Cup display by reaching the final of the following year's Copa America, only losing in the end to Uruguay (3-0).

HIGH LIFE

Bolivia and Ecuador play their home internationals at higher altitudes than any other teams on earth. Bolivia's showpiece Estadio Hernando Siles stadium, in the capital La Paz, is 3,637 metres (11,932ft) above sea level, while Ecuador's main Estadio Olimpico Atahualpa, in Quito, sits 2,800 metres (9,185ft) above sea level. Opposing teams have complained that the rarefied nature of the air makes it difficult to breathe, let alone play, but a FIFA ban on playing competitive internationals at least 2,500 metres (8,200ft) above sea level, first introduced in May 2007, was amended a month later – adjusting the limit to 3,000 metres (9,840ft) and allowing Estadio Hernando Siles to be used as a special case. The altitude ban was suspended entirely in May 2008. FIFA had changed its mind after protests by Bolivia, Ecuador and other affected nations Colombia and Peru. Other campaigners to overturn the law included Argentina legend Diego Maradona. He may have regretted his decision. In March 2009 Bolivia scored a 6-1 home win against Argentina in a FIFA World Cup qualifier. The Argentina coach was ... Maradona.

HERO GUERRERO

Paolo Guerrero's four goals at the 2015 Copa America – including a hat-trick in Peru's 3-1 quarter-final defeat of Bolivia – helped his side to a second straight third-place finish and he shared the Golden Boot with Chile's Eduardo Vargas. He then became Peru's all-time leading scorer with the only goal of their victory over Haiti in the first round of the 2016 Copa America Centenario – taking him to 27, one more than Teofilo Cubillas.

BIGGEST DEFEATS

Brazil 10 Bolivia 1
(10 April 1949)

Brazil 9 Colombia 0
(24 March 1997)

Argentina 12 Ecuador 0
(22 January 1942)

Argentina 8 Paraguay 0
(20 October 1926)

Brazil 7 Peru 0
(26 June 1997)

Argentina 11 Venezuela 0
(10 August 1975)

TIM'S TIME

Peru were coached at the 1982 FIFA World Cup by Tim, who had been waiting an unprecedented 44 years to return to the FIFA World Cup finals – after playing once as striker for his native Brazil in the 1938 tournament.

BIGGEST WINS

Bolivia 7 Venezuela 0
(22 August 1993)

Argentina 0 Colombia 5
(5 September 1993)

Colombia 5 Uruguay 0
(6 June 2004)

Colombia 5 Peru 0
(4 June 2006)

Ecuador 6 Peru 0
(22 June 1975)

Paraguay 7 Bolivia 0
(30 April 1949)

Hong Kong 0 Paraguay 7
(17 November 2010)

Peru 9 Ecuador 1
(11 August 1938)

Venezuela 6 Puerto Rico 0
(26 December 1946)

BOTERO'S ERA

Bolivia failed to reach the 2010 FIFA World Cup but did pull off one of the most eye-catching results of the qualifying campaign – a 6-1 thrashing of Argentina, who had previously been unbeaten under new coach Diego Maradona. The 1 April 2009 game in La Paz made an April fool of Maradona but a national icon of striker **Joaquin Botero,** who hit a hat-trick. A month later, however, the 31-year-old decided to quit international football, bowing out after 48 caps and a Bolivian-record 20 goals.

NOT SO FAB

Colombia full-back Frank Fabra endured a bittersweet Copa America first at the 2016 Centenario tournament when he scored for both teams in one match – no other player had done this in the competition's 100-year history. He found the net at both ends as his side lost 3-2 to Costa Rica in the first round, although Colombia did recover to qualify for the next stage and ultimately reached the semi-finals.

COOL DUDAMEL

Venezuela suffered some bad defeats when missing out on the 1998 FIFA World Cup. They ended with no wins and 13 defeats in 16 games, scoring 13 and conceding 41 goals. The losses included 4-1 to Peru, 6-1 to Bolivia and 6-0 to Chile, for whom Ivan Zamorano scored five. But their goalkeeper Rafael Dudamel had a moment to savour against Argentina in October 1996, when he scored with a direct free-kick late in the game. Venezuela still lost 5-2. Dudamel became Venezuela coach in April 2016 and, two months later, led them to the second round of the Copa America Centenario.

HOT ROD

Colombia's once most expensive ever player sadly missed the 2014 FIFA World Cup. Star striker Radamel Falcao failed to recover in time from a knee injury suffered at the start of that year. This gave the chance for his AS Monaco team-mate **James Rodriguez** to emerge as Colombia's main man, and one of the tournament's most dazzling players. He scored in all five of Colombia's matches, six goals in all – including a long-range volley against Uruguay, which opposing manager Oscar Tabarez described as one of the finest the FIFA World Cup had ever seen. Rodriguez joined Monaco for €45 million from FC Porto in May 2013. There he was joined, a few weeks later, by compatriot Falcao, who cost Monaco €60 million when they signed him from Atletico Madrid. The striker – named after the 1980s Brazil midfielder Falcao – matched Arnoldo Iguaran's Colombian scoring record against Costa Rica in June 2015, his 25th international goal. Rodriguez had already usurped Falcao as Colombia's most expensive player when Real Madrid paid Monaco a reported €80 million transfer fee in July 2014.

CHRISTIAN TRIBUTE

Ecuador's footballers dedicated their 2014 FIFA World Cup campaign to former team-mate Christian "Chucho" Benitez, who died suddenly from a cardiac arrest in July 2013 at the age of only 27. Teammate, and Ecuador's captain at the 2014 FIFA World Cup finals, Antonio Valencia had Benitez's number 11 tattooed on his arm in tribute and the number was officially "retired" by the Ecuador FA. FIFA World Cup rules, however, meant the number had to be worn, and it was given to striker Felipe Caicedo at the 2014 finals.

MOST INTERNATIONAL CAPS

Bolivia	Luis Cristaldo	93
	Marco Sandy	93
Colombia	Carlos Valderrama	111
Ecuador	Ivan Hurtado	168
Paraguay	Paulo Da Silva	137
Peru	Roberto Palacios	128
Venezuela	Juan Arango	127

RUID AWAKENING

Peru ended a 31-year wait to beat Brazil with a 1-0 win in the first round of the 2016 Copa America Centenario. It put Ricardo Gareca's side in the second round and eliminated Dunga's Brazilians. The goal was contentious, however, as Raul Ruidiaz seemed to knock the ball into the goal with his hand from Andy Polo's cross. Ruidiaz insisted he had used his thigh and denied comparisons to Diego Maradona's "Hand Of God" goal at the 1986 FIFA World Cup, claiming his strike was "thanks to God". Peru's previous win over Brazil – 2016 was only the fourth ever – had been in April 1985, when Julio Cesar Uribe got the only goal in a friendly in Brasilia. Their other Copa America defeats of Brazil were in 1953 and 1975.

CANIZA CAN DO

Centre-back and captain **Denis Caniza**, 36, became the first Paraguayan to play at four different FIFA World Cups, with his one appearance against New Zealand during the 2010 tournament. The same event brought a milestone for team-mate Roque Santa Cruz – his goal in the first-round game against Brazil equalled Jose Saturnino Cardozo's all-time Paraguayan scoring record of 25. Fellow striker Salvador Cabanas missed out on the tournament after being shot in the head with a gun in a nightclub five months earlier – though he did recover well enough to return to professional football in 2012.

MARKSMAN SPENCER

Ecuador's greatest player of all time is arguably prolific striker **Alberto Spencer**, even though he played much of his club football in Uruguay. Spencer holds the record for most goals in South America's Copa Libertadores club championship, scoring 54 times between 1960 and 1972 and lifting the trophy three times with Uruguay's Penarol. He also scored four goals in 11 games for Ecuador and once in four appearances for Uruguay. Spencer was nicknamed "Magic Head" and was even praised as a better header of the ball than Pele – the tribute coming from Pele himself.

MOST INTERNATIONAL GOALS

Bolivia	Joaquin Botero	20
Colombia	Radamel Falcao	25
	Arnoldo Iguaran	25
Ecuador	Agustin Delgado	31
Paraguay	Roque Santa Cruz	32
Peru	Paulo Guerrero	27
Venezuela	Juan Arango	23

SAFE HANDS OSCAR

Keeping clean sheets for Colombia all the way through the 2001 Copa America was **Oscar Cordoba**, who went on to become his country's most-capped goalkeeper – with 73 appearances between 1993 and 2006.

HIGHS AND LOWS FOR LOLO

Teodoro "Lolo" Fernandez scored six goals in two games for Peru at the 1936 Summer Olympics, including five in a 7–3 defeat of Finland and another in a 4–2 victory over Austria. But Peru were outraged when the Austrians claimed that fans had been invading the pitch and were even more upset when officials ordered the match to be replayed. Peru withdrew from the tournament in protest, while Austria went on to claim silver. But Fernandez and his team-mates had a happier ending at the Copa America three years later, with Peru crowned champions and Fernandez finishing as top scorer with seven goals. Only Teofilo Cubillas, with 26 goals in 81 games, has scored more for Peru than Fernandez's 24 from 32 appearances.

IVAN THE ADMIRABLE

Ecuador defender Ivan Hurtado is South America's most-capped footballer, playing 168 games after making his debut in 1992 – including five goals. He was one of Ecuador's most influential players at their first FIFA World Cup finals, in 2002, and captained them as they reached the second round of the competition four years later. Hurtado retired after an October 2014 friendly, a 5-1 away victory against El Salvador.

 AFRICA

The African confederation organized its inaugural Cup of Nations in 1957, only a year after it was founded. Egypt, with a record seven victories, were the first winners while most recent include first-timers Zambia, Nigeria in 2013 and the Ivory Coast in Equatorial Guinea in 2015. In the FIFA World Cup, South Africa, in 2010, were Africa's first finals hosts but it is still waiting for a semi-finalist (Cameroon, Senegal and Ghana have all lost quarter-finals). And in 2014, only two teams made it to the second round, where Algeria and Nigeria both lost.

Ivory Coast players celebrate after the Elephants won their second Africa Cup of Nations in Equatorial Guinea in 2015 with a penalty shoot-out success against Ghana.

FAWZI'S FIRST

Abdelrahman Fawzi became the first African footballer to score at a FIFA World Cup, when he pulled a goal back for Egypt against Hungary in the first round of the 1934 tournament – then scored an equalizer eight minutes later, to make it 2-2 at half-time. Egypt went on to lose the match 4-2, and would not return to the finals for another 56 years.

PLAY–OFF PIQUE

Morocco's qualification for the 1970 FIFA World Cup ended a 36-year African exile from the finals. No African countries played at the 1966 FIFA World Cup in Africa, with 16 possible candidate countries all boycotting the event because FIFA wanted the top African team to face a side from Asia or Oceania in a qualification play-off.

HAIL HALLICHE

Algeria became the first African nation to score four goals in one game at a FIFA World Cup finals when they defeated South Korea 4-2 at Porto Alegre in their Group H contest in the Brazil 2014 tournament. The Algerians went on to finish second in the group, behind winners Belgium, and thus qualified for the knock-out stages for the first time. In the second round they faced one of the tournament favourites, Germany, and Algeria only departed after losing a thrilling match 2-1 after extra time. One of Algeria's scorers in the victory over South Korea on 22 June – they had raced into a 3-0 half-time lead – was centre-back **Rafik Halliche** (he headed the second goal), who by the end of the 2014 tournament had made eight FIFA World Cup appearances – a new Algerian record.

AGELESS ALI

Tunisian goalkeeper **Ali Boumnijel** played in all three of his country's games at the 2006 FIFA World Cup – making him the oldest player to feature in Germany that summer, as well as only the fifth man over the age of 40 to play at a FIFA World Cup. Boumnijel conceded six goals in those three matches, against Saudi Arabia (two, in a 2-2 draw), Spain (three, in a 3-1 defeat) and Ukraine (one, in a 1-0 loss).

REDS IN A ROW

When Antar Yahia was sent off for a second bookable offence, three minutes into stoppage-time of Algeria's 1-0 defeat to the USA at the 2010 FIFA World Cup, it was not only the latest red card shown in any World Cup game not featuring extra-time. It also meant at least one player had been sent off on eight consecutive days of the 2010 tournament – a record run for any FIFA World Cup.

DJAB FAB

Barring penalty shoot-outs, no African has scored a later FIFA World Cup goal than Algerian midfielder **Abdelmoumene Djabou**. His consolation strike in a 2-1 second-round loss to Germany on 30 June 2014 was timed at 120 minutes and 50 seconds. This was the third meeting between the two teams. Algeria had followed a 2-0 friendly win in 1964 with a shock 2-1 success at the 1982 FIFA World Cup.

MOROCCAN ROLL

Morocco were the first North African country to reach the second round of a FIFA World Cup, though they were knocked out, 1-0, by eventual finalists West Germany. It was in Mexico in 1986 that Morocco were the first African team to top a FIFA World Cup group, finishing above England, Poland and Portugal. Crucial was their 3-1 victory over Portugal in their final group game, following goalless draws against the other two teams – including an England side who lost captain Bryan Robson to a dislocated shoulder and vice-captain Ray Wilkins to a red card. **Abderrazak Khairi** scored two of the goals against Portugal, while Lothar Matthaus's winning strike for Germany came with just three minutes remaining.

NORTH AFRICAN COUNTRIES' BEST FIFA WORLD CUP PERFORMANCES

ALGERIA: Second round 2014
EGYPT: First round 1934, 1990
MOROCCO: Second round 2006
TUNISIA: First round 1978, 1998, 2002, 2006

NORTH AFRICAN COUNTRIES' FIFA WORLD CUP QUALIFICATIONS

ALGERIA: 4 (1982, 1986, 2010, 2014)
MOROCCO: 4 (1970, 1986, 1994, 1998)
TUNISIA: 4 (1978, 1998, 2002, 2006)
EGYPT: 2 (1934, 1990)

NORTH AFRICA: TOP FIFA WORLD CUP GOALSCORERS

Salah Assad	(Algeria)	2
Salaheddine Bassir	(Morocco)	2
Abdelmoumene Djabou	(Algeria)	2
Abdelrahman Fawzi	(Egypt)	2
Abdeljalil Hadda	(Morocco)	2
Abderrazak Khairi	(Morocco)	2
Islam Slimani	(Algeria)	2

HOMEGROWN HERO

Of the six African countries at the 2010 FIFA World Cup, Algeria's was the only squad with an African coach – **Rabah Saadane**, in his fifth separate stint in charge since 1981. He previously led his country to the 1986 FIFA World Cup in Mexico, where they were also eliminated in the first round. Along with Honduras, the Algeria team of 2010 were one of only two countries failing to score a single goal. However, they did concede just twice in their three games: 1-0 defeats to Slovakia and the USA, and a surprise goalless draw with England – Algeria's first-ever FIFA World Cup clean sheet.

MOKHTAR RUNS AMOK

Egypt had to play only two matches to qualify for the 1934 FIFA World Cup, becoming the first African representatives at the tournament. Both games were against a Palestine side under the British mandate – and the Egyptians won both games handsomely, 7-1 in Cairo and 4-1 in Palestine. Captain and striker Mahmoud Mokhtar scored a hat-trick in the first leg, a brace in the second. Turkey were also meant to contest qualifiers against the two sides, but withdrew, leaving the path to the finals free for Egypt.

TUNISIA IN TUNE

Tunisia became the first African team to win a match at a FIFA World Cup finals, when they beat Mexico 3-1 in Rosario, Argentina, in 1978 – thanks to goals from Ali Kaabi, Nejib Ghommidh and Mokhtar Dhouib. While they share with Morocco and Algeria the North African record of reaching four different FIFA World Cups, they are the only nation from that part of the continent to qualify for three finals in a row – in 1998, 2002 and 2006. Among the players to feature in all three tournaments were 2006 captain Riadh Bouazizi, Hatem Trabelsi and **Radhi Jaidi**.

NO WAITING GAME

Morocco's 2-1 defeat to Saudi Arabia in 1994 was one of the last two games to be played simultaneously at a FIFA World Cup, without falling on a final match-day of a group. Belgium were beating Holland 1-0 at the same time, with every team in Group F having still one game to play. At later tournaments, every match has been played separately until the climactic two fixtures of any group.

NORTH AFRICA NATIONAL RECORDS

MAHREZ THE MARVEL

In spring 2016 Algeria's French-born winger **Riyad Mahrez** became the first African to be voted England's Footballer of the Year by his fellow professionals after helping minnows Leicester City to a surprise first Premier League title. When first approached by Leicester in January 2014, Mahrez thought it was Leicester Tigers rugby club showing interest, but he still signed for just £380,000. His slight build had raised doubts about his ability to thrive in England. The first Algerian to win a Premier League winners medal recalled growing up as a sports-mad "street footballer", saying: "I was always with a ball – that's why I was so skinny, I would miss dinner."

ABOUD AWAKENING

After the political upheaval in Libya in 2011, little was expected of the country's footballers at the 2012 Africa Cup of Nations. Yet they brought some joy to supporters with a surprise 2-1 victory over Senegal in their final first-round match – the first time Libya had ever won an Africa Cup of Nations match outside their own country. Their kit bore the new flag of the country's National Transitional Council. Among the star performers were Ihaab al Boussefi – scorer of both goals against Senegal – and goalkeeper and captain **Samir Aboud**, at 39 the oldest player at the tournament. Libya played their first competitive home game in the capital Tripoli since 2010 when they hosted the Democratic Republic of Congo in a 2014 FIFA World Cup qualifier in June 2013, the game ending in a 0-0 draw.

OFFICIAL INFLUENCE

The first African to referee a FIFA World Cup final was Morocco's Said Belqola, who controlled the 1998 climax in which hosts France beat Brazil 3-0. Perhaps his most notable moment was sending off France's Marcel Desailly in the 68th minute – brandishing only the third red card to be shown in a FIFA World Cup final. Belqola was 41 at the time. He died from cancer just under four years later.

STRIKING RIVALS

A homegrown hero is back at the top of Tunisia's scoring ranks after Gabes-born **Issam Jemaa** passed Francileudo Santos and now has 36 goals from 84 appearances since his debut in 2005. Jemaa began his career with Esperance but since 2005 has played his club football in France for Lens, Caen, Auxerre and Brest, in Kuwait for Kuwait SC and in Qatar for Al-Sailiya. Brazil-born Santos, by contrast, did not visit Tunisia until his late teens and only accepted citizenship at the age of 24 in 2004. Within weeks he was helping his new nation not only to host but win the 2004 Africa Cup of Nations, scoring four goals including the opener in the final against Morocco. Both Jemaa and Santos were hampered by injury ahead of the 2006 FIFA World Cup – Santos played only 11 minutes at the tournament, while while Jemaa missed out altogether. Jemaa's last two goals came in a 3–0 friendly win over Congo in August 2013, but he has not played for Tunisia since late in 2014.

NORTH AFRICA: SELECTED TOP GOALSCORERS

ALGERIA: Abdelhafid Tasfaout	35
EGYPT: Hossam Hassan	68
LIBYA: Tarik El Taib	23
MOROCCO: Ahmed Faras	42
SUDAN: Haytham Tambal	26
TUNISIA: Issam Jemaa	36

THE BLACK EAGLES HAVE LANDED

The Confederation of African Football welcomed a new and 54th member state on 10 February 2012, when the newly-independent nation of South Sudan created a new team and football association. The "Black Eagles" were not admitted in time to take part in qualifiers for the 2013 Africa Cup of Nations but hope to take part in future events – and win FIFA membership as well. Football association president Oliver Benjamin said: "We are a country that has just come out of war. We lack even the balls and the T-shirts – we don't have these in our country. Some of our players use their socks, put clothes in them, wrap them up and play with them. That is our love of football."

HURRAH FOR SALAH

Egypt have a rising star in **Mohamed Salah**. His performances at the London 2012 Olympic Games helped win him that year's Most Promising Talent award from the African Football Confederation. A week before his 21st birthday in June 2013 he scored a hat-trick against Zimbabwe in a 4-2 FIFA World Cup qualifier win and ended the campaign with six goals – only equalled by compatriot Mohamed Aboutrika and Ghana's Asamoah Gyan in Africa's 2014 qualifying rounds. His performances for both country and Swiss club Basel earned him an £11million move to English Premier League giants Chelsea in January 2014 although he subsequently moved to Italy with loans to first Fiorentina and then Roma.

HEAD–TO–HEAD

The international career of Algeria's leading scorer **Abdelhafid Tasfaout** came to an end at the 2002 Africa Cup of Nations – though it could have been a lot worse. Tasfaout was knocked out by a collision with Mali defender Boubacar Diarra which caused him to swallow his tongue, prompting fears he might not even survive – though, thankfully, he did recover. Tasfaout, who played French league football for six years, scored 34 goals in 62 games for Algeria between 1990 and 2002.

SORE LOSERS

Libya could claim the record for highest-scoring victory by an African side, having racked up a 21-0 lead over Oman during the Arab Nations Cup in April 1966. But the Oman players walked off with 10 minutes remaining, in protest at Libya being awarded a penalty, and played no further part in the competition.

NORTH AFRICA: SELECTED TOP APPEARANCES

ALGERIA: Lakhdar Belloumi	101
EGYPT: Ahmed Hassan	184
LIBYA: Tarik El Taib	77
MOROCCO: Abdelmajid Dolmy	140
SUDAN: Haitham Mustafa	103
TUNISIA: Radhi Jaidi	105

SO FARAS, SO GOOD

Ahmed Faras not only heads Morocco's all-time scoring charts, with 42 goals between 1965 and 1979, he was also the captain who lifted the country's only Africa Cup of Nations trophy in 1976 – and was named the tournament's best player after scoring three goals in six games. He had previously come on twice as a sub when Morocco made their FIFA World Cup finals debut in 1970, the first African representatives since 1934.

SUDAN IMPACT

After two second-place and one third-place finishes, Sudan became the third and last of the Africa Cup of Nations founders to lift the trophy, when they beat Ghana in the 1970 final. Hosts Sudan left it late to reach the final, with two goals from El-Issed – the second 12 minutes into extra-time – seeing off Egypt. The same player scored the only goal of the final, after 12 minutes.

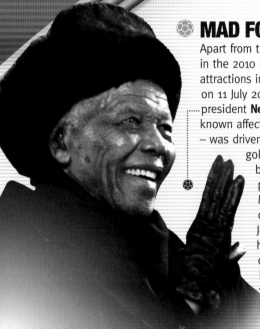

SUB-SAHARAN AFRICA FIFA WORLD CUP RECORDS

MAD FOR 'MADIBA'

Apart from the Dutch and Spanish sides competing in the 2010 FIFA World Cup final, one of the star attractions in Johannesburg's Soccer City stadium on 11 July 2010 was South Africa's legendary former president **Nelson Mandela**. The frail 91-year-old – known affectionately by his tribal name of "Madiba" – was driven on to the pitch before the game in a golf cart and given a rapturous reception by the crowd. It marked his one and only public appearance at the tournament. Mandela had hoped to attend the opening ceremony and game on 11 June, but was mourning the death of his 13-year-old great-granddaughter in a car crash the previous evening. He had been a high-profile presence at the FIFA vote in 2004 which awarded South Africa hosting rights for 2010.

GOING FOR A SONG

Two players have been sent off at two separate FIFA World Cups: Cameroon's Rigobert Song, against Brazil in 1994 and Chile four years later, and France's Zinedine Zidane – red-carded against Saudi Arabia in 1998 and against Italy in the 2006 final. Song's red card against Brazil made him the youngest player to be dismissed at a FIFA World Cup – he was just 17 years and 358 days old. Song, born in Nkanglikock on 1 July 1976, is Cameroon's most-capped player, with 137 appearances – including winning displays in the 2000 and 2002 finals of the Africa Cup of Nations. He has been joined in the national team by his nephew, Arsenal utility player Alexandre Song Billong.

MORE FOR ASAMOAH

Ghana's Asamoah Gyan has scored more FIFA World Cup goals than any other player representing an African nation. He took his overall tally to six with two strikes at the Brazil 2014 FIFA World Cup – putting him one ahead of Cameroon's Roger Milla. He also became the first African to score at three separate FIFA World Cups and his 11 matches took him level with Cameroon's Francois Omam-Biyik.

SUB–SAHARAN AFRICAN COUNTRIES' BEST FIFA WORLD CUP PERFORMANCES

ANGOLA:	First round 2006
CAMEROON:	Quarter-finals 1990
GHANA:	Quarter-finals 2010
IVORY COAST:	First round 2006, 2010, 2014
NIGERIA:	Second round 1994, 1998, 2014
SENEGAL:	Quarter-finals 2002
SOUTH AFRICA:	First round 1998, 2002, 2010
TOGO:	First round 2006
ZAIRE/CONGO DR:	First round 1974

JOLLY ROGER

Cameroon striker **Roger Milla**, famous for dancing around corner flags after each goal, became the FIFA World Cup's oldest scorer against Russia in 1994 – aged 42 years and 39 days. He came on as substitute during that tournament with his surname handwritten, rather than printed, on the back of his shirt. Milla, born in Yaounde on 20 May 1952, had retired from professional football for a year before Cameroon's president, Paul Biya, persuaded him to join the 1990 FIFA World Cup squad. His goals in that tournament helped him win the African Footballer of the Year award for an unprecedented second time – 14 years after he had first received the trophy. He finally ended his international career after the 1994 FIFA World Cup in the United States, finishing with 102 caps and 28 goals to his name.

SUB–SAHARAN AFRICAN COUNTRIES' FIFA WORLD CUP QUALIFICATIONS

CAMEROON:	7	(1982, 1990, 1994, 1998, 2002, 2010, 2014)
NIGERIA:	5	(1994, 1998, 2002, 2010, 2014)
SOUTH AFRICA:	3	(1998, 2002, 2010)
GHANA:	3	(2006, 2010, 2014)
IVORY COAST:	3	(2006, 2010, 2014)
ANGOLA:	1	(2006)
SENEGAL:	1	(2002)
TOGO:	1	(2006)
ZAIRE/CONGO DR:	1	(1974)

OH NO, YOBO

Nigeria captain Joseph Yobo set two national records when he played a second-round tie against France at the 2014 FIFA World Cup – yet his late own goal in a 2-0 defeat may make it a match he would rather forget. His appearance that day not only made him the first Nigerian international to reach a century of caps, but also meant he had played 10 FIFA World Cup games – one more than previous national record-holder Jay-Jay Okocha.

RATOMIR GETS IT RIGHT

Ghana went through four different managers during qualifiers for the 2006 FIFA World Cup, with Serbian coach Ratomir Dujkovic finally clinching the country a place at the finals for the very first time. He led them through the whole of 2005 unbeaten, winning a FIFA prize for being the most-improved team of the year. Ghana were the only African country to make it through the first round of both the 2006 and 2010 FIFA World Cups, despite having the youngest average age of any squad each time. They were again coached by a Serb in 2010, this time Milovan Rajevac.

BROTHERS AT ARMS

The Boateng brothers made FIFA World Cup history in playing against each other at the 2010 finals in South Africa. Both were also selected for the 'replay' in 2014. In 2010 Jerome played left-back for Germany while elder half-brother **Kevin-Prince**, who had switched nationalities a month earlier, was in the Ghana midfield. In the group match in 2010 Jerome Boateng switched to right-back. Germany won 1-0 in South Africa while the return in Brazil ended up 2-2. Kevin-Prince was the only brother to play a full 90 minutes, in South Africa. He was substituted during the game in Brazil while Jerome was replaced during both games. In the total 180 minutes they were on the pitch together for 'only' 117 minutes.

SUB–SAHARAN AFRICAN COUNTRIES: TOP FIFA WORLD CUP GOALSCORERS

Asamoah Gyan (Ghana) 6
Roger Milla (Cameroon) 5
Papa Bouba Diop (Senegal) 3
Samuel Eto'o (Cameroon) 3
Daniel Amokachi (Nigeria) 2
Emmanuel Amunike (Nigeria) 2
Andre Ayew (Ghana) 2
Shaun Bartlett (South Africa) 2
Wilfried Bony (Ivory Coast) 2
Henri Camara (Senegal) 2
Aruna Dindane (Ivory Coast) 2
Didier Drogba (Ivory Coast) 2
Gervinho (Ivory Coast) 2
Patrick Mboma (Cameroon) 2
Benni McCarthy (South Africa) 2
Sulley Muntari (Ghana) 2
Ahmed Musa (Nigeria) 2
Francois Omam-Biyik (Cameroon) 2

KESHI JOB

Nigeria's Stephen Keshi became the first African manager to reach the knock-out stages of a FIFA World Cup when he steered his country through Group F at the 2014 tournament in Brazil. The feat also meant Nigeria were the first African country to reach the second round of three separate FIFA World Cups, having previously done so in 1994 – when Keshi was in the team – and 1998. He announced his resignation after their second-round 2-0 defeat to France, which came despite one of several brave displays by goalkeeper **Vincent Enyeama**.

THE FOURMOST

The only two African footballers to play at four FIFA World Cups – and the only three to be named in the squads for four – are all from Cameroon. Striker Samuel Eto'o became the latest in 2014, after playing in 1998, 2002 and 2010. He emulated defender Rigobert Song, who was in the Cameroon team in 1994, 1998, 2002 and 2010. Goalkeeper Jacques Songo'o was named in the country's squads for the four FIFA World Cups between 1990 and 2002, but he only actually played in the 1994 and 1998 versions.

HOT DROG

Didier Drogba may have been raised in France but he was born in Ivory Coast and remains one of the African country's favourite sons for his actions both on and off the pitch. The Ivory Coast captain has a record 65 goals in 104 appearances for the Elephants. He has been credited with influence off the pitch, too, when he called for a ceasefire in the civil war-torn nation. He also pushed for an Africa Cup of Nations qualifier against Madagascar in June 2007 to be moved from the capital Abidjan to rebel army stronghold Bouake, in an effort to encourage reconciliation. Drogba, a two-time CAF African Footballer of the Year, captained the Ivory Coast team at the three FIFA World Cups they have reached, in 2006, 2010 and 2014, but he started only the third game in 2014.

SUB-SAHARAN AFRICA: SELECTED TOP GOALSCORERS

ANGOLA: Akwa		36
BOTSWANA: Jerome Ramatlhakwane		19
CAMEROON: Samuel Eto'o		56
GHANA: Asamoah Gyan		48
IVORY COAST: Didier Drogba		65
NIGERIA: Rashidi Yekini		37
SENEGAL: Henri Camara		29
SOUTH AFRICA: Benni McCarthy		32
TOGO: Emmanuel Adabayor		30
ZAMBIA: Godfrey Chitalu		76
ZIMBABWE: Peter Ndlovu		38

FIFTEEN LOVE

Fifteen-year-old Samuel Kuffour became the youngest footballer to win an Olympic medal when Ghana took bronze at the 1992 Olympics in Barcelona – 27 days before his 16th birthday.

KNOCKED OUT ON PENALTIES

Botswana goalkeeper and captain Modiri Marumo was sent off in the middle of a penalty shoot-out against Malawi in May 2003, after punching the opposing goalkeeper Philip Nyasulu in the face. Botswana defender Michael Mogaladi had to go in goal for the rest of the shoot-out, which Malawi won 4-1.

EAGLETS SOAR

The first African country to win an official FIFA tournament was Nigeria, when their "Golden Eaglets" beat Germany 2-0 in the final of the 1985 World Under-17 Championships.

FIRST ADE

Togo's all-time leading goalscorer – and 2008 African Footballer of the Year – **Emmanuel Adebayor** was captain during the country's only FIFA World Cup finals appearance, in Germany in 2006. They failed to win a game, but Adebayor's European club career has been more successful, with stints in France with Metz and Monaco, Spain with Real Madrid and England with north London rivals Arsenal and Tottenham Hotspur. His 2014–15 season at Spurs was disrupted, however, by a family row in which he accused his own mother of plotting witchcraft against him.

GENEROUS GEORGE

In 1995 Liberia's George Weah became the first African to be named FIFA World Player of the Year, an award that recognized his prolific goalscoring exploits for Paris Saint-Germain and AC Milan. That same year he added the European Footballer of the Year and African Footballer of the Year prizes to his collection. Weah not only captained his country, but often funded the team's travels – though he remains the only FIFA World Player of the Year whose country has never qualified for a FIFA World Cup. After retiring in 2003 after 60 caps and 22 international goals, he moved into politics and ran unsuccessfully for the Liberian presidency in 2005.

SUPER FRED

In 2007, Frederic Kanoute became the first non-African-born player to be named African Footballer of the Year. The striker was born in Lyon, France, and played for France U-21s. But the son of a French mother and Malian father opted to play for Mali in 2004, scoring 23 goals in 37 appearances before retiring from international football after the 2010 Africa Cup of Nations. As well as going down in history as one of Mali's greatest-ever players, he is also a hero to fans of Spanish side CF Sevilla, for whom he scored 143 goals, winning two UEFA Cups along the way. Only three men have scored more goals for the club.

GABON ON SONG

Gabon's leading international goalscorer **Pierre-Emerick Aubameyang** ended Yaya Toure's four-year reign as CAF African Footballer of the Year in 2016. Toure had joined Cameroon's Samuel Eto'o as a four-time winner, but Aubameyang's 41 goals for club Borussia Dortmund and country relegated him to second. Born in Laval, France, Aubameyang launched his career in Italy with AC Milan, and was the first Bundesliga player to win the award. He made his Gabon debut in March 2009, having rejected an invite to represent Italy U-19s but did play in a friendly for France U-21s.

SUB–SAHARAN AFRICA: SELECTED TOP APPEARANCES

ANGOLA: Akwa	80
BOTSWANA: Mompati Thuma	73
CAMEROON: Rigobert Song	137
GHANA: Asamoah Gyan	95
IVORY COAST: Didier Zokora	123
NIGERIA: Vincent Enyeama / Joseph Yobo	101
SENEGAL: Henri Camara	99
SOUTH AFRICA: Aaron Mokoena	107
TOGO: Abdoul-Gafar Mamah	76
ZAMBIA: David Chabala	108
ZIMBABWE: Peter Ndlovu	100

MAESTRO'S MEMORIALS

Didier Zokora, the Ivory Coast's most-capped player, bears several tattoos cherishing members of his family – chiefly his tragic younger brother Armand, whose name is inked on Didier's right forearm. The duo had both just signed professional contracts with local side ASEC Mimosas when Armand drowned off a beach in 1997 at the age of 14. On his left forearm Zokora – himself nicknamed "Maestro" – has the names of his children Sarah and Nadya while a tattoo of his wife Mariam is just above his heart. Zokora scored just once in 123 international appearances, in a 4-0 FIFA World Cup qualifier victory over Botswana in June 2008.

SHOOTING STAR

Zimbabwe's leading scorer **Peter Ndlovu** was the first African footballer to appear in the English Premier League when he made his Coventry City debut in August 1992. He ended his international career with 38 goals in 100 games for his country between 1991 and 2007 – before being appointed Zimbabwe's assistant manager in 2011. The man nicknamed "the Bulawayo Bullet" had spearheaded in 2004 the first Zimbabwe side to reach an Africa Cup of Nations finals, following that up with repeat qualification two years later. His international team-mates included brother Adam and flamboyant ex-Liverpool goalkeeper Bruce Grobbelaar. Adam Ndlovu tragically died in a car accident near Victoria Falls in Zimbabwe in December 2012. Peter was also in the car and although he suffered very serious head injuries and broken bones he managed to survive.

⚽ ASIA & OCEANIA

Asia created football history in 2002 when Japan and South Korea were the FIFA World Cup's first co-hosts and the Koreans produced Asia's best-ever finish, fourth. Australia's switch from Oceania in 2006 strengthened Asia, but the 2014 FIFA World Cup was depressing as its four nations made group-stage exits, and no Oceania team qualified. But Australia successfully staged, and won, the 2014 AFC Asian Cup. Huge funds are now being poured into Chinese football, for too long under-performing for the country's vast size and population.

Hosts of the Asian Cup for the first time in 2015, Australia became the first nation to win two different continental titles; they won the Oceania championship before becoming part of the Asian confederation.

AUSTRALIA

Victims, perhaps, of an overcomplicated qualifying system that has limited the country's FIFA World Cup finals appearances, and hampered by its geographical isolation that, in the early years, saw other sports prosper in the country at football's expense, it has taken many years for Australia to establish itself on the world football map. However, driven by new generations of players, many based with top European clubs, Australia have become regular FIFA World Cup qualifiers and in 2015 hosted and lifted the AFC Asian Cup for the first time.

AUSTRALIA RECORDS

Honours: Oceania champions 1980, 1996, 2000, 2004; Asian champions 2015
First international: v New Zealand (lost 3-1), Auckland, 17 June 1922
Biggest win: 31-0 v American Samoa, Coffs Harbour, 11 April 2001
Biggest defeat: 7-0 v Croatia, Zagreb, 6 June 1998

NATIVE HERO

Harry Williams holds a proud place in Australian football history as the first Aboriginal player to represent the country in internationals. He made his debut in 1970 and was part of the first Australian squad to compete at a FIFA World Cup finals, in West Germany in 1974.

MOMENTOUS MORI

Damian Mori's then-Australian record tally of 29 goals, in just 45 internationals, included no fewer than five hat-tricks: trebles against Fiji and Tahiti, four-goal hauls against the Cook Islands and Tonga, and five in Australia's 13-0 trouncing of the Solomon Islands in a 1998 FIFA World Cup qualifier. His international career spanned from 1992 to 2002, but he never played in a FIFA World Cup finals as Australia didn't qualify. He did, though, claim a world record for scoring the fastest goal – after just 3.69 seconds for his club side Adelaide City against Sydney United in 1996.

NEILL APPEAL

Tough-tackling Australia veteran **Lucas Neill** had to wait until his 91st international appearance before scoring his first goal for his country: the final strike in a 4-0 victory over Jordan in June 2013 that boosted their chances of reaching the 2014 FIFA World Cup. Qualification was clinched in the next game. Neill, however, was omitted from Australia's squad for Brazil and his international career ended after 96 apppearances for the Socceroos. Former Blackburn Rovers, West Ham United and Galatasary defender Neill made his Australia debut in October 1996, becoming the country's third-youngest international. His scoring record, though, pales alongside that of fellow centre-back Robbie Cornthwaite, his goal against Romania in February 2013 was his third in his first six games for Australia.

TOP CAPS

1	Mark Schwarzer	109
2	Lucas Neill	96
3	Brett Emerton	95
4	Tim Cahill	91
5	Alex Tobin	87
6	Mark Bresciano	84
=	Paul Wade	84
8	Luke Wilkshire	80
9	Tony Vidmar	76
10	Scott Chipperfield	68

CAHILL MAKES HISTORY

Tim Cahill's FIFA World Cup finals goals total is only one fewer than all other Australians combined. He scored the Socceroos' first ever finals goals, netting in the 84th (and 89th) minutes of a 3-1 win over Japan in 2006. His most spectacular was his last, a first-time volley in a 3-2 loss to the Netherlands at Porto Alegre in 2014. Sadly for him he later received a second yellow card of the finals, and so missed Australia's final match. He scored twice in 2006, once in 2010 – and received a red card in Australia's opening game – and twice in 2014. Australia's other FIFA World Cup finals scorers are Brett Holman (two), John Aloisi, Craig Moore, Harry Kewell and Mile Jedinak (all one).

AUSTRALIA'S SHOOT-OUT RECORD

Australia are the only team to reach the FIFA World Cup finals via a penalty shoot-out – in the final qualifying play-off in November 2005. They had lost the first leg 1-0 to Uruguay in Montevideo. Mark Bresciano's goal levelled the aggregate score, which remained 1-1 after extra-time. Goalkeeper **Mark Schwarzer** made two crucial saves as Australia won the shoot-out 4-2, with John Aloisi scoring the winning spot-kick. Schwarzer passed Alex Tobin to become Australia's most-capped footballer with his 88th appearance, in January 2011, in the AFC Asian Cup final defeat to Japan. Tobin had been in defence when Schwarzer made his Australia debut against Canada in 1993.

COME TO A LAND DOWN UNDER

After two near misses, **Australia** – as hosts – lifted the AFC Asian Cup for the first time in 2015, beating South Korea 2-1 after extra-time in Sydney. Juventus midfielder John Troisi scored the winner, and the other goalscorer, Massimo Luongo, was named the tournament's most valuable player. Australia became the first country to become champions of two federations, having won the OFC Nations Cup four times as members of the Oceania federation. Tim Cahill and Mark Bresciano became the first two players to have done so.

MILE 1,000

Australia captain Mile Jedinak had the honour of scoring his country's 1,000th international goal, a stunning free-kick in a 2-2 friendly draw against reigning world champions Germany in March 2015. Bill Maunder had scored the first, in a touring game against New Zealand in June 1922.

THREE-CARD TRICK

Graham Poll, in 2006, was not the first referee at a FIFA World Cup to show the same player three yellow cards. It happened in another game involving Australia, when their English-born midfielder Ray Richards was belatedly sent off against Chile at the 1974 FIFA World Cup. Reserve official Clive Thomas, from Wales, informed Iranian referee Jafar Namdar he had booked Richards three times without dismissing him. Richards played four unwarranted minutes before eventually receiving his marching orders.

BET ON BRETT

Brett Holman's goal against Ghana, in a 1-1 draw at the 2010 tournament, made him Australia's youngest marksman at a FIFA World Cup. He was 26 years 84 days old at the time, 105 days younger than Tim Cahill had been when striking against Japan in 2006. Holman added to his tally five days later, when Australia beat Serbia 2-1. Cahill himself was also on the scoresheet, though goal difference meant Australia failed to reach the second round.

TOP SCORERS

1	Tim Cahill	47
2	Damian Mori	29
3	Archie Thompson	28
4	John Aloisi	27
5	Attila Abonyi	25
=	John Kosima	25
7	Brett Emerton	20
=	David Zdrilic	20
9	Graham Arnold	19
10	Ray Baartz	18

KEWELL AND THE GANG

Alex Tobin was the captain and Englishman Terry Venables the manager when Australia surprised many and reached the first official FIFA Confederations Cup final in 1997 – although the experiences ended in a disappointing 6-0 defeat to Brazil. The two sides had drawn 0-0 in the tournament's opening group-stage, before Australia defeated Uruguay 1-0 in the semi-finals thanks to an extra-time winner by winger **Harry Kewell.**

JAPAN

The past two decades have seen great breakthroughs for Japanese football. Until the first professional league was introduced in 1993, clubs had been amateur and football was overshadowed in Japan's affections by other sports such as baseball, martial arts, table tennis and golf. Even more significantly, Japan co-hosted the 2002 FIFA World Cup – where the team reached the second round for the first time. And AFC Asian Cup wins in 1992, 2000, 2004 and 2011 were celebrated keenly as proof of surging standards.

TOP SCORERS

1	Kunishige Kamamoto	80
2	Kazuyoshi Miura	55
3	Shinji Okazaki	48
4	Hiromi Hara	38
5	Keisuke Honda	35
6	Takuya Takagi	27
7	Kazushi Kimura	26
8	Shinji Kagawa	25
9	Shunsuke Nakamura	24
10	Naohiro Takahara	23

NAKATA BLAZES THE TRAIL

Hidetoshi Nakata ranks among Japan's best-ever players. The midfielder set up all three goals in a 3-2 FIFA World Cup qualifying play-off win over Iran in November 1997. Nakata moved to Perugia in Italy after the 1998 finals, becoming the first Japanese player to star in Europe, and won a Serie A championship medal with Roma in 2001. He was followed abroad by international team-mates such as Shinji Ono, who joined Feyenoord in the Netherlands, and midfielder Shunsuke Nakamura, whose European employers included Reggina in Italy, Celtic in Scotland and Espanyol in Spain. Nakata started in three FIFA World Cup finals tournaments, making ten appearances and scoring one goal – the second in a 2-0 win over Tunisia that took Japan to the last 16 in 2002. Nakata won 77 caps and scored 11 goals, before surprisingly retiring from all forms of football after the 2006 FIFA World Cup, aged just 29.

POLITICAL FOOTBALL

Japan were surprise bronze medallists in the football tournament at the 1968 Olympic Games in Mexico City. Star striker **Kunishige Kamamoto** finished top scorer overall with seven goals. He remains Japan's all-time leading scorer, with 80 goals in 84 matches (Japan consider Olympic Games matches full internationals). Since retirement, he has combined coaching with being elected to Japan's parliament and serving as vice-president of the country's football association.

HONDA INSPIRES

After hosts Brazil, Japan were the first country to qualify for the 2014 FIFA World Cup, after Keisuke Honda's late penalty secured a 1-1 draw with Australia in June 2013. Honda had previously won two man-of-the-match awards at the 2010 FIFA World Cup and was named player of the tournament when Japan, under Italian-born coach Alberto Zaccheroni, won the 2011 AFC Asian Cup. He scored Japan's first goal at the 2014 finals, against Ivory Coast, but they lost 2-1 and exited the tournament after two defeats and a draw, prompting Zaccheroni's resignation. Honda was the first Japanese player to score at two FIFA World Cups and the first to reach three goals.

⚽ TOP CAPS

1	Yasuhito Endo	152
2	Masami Ihara	122
3	Yoshikatsu Kawaguchi	116
4	Yuji Nakazawa	110
5	Shinji Okazaki	100
6	Shunsuke Nakamura	98
7	Makoto Hasebe	97
8	Kazuyoshi Miura	89
9	Yuto Nagatomo	88
10	Yasuyuki Konno	87

⚽ THE ENDO

Midfielder Yasuhito Endo scored the opening goal of Japan's defence of their AFC Asian Cup crown, as they began the 2015 tournament with a 4-0 win over debutants Palestine. However, after winning their three group matches, without conceding a goal, Japan lost next time out, a quarter-final against the United Arab Emirates, on penalties after a 1-1 draw. It was their worst showing at the AFC Asian Cup for 19 years. Endo had the consolation becoming Japan's first international to reach 150 caps, but he left the international stage after the finals, having scored 15 times in 152 appearances.

⚽ OKAZAKI'S A–OK

Shinji Okazaki became only the fifth man to reach 100 appearances for Japan, in a match against Syria in March 2016. Two months later, the striker ended the season with an English Premier League winner's medal, having scored six goals in Leicester City's 5,000-1 triumph. He was on the scoresheet during Japan's 3-1 victory over Denmark in Bloemfontein at the 2010 FIFA World Cup, along with Keisuke Honda and Yasuhito Endo – the first time an Asian side had scored three goals in one FIFA World Cup match since Portugal had beaten North Korea 5-3 in the 1966 quarter-finals. His 48 goals for his country include hat-tricks in consecutive matches, against Hong Kong and Togo in October 2009.

⚽ SHINJI BENEFITS

Playmaker Shinji Kagawa became the first Japanese footballer to be part of an English league championship-winning side, when securing the Premier League title with Manchester United in 2012–13 – 12 months after helping his former club Borussia Dortmund win the Bundesliga in Germany. Kagawa was named 2012 AFC International Player of the Year. Yet he suffered for his art during Japan's triumphant 2011 AFC Asian Cup campaign, scoring twice in their victorious quarter-final but breaking his foot in the next game and thus missing the final.

⚽ TA–DA, TADANARI

The goalscoring hero whose extra-time goal won a record fourth AFC Asian Cup for Japan in 2011 was a man who had not even played for his country before the tournament kicked off. Striker **Tadanari Lee** made his international debut in the first-round match against Jordan – and conjured perfect timing for his first Japan goal, with 11 minutes of extra-time left in the final against Australia. His midfield team-mate Kaisuke Honda took the prize for the event's most valuable player, while forward Shinji Okazaki's first-round hat-trick against Saudi Arabia helped earn him a place in the team of the tournament.

⚽ JAPANESE GOAL GLUT

No team have scored more goals in one AFC Asian Cup tournament than Japan's 21 in six games on their way to winning the title for the second time, in Lebanon in 2000 – though the final against Saudi Arabia was settled with just a single goal, by Shigeyoshi Mochizuki. Nine different players scored for Japan during the tournament – including Akinori Nishizawa and Naohiro Takahara, who each managed five – while their team-mate Ryuzo Morioka scored once in his own net. Japan's most emphatic victory of the tournament came in the first round, 8-1 against Uzbekistan, with both Nishizawa and Takahara hitting hat-tricks.

SOUTH KOREA

"Be the Reds!" was the rallying cry of South Korea's fervent fans as they co-hosted the 2002 FIFA World Cup – and saw their energetic team become the first Asian side to reach the semi-finals, ultimately finishing fourth. South Korea also won the AFC Asian Cup the first two times it was staged (in 1956 and 1960). South Korea could well claim to be the continent's leading football side, even if AFC Asian Cup triumphs have been thin on the ground since then. The country's professional K-League is making progress and South Korean teams have won the Asian club championship 10 times.

PARK LIFE

The tirelessly-energetic midfielder **Park Ji-Sung** can claim to be the most successful Asian footballer of all time. He became the first Asian player to lift the UEFA Champions League trophy when his club Manchester United beat Chelsea in 2008, despite missing the final. He also became the first Asian footballer to score at three successive FIFA World Cups – beginning on home turf in 2002, when his goal broke the deadlock in a first-round game against Portugal, putting South Korea through to the knock-out stages for the first time ever. International team-mate Ahn Jung-Hwan and Saudi Arabia's Sami Al-Jaber are the only other Asian footballers to have scored three FIFA World Cup goals. Park became the eighth South Korean to reach a century of caps when he captained the side in their 2011 AFC Asian Cup semi-final defeat to Japan, before announcing his international retirement to allow a younger generation to emerge.

HERE COMES THE SON

South Korea have played more FIFA World Cup finals matches than any other Asian team, taking their tally to 31 with three games in 2014 – though they finished bottom of Group H. Only twice has South Korea made it past the first round and their overall record is five wins, nine draws and 17 defeats. Their 30th game, which fell on 22 June 2014, a 4-2 defeat to Algeria, was an unhappier outcome than their two previous matches on the same date: a penalty shoot-out victory over Spain in a 2002 quarter-final and a 2-2 group-stage draw with Nigeria eight years later. South Korea's second goal against Algeria was scored by Bayer Leverkusen striker **Son Heung-Min**. His father, Son Woong-Chun, a former international footballer, had unsuccessfully urged coaches during qualifying to leave his son out of the team and allow him more time to develop as a player.

SPIDER CATCHER

Goalkeeper **Lee Woon-Jae** – nicknamed "Spider Hands" – made himself a national hero by making the crucial penalty save that took co-hosts South Korea into the semi-finals of the 2002 FIFA World Cup. He blocked Spain's fourth spot-kick, taken by winger Joaquin, in a quarter-final shoot-out. Lee, who also played in the 1994, 2006 and 2010 FIFA World Cups, provided more penalty saves at the 2007 AFC Asian Cup – stopping three spot-kicks in shoot-outs on South Korea's way to third place. Lee's form restricted his frequent back-up, Kim Byung-Ji, to just 62 international appearances. But Kim did at least set a new South Korean top-flight landmark of 200 clean sheets in June 2012, at the age of 42.

SOUTH KOREAN "SUPERMAN"

Striker **Lee Dong-gook's** 16-year international career has included appearances at the 1998 and 2010 FIFA World Cups, omission from the squads in 2002 and 2014 and an injury that ruled him out of the 2006 tournament – as well as a 12-month ban in 2007 for a night out drinking during his country's third-place-finish campaign at that year's AFC Asian Cup. He also had spells with Werder Bremen in Germany and England's Middlesbrough, before returning home and becoming the all-time top scorer in South Korea's K-League – and appearing with his family in a reality TV show named The *Return Of Superman*.

TOP CAPS

1	Hong Myung-Bo	136
2	Cha Bum-kun	135
3	Lee Woon-jae	133
4	Lee Young-pyo	127
5	Yoo Sang-chul	124
6	Kim Ho-gon	120
7	Cho Young-jeung	109
8	Kim Tae-young	105
9	Lee Dong-gook	103
=	Hwang Sun-hong	103
=	Park Sung-hwa	103

TOP SCORERS

1	Cha Bum-kun	58
2	Hwang Sun-hong	50
3	Park Lee-chun	36
4	Lee Dong-gook	33
=	Kim Jae-han	33
6	Kim Do-hoon	30
=	Huh Jung-moo	30
=	Choi Soon-ho	30
9	Kim Jin-kook	27
=	Choi Yong-soo	27
=	Lee Young-moo	27

HONG SETS FIFA WORLD CUP RECORD

South Korea defender **Hong Myung-Bo** was the first Asian footballer to appear in four consecutive FIFA World Cup finals tournaments. He played all three games as South Korea lost to Belgium, Spain and Uruguay in 1990. He scored twice in three appearances in 1994 – his goal against Spain sparking a Korean fightback from 2-0 down to draw 2-2. In 1998 he started all three group games as South Korea were eliminated at the group stage. Four years later, on home soil, he captained South Korea to fourth place in the finals and was voted third-best player of the tournament. Hong coached South Korea's U-23 side to Olympic bronze at the 2012 Summer Games – beating Japan 2-0 in the medal play-off. Those goals were scored by Arsenal's Park Chu-Young and WfL Wolfsburg Koo Ja-Cheol. Hong became South Korea manager in June 2013, and was in charge of the team at the 2014 FIFA World Cup, where one group game pitted him against Belgium and their coach Marc Wilmots – the pair having played against each other at the 1998 finals.

CHA BOOM AND BUST

Even before South Korea made their FIFA World Cup breakthrough under Guus Hiddink, the country had a homegrown hero of world renown – thunderous striker **Cha Bum-Kun**, known for his fierce shots and suitable nickname "Cha Boom". He helped pave the way for more Asian players to make their name in Europe by signing for German club Eintracht Frankfurt in 1979 and later played for Bundesliga rivals Bayer Leverkusen. His achievements in Germany included two UEFA Cup triumphs – with Frankfurt in 1980 and with Leverkusen eight years later – while his performances helped make him a childhood idol for future German internationals such as Jurgen Klinsmann and Michael Ballack. His record 58 goals for the national team, in 135 appearances, included a seven-minute hat-trick against Malaysia in the 1977 Park's Cup tournament – levelling the score after South Korea had been trailing 4-1. "Cha Boom" later served as national coach, winning 22, losing 11 and drawing eight during his time in charge between January 1997 and June 1998 – but there was an unhappy ending when he was sacked two games into the 1998 FIFA World Cup, after South Korea's 5-0 defeat to the Netherlands.

OTHER ASIAN COUNTRIES

The lesser-known Asian footballing nations represent the true backwaters of world football. These may well be the countries in which true football obsession has yet to take hold, but competition between, and achievements by, these teams are no less vibrant. The regions are the home to many of the game's record-breakers – from the most goals in a single game to the most career appearances – and some of these records may never be broken.

SAUDI SURGE

Saudi Arabia marked their FIFA World Cup finals debut in 1994 by reaching the last 16, with Saeed Al-Owairan's 60-yard solo goal against Belgium in the first round a particular highlight. They have qualified three times since then but not yet reached the knock-out stages again. But they may have higher hopes for 2018. In November 2015 they set a national record by trouncing Timor-Leste 10-0, including five goals by striker **Mohammed Al-Sahlawi**. Just two months earlier he had scored his first international hat-trick when his side beat the same opponents 7-0.

IRAN TOP SCORERS

1	Ali Daei	109
2	Karim Bagheri	50
3	Javad Nekounam	39
4	Ali Karimi	38
5	Gholam Hossein Mazloomi	19
=	Farshad Pious	19
7	Nasser Mohammadkhani	18
=	Ali Asghar Modir Roosta	18
9	Vahid Hashemian	15
10	Hamid Alidoosti	14

READY NEK

Javad Nekounam is second behind Ali Daei in matches as Iran's captain (56 to 80) but he replaced his former team-mate at the top of the appearances table. Nekounam captained Iran at the 2014 FIFA World Cup, surpassed Daei's record with his 150th cap against Chile in March 2015 and bowed out with his final game against Sweden five days later. He was promptly appointed as assistant to Iran's national coach Carlos Queiroz.

IRAN'S WINNING RUN

Iran won all 13 matches across their hat-trick of AFC Asian Cup triumphs in 1968, 1972 and 1976 – and their 8-0 win over South Yemen in 1976 remains a tournament record. Among the players who enjoyed repeat success was Homayoun Behzadi, who scored in all four games in 1968 and was again on the winning side four years later. Iran's manager in 1976 was Heshmat Mohajerani, who also led the team to the quarter-finals of that year's Summer Olympics in Montreal before steering Iran to their first-ever FIFA World Cup appearance in 1978. Iran's captain at the tournament in Argentina was midfielder Ali Parvin – who had scored the only goal of the 1976 AFC Asian Cup final against Kuwait.

RANK OUTSIDERS

North Korea only narrowly lost their first game of the 2010 FIFA World Cup, 2-1 to Brazil – **Ji Yun-Nam** scoring late on for the Koreans. The match was between the tournament's highest- and lowest-ranked qualifying teams. Brazil were in first place in the FIFA rankings, while North Korea were 105th.

IRAN TOP CAPS

1	Javad Nekounam	151
2	Ali Daei	149
3	Ali Karimi	127
4	Mehdi Mahdavikia	110
5	Jalal Hosseini	101
6	Andranik Teymourian	97
7	Karim Bagheri	87
8	Hossein Kaebi	84
9	Hamid Reza Estili	82
10	Mohammad Nosrati	81

APPEARANCES IN THE FIFA WORLD CUP FINALS

Iran	4	(1978, 1998, 2006, 2014)
Saudi Arabia	4	(1994, 1998, 2002, 2006)
New Zealand	2	(1982*, 2010*)
North Korea	2	(1966, 2010)
China	1	(2002)
Indonesia**	1	(1938)
Iraq	1	(1986)
Israel	1	(1970)
Kuwait	1	(1982)
United Arab Emirates	1	(1990)

* Qualified for FIFA World Cup as Oceania Confederation member
** Played in the 1938 FIFA World Cup as Dutch East Indies

SHAKEN SHEIKH

Kuwait have qualified for the FIFA World Cup just once, in 1982 – though they made a memorable appearance when they almost walked off the field in protest at a decision. Kuwait's chief Olympic official, Sheikh Fahad Al-Ahmed, even stomped on to the pitch in Valladolid, Spain, when France's Alain Giresse scored a goal that would have given les Bleus a 4-1 lead. The Kuwaitis claimed they had heard a whistle and stopped playing and ultimately convinced referee Myroslav Stupar to disallow the strike. The game still finished 4-1 to France, though, and Kuwait were eliminated in the first round.

CHINA YET TO REALIZE POTENTIAL

China have qualified just once for the FIFA World Cup finals, in 2002, but they suffered in the finals, failing to score a goal in defeats by Costa Rica (2-0), Brazil (4-0) and Turkey (3-0). Their 2002 side included record caps-holder Li Weifeng (112 appearances) and all-time leading scorer Hao Haidong (37 goals). Better times may lie ahead, however – China were one of a record three teams (the others being Japan and South Korea) to complete the first round of the 2015 AFC Asian Cup with three wins out of three and no goals conceded, the first time they had achieved maximum points in an opening stage. The side coached by Frenchman Alain Perrin then lost 2-0 to eventual champions Australia in the quarter-finals.

MAB RULE

United Arab Emirates striker **Ali Mabkhout** became, in 2015, the first player from his nation to top the scoring charts at an AFC Asian Cup. His five goals included a strike just 14 seconds into a 2-1 victory over Bahrain – the fastest ever in the competition. His final goal was the winner in the 3-2 third-place play-off victory over Iraq and took him to 25 goals in just 37 appearances for the UAE, who enjoyed their most successful AFC Asian Cup since finishing runners-up as hosts in 1996.

PALESTINE THE PIONEERS

Palestine, then under British rule, were the first Asian team to enter the FIFA World Cup qualifiers. They lost 7-1 away to Egypt on 16 March 1934. They lost the return match at home on 6 April, 4-1. Four years later, they were eliminated by Greece, who won 3-1 in Tel Aviv and 1-0 at home. The former Palestine was split by partition in 1948. A "new" Palestine made their debut in the Asian Cup finals in 2015 in Australia, but lost all three first round games.

WORLD'S WORST

On the same day that Brazil and Germany contested the FIFA World Cup final on 30 June 2002, the two lowest-ranked FIFA countries were also taking each other on. Asian side Bhutan ran out 4-0 winners over CONCACAF's Montserrat, in a match staged in the Bhutan capital Thimphu. The winning side's captain, striker Wangay Dorji, scored a hat-trick.

IRAQ AND ROLL

One of the greatest – and most heart-warming – surprises of recent international football was Iraq's unexpected triumph at the 2007 AFC Asian Cup, barely a year after the end of the war that ravaged the country and forced them to play "home" games elsewhere. Despite disrupted preparations, they eliminated Vietnam and South Korea on the way to the 2007 final in which captain **Younis Mahmoud**'s goal proved decisive against Saudi Arabia. They were unable to retain their title four years later, losing to Australia in the quarter-finals. Mahmoud retired from international football in March 2014, ending his Iraq career with 50 goals in 124 matches – second in both categories – behind only Hussein Saeed, who scored 61 goals in 126 appearances between 1977 and 1990.

MOKH STAR

Mokhtar Dahari, who died from muscular dystrophy aged just 37 in 1991, remains Malaysia's record scorer – with 125 goals in 167 games between 1972 and 1985 – and a national hero. In 1978 Dahari, known as "Super Mokh", scored with a solo run for the halfway line in a 1-1 draw with England B, a game played before a 45,000-strong crowd in Kuala Lumpur. He is one of 11 people in the AFC's Hall of Fame, alongside compatriot Soh Chin Aun, Australia's Harry Kewell, China's Sun Wen, India's Baichung Bhutia, Iran's Homayoun Behzadi and Ali Daei, Japan's Homare Sawa and Yasuhiko Okudera, Saudi Arabia's Sami Al-Jaber and South Korea's Hong Myung-bo.

HAPPY DAEI

Iran striker **Ali Daei** became the first footballer to score a century of international goals, when his four in a 7-0 defeat of Laos on 17 November 2004 took him to 102. He ended his career having scored 109 times for Iran in 149 internationals between 1993 and 2006 – though none of his goals came during FIFA World Cup appearances in 1998 and 2006. He is also the all-time leading scorer in the AFC Asian Cup, with 14 goals, despite failing ever to win the tournament. His time as national coach was less auspicious – he lasted only a year from March 2008 to March 2009 before being fired, as Iran struggled in qualifiers for the 2010 FIFA World Cup.

ONE OF BARCA'S BEST

The first Asian footballer ever to play for a European club was also, for almost a century, the all-time leading scorer for Spanish giants Barcelona, before being finally overtaken by Lionel Messi in March 2014. Paulino Alcantara, from the Philippines, scored 369 goals in 357 matches for the Catalan club between 1912 and 1927. He made his debut aged just 15, and remains Barcelona's youngest-ever first-team player. Alcantara was born in the Philippines, but had a Spanish father, and appeared in internationals for Catalonia, Spain and the Philippines, for whom he featured in a record 15-2 trouncing of Japan in 1917. Alcantara became a doctor after retiring from football at the age of 31, though he did briefly manage Spain in 1951.

SURPRISE SEVEN

The top scorer in the Asian qualification campaign for the 2014 FIFA World Cup was Japan's eight-goal Shinji Okazaki, but he was followed by players from outside the Asian Confederation's traditional superpowers. Tied on seven goals apiece were Iraq's Younis Mahmoud, Jordan's Ahmad Hayel and Hassan Abdel-Fattah and Vietnam's **Le Cong Vinh**, whose strikes helped him to an all-time national record of 31. Jordan had never reached the fourth and final round of AFC qualifiers before and did so this time coached by Adnan Hamad, who had previously served five different stints as manager of his native Iraq.

KUWAIT IN GOLD

Kuwait's only AFC Asian Cup triumph came in 1980 – as tournament hosts. They beat South Korea 3-0 in the final, having lost by the same scoreline, to the same opponents, in a first-round group game. Faisal Al-Dakhil was Kuwait's hero in the final, scoring twice, his fourth and fifth goals of the tournament. His third proved to be the winner in a 2-1 semi-final victory over Iran.

TIE LACK

The 2015 AFC Asian Cup set a new international tournament record for consecutive matches without a draw. All 24 first-round group matches and the first two quarter-finals had a positive result after 90 minutes. Uniquely, the inaugural FIFA World Cup, in 1930, saw all 18 contests end in a decisive result. In 2015, however, Iraq (over Iran) and the United Arab Emirates (against Japan) needed penalty shoot-outs to reach the last four – and the final required extra-time.

AFC ASIAN CUP TOP SCORERS

1	**Ali Daei** (Iran)	14
2	**Lee Dong-Gook** (South Korea)	10
3	**Naohiro Takahara** (Japan)	9
4	**Jassem Al-Houwaidi** (Kuwait)	8
=	**Younis Mahmoud** (Iraq)	8
6	**Behtash Fariba** (Iran)	7
=	**Hossein Kalani** (Iran)	7
=	**Choi Soon-Ho** (South Korea)	7
=	**Faisal Al-Dakhil** (Kuwait)	7
10	**Yasser Al-Qahtani** (Saudi Arabia)	6
=	**Tim Cahill** (Australia)	6
=	**Alexander Geynrikh** (Uzbekistan)	6

PAK STRIKE MAKES HISTORY

North Korea's **Pak Doo Ik** earned legendary status by scoring the goal that eliminated Italy from the 1966 FIFA World Cup finals. The shockwaves caused by the victory were comparable to those caused by the United States' 1-0 win over England in 1950. Pak netted the only goal of the game in the 42nd minute at Middlesbrough on 19 July. North Korea thus became the first Asian team to reach the quarter-finals. Pak, an army corporal, was promoted to sergeant after the victory and later became a gymnastics coach.

ASIAN FOOTBALLER OF THE YEAR

Year	Player	Country
1988	Ahmed Radhi	Iraq
1989	Kim Joo-Sung	South Korea
1990	Kim Joo-Sung	South Korea
1991	Kim Joo-Sung	South Korea
1992	not awarded	
1993	Kazuyoshi Miura	Japan
1994	Saeed Owarain	Saudi Arabia
1995	Masami Ihara	Japan
1996	Khodadad Azizi	Iran
1997	Hidetoshi Nakata	Japan
1998	Hidetoshi Nakata	Japan
1999	Ali Daei	Iran
2000	Nawaf Al Temyat	Saudi Arabia
2001	Fan Zhiyi	China
2002	Shinji Ono	Japan
2003	Mehdi Mahdavikia	Iran
2004	Ali Karimi	Iran
2005	Hamad Al-Montashari	Saudi Arabia
2006	Khalfan Ibrahim	Qatar
2007	Yasser Al-Qahtani	Saudi Arabia
2008	Server Djeparov	Uzbekistan
2009	Yasuhito Endo	Japan
2010	Sasa Ognenovski	Australia
2011	Server Djeparov	Uzbekistan
2012	Lee Keun-Ho	South Korea
2013	Zheng Zhi	China
2014	Nasser Al-Shamrani	Saudi Arabia
2015	Ahmed Khalil	UAE

AFC ASIAN CUP–WINNING COACHES

1956	**Lee Yoo-Hyung**	(South Korea)
1960	**Wi Hye-Deok**	(South Korea)
1964	**Gyula Mandl**	(Israel)
1968	**Mahmoud Bayati**	(Iran)
1972	**Mohammad Ranjbar**	(Iran)
1976	**Heshmat Mohajerani**	(Iran)
1980	**Carlos Alberto Parreira**	(Kuwait)
1984	**Khalil Al-Zayani**	(Saudi Arabia)
1988	**Carlos Alberto Parreira**	(Saudi Arabia)
1992	**Hans Ooft**	(Japan)
1996	**Nelo Vingada**	(Saudi Arabia)
2000	**Philippe Troussier**	(Japan)
2004	**Zico**	(Japan)
2007	**Jorvan Vieira**	(Iraq)
2011	**Alberto Zaccheroni**	(Japan)
2015	**Ange Postecoglou**	(Australia)

AL-JABER TO THE FORE

Sami Al-Jaber (born on 11 December 1972 in Riyadh) became only the second Asian player to appear in four FIFA World Cup finals tournaments when he started against Tunisia in Munich on 14 June 2006. He scored in a 2-2 draw, his third goal in nine appearances at the finals. Al-Jaber played only one game in 1998 before he was rushed to hospital with a burst appendix, which ruled him out of the competition. He became Saudi Arabia's record scorer, with 44 goals in 163 matches.

A LONG JOURNEY FOR A BEATING

The first Asian country to play in a FIFA World Cup finals was Indonesia, who played in France in 1938 as the Dutch East Indies. The tournament was a straight knockout and, on 5 June in Reims, Hungary beat them 6-0, with goals from Gyorgy Sarosi, Gyula Zsengeller (two each), Vilmos Kohut and Geza Toldi.

BHUTAN DO THE BEATING

Bhutan enjoyed an unprecedented winning streak in March 2015. The world's then-lowest-ranked nation had won only two official internationals in 34 years before they beat Sri Lanka twice in a two-legged 2018 FIFA World Cup qualifier. The only goal of the first leg came from Tshering Dorji, while **Chencho Gyeltshan** – the nation's only professional footballer – struck both for Bhutan in a 2-1 victory a week later. The Himalayan nation reached the second round of the AFC qualification for the first time, but lost all three matches in this round. The reign of their Japanese coach Norio Tsukitate's ended in strange circumstances. He was fired at half-time when Bhutan trailed the Maldives 4-0 but the match ended 4-3.

A RESULT FOR REZA

No AFC nation reached the 2014 FIFA World Cup knock-out stages for the first time since 1998. Japan, South Korea, Australia and Iran all went out in the first-round, but Iran forward **Reza Ghoochannejhad**'s consolation goal in their final game, a 3-1 loss to Bosnia-Herzegovina, meant that all the finalists had scored. This had not happened at a FIFA World Cup since 1998, when the tournament first expanded to 32 teams. Ghoochannejhad also scored Iran's goal in the 1-0 win against South Korea in June 2013 that ensured they finished at the top of their final Asian qualification group.

HONG KONG HISTORY-MAKER

Chan Yuen-Ting made history when Hong Kong club Eastern won the national title in May 2016 – the 27-year-old became the first woman in the world to win a top-flight league crown as coach of a men's team. Her side pipped 41-time champions South China to the prize.

CHINA'S 4X4

Four teams carry the name of China. The China national team receives the most attention, but Hong Kong (a former British colony) and Macau (a former Portuguese colony) both retain their autonomous status for football – as Hong Kong China and Macau China respectively. Meanwhile, the independent island state of Taiwan competes in the FIFA World Cup and other competitions as Chinese Taipei.

COACH WITH THE MOST

Only one coach has twice led a team to victory in the AFC Asian Cup and he did it with two different countries. Carlos Alberto Parreira first won the trophy with Kuwait in 1980 and repeated the feat in 1988, this time in charge of Saudi Arabia. He then managed his native Brazil to FIFA World Cup glory in the USA in 1994.

AFC A-OK FOR UAE

Iran dominate AFC Asian Cup records. The have the most victories (37), most draws (18) and most goals scored (119), and share with South Korea the top tally of 62 games played. South Korea have conceded the most goals (62), Singapore and Myanmar the fewest (four), while 2015 debutants Palestine must wait to add to their record low of one goal in their favour. The next AFC Asian Cup is due to be staged by the United Arab Emirates in 2019, their first time as hosts since finishing runners-up in 1996.

LOCAL COACHES MAKE THEIR MARK

No one has won the AFC Coach of the Year award more than once since it was introduced in 1994 – though Asians have claimed the prize every year except when it went to Japan's French boss Philipppe Troussier in 2000 and South Korea's Dutch manager Guus Hiddink two years later. The women's game was recognized with triumphs for China coach Ma Yuanan in 1996, North Korea's U-20 manager Choe Kwang-Sok ten years later and Japan's FIFA Women's World Cup-winning coach Norio Sasaki in 2011. The award 12 months later went to Kim Ho-Gon, in charge of South Korean club Ulsan Hyundai.

HIGHEST ... AND LOWEST

The highest attendance for an Asian team in a home FIFA World Cup qualifier was the 130,000 who watched Iran draw 1-1 with Australia in the Azadi Stadium, Tehran, on 22 November 1997. The game was the first leg of a final playoff for the last place in the 1998 finals. Iran advanced on away goals after drawing the second leg 2-2 in Melbourne. The lowest attendance was the "crowd" of 20 that turned out for Turkmenistan's 1-0 win over Taiwan, played in Amman, Jordan, on 7 May 2001.

LOYAL UKBEKS KEEP ON GOING

Uzbekistan's seven most-capped internationals are all still active in internationals, led by midfielders Timur Kapadze (119 appearances) and two-time AFC Asian Footballer of the Year **Server Djeparov** (113) and goalkeeper Ignatiy Nesterov (92).

UAE KO ZAGALLO

Brazilian great Mario Zagallo, who won the FIFA World Cup as both player and manager, coached the United Arab Emirates when they qualified for their one and only FIFA World Cup finals in 1990. But despite his success in the Asian qualifiers, he was sacked on the eve of the FIFA World Cup itself. Zagallo was replaced by Polish coach Bernard Blaut, whose UAE team lost all three matches at Italia 90. Other big names to have managed the UAE over the years include Brazil's Carlos Alberto Parreira (another FIFA World Cup winner with Brazil), England's Don Revie and Roy Hodgson, Ukraine's Valery Lobanovsky and Portugal's Carlos Queiroz.

UZBEK RECORD-BREAKERS

Uzbekistan's Maksim Shatskikh retired from international football after winning his 61st cap, in a friendly against Oman in May 2014. He did not add to his national 34 goals that day. He equalled the top tally – 31 set by **Mirjalol Qosimov** – in a 7-3 defeat of Singapore in June 2008, and also holds the Uzbek single-game record with five goals against Taiwan in October 2007. Shatskikh has also enjoyed club success in Ukraine and, at Dynamo Kiev, he joined Qosimov as the only Uzbeks to score in a UEFA club competition. Qosimov was twice Uzbekistan's coach, 2008–10 and 2012–15, when the team were 2015 AFC Asian Cup quarter-finalists.

DOUBLE AGENT

Although North Korea's Kim Myong-Won usually plays as a striker, he was named as one of three goalkeepers in the country's 23-man squad for the 2010 FIFA World Cup. FIFA told North Korea he would only be able to play in goal, rather than outfield, though he failed to make it on to the pitch in any form during his country's three Group G matches.

THE ISRAEL ISSUE

Israel is, geographically, an Asian nation. It hosted – and won – the Asian Cup in 1964. But, over the years, many Asian confederation countries refused to play Israel on political grounds. When Israel reached the 1970 FIFA World Cup finals they came through a qualifying tournament involving two Asian nations – Japan and South Korea – and two from Oceania – Australia and New Zealand. In 1989, Israel topped the Oceania group, but lost a final play-off to Colombia for a place in the 1990 finals. They switched to the European zone qualifiers in 1992 and have been a full member of the European federation, UEFA, since 1994.

ASIAN CUP WINNERS

The Asian Cup is Asia's continental championship

Year	Winners
1956	South Korea
1960	South Korea
1964	Israel
1968	Iran
1972	Iran
1976	Iran
1980	Kuwait
1984	Saudi Arabia
1988	Saudi Arabia
1992	Japan
1996	Saudi Arabia
2000	Japan
2004	Japan
2007	Iraq
2011	Japan
2015	Australia

FROZEN OUT

Mongolia went 38 years without playing a single international between 1960 and 1998 and the country still barely stages any action, international or domestic, due to below-freezing conditions between October and June.

OCEANIA

Football in Oceania can claim some of the most eye-catching football statistics – though not necessarily in a way many there would welcome, especially the long-suffering goalkeepers from minnow islands on the end of cricket-style scorelines. The departure to the Asian Football Confederation of Australia, seeking more testing competition, was a morale blow – but benefited New Zealand out on the pitch. The finals tournament of the 2010 FIFA World Cup was the first to feature both Australia and New Zealand.

PAIA FIRE IN VAIN

No team from Oceania other than Australia or New Zealand has ever qualified for the men's football tournament at the Summer Olympics – but Fiji came close to reaching the 2012 event, only losing 1-0 to New Zealand in the final of the qualifying competition. The top scorers were the Solomon Islands, but they didn't make it out of their opening group. They recorded a best first-round goal difference of +12 – thanks to a 16-1 destruction of American Samoa, including seven goals by Ian Paia. However, defeats by Fiji and Vanuatu left them third in the four-team section.

MR SMITH GOES TO WELLINGTON

Defender **Tommy Smith** was born in Macclesfield, England, but grew up in New Zealand, giving him dual nationality. Although he played for England U-17s and U-18s, including at the 2007 FIFA U-17 World Cup, he switched his allegiance and not only played for New Zealand at senior international level, but also became their youngest ever captain. In May 2012, with senior colleagues Ryan Nelsen and Winston Reid both absent, Smith, aged 22 years and 53 days was given the armband for a game against El Salvador.

TOP SCORERS: NEW ZEALAND

1	Vaughan Coveney	28
2	Shane Smeltz	24
3	Steve Sumner	22
4	Brian Turner	21
5	Chris Killen	16
=	Keith Nelson	16
=	Jock Newall	16
8	Grant Turner	14
9	Chris Wood	13
10	Darren McLennan	12
=	Michael McGarry	12
=	Wynton Rufer	12

TOP CAPS: NEW ZEALAND

1	Ivan Vicelich	88
2	Simon Elliott	69
3	Vaughan Coveney	64
4	Ricki Herbert	61
5	Chris Jackson	60
6	Brian Turner	59
7	Duncan Cole	58
=	Steve Sumner	58
9	Chris Zoricich	57
10	Leo Bertos	56
=	Ceri Evans	56

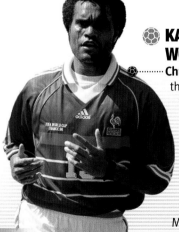

KAREMBEU A FIFA WORLD CUP WINNER

Christian Karembeu, born in New Caledonia, is the only FIFA World Cup winner to come from the Oceania region. He started for France in their 3-0 final victory over Brazil on 12 July 1998. The defensive midfielder had earlier begun against Denmark (group), Italy (quarter-finals) and Croatia (semi-finals). He played 53 times for France, scoring one goal, and was also a double European Champions League Cup winner with Real Madrid in 1998 in 2000.

RETURNING RICKI

Ricki Herbert is the only New Zealander to reach two FIFA World Cup finals. A left-back at the 1982 tournament in Spain, he then coached the country to their second World Cup appearance, in 2010. This second qualifcation came after a play-off defeat of Asian Football Confederation representatives Bahrain. Herbert resigned in November 2013 after losing a 2014 FIFA World Cup qualifying play-off to Mexico, but later took charge of The Maldives. He was succeeded by former Tottenham Hotspur reserve team coach and Bahrain manager Anthony Hudson. Herbert is one of only two New Zealand-born men to be national coach, along with Barrie Truman who was in charge between 1970 and 1976.

FLYING KAI

Australia (12) and New Zealand (nine) dominated the 25 OFC Oceania men's Player of the Year awards 1988–2012. Christian Karembeu, a French international, won in 1995 and 1998 – and compatriot **Bertrand Kai** emulated him in 2011. Kai scored 20 goals in 31 internationals, and was ten-goal top scorer when New Caledonia won the 2011 Pacific Games. Former Nantes, Nice and Monaco forward Marama Vahirua won the award as a Tahiti player in 2005.

TEHAU ABOUT THAT?

The Pacific Island underdogs of Tahiti finally broke the stranglehold Australia and New Zealand had over the OFC Nations Cup by winning the tournament when it was held for the ninth time in 2012, following four previous triumphs for Australia and four for New Zealand. Tahiti scored 20 goals in their five games at the event in the Solomon Islands – 15 of which came from the Tehau family: brothers Lorenzo (five), Alvin and Jonathan Tehau (four each) and their cousin Teaonui (two). Steevy Chong Hue scored the only goal of the final, against New Caledonia, to give the team managed by Eddy Etaeta not only the trophy but a place at the 2013 FIFA Confederations Cup in Brazil.

BAD LUCK OF THE DRAW

Despite featuring at only their second-ever FIFA World Cup – and their first since 1982 – New Zealand did not lose a game in South Africa in 2010. They drew all three first-round matches, against Slovakia, Italy and Paraguay. The three points were not enough to secure a top-two finish in Group F, but third-placed New Zealand did finish above defending world champions Italy. The only other three teams to have gone out despite going unbeaten in their three first-round group games were Scotland (1974), Cameroon(1982) and Belgium (1998).

LAUGHING ALL THE WAY TO THE BANK

New Zealand went to the 2010 FIFA World Cup with four amateur players in their 23-man squad. Midfielder Andy Barron, who worked as an investment adviser at a bank in Wellington, even made it on to the pitch as a stoppage-time substitute against reigning world champions Italy.

FIJI TIPS

Fiji – with a population of just 900,000 – secured their first ever victory at a FIFA tournament with an unexpected 3-0 defeat of Honduras at the 2015 FIFA U-20 World Cup in New Zealand. Their victory, thanks to efforts from Iosefo Verevou, Saula Waqa and a Kevin Alvarez own goal, came days after an 8-1 trouncing by Germany. Although the hosts reached the round of 16, Fiji made the relatively short trip home after a 3-0 loss to Uzbekistan.

"WORLD'S WORST TEAM" TO SILVER SCREEN

Nicky Salapu was in goal when American Samoa set an unwanted international record, losing 31-0 to Australia in April 2001 – two days after Australia had crushed Tonga 22-0. Passport problems had denied American Samoa some of their best players for the Australia game and they had to field three 15-year-olds in a side with an average age of 18. Salapu was also playing when American Samoa finally won their first competitive international, 2-1 against Tonga in November 2011 thanks to goals by Ramin Ott and Shamin Luani. This was followed by a 1-1 draw with the Cook Islands, during a 2014 FIFA World Cup qualification campaign during which American Samoa were managed by Dutch coach Thomas Rongen and followed by film crews making a documentary movie, *Next Goal Wins*. It was released in 2014 to widespread critical acclaim – including for Jaiyah Saelua, the world's first transgender international footballer. He was born biologically male but is from the Fa'afafine people, a traditional American Samoan group with both masculine and feminine traits and often described as "third-gender".

CONCACAF

The power and passion of football in the Caribbean, central and North America was illustrated dramatically at the 2014 FIFA World Cup finals. Costa Rica, Mexico and the United States all progressed beyond the group stage in Brazil, with Costa Rica's popular adventure lasting the longest. Los Ticos reached the quarter-finals for the first time in their history, only to lose to Netherlands on the lottery of a penalty shoot-out. Keeping CONCACAF squarely in focus, the United States hosted the centenary edition of the Copa America in 2016.

The opening ceremony for Copa America Centenario 2016, held in the United States, took place at Levi's Stadium, Santa Clara, California.

MEXICO

Mexico may well be the powerhouse of the CONCACAF region and are regular qualifiers for the FIFA World Cup – they did not play in the finals of the tournament on just three occasions (1934, 1974 and 1982) – but they have always struggled to impose themselves on the international stage. Two FIFA World Cup quarter-final appearances (both times as tournament hosts, in 1970 and 1986) represent their best performances to date. A football-mad nation expects more.

TOP SCORERS

1	Jared Borghetti	46
2	Javier Hernandez	45
3	Cuauhtemoc Blanco	39
4	Carlos Hermosillo	35
=	Luis Hernandez	35
6	Enrique Borja	31
7	Luis Roberto Alves	30
8	Luis Flores	29
=	Benjamin Galindo	29
=	Luis Garcia	29
=	Hugo Sanchez	29

VICTOR HUGO

Jared Borgetti may hold the record as Mexico's all-time leading scorer, but perhaps the country's most inspirational striker remains **Hugo Sanchez,** famed for his acrobatic bicycle-kick finishes and somersaulting celebrations. Sanchez played for Mexico at the 1978, 1986 and 1994 FIFA World Cups and would surely have done so had they qualified in 1982 and 1990. During spells in Spain with Atletico Madrid and Real Madrid he finished as La Liga's top scorer five years out of six between 1985 and 1990. He was less successful as Mexico coach from 2006 to 2008, the best result being third in the 2007 Copa America.

MAKING HIS MARQUEZ

Commanding centre-back Rafael Marquez made history in 2014 as the first player to captain his country at four consecutive FIFA World Cups. His four games in 2014 took him to 16 FIFA World Cup appearances, beyond Antonio Carbajal – whose 11 were spread across five not four tournaments. Marquez, who scored against Cameroon in 2014, having also registered in 2006 and 2010, is also the second Mexican to score at three different FIFA World Cups, after Cuauhtemoc Blanco. Marquez, aged 37, was a surprise choice to some when included by coach Juan Carlos Osorio in Mexico's squad for the 2016 Copa America Centenario. But in their first game against Uruguay he gave his side a 2-1 lead with just five minutes remaining, Mexico going on to win 3-1. And he oversaw their progress to the quarter-finals despite being given some brief time off to return to Guadalaraja when his wife Jayde Michel gave birth to their third child.

PRECOCIOUS PEREZ

Mexico's youngest international remains midfielder **Luis Ernesto Perez,** who won the first of his 69 caps at the age of 17 years and 308 days, against El Salvador on 17 November 1998. Less impressive was his red card in Mexico's third first-round match against Portugal at the 2006 FIFA World Cup. Hugo Sanchez was the nation's oldest player, 39 years and 251 days old for his final international, against Paraguay on 19 March 1998 – though this was a farewell game for Sanchez, four years after his previous Mexico appearance, and he was replaced in the first minute by Luis Garcia.

TOP CAPS

1	Claudio Suarez	178
2	Pavel Pardo	148
3	Gerardo Torrado	146
4	Rafael Marquez	132
5	Jorge Campos	130
6	Andres Guardado	129
7	Carlos Salcido	124
8	Ramon Ramirez	121
9	Cuauhtemoc Blanco	120
10	Alberto Garcia-Aspe	109

SUAREZ IS NUMBER THREE ALL-TIME

Only Egypt's Ahmed Hassan and Mohamed Al-Deayea of Saudi Arabia played more internationals than Mexico defender **Claudio Suarez**, who made 178 appearances. Suarez – nicknamed "The Emperor" – played in all of Mexico's four games at the 1994 and the 1998 FIFA World Cups, but had to miss the 2002 finals after suffering a broken leg. He was a member of the squad for the 2006 tournament in Germany, but did not play.

LITTLE PEA FROM A POD

When **Javier Hernandez** appeared for Mexico against South Africa on 11 June 2010, he became the third generation of his family to play at a FIFA World Cup. Hernandez – nicknamed "Chicharito", or "Little Pea" – is the son of Javier Hernandez, who reached the quarter-finals with Mexico in 1986, and the grandson of Tomas Balcazar, a member of the country's 1954 squad. Another Mexican pair were the first grandfather-grandson pairing to play at the finals. Luis Perez represented Mexico in 1930. His grandson Mario Perez played for Mexico 40 years later. Hernandez scored all three of Mexico's goals at the 2013 FIFA Confederations Cup, putting him level with Carlos Hermosillo and Luis Hernandez on 35 goals for his country – albeit in only 53 games, compared to Hernandez's 85 and Hermosillo's 90. He was ruled out of the 2015 CONCACAF Gold Cup with a fractured collarbone, but was fit for the 2016 Copa America Centenario and his goal against Jamaica moved him to within one goal of Jared Borghetti's national record 46.

SEVEN DOWN

Mexico's shock 7-0 trouncing by Chile in the quarter-finals of the 2016 Copa America Centenario was their heaviest defeat in an official competition – and brought to an end a 22-match unbeaten run, a Mexican international record. Their previous biggest tournament defeat had been a 6-0 loss to West Germany at the 1978 FIFA World Cup. What made this defeat against Chile even more painful was that it came in front of a 70,547 crowd of mainly Mexican supporters in the Levi's Stadium in Santa Clara, California.

MEXICO BEATS EARTHQUAKE

Mexico stepped in to host the 1986 FIFA World Cup finals after the original choice, Colombia, pulled out in November 1982. FIFA chose Mexico as the replacement venue because of its stadiums and infrastructure, still in place from the 1970 finals. The governing body turned down rival bids from Canada and the United States. Mexico had to work overtime to be ready for the finals, after the earthquake of 19 September 1985, which killed an estimated 10,000 people in central Mexico and destroyed many buildings in Mexico City.

ROSAS NETS HISTORIC PENALTY

Mexico's Manuel Rosas scored the first penalty ever awarded in the FIFA World Cup finals when he converted a 42nd-minute spot-kick in his country's match against Argentina in 1930. Rosas scored again in the 65th minute, but it was too little too late for the Mexicans: they crashed to a 6-3 defeat.

GUARD OF HONOUR

Versatile wide man **Andres Guardado** was just 19 when making his Mexico debut in December 2005. He featured in three FIFA World Cups – in 2006, 2010 and 2014, and scored crucial goals during Mexico's triumphant 2011 CONCACAF Gold Cup run. For the tournament's 2015 edition, the 28-year-old was captain and elder statesman. He and other senior players were saved for the 2015 CONCACAF Gold Cup rather than taking part in the Copa America as guests earlier that summer. Others given similar treatment included Giovani, Jonathan Dos Santos, Carlos Vela and Guillermo Ochoa. Guardardo scored the opening goal of the 2015 CONCACAF Gold Cup final as Mexico beat Jamaica 3-1. After the 2016 Copa America Centenario he was sixth all-time on the caps list with 129.

UNITED STATES

Some of football's biggest names – from Pele to David Beckham – have graced the United States' domestic leagues over the years, and the country is one of only 15 countries to have had the honour of hosting a FIFA World Cup, but it is still a minority sport in the world's most powerful country. However, following a series of impressive performances on the world stage, especially at the Brazil 2014 World Cup, and a huge upsurge in support, the expectation is that the situation will soon change.

TOP CAPS

1	Cobi Jones	164
2	Landon Donovan	157
3	Jeff Agoos	134
4	Clint Dempsey	130
5	Marcelo Balboa	127
6	DaMarcus Beasley	123
7	Michael Bradley	121
8	Claudio Reyna	112
9	Carlos Bocanegra	110
=	Paul Caligiuri	110

ALTIDORE OPENS THE FLOODGATES

Jozy Altidore became the United States' youngest scorer of an international hat-trick in a 3-0 victory over Trinidad and Tobago on 1 April 2009, aged 19 years and 146 days. But he endured a 15-month barren spell between November 2011 and June 2013, when he scored the opener in a 4-3 defeat of Germany in a Washington DC friendly marking America's Centennial. He then scored against Jamaica, Panama and Honduras to equal a national record of scoring four games in a row, joining William Lubb, Eric Wynalda, Eddie Johnson, **Brian McBride** and Landon Donovan. Altidore's scoring spree came in a 2012–13 season in which he also set a US record for goals in a European club league, with 31 for Dutch club AZ Alkmaar. Sadly his 2014 FIFA World Cup was ended by a hamstring injury 23 minutes into the opening game against Ghana.

CALIGIURI'S SHOT MAKES HISTORY

The US's FIFA World Cup qualifying win in Trinidad, on 19 November 1989, is regarded as a turning point in the country's football history. The team included just one full-time professional, Paul Caligiuri, of (West) German second division club Meppen. He scored the only goal of the game with a looping shot after 31 minutes to take the US to their first finals for 40 years. Trinidad's goalkeeper, Michael Maurice, claimed to have been blinded by the sun, but the win raised the profile of the US team hugely, despite a first-round elimination in the 1990 FIFA World Cup.

LANDON HOPE AND GLORY

The US's all-time leading scorer **Landon Donovan** was the star of their 2010 FIFA World Cup campaign. He scored three goals in four matches, including a stoppage-time winner against Algeria that meant his side finished top of Group C. His four displays at the tournament meant he featured in 13 FIFA World Cup matches for the USA, two ahead of Earnie Stewart, Cobi Jones and DaMarcus Beasley. His goal in the second-round loss to Ghana also made him the USA's all-time top scorer in the finals, with five – one more than 1930 hat-trick hero Bert Patenaude and Clint Dempsey, who scored twice in 2014. He was the first man to score more than one hat-trick for the US, with four goals against Cuba in July 2003 and trebles versus Ecuador in March 2007 and Scotland in May 2012. Jozy Altidore registered two hat-tricks, against Trinidad & Tobago in April 2009 and Bosnia & Herzegovina in August 2013, while 10 others have one each.

HIGH–POWERED BACKING

US president Barack Obama was among the millions of Americans who enthused over the 2014 FIFA World Cup like never before. Many millions tuned in to watch the games in their homes – it was estimated 25 million for the team's 2-2 draw with Portugal in the group stage – and millions more watched in bars and clubs. Team USA also faced Joachim Low's Germany in the first round – pitting coach Jurgen Klinsmann against his native land, the country he had led at the 2006 FIFA World Cup with Low as his assistant. Low's men won 1-0 to top Group G, with the USA second. Then some 28,000 fans crowded into Chicago's Soldier Field for big-screen coverage of the USA's second-round match against Belgium. They lost, bravely, 2-1 after extra-time – despite goalkeeper Tim Howard making a FIFA World Cup record 16 saves.

PAYING HIS DEUCE

The United States became the first CONCACAF nation to have two players who have now reached a half-century of goals apiece. **Clint Dempsey** is now closing in on Landon Donovan's national record, after scoring his 50th for his country from the penalty spot against Costa Rica in the first round of the 2016 Copa America Centenario. Dempsey – nicknamed "Deuce" - previously scored just 30 seconds into the USA's first game at the 2014 FIFA World Cup, against Ghana – the fifth fastest goal in the tournament's history. Also that summer, DaMarcus Beasley became the first American to play at four different FIFA World Cups.

ENGLAND STUNNED BY GAETJENS

The US's 1-0 win over England on 29 June 1950 ranks among the biggest surprises in FIFA World Cup history. England, along with hosts Brazil, were joint favourites to win the trophy. The US had lost their last seven matches, scoring just two goals. Joe Gaetjens scored the only goal, in the 37th minute, diving to head Walter Bahr's cross past goalkeeper Bert Williams. England dominated the game, but US keeper Frank Borghi made save after save. Defeats by Chile and Spain eliminated the US at the group stage, but their victory over England remains the greatest result in the country's football history.

MAGIC CHRISTIAN

Striker **Christian Pulisic** became the United States' youngest international goalscorer when he netted against Bolivia, aged 17 years and 253 days, in May 2016. The Philadelphia native moved to Germany as a 16-year-old in 2015 to sign for Borussia Dortmund. He was joined there a year later by his cousin Will, a goalkeeper who has played for the USA's U-17s. A month before Christian Pulisic's first goal for his country, he got his first for Dortmund, becoming the youngest non-German to score in the Bundesliga.

TOP SCORERS

1	Landon Donovan	57
2	Clint Dempsey	52
3	Jozy Altidore	34
=	Eric Wynalda	34
5	Brian McBride	30
6	Joe-Max Moore	24
7	Bruce Murray	21
8	Eddie Johnson	19
9	DaMarcus Beasley	17
=	Earnie Stewart	17

"OLD MAN" HAHNEMANN

Goalkeeper Marcus Hahnemann became the US's oldest international when he faced Paraguay on 29 March 2011 at the age of 38 years and 286 days. That was the last of his nine caps, testament to the US's goalkeeping strength in depth – Kasey Keller (101 caps), Tim Howard (104) and Brad Friedel (82) were among his contemporaries. Howard has played in the most USA wins – 55 in 109 appearances – two more than Keller (53 in 102). But Keller still holds the US record for clean sheets with 37, followed by Howard's 36 and Tony Meola's 32.

KEEPING UP WITH JONES

His dreadlocked hair helped catch the attention, but **Cobi Jones**'s raiding runs down the wing also made him one of the host country's most high-profile performers at the 1994 FIFA World Cup. Jones went on to become the US's most-capped player, with 164 international appearances between 1992 and 2004. When he finally retired from all forms of the game in 2007, his number 13 shirt was officially "retired" by the Los Angeles Galaxy – the first time a Major League Soccer club had honoured a player in such a way. Jones had been with the Galaxy since the MLS was launched in 1996 and later served the club as assistant coach and caretaker manager.

Mexico and the United States (with 25 FIFA World Cup finals appearances between them) are clearly the powerhouses of the CONCACAF region, which takes in North and Central America and the Caribbean. But Mexico only reached the 2014 finals via a play-off, after finishing behind automatic qualifiers USA, Honduras and Costa Rica. The surprising Costa Ricans were one of the stand-out performers in the finals, outdoing their Confederation rivals by reaching the quarter-finals.

DWAYNE'S REIGN

Canada's all-time leading goalscorer with 22, **Dwayne De Rosario** ended his footballing career in fitting style, playing in a January 2015 international friendly against Iceland – and he scored his team's goal in a 1-1 draw. De Rosario's 18-year playing career took in five different Major League Soccer clubs – including two stints with Toronto FC. When he played for DC United, he registered the fastest ever MLS hat-trick, in nine minutes. He was part of the Canada side which lifted their first CONCACAF Gold Cup in 2000, although team-mate Carlo Carazzin finished tournament top scorer with four goals. De Rosario could also claim to be a footballing rarity in being vegetarian and was even vegan for ten years until taking up fish in 2004.

KEYLOR IS KEY

Costa Rica made their FIFA World Cup finals debut in 1990 and goalkeeper Luis Gabelo Conejo shared the best goalkeeper award with Argentina's Sergio Goycochea as his displays helped his team reach the knock-out stages. "Los Ticos" did even better in 2014 and while goalscorers **Joel Campbell** and Bryan Ruiz impressed, again a goalkeeper was crucial: **Keylor Navas** was named man of the match four times in five games. Costa Rica went to the quarter-finals, where the Netherlands beat them, but only on penalties. They had topped the so-called "Group Of Death" by beating two former FIFA World Cup winners, Uruguay and Italy, and drawing with another, England. Navas conceded only two goals at the finals and his penalty shoot-out save from Theofanis Gekas helped his side past Greece in the second-round. Costa Rica became only the second CONCACAF side, after Mexico in 1986, to go out without losing a game in regulation-time.

ALL FOR EL SALVADOR

El Salvador can claim to be the first Central American country – other than Mexico or the United States – to have qualified for the FIFA World Cup twice, doing so in 1970 and 1982. Recent years have brought more struggles, however, although left-back Alfredo Pacheco became his country's pride and most-capped player with 86 appearances between 2002 and 2013. His life ended tragically, however, with a life ban for match-fixing in 2013 followed by his fatal shooting at a petrol station two years later at the age of 33.

COSTA RICA WIN WITHOUT A CROWD

The lowest-ever attendance for a CONCACAF FIFA World Cup qualifier was for the Costa Rica–Panama game on 26 March 2005. FIFA ordered the game, staged at the Saprissa Stadium in San Jose, to be played behind closed doors after missiles were thrown at visiting players and the match officials when Mexico won there 2-1 on 9 February. The game was known as "the ghost match". Costa Rica beat Panama 2-1, thanks to a Roy Myrie goal in the first minute of stoppage time.

CELSO LIKE HIS FATHER

Costa Rica playmaker Celso Borges was delighted, in 2014, to emulate his father by reaching the knock-out stages of the FIFA World Cup. He actually went one better as he scored the first penalty of Los Ticos' 5-3 shoot-out defeat of Greece in the second round. His Brazilian-born father, Alexandre Borges Guimares, played at the 1990 FIFA World Cup and set up the late winner scored by Hernan Medford against Sweden to take the FIFA World Cup finals debutants beyond the first round. The man affectionately known as "Guima" was Costa Rica's coach at both the 2002 and 2006 FIFA World Cup finals, but they failed to go beyond the group stage on either occasion.

REGGAE BOYZ STEP UP

In 1998, Jamaica became the first team from the English-speaking Caribbean to reach the FIFA World Cup finals. The "Reggae Boyz", as they were nicknamed, included several players based in England. They were eliminated at the group stage, despite beating Japan 2-1 in their final game thanks to two goals by Theodore Whitmore. They had earlier lost 3-1 to Croatia and 5-0 against Argentina.

CONCACAF TEAMS IN THE FIFA WORLD CUP FINALS

Appearances made by teams from the CONCACAF region at the FIFA World Cup finals

1	Mexico	15
2	US	10
3	Costa Rica	4
4	Honduras	3
5	El Salvador	2
6	Canada	1
=	Cuba	1
=	Haiti	1
=	Jamaica	1
=	Trinidad & Tobago	1

BROTHERS IN ARMS

Honduras became the first team to field not one, not two, but three siblings at a FIFA World Cup, when they picked defender Johnny, midfielder Wilson and striker Jerry Palacios in the 2010 squad. Stoke City defensive midfielder **Wilson Palacios** was perhaps the most famous and acclaimed player in the first Honduras side to reach a FIFA World Cup in 28 years. Like the 1982 side, though, Reinaldo Rueda's men went three games without a win. An older brother, Milton Palacios, played 14 times as a defender for Honduras between 2003 and 2006. Both Jerry and Wilson made it into the 2014 FIFA World Cup squad, but it was not a happy time, especially for Wilson, who was sent off in the opener against France, and Honduras lost all three matches, but did at least score in the defeat against Ecuador.

CUBA SHOW THE WAY

In 1938, Cuba became the first island state of the CONCACAF region to reach the FIFA World Cup quarter-finals. They drew 3-3 with Romania after extra-time in the first round, then won the replay 2-1 with goals by Hector Socorro and Carlos Oliveira after trailing at half-time. They were thrashed 8-0 by Sweden in the last eight. Haiti were the next Caribbean island to play in the finals, in 1974. They lost all three group games, 3-1 to Italy, 7-0 against Poland and 4-1 to Argentina.

SCALING THE HEIGHTS

In the school of Guatemalan goalscorers, **Carlos Ruiz** – nicknamed "Pescado" or "Fish" – swims alone. His earned his 100th cap, scoring twice in a 3-3 draw with Paraguay in August 2012, giving him 50 goals. Despite a few international retirements, his latest return, for the 2018 FIFA World Cup qualifiers, made him the second Guatemalan – after Juan Manuel Funes – to appear in five qualification campaigns. No one has scored more FIFA World Cup qualifiers goals (32) without reaching the tournament itself. His 61st international goal was in a 7-1 defeat to Armenia in May 2016.

STERN OPPOSITION

Only ten men have netted more than the 70 international goals – in 114 matches – scored by Trinidad and Tobago's **Stern John** between his debut in 1995 and his final game in 2011. He was Trinidad and Tobago's top scorer and second-highest appearance-maker, behind midfielder Angus Eve – who quit the international scene with 117 caps when omitted from the squad for the 2006 FIFA World Cup. John played in Germany and, after a brief retirement from club football, returned at the age of 34 in January 2014 to play for WASA FC in his homeland's top-flight.

LOVE HAITI

Italy goalkeeper Dino Zoff's international record of 1,142 minutes without conceding a goal was broken at the 1974 FIFA World Cup by Emmanuel Sanon, Haiti's all-time leader in caps (100) and goals (47). He also scored Haiti's other goal at those finals, against Argentina. Recent promise saw a 2-2 friendly draw with Italy in June 2013 and a place at the 2016 Copa America Centenario.

PART 2:
FIFA ALL-TIME RECORDS
WORLD CUP

Germany, in Brazil, became the third country to win the FIFA World Cup at least four times, the same as Italy. However, Brazil remain the record-holders, with five victories, inspired by superstars from Pele and Garrincha to Ronaldo and Ronaldinho. Argentina and Uruguay (two each) are the other South American winners, with past champions from Europe being England, France and Spain (one apiece). Germany's 2014 glory in Brazil was their first FIFA World Cup as Germany, their first three coming as West Germany.

Four-star joy for Germany as their players show off the FIFA World Cup after winning the 2014 Final in Brazil and thus earning the right to have four stars on their shirts – one for each FIFA World Cup won by the nation.

FIFA QUALIFIERS
WORLD CUP

BALLON D'ORIBE

Mexico booked the final spot at the 2014 FIFA World Cup by beating Oceania representatives New Zealand 9-3 on aggregate in a two-legged November 2013 play-off. Caretaker manager Miguel Herrera – Mexico's fourth boss of the year – earned himself the job permanently by masterminding wins by 5-1 at home and 4-2 away. His squad relied purely on domestic-based players, meaning there were no European-based stars such as Villarreal's Giovani dos Santos or Manchester United's Javier Hernandez. The goalscoring hero was **Oribe Peralta**, who scored five goals in the two games – including the first three of the 4-2 victory in Wellington's Westpac Stadium.

T&T AT FULL STRETCH

Trinidad and Tobago share the record for the most games played to qualify for a FIFA World Cup finals. They played 20 in reaching the 2006 finals, beginning with 2-0 away and 4-0 home wins over the Dominican Republic in the preliminaries. T&T then finished second behind Mexico at the four-team first group stage to reach the six-team final group. After finishing fourth, they had to play off against Bahrain and won 2-1 on aggregate. Uruguay matched that figure in 2010, with 18 South America group matches and a two-legged play-off.

UAE IN A SQUEEZE

The **United Arab Emirates** reached the finals in 1990 by recording just one win and scoring only four goals in the Asian final round. They drew four of their five matches, but beat China 2-1 to qualify in second place behind South Korea.

BIG BOS MAN

Bosnia and Herzegovina were the only first-time qualifiers among the 32 nations at the 2014 FIFA World Cup. After losing to Portugal in play-offs for both the 2010 FIFA World Cup and the 2012 UEFA European Championship, they secured a place at the 2014 tournament by topping their qualification group ahead of Greece on goal difference. Their coach since 2009 was Bosnian-born former Yugoslavia and Paris Saint-Germain midfielder Safet Susic.

FIFA OPENS WORLD CUP TO THE WORLD

FIFA has enlarged the World Cup finals twice since 1978, to take account of the rising football nations of Africa and Asia. The rise in interest is reflected in the massive number of sides entering the competition – 204 for the 2014 event. Brazilian **João Havelange**, FIFA president from 1974 to 1998, enlarged the organization both to take advantage of commercial opportunities and to give smaller nations a chance. The number of teams in the finals was first increased from 16 to 24 for the 1982 finals in Spain, with an extra place given for Africa and Asia and a chance for a nation from Oceania to reach the finals. The number of finalists was further increased to 32 for the 1998 tournament in France.

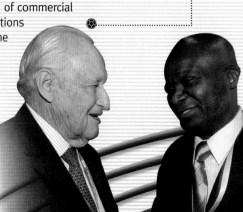

TAKING AIM

The 2014 World Cup culminated in a final staged in Rio's Maracana Stadium. Some 203 initially entered the qualifying competition – two fewer than the record 205 tilting at South Africa in 2010. The Bahamas and Mauritius subsequently later withdrew from the 2014 running, bringing the Brazil-bound contenders down to 201. Six more FIFA member states were missing, including the already-qualified hosts. New independent country South Sudan joined FIFA too late to compete, while four more nations opted not to take part this time: Bhutan, Brunei, Guam and Mauritania.

ALL–TIME QUALIFICATIONS BY REGIONAL CONFEDERATION

1	Europe	231
2	South America	80
3	Africa	39
=	North/Central America & Caribbean	39
5	Asia	32
6	Oceania	4

THE FIRST SHOOT–OUT

The first penalty shoot-out in qualifying history came on 9 January 1977 when Tunisia beat Morocco 4-2 on spot-kicks after a 1-1 draw in Tunis. The first game, in Casablanca, had also finished 1-1. Tunisia went on to qualify for the finals.

SPANISH INVINCIBLES

Several countries have qualified for a FIFA World Cup without losing or even drawing a single game. But the Spain side who cruised their way through to the 2010 tournament in South Africa were the first to do so while playing as many as 10 matches. Qualifying for the same finals from a smaller group, Holland won eight games out of eight. West Germany also went through eight matches without dropping a point in reaching the 1982 FIFA World Cup in Spain, and Brazil won six out of six in qualifying for the 1970 competition – at which Mario Zagallo's men won another six out of six on their way to lifting the trophy.

BAH HUMBUG

The Bahamas failed to qualify for Brazil despite winning all their matches – that is, both of them. The CONCACAF country beat Turks and Caicos Islands 4-0 and then 6-0 in their first-round tie, but then withdrew from the competition because rebuilding work on their Thomas A Robinson Stadium was not completed in time for their second-round group games.

THE GROWTH OF THE QUALIFYING COMPETITION

This charts the number of countries entering qualifiers for the FIFA World Cup finals. Some withdrew before playing.

World Cup	Teams entering
Uruguay 1930	-
Italy 1934	32
France 1938	37
Brazil 1950	34
Switzerland 1954	45
Sweden 1958	55
Chile 1962	56
England 1966	74
Mexico 1970	75
West Germany 1974	99
Argentina 1978	107
Spain 1982	109
Mexico 1986	121
Italy 1990	116
USA 1994	147
France 1998	174
Japan/South Korea 2002	199
Germany 2006	198
South Africa 2010	205
Brazil 2014	203
Russia 2018	210

BYERS MARKS IT

Three players shared the title of 11-goal top scorer in qualifiers for the 2014 FIFA World Cup: Dutch striker Robin van Persie and Uruguay's Luis Suarez, whose sides both qualified for Brazil, and Belize's **Deon McCaulay**. Antigua and Barbuda's Peter Byers was the only man to score two separate hat-tricks during the campaign, both against the United States Virgin Islands.

THE FASTEST SUBSTITUTION

The quickest-ever substitution in the history of FIFA World Cup qualifiers came on 30 December 1980, when North Korea's Chon Byong Ju was substituted in the first minute of his country's home game against Japan.

KOSTADINOV STUNS FRANCE

On 17 November 1993, in the last game of the Group Six schedule, Bulgaria's Emil Kostadinov scored one of the most dramatic goals in qualifying history to deny France a place at the 1994 finals. France seemed to be cruising with the score at 1-1 in stoppage time, but Kostadinov earned Bulgaria a shock victory after David Ginola lost possession. The Bulgarians reached the semi-finals of the tournament in the United States, losing 2-1 to Italy.

PALMER BEATS THE WHISTLE

Carl Erik Palmer's second goal in Sweden's 3-1 win over the Republic of Ireland in November 1949 was one of the most bizarre in qualifying history. The Irish defenders stopped, having heard a whistle, while Palmer ran on and put the ball in the net. The goal stood, because the whistle had come from someone in the crowd, not the referee. The 19-year-old forward went on to complete a hat-trick.

BWALYA LEAVES IT LATE

Zambia's **Kalusha Bwalya** is the oldest player to have scored a match-winning goal in a FIFA World Cup qualifying match. The 41-year-old netted the only goal against Liberia on 4 September 2004 after coming on as a substitute. He had also scored in his first qualifier, 20 years previously, in Zambia's 3-0 win over Uganda.

AUSTRALIA'S INCREDIBLE GOAL SPREE

Australia set a FIFA World Cup qualifying record in 2001, one that is unlikely to be beaten, as the Socceroos scored 53 goals in the space of two days. The details:

9 April 2001, Sydney: Australia 22, Tonga 0
Australia scorers: Scott Chipperfield 3, 83 mins; Damian Mori 13, 23, 40; John Aloisi 14, 24, 37, 45, 52, 63; **Kevin Muscat** (No. 2, right) 18, 30, 54, 58, 82; Tony Popovic 67; Tony Vidmar 74; David Zdrilic 78, 90; Archie Thompson 80; Con Boutsiania 87

11 April 2001, Sydney: Australia 31, American Samoa 0
Australia scorers: Boutsiania 10, 50, 84 mins; Thompson 12, 23, 27, 29, 32, 37, 42, 45, 56, 60, 65, 68, 88; Zdrilic 13, 21, 25, 33, 58, 66, 78, 89; Vidmar 14, 80; Popovic 17, 19; Simon Colosimo 51, 81; Fausto De Amicis 55

THOMPSON SETS UNLIKELY MARK

Archie Thompson eased past Iran striker Karim Bagheri's record for the number of goals in a single qualifying match (seven) as Australia thrashed American Samoa 31-0 on 11 April 2001. He netted 13 goals. David Zdrilic also beat Bagheri's total with eight goals. Two days earlier, Australia had previously smashed Iran's scoring record after completing a 22-0 victory over Tonga.

THE FASTEST GOAL

Davide Gualtieri, of minnows San Marino, scored the fastest goal in qualifying history when he netted after just nine seconds against England on 17 November 1993. England went on to win 7-1 but still failed to qualify.

CRIS IS IT

The UEFA play-off between Portugal and Sweden was widely billed as Cristiano Ronaldo versus Zlatan Ibrahimovic. Neither player disappointed and the pair were the only ones to hit the scoresheet, as Portugal won 1-0 at home and then 3-2 away. Ibrahamovic's second-leg double was not enough since two late goals from Ronaldo completed his second hat-trick of the campaign. His first international hat-trick had come in 15 minutes against Northern Ireland during the group stages, taking him above Eusebio in Portugal's list of all-time scorers – and his Sweden treble put him joint top with Pauleta.

REPEAT OFFENDERS

Three players were sent off twice during qualifiers for the 2014 FIFA World Cup: Bulgaria's Svetoslav Dyakov, Tanzania's Aggrey Morris and Montenegro's Savo Pavicevic. A total of 100 red cards and 2,916 yellow cards were shown throughout the campaign, while 2,286 goals were scored – an average of 2.8 per game. The highest-scoring teams were Germany and New Caledonia (36 apiece), Argentina (35), the Netherlands (34) and England (31).

RECORD HAT–TRICK

Abdel Hamid Bassiouny of Egypt scored the fastest-ever hat-trick in qualifying history in their 8-2 win over Namibia on 13 July 2001. He netted three times in just 177 seconds between the 39th and 42nd minutes.

YOUNGEST AND OLDEST

The youngest player to appear in the FIFA World Cup qualifiers is Souleymane Mamam of Togo, who was 13 years 310 days when he played against Zambia on 6 May 2001. The oldest was MacDonald Taylor, who was 46 years, 180 days when he played for the Virgin Islands against St Kitts Nevis on 18 February 2004.

DAEI TOPS THE SCORERS

Iran's **Ali Daei** is the all-time top scorer in FIFA World Cup qualifiers. His nine goals in the 2006 qualifying campaign took his total to 30, nine ahead of the previous joint record-holder, Japan's Kazu Miura. Daei also scored seven goals in the 1994 qualifiers, four in the 1998 preliminaries and ten in 2002.

HORST THE FIRST TO GIVE WAY

The first player to be substituted during a FIFA World Cup qualifier was West Germany's **Horst Eckel**, when he was replaced by Richard Gottinger in their 3-0 victory over the short-lived protectorate of Saarland in October 1953. Eckel would go on to play on the right side of midfield in the side that beat Hungary in the 1954 FIFA World Cup final, while Gottinger's delayed appearance against Saarland was his first and last for his country. By the time of the 1958 FIFA World Cup qualifiers, Saarland had been integrated within West Germany.

UNITED STATES LEAVE IT LATE

The latest of all qualifying play-offs took place in Rome on 24 May 1934, when the USA beat Mexico 4-2 to clinch the last slot in the FIFA World Cup finals. Three days later, the Americans were knocked out 7-1 by hosts Italy in the first round of the tournament.

ITALY FORCED TO QUALIFY

Italy are the only host country who have been required to qualify for their own tournament. The 1934 hosts beat Greece 4-0 to go through. FIFA decided that, for the 1938 finals, the holders and the hosts would qualify automatically. That decision was changed for the 2006 finals. Since then, only the hosts have been exempt from qualifying, though South Africa played in the second round of qualifying for 2010. This is because it doubled up as qualifiers for the 2010 Africa Cup of Nations.

TURKEY THROUGH ON LUCK OF THE DRAW

Turkey were the first team to qualify for the FIFA World Cup finals after the drawing of lots. Their play-off against Spain, in Rome on 17 March 1954, ended 2-2. Qualification was decided by a 14-year-old Roman boy, Luigi Franco Gemma. He was blindfolded to draw the lots – and pulled out Turkey, instead of much-fancied Spain.

THE "FOOTBALL WAR"

War broke out between El Salvador and Honduras after El Salvador beat Honduras 3-2 in a play-off on 26 June 1969 to qualify for the 1970 finals. Tension had been running high between the neighbours over a border dispute and there had been rioting at the match. On 14 July, the Salvador army invaded Honduras.

FIRST–TIME QUALIFIERS

1930: Argentina, Belgium, Bolivia, Brazil, Chile, France, Mexico, Paraguay, Peru, Romania, USA, Uruguay, Yugoslavia

1934: Austria, Czechoslovakia, Egypt, Germany, Hungary, Italy, Netherlands, Spain, Sweden, Switzerland

1938: Cuba, Dutch East Indies, Norway, Poland

1950: England

1954: Scotland, South Korea, Turkey, West Germany

1958: Northern Ireland, Soviet Union, Wales

1962: Bulgaria, Colombia

1966: North Korea, Portugal

1970: El Salvador, Israel, Morocco

1974: Australia, East Germany, Haiti, Zaire

1978: Iran, Tunisia

1982: Algeria, Cameroon, Honduras, Kuwait, New Zealand

1986: Canada, Denmark, Iraq

1990: Costa Rica, Republic of Ireland, United Arab Emirates

1994: Greece, Nigeria, Russia, Saudi Arabia

1998: Croatia, Jamaica, Japan, South Africa, Yugoslavia

2002: China, Ecuador, Senegal, Slovenia

2006: Angola, Czech Republic, Ghana, Ivory Coast, Serbia and Montenegro, Togo, Trinidad and Tobago, Ukraine

2010: Serbia, Slovakia

2014: Bosnia and Herzegovina

PLAY–OFF YOU GO

For the fourth FIFA World Cup in a row, Uruguay reached the 2014 tournament via a play-off, this one an easy aggregate win over Jordan. They won the away leg 5-0, the fifth scored by **Edinson Cavani** – the largest away win in the history of FIFA World Cup intercontinental play-offs – and eased through with a goalless draw on home soil. Jordan, aiming for their first FIFA World Cup finals, played 20 qualifying matches, including a 2-2 aggregate Asian play-off tie against Uzbekistan, which they won 9-8 on penalties.

THIERRY'S TRICKERY

France qualified for the 2010 FIFA World Cup finals thanks to one of the most controversial international goals of recent history. The second leg of their play-off against the Republic of Ireland in November 2009 was 14 minutes into extra-time when striker **Thierry Henry** clearly controlled the ball with his hand, before crossing to William Gallas who gave his side a decisive 2-1 aggregate lead. After Swedish referee Martin Hansson allowed the goal to stand, the Football Association of Ireland first called for the game to be replayed, then asked to be allowed into the finals as a 33rd country – but both requests proved in vain.

NICE ONE, SON

The latest goal of 2014 FIFA World Cup qualifiers was **Son Heung-Min's** winner for South Korea, six minutes into stoppage-time of their crucial March 2013 match against Qatar. The strike not only secured a 2-1 win, but also South Korea's qualification for the finals in Brazil.

GOING UNDERCOVER

The Kingdome in Seattle, United States, hosted the first FIFA World Cup qualifier to be played indoors, when the US beat Canada 2-0 in October 1976 – just a few months after the same venue had staged its first rock concert, by Paul McCartney's post-Beatles band Wings, and a religious rally featuring evangelist Billy Graham and country singer Johnny Cash. Canada gained revenge by beating the US 3-0 in a play-off, hosted in Haiti, to reach the next stage of the CONCACAF qualifying round. But only Mexico would go on to represent the Confederation at the 1978 FIFA World Cup in Argentina.

MAMADOU CAN DO

No European team had ever come from two goals down to win a FIFA World Cup play-off until November 2013, when France lost 2-0 in Ukraine but then won 3-0 in Paris thanks to a goal by striker Karim Benzema and a surprise brace by centre-back Mamadou Sakho, including a 72nd-minute winner.

NOT SO FASO

Burkina Faso lost their final qualifying play-off in the Africa section on away goals to Algeria, following a 3-2 victory at home and a 1-0 defeat away. They then tried to have Algeria disqualified, claiming that crucial goalscorer **Madjid Bougherra** was ineligible. Burkina Faso officials, hoping to reach their first FIFA World Cup, claimed he should have been suspended following two yellow cards in previous matches but FIFA ruled he had been booked only the once.

FIFA TEAM RECORDS
WORLD CUP

EXTRA SPECIAL GERMANS

Germany, in beating Argentina 1-0 in the Maracana stadium in 2014, became the fifth team to win the FIFA World Cup Final in extra time after Italy (1934), England (1966), Argentina (1978) and Spain (2010). In both 2010 and 2014, the Final had finished goalless after 90 minutes. Andres Iniesta, for Spain in 2010, and Mario Gozte, for Germany in Rio de Janeiro, both struck their lone winning goals in the second period of the additional 30 minutes. Extra time was not enough in 1994 and 2006, when Brazil and Italy, respectively, won on penalties.

SHARING THE GOALS

France in 1982 and winners Italy, in 2006, supplied the most individual goalscorers during a FIFA World Cup finals tournament – ten. Germany's 17 goals were shared among seven players on their way to ultimate success in Brazil in 2014: Thomas Muller (five), Andre Schurrle (three), Mats Hummels (two), Miroslav Klose (two), Toni Kroos (two), Mario Gotze (two) and Mesut Ozil (one).

BRAZIL COLOUR UP

Brazil's yellow shirts are famous around the world. But they wore **white shirts** at the first four FIFA World Cup finals. However, their 2-1 loss to Uruguay in the 1950 tournament's final match – when a draw would have given Brazil the Cup – was such a shock they switched to yellow. The Brazilian confederation insisted no further colour change would follow the shock of the 7-1 semi-final defeat by Germany and 3-0 third-place play-off loss to Holland in 2014.

COLOUR CODE CONNECTION

Germany sought to engage with Brazilian fans by incorporating the colours of one of the country's most popular clubs, Flamengo, when Die Nationalelf wore red-and-black hoops as their second kit in the 2014 FIFA World Cup.

ITALY KEEP IT TIGHT

Italy set the record for the longest run without conceding a goal at the FIFA World Cup finals. They went five games without conceding at the 1990 finals, starting with their 1-0 group win over Austria. Goalkeeper Walter Zenga was not beaten until Claudio Caniggia scored Argentina's equalizer in the semi-final. And a watertight defence did not bring Italy the glory it craved: Argentina reached the final by winning the penalty shoot-out 4-3.

TODAY EUROPE, TOMORROW THE WORLD

Spain's 2010 trophy-lifting coach **Vicente del Bosque** became only the second manager to have won both the FIFA World Cup and the UEFA Champions League or its previous incarnation, the European Champions' Cup. Marcello Lippi won the UEFA prize with Juventus in 1996, 10 years before his Italy team became world champions. Del Bosque won the UEFA Champions League twice with Real Madrid, in 2000 and 2002, though he was sacked in summer 2003 for "only" winning the Spanish league title the previous season.

SUPER EIGHT FOR 2014

The 2014 FIFA World Cup saw all eight group-winners win in the round-of-16 to reach the quarter-finals for the first time in the tournament's history. However there was an unwanted record, as well. Spain and 2010 Cup-winning skipper **Iker Casillas** exited in the first-round, meaning three of the last four FIFA World Cup winners have gone out in the following group stage (emulating France in 2002 and Italy in 2010). Only three countries have never exited at the first round group stage: Germany/West Germany, the Netherlands and the Republic of Ireland.

MOST APPEARANCES IN THE FIFA WORLD CUP FINAL

1	Germany/West Germany	8
2	Brazil	7
3	Italy	6
4	Argentina	5
5	Netherlands	3
6	Czechoslovakia	2
=	France	2
=	Hungary	2
=	Uruguay	2
10	England	1
=	Spain	1
=	Sweden	1

BRAZIL PROFIT FROM RIMET'S VISION

Jules Rimet, president of FIFA 1921–54, was the driving force behind the first FIFA World Cup, in 1930. The tournament, in Uruguay, was not high-profile, with only 13 nations taking part. The long sea journey kept most European teams away, and only Belgium, France, Romania and Yugoslavia made the trip. Rimet's dream has been realized and the FIFA World Cup has grown enormously in popularity. Brazil have been the competition's most successful team, winning five times. The only FIFA World Cup finals ever-presents, Brazil have more wins (70) than any other country, though Germany (66 wins) have played more matches: 106 to Brazil's 104. Germany and Italy are the most successful European nations with four World Cup wins apiece. The original finalists, Uruguay and Argentina, are both two-time champions, though Argentina have also lost two Finals. England (1966) and France (1998) both won once as hosts. Spain failed as hosts in 1982 but won in South Africa in 2010.

WHY THE BRITISH TEAMS STAYED OUT

England and Scotland are considered the homelands of football, but neither country entered the FIFA World Cup until the qualifiers for the 1950 finals. The four British associations – England, Scotland, Wales and Northern Ireland – quit FIFA in the 1920s over a row over broken-time (employment compensation) payments to amateurs. The British associations did not rejoin FIFA until 1946.

ONE-TIME WONDERS

Indonesia, then known as the Dutch East Indies, made one appearance in the finals, in the days when the tournament was a strictly knockout affair. On 5 June 1938, they lost 6-0 to Hungary in the first round, and have never qualified for the tournament since.

MOST APPEARANCES IN FIFA WORLD CUP FINALS TOURNAMENTS

1	Brazil	20
2	Germany/West Germany	18
=	Italy	18
4	Argentina	16
5	Mexico	15

FIFA WORLD CUP STOPS THE WORLD

The FIFA World Cup finals is the world's biggest single-sport event. Television was in its infancy when the first finals were held in 1930, and they have since become one of the most popular TV sporting events of all. The 2014 finals set ratings records around the world. In Germany, an all-time high of 41.89 million viewers (an 86.3 per cent share) watched the victory over Argentina in the final. The global audience for the match was expected to top the 909 million who watched Spain beat the Netherlands in 2010. A further 12 million German fans were estimated to have watched the final in a public space back home. All manner of online records were set. Germany's 7-1 thrashing of Brazil in the semi-final generated a world sports record of 35 million tweets.

GOLDEN NARROWS

Before 2010, no country had won five consecutive FIFA World Cup matches by a one-goal margin – but **Arjen Robben** and the Netherlands and became the first, thanks to their 3-2 semi-final victory over Uruguay. Before then, the record rested with Italy, who managed four single-goal wins in a row across the 1934 and 1938 FIFA World Cups. Spain's 1-0 defeat of the Dutch in the 2010 FIFA World Cup was also their fifth consecutive single-goal victory and fourth in the knockout stages.

BRAZIL'S GOALS GLOOM

The 14 goals conceded by Brazil in the 2014 FIFA World Cup finals are the most ever conceded by the host nation. The overall record was 16 goals shipped by South Korea in Switzerland in 1954. In those finals, West Germany let in 14 but still won the tournament for the first time. It included eight in a group match against beaten finalists Hungary.

EVER RED

England's victory in 1966 was not just the only time they have won the FIFA World Cup – it also now remains the only time the prize has been clinched by a side wearing red shirts in the final. Spain might have emulated England's fashion sense in 2010 but had to wear blue to avoid clashing with the Netherlands' bright orange – they did, however, change back into their usual red to receive the trophy from FIFA president **Joseph S. Blatter**.

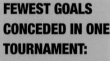

THE FEWEST GOALS CONCEDED

FIFA World Cup winners France (1998), Italy (2006) and Spain (2010) hold the record for the fewest goals conceded on their way to victory. All three conceded just two. Spain also hold the record for fewest goals scored by FIFA World Cup winners. They netted just eight in 2010, below the 11 scored by Italy in 1938, England in 1966 or Brazil in 1994.

SPONSORS MAKE THE FINALS PAY

The Brazil 2014 FIFA World Cup was the most lucrative ever, with world football's governing body, FIFA, achieving a surplus of more than $2 billion. Two-thirds of FIFA World Cup revenues come from TV rights. This was the fifth finals played with 32 teams, the number going up from 24 for the France 1998 FIFA World Cup.

> **FEWEST GOALS CONCEDED IN ONE TOURNAMENT:**
> Switzerland: 0, 2006

MOST GOALS SCORED IN ONE TOURNAMENT
Hungary: 27, 1954

MOST WINS IN ONE TOURNAMENT
Brazil: 7, 2002

MOST GOALS SCORED IN ONE TOURNAMENT
Just Fontaine (France): 13, 1958

MOST CONSECUTIVE MATCHES SCORING A GOAL AT FIFA WORLD CUP FINALS

18	Brazil	1930–58
18	Germany	1934–58, 1986–98
17	Hungary	1934–62
16	Uruguay	1930–62
15	Brazil	1978–90
15	France	1978–86

PERFORMANCES BY HOST NATION AT FIFA WORLD CUP FINALS

1930	Uruguay	Champions
1934	Italy	Champions
1938	France	Quarter-finals
1950	Brazil	Runners-up
1954	Switzerland	Quarter-finals
1958	Sweden	Runners-up
1962	Chile	Third place
1966	England	Champions
1970	Mexico	Quarter-finals
1974	West Germany	Champions
1978	Argentina	Champions
1982	Spain	Second round
1986	Mexico	Quarter-finals
1990	Italy	Third place
1994	United States	Second round
1998	France	Champions
2002	South Korea	Fourth place
	Japan	Second round
2006	Germany	Third place
2010	South Africa	First round
2014	Brazil	Fourth place

SAFE EUROPEAN HOME

Germany's 1-0 victory over Argentina in the 2014 FIFA World Cup final meant they became the first European nation to win the FIFA World Cup in any of the eight tournaments staged in North, Central or South America, going back to 1930. Spain, winners of the 2010 FIFA World Cup in South Africa, were the first European victors to achieve it outside their home continent.

HOLDERS CRASH OUT

France produced the worst performance by a defending FIFA World Cup winner in Japan and South Korea in 2002: they lost their opening game 1-0 to Senegal, drew 0-0 against Uruguay and were eliminated after losing 1-0 to Denmark. They were the first defending champions to be knocked out without scoring a goal. In 2010 Italy emulated France by exiting at the first-round stage, and without winning a match – nor indeed ever taking the lead. At least Italy did achieve two draws – and scored four goals. They opened with a 1-1 draw against Paraguay, needed a penalty to force another 1-1 draw against minnows New Zealand, and they were on their way home after losing 3-2 to Slovakia.

THREE AND OUT

The Netherlands, coached by **Bert van Marwijk** in 2010, became the only country to have reached the final of three FIFA World Cups without managing to lift the trophy once. Their six victories en route to the 2010 final are also more than any other team has managed in one tournament without going on to claim the main prize.

BRAZIL LEAD THE WAY

Brazil scored the most victories in finals tournaments when they won all their seven games in 2002. They began with a 2-1 group win over Turkey and ended with a 2-0 final triumph over Germany. They scored 18 goals in their unbeaten run and conceded on only four occasions.

HOME DISCOMFORT

South Africa became the first host nation to fail to reach the second round of a FIFA World Cup, when staging the 2010 tournament – though their first-round record of one win, one draw and one defeat was only inferior on goal difference to the opening three games played by hosts Spain, in 1982, and the USA, in 1994, both of whom reached the second round. Uruguay's 3–0 victory over South Africa in Pretoria on 16 June 2010 equalled the highest losing margin suffered by a FIFA World Cup host, following Brazil's 5–2 win over Sweden in the 1958 final and Italy's 4–1 trouncing of Mexico in their 1970 quarter-final.

HOST WITH THE MOST

Brazil have scored more goals (nine) in the opening matches of the FIFA World Cup than any other nation, though their status as double hosts in 1950 and 2014 certainly helped. Between 1974 and 2002 the holders, rather than the hosts, also had the honour of kicking off proceedings. Brazil beat Mexico easily by 4-0 in the 1950 opener in the Maracana stadium, with goals from Jair, Baltazar and Ademir (two). They defeated Scotland 2-1 in the Opening Match of France 1998 (Cesar Sampaio and Tom Boyd, own goal) and then Croatia, 3-1, in 2014, thanks to a double (one a penalty) from **Neymar** and a third from Oscar. A Brazilian also netted the very first goal of the 2014 finals, as left-back Marcelo gave Croatia the lead with an own goal. Italy's total of eight goals in the Opening Match was mainly thanks to a 7-1 beating of the United States in 1934 – they drew 1-1 with Bulgaria in 1986.

HIGHEST SCORES

The highest-scoring game in the FIFA World Cup finals was the quarter-final between Austria and Switzerland on 26 June 1954. Austria staged a remarkable comeback to win 7-5, with centre-forward **Theodor Wagner** scoring a hat-trick, after trailing 3-0 in the 19th minute. Three other games have produced 11 goals – Brazil's 6-5 win over Poland in the 1938 first round, Hungary's 8-3 win over West Germany in their 1954 group game and the Hungarians' 10-1 rout of El Salvador at the group stage in 1982.

LOW-SCORING SPAIN

Spain won the 2010 FIFA World Cup despite scoring just eight goals in seven games on their way to the title – fewer than any world champions in history, including 11-goal Italy in 1934, England in 1966 and Brazil in 1994. Vicente del Bosque's Spain were also the first team to win 1-0 in all four of their knockout matches. David Villa scored the decisive goal in two of those matches.

GENEROUS OPPONENTS

Chile was the first team to benefit from an opponent's own goal at the FIFA World Cup. Mexico's Manuel Rosas put the ball into his own net during the Chileans' 3-0 win at the inaugural 1930 finals in Uruguay. France, Germany and Italy share the record for receiving the most FIFA World Cup finals own goals, with four each. At the 2014 World Cup, France profited from two own goals, the first courtesy of Honduras goalkeeper Noel Valladares in a 3-0 group stage win; the second was by Nigeria's Joseph Yobo, to make it 2-0 in the second-round. Valladares's own goal – the ball struck him off a goal-post and thus denied Karim Benzema a hat-trick – was ratified by goal-line technology, in operation in the finals in Brazil for the first time.

ZERO TOLERANCE

Four is the most number of penalty shootouts in the knockout phases of the FIFA World Cup since the first one in 1982. A further 25 have been needed in the eight finals thereafter. The record of four came at Italy 1990, Germany 2006 and Brazil 2014, where 26 of 36 kicks succeeded. The most crucial failures came after the goalless **Argentina** v Netherlands semi-final, and Dutchmen Ron Vlaar and Wesley Sneijder both were denied by keeper Sergio Romero.

THE FASTEST GOAL

Turkey's **Hakan Sukur** holds the record for the quickest goal scored in the FIFA World Cup finals. He netted after 11 seconds against South Korea in the 2002 third-place play-off. Turkey went on to win 3-2. The previous record was held by Vaclav Masek of Czechoslovakia, who struck after 15 seconds against Mexico in 1962.

BIGGEST FIFA WORLD CUP FINALS WINS

Hungary 10, El Salvador 1 (15 June 1982)
Hungary 9, South Korea 0 (17 June 1954)
Yugoslavia 9, Zaire 0 (18 June 1974)
Sweden 8, Cuba 0 (12 June 1938)
Uruguay 8, Bolivia 0 (2 July 1950)
Germany 8, Saudi Arabia 0 (1 June 2002)

MOST GOALS IN ONE FIFA WORLD CUP

Goals	Country	Year
27	Hungary	1954
25	West Germany	1954
23	France	1958
22	Brazil	1950
19	Brazil	1970

MOST GOALS IN FIFA WORLD CUP FINALS (MINIMUM 100)

1	Germany/W Germany	224
2	Brazil	221
3	Argentina	131
4	Italy	128
5	France	103

MOST AND LEAST

Mario Gotze's winner for Germany in the 2014 FIFA World Cup Final meant the tournament matched the record aggregate of 171 goals at the 1998 finals in France, the first expanded to 32 teams and 64 games. The two finals shared a goals average of 2.67 per game. The record goals per match average is 5.38, set at the 1954 finals, when there were 140 goals in 26 matches in Switzerland. The lowest average came at the 1990 FIFA World Cup in Italy, when the 52 matches generated only 115 goals, an average of only 2.21.

YOUNGEST AND OLDEST

The youngest-ever scorer of a goal in FIFA World Cup finals history is **Pele.** He was 17 years and 239 days old when he notched Brazil's winner against Wales in the 1958 quarter-finals. Cameroon's **Roger Milla** – aged 42 years and 39 days – became the oldest scorer when he netted his country's only goal in a 6-1 defeat by Russia in 1994.

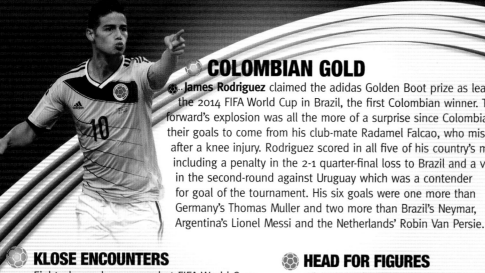

COLOMBIAN GOLD

James Rodriguez claimed the adidas Golden Boot prize as leading scorer at the 2014 FIFA World Cup in Brazil, the first Colombian winner. The AS Monaco forward's explosion was all the more of a surprise since Colombia had expected their goals to come from his club-mate Radamel Falcao, who missed the finals after a knee injury. Rodriguez scored in all five of his country's matches, including a penalty in the 2-1 quarter-final loss to Brazil and a volley in the second-round against Uruguay which was a contender for goal of the tournament. His six goals were one more than Germany's Thomas Muller and two more than Brazil's Neymar, Argentina's Lionel Messi and the Netherlands' Robin Van Persie.

KLOSE ENCOUNTERS

Eight players have scored at FIFA World Cups 12 years apart. The most notable was Miroslav Klose. The Polish-born centre-forward opened with a hat-trick when Germany beat Saudi Arabia 8-0 in Japan in 2002 and scored a 16th goal in the 7-1 destruction of hosts Brazil in the 2014 semi-finals. That established Klose as the finals' all-time record marksman with one more goal than Brazil's Ronaldo. The other seven men to have scored in FIFA World Cups 12 years apart are: Pele (Brazil), Uwe Seeler (West Germany), Diego Maradona (Argentina), Michael Laudrup (Denmark), Henrik Larsson (Sweden), Sami Al-Jaber (S Arabia) and Cuauhtemoc Blanco (Mexico).

EUSEBIO THE STRIKE FORCE

Portugal's **Eusebio** was the striking star of the 1966 FIFA World Cup finals. Ironically, he would not be eligible to play for Portugal now. He was born in Mozambique, then a Portuguese colony, but now an independent country. He finished top scorer with nine goals, including two as Portugal eliminated champions Brazil and four as they beat North Korea 5-3 in the quarter-finals after trailing 3-0.

HEAD FOR FIGURES

When **Jermaine Jones** thundered home from 30 metres for the United States in their 2-2 draw with Portugal in a Group G clash at the 2014 FIFA World Cup, he registered the 2,300th goal of the finals. Mario Gotze's winning goal for Germany in the Final against Argentina lifted the overall tally to 2,379.

FIFA WORLD CUP FINALS TOP SCORERS

Maximum 16 teams in finals

Year	Venue	Top Scorer	Country	Goals
1930	Uruguay	**Guillermo Stabile**	Argentina	8
1934	Italy	**Oldrich Nejedly**	Czechoslovakia	5
1938	France	**Leonidas**	Brazil	7
1950	Brazil	**Ademir**	Brazil	9
1954	Switzerland	**Sandor Kocsis**	Hungary	11
1958	Sweden	**Just Fontaine**	France	13
1962	Chile	**Garrincha**	Brazil	4
		Vava	Brazil	
		Leonel Sanchez	Chile	
		Florian Albert	Hungary	
		Valentin Ivanov	Soviet Union	
		Drazen Jerkovic	Yugoslavia	
1966	England	**Eusebio**	Portugal	9
1970	Mexico	**Gerd Muller**	West Germany	10
1974	West Germany	**Grzegorz Lato**	Poland	7
1978	Argentina	**Mario Kempes**	Argentina	6

24 teams in finals

Year	Venue	Top Scorer	Country	Goals
1982	Spain	**Paolo Rossi**	Italy	6
1986	Mexico	**Gary Lineker**	England	6
1990	Italy	**Salvatore Schillaci**	Italy	6
1994	United States	**Oleg Salenko**	Russia	6
		Hristo Stoichkov	Bulgaria	6

32 teams in finals

Year	Venue	Top Scorer	Country	Goals
1998	France	**Davor Suker**	Croatia	6
2002	Korea/Japan	**Ronaldo**	Brazil	8
2006	Germany	**Miroslav Klose**	Germany	5
2010	South Africa	**Thomas Muller***	Germany	5
		Diego Forlan	Uruguay	5
		Wesley Sneijder	Netherlands	5
		David Villa	Spain	5
2014	Brazil	**James Rodriguez**	Colombia	6

* = Won Golden Boot (had most assists)

KEMPES MAKES HIS MARK

Mario Kempes was Argentina's only foreign-based player in the hosts' squad at the 1978 finals. Twice top scorer in the Spanish league, Valencia's Kempes was crucial to Argentina's success. Coach Cesar Luis Menotti told him to shave off his moustache after he failed to score in the group games. Kempes then netted two against Peru, two more against Poland, and two decisive goals in the final against the Netherlands.

NO GUARANTEES FOR TOP SCORERS

Topping the FIFA World Cup finals scoring chart is a great honour for all strikers, but few have gained the ultimate prize and been leading scorer. Argentina's Guillermo Stabile started the luckless trend in 1930, topping the scoring charts but finishing up on the losing side in the final. The list of top scorers who have played in the winning side is small: Garrincha and Vava (joint top scorers in 1962), Mario Kempes (top scorer in 1978), Paolo Rossi (1982) and Ronaldo (2002). Gerd Muller, top scorer in 1970, gained his reward as West Germany's trophy winner four years later. Other top scorers, such as Sandor Kocsis, 1954, Just Fontaine, 1958, and Gary Lineker, 1986, have been disappointed in the final stages. Kocsis was the only one to reach the final – and Hungary were defeated. Four players finished tied on five goals at the 2010 FIFA World Cup and one – David Villa – collected a winner's medal, but the Golden Boot went to Germany's Thomas Muller.

STABILE MAKES AN IMPACT

Guillermo Stabile, top scorer in the 1930 FIFA World Cup finals, had never played for Argentina before the tournament. He made his debut – as a 25-year-old – against Mexico because first-choice Roberto Cherro had suffered a panic attack. He netted a hat-trick then scored twice against both Chile and the United States as Argentina reached the final. He struck one of his side's goals in the 4-2 defeat by Uruguay in the final.

SUPER SUBS

Germany's winner in the 2014 FIFA World Cup Final was scored by **Mario Gotze** and created by a pass from Andre Schurrle. This was the first time both the assist and goal itself in a FIFA World Cup Final had come from two substitutes. It was also the first winning goal scored by a substitute.

HURST MAKES HISTORY

England's **Geoff Hurst** became the first and to date only player to score a hat-trick in a FIFA World Cup final when he netted three in the hosts' 4-2 victory over West Germany in 1966. Hurst headed England level after the Germans took an early lead, then scored the decisive third goal with a shot that bounced down off the crossbar and just over the line, according to the Soviet linesman. Hurst hit his third in the last minute. The British TV commentator Kenneth Wolstenholme described Hurst's strike famously with the words: "Some people are on the pitch ... They think it's all over ... It is now!"

THREE OUT OF 10

Only three players wearing the iconic No.10 shirt have won the FIFA World Cup finals Golden Boot: Argentina's Mario Kempes in 1978, England's Gary Lineker in 1986 and Colombia's six-goal James Rodriguez at Brazil 2014. Lionel Messi and Neymar, Argentina's and Brazil's No.10s, both scored four goals, one behind Germany's No.13, Thomas Muller.

ANDRES THE GIANT

Spain's hero in the 2010 FIFA World Cup final was **Andres Iniesta** (right), whose 116th-minute goal was also the latest trophy-winning strike in the tournament's history – not counting penalty shoot-outs, that is.

FIFA WORLD CUP FINALS ALL–TIME LEADING GOALSCORERS

	Name	Country	Tournaments	Goals
1	Miroslav Klose	Germany	2002, 2006, 2010, 2014	16
2	Ronaldo	Brazil	1998, 2002, 2006	15
3	Gerd Muller	West Germany	1970, 1974	14
4	Just Fontaine	France	1958	13
5	Pele	Brazil	1958, 1962, 1966, 1970	12
6	Jurgen Klinsmann	Germany	1990, 1994, 1998	11
=	Sandor Kocsis	Hungary	1954	11
8	Gabriel Batistuta	Argentina	1994, 1998, 2002	10
=	Teofilo Cubillas	Peru	1970, 1978	10
=	Grzegorz Lato	Poland	1974, 1978, 1982	10
=	Gary Lineker	England	1986, 1990	10
=	Thomas Muller	Germany	2010, 2014	10
=	Helmut Rahn	West Germany	1954, 1958	10

THE BRADLEY BUNCH

Michael Bradley's late equalizer for the United States, in their Group C 2-2 draw with Slovenia in June 2010, made him the first person to score a FIFA World Cup goal for a team coached by his own father – in this case, Bob Bradley.

MESSI MISSING OUT

Argentina's captain **Lionel Messi** left the 2014 FIFA World Cup with a runners-up medal and the Golden Ball, awarded to the finals' best player. The winner, once chosen by a poll of journalists, was judged in Brazil by the technical study group. This comprises present and former coaches appointed by FIFA to monitor football trends. The last player to win both the award and the FIFA World Cup was Romario, back in 1994.

PELE SO UNLUCKY

Pele would surely have been the all-time FIFA World Cup top scorer but for injuries. He was sidelined early in the 1962 finals, and again four years later. He scored six goals in Brazil's 1958 triumph, including two in the 5-2 final victory over Sweden. He also netted Brazil's 100th FIFA World Cup goal as they beat Italy 4-1 in the 1970 final.

MULLER'S SCORING HABIT

West Germany's **Gerd Muller** had the knack of scoring in important games. He struck the winner against England in the 1970 quarter-final and his two goals in extra-time against Italy almost carried his side to the final. Four years later, Muller's goal against Poland ensured that West Germany reached the final on home soil. Then he scored the winning goal against the Netherlands in the FIFA World Cup final. He also had a goal disallowed for offside – wrongly, as TV replays proved.

RONALDO SO CONSISTENT

Ronaldo was a consistent scorer in the three FIFA World Cup finals tournaments he played in. He netted four times in 1998, when they were runners-up to France, eight as Brazil won the 2002 tournament – including both goals in the final – and three more in 2006. He became the all-time top scorer when netting Brazil's opener in a 3-0 win over Ghana in the last-16 round at Dortmund on 27 June 2006. As a teenager, Ronaldo had been a member of Brazil's FIFA World Cup winning squad in the United States in 1994, but did not play.

WHO SCORED THE FIRST HAT-TRICK?

For many years, Argentina's Guillermo Stabile was considered the first hat-trick scorer in the FIFA World Cup finals. He netted three in Argentina's 6-3 win over Mexico on 19 July 1930, but has since been superseded by Bert Patenaude of the United States. FIFA changed its records in November 2006, to acknowledge that Patenaude's treble two days earlier, in the Americans' 3-0 win over Paraguay, had been the tournament's first hat-trick.

KLINSMANN'S CONTRIBUTION

Jurgen Klinsmann has been one of the most influential personalities at the modern FIFA World Cup. He scored three goals when West Germany won the FIFA World Cup in 1990 and a further eight in 1994 and 1998. As team coach he then led Germany to third place in 2006, and the United States to the second round in 2014.

HIGH FIVES

Germany forwards **Thomas Muller** (in 2010 and 2014) and Miroslav Klose (2002 and 2006) are the only men to have scored five or more goals at successive FIFA World Cup finals. Muller's 10 goals have come in only 13 matches and he will be only 28 years old when the Russia 2018 FIFA World Cup kicks-off.

FIFA WORLD CUP APPEARANCES

Goalkeeper Gianluigi Buffon was in Italy's squad for his fifth FIFA World Cup in Brazil in 2014 and, after missing the victory over England, he captained the Azzurri in losses to Costa Rica and Uruguay. Buffon actually played in only four tournaments, however, having been an unused substitute in 1998. Two players have appeared in matches in five FIFA World Cups: Mexico's Antonio Carbajal (1950–66) and West Germany/Germany's Lothar Matthaus (1982–98).

YOUNGEST AND OLDEST

Northern Ireland's Norman Whiteside is the youngest player in FIFA World Cup finals history, being just 17 years and 41 days when he started against Yugoslavia in 1982. The oldest player to feature is Colombia goalkeeper Faryd Mondragon as a late substitute in a 4-1 win over Japan in 2014. Aged 43 years and three days, he outdid the 42 years 39 days of Cameroon's Roger Milla.

THIS IS ENGLAND

England captain **Steven Gerrard** led the 110 players from the top-represented English Premier League at the 2014 FIFA World Cup. This was down seven on 2010. Celtic goalkeeper Fraser Forster was the England squad's only non-Premier League player. Belgium had 12 Premier League players and France 10. Chelsea sent 17 players, Manchester United 14, Liverpool 12 and champions Manchester City 10.

MOST APPEARANCES IN FIFA WORLD CUP FINALS

25	**Lothar Matthaus** (West Germany/Germany)
24	**Miroslav Klose** (Germany)
23	**Paolo Maldini** (Italy)
21	**Diego Maradona** (Argentina)
	Uwe Seeler (West Germany)
	Wladyslaw Zmuda (Poland)
20	**Cafu** (Brazil)
	Philipp Lahm (Germany)
	Grzegorz Lato (Poland)
	Bastian Schweinsteiger (Germany)

DOUBLE WINNERS

Players who have played on the winning side in two FIFA World Cup finals:

Giovanni Ferrari (Italy), 1934, 1938
Giuseppe Meazza (Italy), 1934, 1938
Pele (Brazil), 1958, 1970
Didi (Brazil), 1958, 1962
Djalma Santos (Brazil), 1958, 1962
Garrincha (Brazil), 1958, 1962
Gilmar (Brazil), 1958, 1962
Nilton Santos (Brazil), 1958, 1962
Vava (Brazil), 1958, 1962
Zagallo (Brazil), 1958, 1962
Zito (Brazil), 1958, 1962
Cafu (Brazil), 1994, 2002

THE "DOUBLE" CHAMPIONS

Franz Beckenbauer and Mario Zagallo are a unique duo. They have both won the FIFA World Cup as a player and a coach. Beckenbauer also had the distinction of captaining West Germany to victory on home soil in 1974. As coach, he steered them to the final in Mexico in 1986 and to victory over Argentina in Italy four years later. He was nicknamed "Der Kaiser" (The Emperor) both for his style and his achievements. Zagallo gained two winners' medals as a player. He was the left-winger in Brazil's triumphant march to the 1958 championship, before playing a deeper role in their 1962 victory. He took over from the controversial Joao Saldanha as Brazil coach three months before the 1970 finals and guided the side to victory in all six of its games, scoring 19 goals and routing Italy 4-1 in the final. Zagallo later filled the role of the team's technical director when Brazil won the FIFA World Cup for a fourth time in 1994.

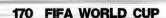

MOST FIFA WORLD CUP FINALS TOURNAMENTS

The following all played in at least four FIFA World Cup finals.

5 **Antonio Carbajal** (Mexico) 1950, 1954, 1958, 1962, 1966
   Lothar Matthaus (W Germany/Germany) 1982, 1986, 1990, 1994, 1998

4 **Sami Al-Jaber** (Saudi Arabia) 1994, 1998, 2002, 2006
   DaMarcus Beasley (United States) 2002, 2006, 2010, 2014
   Giuseppe Bergomi (Italy) 1982, 1986, 1990, 1998
   Gianluigi Buffon (Italy) 2002, 2006, 2010, 2014
   Cafu (Brazil) 1994, 1998, 2002, 2006
   Denis Caniza (Paraguay) 1998, 2002, 2006, 2010
   Fabio Cannavaro (Italy) 1998, 2002, 2006, 2010
   Iker Casillas (Spain) 2002, 2006, 2010, 2014
   Samuel Eto'o (Cameroon) 1998, 2002, 2010, 2014
   Thierry Henry (France) 1998, 2002, 2006, 2010
   Miroslav Klose (Germany) 2002, 2006, 2010, 2014
   Paolo Maldini (Italy) 1990, 1994, 1998, 2002
   Diego Maradona (Argentina) 1982, 1986, 1990, 1994
   Rafael Marquez (Mexico) 2002, 2006, 2010, 2014
   Hong Myung-Bo (South Korea) 1990, 1994, 1998, 2002
   Pele (Brazil) 1958, 1962, 1966, 1970
   Gianni Rivera (Italy) 1962, 1966, 1970, 1974
   Pedro Rocha (Uruguay) 1962, 1966, 1970, 1974
   Djalma Santos (Brazil) 1954, 1958, 1962, 1966
   Karl-Heinz Schnellinger (W. Germany) 1958, 1962, 1966, 1970
   Enzo Scifo (Belgium) 1986, 1990, 1994, 1998
   Uwe Seeler (West Germany) 1958, 1962, 1966, 1970
   Rigobert Song (Cameroon) 1994, 1998, 2002, 2010
   Franky van der Elst (Belgium) 1986, 1990, 1994, 1998
   Xavi (Spain) 2002, 2006, 2010, 2014
   Wladyslaw Zmuda (Poland) 1974, 1978, 1982, 1986
   Andoni Zubizarreta (Spain) 1986, 1990, 1994, 1998

BAYERN BEAT

Seven of Germany's 2014 FIFA World Cup-winning squad came from champions Bayern Munich: Manuel Neuer, Philipp Lahm, Jerome Boateng, Bastian Schweinsteiger, Toni Kroos, Thomas Muller and Mario Gotze. All started the final against Argentina – except match-winner Gotze. Immediately after the final the Bayern contingent was reduced when Kroos joined Real Madrid.

KHEDIRA'S DOUBLE PAIN

Sami Khedira was in a world of his own in Brazil in 2014 as he ended the season with a winner's medal from both the FIFA World Cup and the UEFA Champions League. First Khedira lined up in midfield as Spanish club Real Madrid scored a 4-1 extra-time win over neighbours Atletico in Europe's club season climax. He then joined up with Germany's World Cup squad in Brazil. Here he won a second medal, despite withdrawing from the final just before kick-off after aggravating a muscle injury in the warm-up. Khedira was the 10th player to clinch the World Cup/European Cup double.

SONG FAMILY GOES OFF KEY

In playing 17 minutes at the 2010 FIFA World Cup, Cameroon defender **Rigobert Song** became the first African to play in four finals tournaments – nine matches, across 16 years and nine days. He featured in 1994, 1998, 2002 and 2010 – Cameroon failed to qualify in 2006. He, and Colombia's Faryd Mondragon, share the fourth-longest FIFA World Cup career-spans, bettered only by Mexicans Antonio Carbajal (spanning 16 years, 25 days) and Hugo Sanchez (16 years, 17 days) and West Germany/Germany's Lothar Matthaus (16 years, 14 days). On the down side, Song was sent off twice at World Cups and cousin Alex Song was dismissed at the 2014 finals for elbowing Mario Mandzukic in a 4-0 loss to Croatia. Thus, the Song family is responsible for three of Cameroon's eight FIFA World Cup finals red cards.

MOST FIFA WORLD CUP FINALS MATCHES (BY POSITION)

Goalkeeper: Sepp Maier (West Germany, 18 matches) and Claudio Taffarel (Brazil, 18 matches)
Defence: Paolo Maldini (Italy, 23); Wladyslaw Zmuda (Poland, 21); Cafu (Brazil, 20); Philipp Lahm (Germany, 20)
Midfielders: Lothar Matthaus (W. Germany/Germany, 25); Bastian Schweinsteiger (Germany, 20)
Forwards: Miroslav Klose (Germany, 24); Diego Maradona (Argentina, 21); Uwe Seeler (West Germany, 21); Grzegorz Lato (Poland, 20)

PROSINECKI'S SCORING RECORD

Robert Prosinecki is the only player to have scored for different countries in FIFA World Cup finals tournaments. He netted for Yugoslavia in their 4-1 win over the United Arab Emirates in the 1990 tournament. Eight years later, following the break-up of the old Yugoslavia, he scored for Croatia in their 3-0 group-game win over Jamaica, and then netted the first goal in his side's 2-1 third-place play-off victory over the Netherlands.

QUICKEST SUBSTITUTIONS

The three fastest substitutions in the history of the FIFA World Cup finals have all come in the fourth minute. In each case the player substituted was so seriously injured that he took no further part in the tournament: Steve Hodge came on for Bryan Robson in England's 0-0 draw with Morocco in 1986; Giuseppe Bergomi replaced Alessandro Nesta in Italy's 2-1 win over Austria in 1998; and Peter Crouch subbed for Michael Owen in England's 2-2 draw with Sweden in 2006.

PRIZE PROBLEM

Winning the FIFA World Player of the Year award, or Ballon d'Or, has not proved a lucky omen for its proud bearers. The winner has never gone on to win the next World Cup. The 2014 FIFA World Cup was no different as **Cristiano Ronaldo**, 2013 FIFA World Player of the Year, and his Portugal team-mates went out in the group stage. His predecessor as Ballon d'Or-holder, Lionel Messi of Argentina, was on the losing side in the 2014 Final. Messi was also the incumbent going into the 2010 FIFA World Cup, but lost in the quarter-finals.

SIMUNIC'S THREE–CARD MATCH

Croatia's Josip Simunic shares (with Ray Richards of Australia in 1974) the record for collecting the most yellow cards in one match at the FIFA World Cup finals – three. He received three yellows against Australia in 2006 before he was sent off by English referee Graham Poll. When Poll showed Simunic his second yellow, he forgot he had already booked him.

LEADING CAPTAINS

Three players have each captained their teams in two FIFA World Cup finals – Diego Maradona of Argentina, Dunga of Brazil and West Germany's Karl-Heinz Rummenigge. Maradona lifted the trophy in 1986, but was a loser four years later. Dunga was the winning skipper in 1994, but was on the losing side in 1998. Rummenigge was a loser on both occasions, in 1982 and 1986. Maradona has made the most appearances as captain at the FIFA World Cup finals, leading out Argentina 16 times between 1986 and 1994.

FIRST ELEVEN

In an age of squad numbers, **Brazil** may have pleased some traditionalists when fielding players wearing shirt numbers one to 11 in the starting line-ups for their first two games of the 2010 FIFA World Cup, against North Korea and the Ivory Coast. Kicking off for coach Dunga on each occasion were: 1 Julio Cesar, 2 Maicon, 3 Lucio, 4 Juan, 5 Felipe Melo, 6 Michel Bastos, 7 Elano, 8 Gilberto Silva, 9 Luis Fabiano, 10 Kaka and 11 Robinho. **the Netherlands** managed a similar starting structure for not only their second-round tie against Slovakia, but the final against Spain: 1 Maarten Stekelenburg, 2 Gregory van der Wiel, 3 Johnny Heitinga, 4 Joris Mathijsen, 5 Giovanni van Bronckhorst, 6 Mark van Bommel, 7 Dirk Kuyt, 8 Nigel de Jong, 9 Robin van Persie, 10 Wesley Sneijder and 11 Arjen Robben. Both Brazil and the Netherlands came close to the same feat when they met in the quarter-finals, though both featured a number 13 – Brazil's Dani Alves, in place of 7 Elano, and the Netherlands' Andre Ooijer instead of 4 Joris Mathijsen (Elano and Mathijsen were unavailable through injury).

FASTEST RED CARDS IN THE FIFA WORLD CUP FINALS

1 min Jose Batista (Uruguay) v Scotland, 1986
8 min Giorgio Ferrini (Italy) v Chile, 1962
14 min Zeze Procopio (Brazil) v Czechoslovakia, 1938
19 min Mohammed Al Khlaiwi (Saudi Arabia) v France, 1998
Miguel Bossio (Uruguay) v Denmark, 1986
21 min Gianluca Pagliuca (Italy) v Rep of Ireland, 1994

FASTEST YELLOW CARDS IN THE FIFA WORLD CUP FINALS

1 min Sergei Gorlukovich (Russia) v Sweden, 1994
Giampiero Marini (Italy) v Poland, 1982
2 min Jesus Arellano (Mexico) v Italy, 2002
Henri Camara (Senegal) v Uruguay, 2002
Michael Emenalo (Nigeria) v Italy, 1994
Humberto Suazo (Chile) v Switzerland, 2010
Mark van Bommel (Netherlands) v Port., 2006

SUPER SUBS IMPOSE THEIR WILL

Substitutes scored more goals in the Brazil 2014 FIFA World Cup than in any previous finals. Mario Gotze's goal in the final was the 32nd by a substitute, extending the record from the previous mark of 24 set in 2006 in Germany. Substitutes, two of them, were first permitted for the 1970 finals in Mexico, and it went up to three from 1998. The 1998 FIFA World Cup finals also saw the fastest goal by a substitute. Denmark's **Ebbe Sand** scored 16 seconds after coming on against Nigeria.

YOUNGEST PLAYERS IN FIFA WORLD CUP FINAL
Pele (Brazil) – 17 years, 249 days, in 1958
Giuseppe Bergomi (Italy) – 18 years, 201 days, in 1982
Ruben Moran (Uruguay) – 19 years, 344 days, in 1950

OLDEST PLAYERS IN FIFA WORLD CUP FINAL
Dino Zoff (Italy) – 40 years, 133 days, in 1982
Gunnar Gren (Sweden) – 37 years, 241 days, in 1958
Jan Jongbloed (Netherlands) – 37 years, 212 days, in 1978
Nilton Santos (Brazil) – 37 years, 32 days, in 1962

PUZACH THE FIRST SUB
The first substitute in FIFA World Cup finals history was Anatoli Puzach of the Soviet Union. He replaced Viktor Serebrianikov at half-time of the Soviets' 0-0 draw with hosts Mexico on 31 May 1970. The 1970 tournament was the first in which substitutes were allowed, with two permitted for each side. FIFA increased this to three per team for the 1998 finals.

FOUR AND OUT
The most players sent off in one FIFA World Cup finals game is four. Costinha and Deco of Portugal and Khalid Boulahrouz and Gio van Bronckhorst of the Netherlands were sent off by Russian referee Valentin Ivanov in their second-round match in Germany in 2006.

CANIGGIA – SENT OFF, WHILE ON THE BENCH...
Claudio Caniggia of Argentina became the first player to be sent off from the substitutes' bench, during the match against Sweden in 2002. Caniggia was dismissed in first-half stoppage time for dissent towards UAE referee Ali Bujsaim. Caniggia carried on protesting after the referee warned him to keep quiet, so Bujsaim showed him a red card.

MALDINI'S MINUTES RECORD
Lothar Matthaus of West Germany/Germany has started the most FIFA World Cup finals matches – 25. But Italy defender **Paolo Maldini** (left) has stayed on the field for longer, despite starting two games fewer. Maldini played for 2,220 minutes, Matthaus for 2,052. According to the stopwatch, the top four are completed by Uwe Seeler of West Germany, who played for 1,980 minutes, and Argentina's Diego Maradona, who played for 1,938.

GERMANY UNITED
Germany and West Germany are counted together in World Cup records because the Deutscher Fussball-Bund, founded in 1900, was the original governing body and the DFB was in charge of the national game before World War 2, during the East–West split and post-reunification. German sides have won the World Cup four times and appeared in the Final a record eight times. In 2014, match-deciding substitutes Andre Schurrle and Mario Gotze were the first players born in Germany since reunification to win the World Cup, while team-mate Toni Kroos was the only 2014 squad-member to have been born in what was East Germany. Kroos was also the first player from the former East Germany to win the World Cup.

UNBEATEN GOALKEEPERS IN THE FIFA WORLD CUP FINALS*

Walter Zenga (Italy)	517 minutes without conceding a goal, 1990
Peter Shilton (England)	502 minutes, 1986–90
Iker Casillas (Spain)	476 minutes, 2010–14
Sepp Maier (W Germany)	475 minutes, 1974–78
Gianluigi Buffon (Italy)	460 minutes, 2006
Emerson Leao (Brazil)	458 minutes, 1978
Gordon Banks (England)	442 minutes, 1966

* Pascal Zuberbuhler did not concede a goal in all 390 minutes played by Switzerland in the 2006 FIFA World Cup.

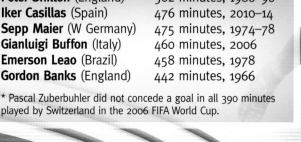

HAIL CESAR!

Brazil goalkeeper **Julio Cesar** wept with relief and joy after his penalty shoot-out defiance helped the 2014 FIFA World Cup hosts beat Chile in a round-of-16 tie in Belo Horizonte. Coach Luiz Felipe Scolari had kept faith with the 34-year-old, even though he had barely played for his English club Queens Park Rangers and gone on loan to FC Toronto of the MLS. Cesar was blamed by many Brazilians for a mistake which led to defeat by Netherlands in the 2010 quarter-finals. In 2014, however, he saved Chile's first two kicks and rocketed from scapegoat to national hero.

NOT THINKING OUTSIDE THE BOX

Italy's Gianluca Pagliuca was the first goalkeeper to be sent off at a FIFA World Cup match – for handball outside his penalty area – against Norway in 1994. Despite sacrificing playmaker Roberto Baggio for goalkeeper Luca Marchegiani, Italy still won 1-0.

ITALY'S ELDER STATESMEN

Dino Zoff became both the oldest player and oldest captain to win the FIFA World Cup when Italy lifted the trophy in Spain in 1982. He was 40 years 133 days old. A predecessor as goalkeeper and captain of both Italy and Juventus, Gianpiero Combi, had led Italy to World Cup glory in 1934.

FIVE-STAR CARBAJAL

Antonio Carbajal, of Mexico, is one of only two men to have appeared at five FIFA World Cup finals – the other was Germany's versatile Lothar Matthaus. Carbajal, who played in 1950, 1954, 1958, 1962 and 1966, conceded a record 25 goals in his 11 FIFA World Cup finals appearances – the same number let in by Saudi Arabia's Mohamed Al-Deayea across ten games in 1994, 1998 and 2002. Al-Deayea was a member of the Saudi squad for the 2006 tournament but did not play.

ZERO TO HERO

One of the unlikeliest stars of the 2014 FIFA World Cup finals was Mexico goalkeeper **Guillermo Ochoa**. He had spent the previous three years in the European shadows at modest French Corsican club Ajaccio. He feared for his World Cup place when Ajaccio were relegated, but Mexico coach Miguel Herrera was unconcerned and Ochoa repaid him with a string of outstanding performances. Best of all was his brilliant defiance of hosts Brazil in a goalless draw in the group phase. Ochoa, who ended the finals with 61 caps for Mexico, conceded just three times in four games as Mexico lost 2-1 to two late Netherlands goals in the round-of-16.

NUMBER-ONE NUMBER ONES

The Lev Yashin Award was introduced in 1994 for the man voted best goalkeeper of the FIFA World Cup – though a goalkeeper was selected subsequently for an all-star team at the end of every tournament dating back to 1930. The all-star team was expanded from 11 to 23 players in 1998, allowing room for more than one goalkeeper, but returned to 11 players in 2010. Players who were picked for the all-star teams but missed out on the Lev Yashin Award were Paraguay's Jose Luis Chilavert in 1998, Turkey's Rustu Recber in 2002, and Germany's Jens Lehmann and Portugal's Ricardo in 2006. The first Lev Yashin Award was presented to Belgium's Michel Preud'homme, even though he only played four games, conceding four goals, at the 1994 competition – his side were edged out 3-2 by Germany in the second round. Legendary Soviet goalkeeper Lev Yashin, after whom the trophy was named, played in the 1958, 1962 and 1966 FIFA World Cups and was a member of his country's 1970 squad as third-choice keeper and assistant coach – although he was never chosen for a FIFA World Cup team of the tournament. From 2010 commercial priorities led to Yashin's name being dropped from the award and it was renamed the Golden Glove award.

OLIVER'S ARMS

Germany's **Oliver Kahn** is the only goalkeeper to have been voted FIFA's Player of the Tournament, winning the award at the 2002 FIFA World Cup – despite taking a share of the blame for Brazil's winning goals in the final.

RIGHT WAY FOR RICARDO

Spain's Ricardo Zamora became the first man to save a penalty in a FIFA World Cup finals match, stopping Valdemar de Brito's spot-kick for Brazil in 1934. Spain went on to win 3-1.

HOWARD'S WAY

Tim Howard wrote his name into the FIFA World Cup history books with his amazing performance in the United States' second round clash with Belgium in 2014. Howard registered 16 superb saves in defying wave upon wave of Belgian attacks. This was the most saves ever recorded in a FIFA World Cup tie since the statistic was first introduced in 1966. It was not enough, however: the United States lost a thriller of a match 2-1 after extra time.

LEADING FROM THE BACK

Iker Casillas became the third goalkeeper to captain his country to FIFA World Cup glory, when Spain became champions in South Africa in 2010. He emulated Italians Gianpiero Combi (in 1934) and Dino Zoff (1982). Casillas was also the first man to lift the trophy after his side had lost their opening match of the tournament.

UNLUCKY BREAK

Goalkeeper Frantisek Planicka broke his arm during Czechoslovakia's 1938 second-round clash against Brazil, but played on, even though the game went to extra-time before ending in a 1-1 draw. Not surprisingly, given the extent of his injury, Planicka missed the replay two days later, which the Czechs lost 2-1, and the goalkeeper of the 1938 FIFA World Cup never added to his tally of 73 caps.

PLAYERS VOTED BEST GOALKEEPER OF THE TOURNAMENT

Year	Player	Year	Player
1930	Enrique Ballestrero (Uruguay)	1978	Ubaldo Fillol (Argentina)
1934	Ricardo Zamora (Spain)	1982	Dino Zoff (Italy)
1938	Frantisek Planicka (Czechoslovakia)	1986	Harald Schumacher (West Germany)
1950	Roque Maspoli (Uruguay)	1990	Sergio Goycoechea (Argentina)
1954	Gyula Grosics (Hungary)	1994	Michel Preud'homme (Belgium)
1958	Harry Gregg (Northern Ireland)	1998	Fabien Barthez (France)
1962	Viliam Schrojf (Czechoslovakia)	2002	Oliver Kahn (Germany)
1966	Gordon Banks (England)	2006	Gianluigi Buffon (Italy)
1970	Ladislao Mazurkiewicz (Uruguay)	2010	Iker Casillas (Spain)
1974	Jan Tomaszewski (Poland)	2014	Manuel Neuer (Germany)

BATTERING RAMON

Argentina's 6-0 win over Peru at the 1978 FIFA World Cup aroused suspicion because the hosts needed to win by four goals to reach the final at the expense of arch-rivals Brazil – and Peruvian goalkeeper Ramon Quiroga had been born in Argentina. He insisted, though, that his saves prevented the defeat from being even more embarrassingly emphatic. Earlier in the same tournament, Quiroga had been booked for a foul on Grzegorz Lato after running into the Polish half of the field.

END TO END STUFF

When Miroslav Klose raced on to a long ball from German team-mate **Manuel Neuer** to score against England in their 2010 FIFA World Cup second round tie, it made Neuer the first goalkeeper to directly set up a finals goal for 44 years. The last before then had been the Soviet Union's Anzor Kavazashvili, providing an assist for Valery Porkuyan's late winner against Chile in the 1966 group stage.

MORE AND MORA

Luis Ricardo Guevara Mora holds the unenviable record for most goals conceded in just one FIFA World Cup finals match. The 20-year-old had to pick the ball out of the net ten times in El Salvador's thrashing by Hungary in 1982 – and his team-mates managed only one goal of their own in reply. In this game he also set the record for being the youngest goalkeeper to participate in the FIFA World Cup finals.

TONY AWARD

United States goalkeeper **Tony Meola** left the national team after the 1994 FIFA World Cup because he wanted to switch sports and take up American football instead. He failed to make it in gridiron and returned to soccer, but did not play for his country again until 1999. He retired for a second time after reaching a century of international appearances and still holds the record for being the youngest FIFA World Cup captain, having worn the armband for the US's 5-1 defeat to Czechoslovakia in 1990, aged 21 years 316 days.

SWEDISH STALEMATE

Gilmar and Colin McDonald were the goalkeepers who made history at the 1958 FIFA World Cup in Sweden when first round group rivals Brazil and England fought out the first goalless draw in the history of the finals.

KEEPING THE FAITH

Switzerland's **Diego Benaglio** was the only goalkeeper to register a shot at the 2014 FIFA World Cup in Brazil. With the Swiss losing their second-round tie 1-0 to Argentina in Sao Paulo, he charged upfield at a corner. The ball fell loose to him in the penalty area, but his effort on goal was blocked. Benaglio's Swiss predecessor, at the 2006 finals, was equally unlucky. Pascal Zuberbuhler kept a clean sheet in all four of their matches, three in the group stage and a goalless draw with Ukraine in the second round. However the Swiss lost the resulting penalty shoot-out 3-0, despite Zuberbuhler saving Ukraine's first kick by Andriy Shevchenko.

TOP GOALS

Year	Goals	Per match
1930	70	(3.89 per match)
1934	70	(4.12 per match)
1938	84	(4.67 per match)
1950	88	(4 per match)
1954	140	(5.38 per match)
1958	126	(3.6 per match)
1962	89	(2.78 per match)
1966	89	(2.78 per match)
1970	95	(2.97 per match)
1974	97	(2.55 per match)
1978	102	(2.68 per match)
1982	146	(2.81 per match)
1986	132	(2.54 per match)
1990	115	(2.21 per match)
1994	141	(2.71 per match)
1998	171	(2.67 per match)
2002	161	(2.52 per match)
2006	147	(2.3 per match)
2010	145	(2.27 per match)
2014	171	(2.67 per match)
Total	**2,379**	(2.85 per match)

THE PETER PRINCIPLE

Peter Shilton became the oldest FIFA World Cup captain when he led England for their 1990 third-place play-off against hosts Italy. He was 40 years and 292 days old as he made his 125th and final appearance for his country – though his day was spoiled by a 2-1 defeat, including a goalkeeping error that gifted Roberto Baggio Italy's opener. Shilton, born in Leicester on 18 September 1949, also played for England at the 1982 and 1986 tournaments. He became captain in Mexico in 1986 after Bryan Robson was ruled out of the tournament by injury and Ray Wilkins by suspension, and featured in one of the FIFA World Cup's all-time memorable moments, when he was out-jumped by Argentina's Diego Maradona for the infamous "Hand of God" goal. Shilton jointly holds the record for most FIFA World Cup clean sheets, with ten – along with France's Fabien Barthez, who played at the 1998, 2002 and 2006 tournaments. Both men made 17 FIFA World Cup finals appearances apiece.

TRADING PLACES

The first goalkeeper to be substituted at a FIFA World Cup was Romania's Stere Adamache, who was replaced by Rica Raducanu 27 minutes into a 3-2 defeat to Brazil in 1970. Romania were 2-0 down at the time.

PLAYING THROUGH THE PAIN BARRIER

The first FIFA World Cup clean sheet was kept by Jimmy Douglas of the United States in a 3-0 win over Belgium in 1930. He followed that up with another, as Paraguay were beaten by the same scoreline – but Argentina proved too good, winning 6-1 in the semi-final. Douglas injured his knee after only four minutes, but had to play on as this occurred in the days before substitutes were allowed.

HOW GOING DUTCH PAYS OFF

Argentina's **Sergio Romero** will never be forgotten in the Netherlands – for using the experience he gained there to put the Dutchmen out of the 2014 FIFA World Cup. Romero had been brought to Europe in 2007 by Louis Van Gaal when the Dutch master coach was boss of AZ Alkmaar. In 2011 Romero moved to Italy to play for Sampdoria. Then he fell out of favour with the Genoese club and was loaned to French club AS Monaco in August 2013. Romero was hardly a regular in Ligue 1 either, indeed he played only three league matches in the season leading up to the FIFA World Cup. However, he did remain the first-choice with Argentina coach Alejandro Sabella. Argentina won all their group matches and then Romero kept clean sheets in initial knockout victories over Switzerland and Belgium. When the semi-final went to penalties, Romero became a national hero, with match-winning saves from the Netherlands' Ron Vlaar and Wesley Sneijder. Romero said later he owed Van Gaal special thanks ... "for teaching me how to save penalties."

FIFA MANAGERS
WORLD CUP

MANAGING SUCCESS

Germany provided the largest single contingent of coaches at the 2014 FIFA World Cup in Brazil. Most successful was Die Nationalelf's boss, **Joachim Low**, who became, following the 1-0 final victory over Argentina, the fourth German coach to win the trophy after Sepp Herberger (1954), Helmut Schon (1974) and Franz Beckenbauer (1990). Low was appointed in 2006 after having been assistant for two years. **Jurgen Klinsmann** (United States) and Ottmar Hitzfeld (Switzerland) both reached the second round, but the group stage was the end of the line for Volker Finke (Cameroon) and Berlin-born Nico Kovac (Croatia).

YOUNG JUAN

Juan Jose Tramutola remains the youngest-ever FIFA World Cup coach, leading Argentina in the 1930 tournament at the age of 27 years and 267 days. Italian Cesare Maldini became the oldest in 2002, taking charge of Paraguay when aged 70 years and 131 days.

DREAM TO NIGHTMARE

Luiz Felipe Scolari quit as Brazil coach after the 2014 FIFA World Cup brought the worst defeat in their history, by 7-1 against Germany in the semi-finals, and then a 3-0 defeat to Holland in the third-place play-off. However, he had won the FIFA World Cup with Brazil in 2002 and went on, with Portugal in 2006, to set an individual record of 11 successive wins at the finals.

PUFF DADDIES

The coaches of the two sides appearing at the 1978 FIFA World Cup final were such prolific smokers that an oversized ashtray was produced for Argentina's Cesar Luis Menotti and the Netherlands's Ernst Happel so they could share it on the touchline.

SOCCER SIX

Only one man has gone to six FIFA World Cups as coach: Brazilian **Carlos Alberto Parreira**, whose greatest moment came when he guided Brazil to the trophy for the fourth time in 1994. His second stint as Brazil coach was less successful – they fell in the quarter-finals in 2006. Parreira also led Kuwait (1982), the United Arab Emirates (1990), Saudi Arabia (1998) and hosts South Africa (2010) at the finals. He had stepped down as South Africa coach in April 2008, for family reasons, but returned late the following year. Parreira was once sacked midway through a FIFA World Cup. In 1998 he led Saudi Arabia for the first two of their three games – losing 1-0 to Denmark and 4-0 to France – before receiving his marching orders.

⚽ ELDEST STATESMAN OTTO

Otto Rehhagel became the oldest coach in FIFA World Cup history in South Africa in 2010. He was 71 years and 317 days old when his Greece team lost 2-0 to Argentina in their final group game. German Rehhagel had led Greece to their UEFA European Championship victory in 2004.

CRASHING BORA

Only one tournament behind record-holder Carlos Alberto Parreira, **Bora Milutinovic** has coached at five different FIFA World Cups – with a different country each time, two of them being the hosts. As well as Mexico in 1986 and the United States in 1994, he led Costa Rica in 1990, Nigeria in 1998 and China in 2002. He reached the knockout stages with every country except China – who failed to score a single goal.

⚽ DIVIDED LOYALTIES

No coach has won the FIFA World Cup in charge of a foreign team, but several have faced their homeland. These include Jurgen Klinsmann, who played for Germany when they won the Cup in 1990 and then managed them to third-place in 2006. Klinsmann, who was German boss 2004–06, having already made his home in California, was appointed United States coach in 2011. In the 2014 FIFA World Cup, "Klinsi" and the US lost 1-0 in a group match to Germany, now led by his former assistant Joachim Low, whom he had appointed in 2004. Other managers to face their native land include Brazilian Didi (with Peru in 1970), Frenchman Bruno Metsu (with Senegal in 2002) and Swede Sven-Goran Eriksson (with England in 2002 and 2006).

⚽ FIFA WORLD CUP– WINNING COACHES

1930	Alberto Suppici
1934	Vittorio Pozzo
1938	Vittorio Pozzo
1950	Juan Lopez
1954	Sepp Herberger
1958	Vicente Feola
1962	Aymore Moreira
1966	Alf Ramsey
1970	Mario Zagallo
1974	Helmut Schon
1978	Cesar Luis Menotti
1982	Enzo Bearzot
1986	Carlos Bilardo
1990	Franz Beckenbauer
1994	Carlos Alberto Parreira
1998	Aime Jacquet
2002	Luiz Felipe Scolari
2006	Marcello Lippi
2010	Vicente del Bosque
2014	Joachim Low

⚽ SCHON SHINES

West Germany's **Helmut Schon** was coach for more FIFA World Cup matches than any other man – 25, across the 1966, 1970, 1974 and 1978 tournaments. He has also won the most games as a coach, 16 in all – including the 1974 final against the Netherlands. The 1974 tournament was third time lucky for Schon. He he had taken West Germany to second place in 1966 and to third in 1970. Before taking charge of the national side, Schon had worked as an assistant to Sepp Herberger, coach of West Germany's 1954 FIFA World Cup-winning team – Schon was coach of the then-independent Saarland regional side at the time. Dog-lover Schon, born in Dresden on 15 September 1915, scored 17 goals in 16 internationals for Germany between 1937 and 1941. He succeeded Herberger in 1964 and spent 14 years in charge of his country. He was the first coach to win both the FIFA World Cup (1974) and the European Championship (1972).

FIFA WORLD CUP DISCIPLINE

FIFA BITES BACK

Uruguay's **Luis Suarez** incurred a record instant FIFA sanction after biting Italy's Giorgio Chiellini during Uruguay's 1-0 win in the 2014 World Cup, a result that put them, and not the Azzurri, into the second round. Suarez missed the subsequent 2-0 defeat by Colombia because he had been banned from all football for four months, from international competition for nine games and fined 100,000 Swiss francs. It was not the first time Suarez had been in trouble at the FIFA World Cup finals, having been banned for one match at the 2010 finals after being dismissed for handball on the goal-line in a quarter-final against Ghana.

REPEAT OFFENDERS

France's **Zinedine Zidane** and Brazil's **Cafu** are both FIFA World Cup winners – and both notched up a record six FIFA World Cup cards, though Cafu escaped any reds, while Zidane was sent off twice. Most famously, Zidane was dismissed for headbutting Italy's Marco Materazzi in extra-time of the 2006 final in Berlin – the final match of the Frenchman's career. He had also been sent off during a first-round match against Saudi Arabia in 1998, but returned from suspension in time to help France win the trophy with a sensational two-goal performance in the final. The only other man to have been sent off twice at two different FIFA World Cups is Cameroon's Rigobert Song. When dismissed against Brazil in 1994, he became the FIFA World Cup's youngest red card offender – aged just 17 years and 358 days. He saw red for the second time against Chile in 1998.

NOT LEADING BY EXAMPLE

The first man to be sent off at a FIFA World Cup was Peru's Placido Galindo, at the first tournament in 1930 during a 3-1 defeat to Romania. Chilean referee Alberto Warnken dismissed the Peruvian captain for fighting.

ARGIE BARGEY

Argentina defender Pedro Monzon became the first player sent off in a World Cup final when he was dismissed in 1990 for a foul on West Germany's Jurgen Klinsmann. Monzon had been on the pitch only 20 minutes after coming on as a half-time substitute. Three minutes from full-time Mexican referee Edgardo Codesal reduced Argentina to nine men by dismissing Gustavo Dezotti after a skirmish with Jurgen Kohler. Marcel Desailly, of France in 1998, is the only member of a winning team to have been sent off in a World Cup final.

CARDS CLOSE TO CHEST

Only one group in FIFA World Cup finals history has featured no bookings at all – Group 4 in 1970, featuring West Germany, Peru, Bulgaria and Morocco. In contrast, the 2006 FIFA World Cup in Germany was the worst for both red and yellow cards, with 28 dismissals and 345 bookings in 64 matches.

FINAL COUNT

England's Howard Webb set a record with one red card and 14 yellow in the 2010 FIFA World Cup Final between Spain and Netherlands. The previous 18 finals had featured 40 bookings and three dismissals between them. Webb's card total of 15 was nine more than the six shown by Brazil's Romualdo Arppi Filho in the 1986 final between Argentina (four) and Germany (two). Italy's Nicola Rizzoli showed four yellow cards (two each) when the same teams met in the 2014 FIFA World Cup Final.

SOLE CHANCE OF GLORY

India withdrew from the 1950 FIFA World Cup because some of their players wanted to play barefoot but FIFA insisted all players must wear football boots. India have not qualified for the tournament since.

FIFA WORLD CUP RED CARDS, BY TOURNAMENT

1930	1
1934	1
1938	4
1950	0
1954	3
1958	3
1962	6
1966	5
1970	0
1974	5
1978	3
1982	5
1986	8
1990	16
1994	15
1998	22
2002	17
2006	28
2010	17
2014	10

BREAKING COVER

Zaire defender Mwepu Llunga was booked for running out of the wall and kicking the ball away as Brazil prepared to take a free-kick, at the 1974 FIFA World Cup. Romanian referee Nicolae Rainea ignored Llunga's pleas of innocence.

GOOD SON, BAD SON

Cameroon's Andre Kana-Biyik served two suspensions during the 1990 FIFA World Cup. The first came after he was sent off in the opening match against Argentina – six minutes before his brother Francois Omam-Biyik scored the only goal. His second ban came after yellow cards in the final group game against Russia and in the second-round defeat of Colombia.

YELLOW MELO'S RED MIST

Felipe Melo's red card for stamping on Arjen Robben, in Brazil's 2010 FIFA World Cup quarter-final defeat to the Netherlands, meant Brazil have had more players sent off in FIFA World Cup history than any other team – one more than Argentina. Melo was Brazil's 11th dismissal, after Kaka had become the 10th in a first-round victory over the Ivory Coast.

Melo could also have gone down as the first player ever to score an own goal and be sent off in the same FIFA World Cup match, but the first Dutch goal was later officially awarded to their own playmaker Wesley Sneijder.

ALL'S FAIR

FIFA World Cup organizers hailed a vast improvement in fair play at the 2014 finals in Brazil. The total of 10 red cards was the lowest since eight in Mexico in 1986 and the tally of 177 yellow cards the fewest since 165 in Italy in 1990 (both finals contained 24 teams and 52 matches). The first dismissal in the group stage was Uruguay's Maxi Pereira against Costa Rica, but the earliest in a game was Portugal defender **Pepe** for a headbutt on Germany's Thomas Muller in the 37th minute of their clash in Salvador. FIFA referee's chief Massimo Busacca also put a sharp reduction in injuries down to greater discipline among players.

THREE LIONS' THREE REDS

Ray Wilkins, David Beckham and Wayne Rooney are the only three England players to have been sent off at the FIFA World Cup. Wilkins was dismissed for a second yellow card in a group game against Morocco in 1986; Beckham incurred a straight red in the second round against Argentina in 1998; and Rooney also received a straight red against Portugal in the 2006 quarter-finals. All three matches ended in draws, but England lost penalty shoot-outs to Argentina and Portugal.

FIFA WORLD CUP ATTENDANCES

CAPACITY PLANNING

If current plans are realised and every seat is occupied, the attendances at the Final of each of the next two FIFA World Cups will exceed significantly the 74,738 who attended the Maracana in Rio de Janeiro for the 2014 climax. Projected capacity for the redeveloped Luzhniki in Moscow, which will stage the 2018 FIFA World Cup Final, is 81,000 while 86,250 is the maximum estimated for the **Lusail** Iconic Stadium in Qatar in 2022. The smallest proposed capacities at the next two World Cups are 43,702 at the Rostov-on-Don stadium in 2018 and then 43,520 at the Qatar University Stadium in Doha in 2022. FIFA regulations insist on a minimum capacity for a finals venue of 40,000.

TWO'S COMPANY, 300'S A CROWD

The 300 people who were recorded as watching Romania beat Peru 3-1 in 1930 formed the FIFA World Cup finals' smallest attendance, with plenty of room for manoeuvre inside the Estadio Pocitos in Montevideo. A day earlier, ten times as many people are thought to have been there to watch France's 4-1 win over Mexico.

BONANZA IN BRAZIL

The 2014 FIFA World Cup in Brazil was watched by a total of 3,429,873 spectators, across the 64 matches in 12 different stadia – the second highest aggregate attendance in the tournament's history, behind only the United States in 1994. The average attendance was 53,592 which meant a 98.4 per cent capacity. That was a marked improvement on South Africa in 2010 when the attendance average was 49,670 with "only" 92.9 per cent of the seats being filled.

CITY SLICKER

The capacity of **Soccer City**, venue for the first FIFA World Cup Final in Africa, was 84,490. This followed a total redevelopment of the original Johannesburg stadium, which had held a maximum 78,000. The design of the new stadium was based on traditional African pottery and nicknamed The Calabash. Soccer City hosted the Opening Match, Final, four group games, and one each in the second round quarter-finals.

GENDER EQUALITY

Only two stadiums have hosted the finals of the FIFA World Cup for both men and women. The **Rose Bowl**, in Pasadena, California, was the venue for the men's final in 1994 – when Brazil beat Italy – and the women's showdown between the victorious US and China five years later, which was watched by 90,185 people. But Sweden's Rasunda Stadium, near Stockholm, just about got there first – though it endured a long wait between the men's final in 1958 and the women's in 1995. Both sets of American spectators got their money's worth, watching games that went into extra-time and which were settled on penalties.

FIFA WORLD CUP FINAL ATTENDANCES

Year	Attendance	Stadium	City
1930	93,000	Estadio Centenario	Montevideo
1934	45,000	Stadio Nazionale del PNF	Rome
1938	60,000	Stade Olympique de Colombes	Paris
1950	173,850	Estadio do Maracana	Rio de Janeiro
1954	60,000	Wankdorfstadion	Berne
1958	51,800	Rasunda Fotbollstadion	Solna
1962	68,679	Estadio Nacional	Santiago
1966	98,000	Wembley Stadium	London
1970	107,412	Estadio Azteca	Mexico City
1974	75,200	Olympiastadion	Munich
1978	71,483	Estadio Monumental	Buenos Aires
1982	90,000	Estadio Santiago Bernabeu	Madrid
1986	114,600	Estadio Azteca	Mexico City
1990	73,603	Stadio Olimpico	Rome
1994	94,194	Rose Bowl	Pasadena
1998	80,000	Stade de France	Paris
2002	69,029	International Stadium	Yokohama
2006	69,000	Olympiastadion	Berlin
2010	84,490	Soccer City	Johannesburg
2014	74,738	Maracana	Rio de Janeiro

TOURNAMENT ATTENDANCES

Year	Total	Average
1930	434,500	24,139
1934	358,000	21,059
1938	376,000	20,889
1950	1,043,500	47,432
1954	889,500	34,212
1958	919,580	26,274
1962	899,074	28,096
1966	1,635,000	51,094
1970	1,603,975	50,124
1974	1,768,152	46,530
1978	1,546,151	40,688
1982	2,109,723	40,572
1986	2,393,331	46,026
1990	2,516,348	48,391
1994	3,587,538	68,991
1998	2,785,100	43,517
2002	2,705,197	42,269
2006	3,359,439	52,491
2010	3,178,856	49,670
2014	3,429,873	53,592
TOTAL	**34,538,837**	**44,903**

FAN FESTS FIND FAVOUR

City centre "**Fan Fests**", including giant television screens, food service and entertainment provision, proved more popular than ever at the 2014 FIFA World Cup in Brazil. Several of the 12 city authorities had been reluctant, initially, to put in the work. But their efforts were rewarded with more than five million fans visiting the sites across Brazil. This was a major improvement on the total of 2.6 million across South Africa in 2010 and the initial fan fests in Germany in 2006. Not surprising, the liveliest party venue in 2014 was the fan fest on **Copacabana** beach in Rio de Janeiro.

ABSENT FRIENDS

Only 2,823 spectators turned up at the Rasunda Stadium in Stockholm to see Wales play Hungary in a first-round play-off match during the 1958 FIFA World Cup. More than 15,000 had attended the first game between the two sides, but boycotted the replay in tribute to executed Hungarian uprising leader Imre Nagy.

MORBID MARACANA

The largest attendance for a FIFA World Cup match was at Rio de Janeiro's Maracana for the last clash of the 1950 tournament – though no one is quite sure how many were there. The final tally was officially given as 173,850, though some estimates suggest as many as 210,000 witnessed the host country's traumatic defeat. Tensions were so high at the final whistle, winning Uruguay captain Obdulio Varela was not awarded the trophy in a traditional manner, but had it surreptitiously nudged into his hands. FIFA president Jules Rimet described the crowd's overwhelming silence as "morbid, almost too difficult to bear". Uruguay's triumphant players barricaded themselves inside their dressing room for several hours before they judged it safe enough to emerge. However, at least Brazil did make it to Maracana in 1950. In the 2014 FIFA World Cup, as hosts again, Brazil played in Sao Paulo, Fortaleza, Brasilia and Belo Horizonte but, after losing in the semi-finals, ended up back in Brasilia for the third-place play-off instead of Maracana for the Final.

FIFA WORLD CUP STADIUMS & HOSTS

BERLIN CALL

Despite later becoming the capital of a united Germany, then-divided Berlin only hosted three group games at the 1974 FIFA World Cup in West Germany – the host country's surprise loss to East Germany took place in Hamburg. An unexploded World War Two bomb was discovered beneath the seats at Berlin's Olympiastadion in 2002, by workers preparing the ground for the 2006 tournament. Germany, along with Brazil, had applied to host the tournament in 1942, before it was cancelled due to the outbreak of World War Two.

TWIN PEAKS

Five stadiums hold the distinction of having staged both the final of a FIFA World Cup and the summer Olympics athletics: Berlin's Olympiastadion (1936 Olympics, 2006 World Cup), Paris's Stade Colombes (1924 Olympics, 1938 World Cup), London's Wembley (1948 Olympics, 1966 World Cup), Rome's Stadio Olimpico (1960 Olympics, 1990 World Cup) and Munich's Olympiastadion (1972 Olympics, 1974 World Cup). The Estadio Azteca (Mexico City) and Rose Bowl (Pasadena) have both hosted World Cup finals as well as Olympic football finals.

OLYMPIC NAMES

The stadium hosting the opening match of the 1930 FIFA World Cup had stands named after great Uruguayan footballing triumphs: Colombes, in honour of the 1924 Paris Olympics venue; Amsterdam, after the site where that title was retained four years later; and Montevideo, even though it would be another fortnight before the home team clinched the first FIFA World Cup in their own capital city.

RIO'S MARIO

Most people know Brazil's largest stadium as the Maracana, named after the Rio neighbourhood and a small nearby river. But, since the mid-1960s, the official title has been "Estadio Mario Filho" after the influential sports journalist and editor who campaigned for the stadium's construction on that site.

TERRITORIAL GAINS

History was made twice over when **FIFA** decided in December 2010 which countries would stage the 2018 and 2022 FIFA World Cups. The 2018 vote went in favour of Russia – ahead of Spain/Portugal, Belgium/Netherlands and England – meaning the first FIFA World Cup to be held in Eastern Europe. The tournament will then go to the Middle East for the first time in 2022, after Qatar emerged ahead of rival bids from the USA, Japan, South Korea and Australia.

MEXICAN SAVE

Mexico was not the original choice to host the 1986 FIFA World Cup, but stepped in when Colombia withdrew in 1982 due to financial problems. Mexico held on to the staging rights despite suffering from an earthquake in September 1985 that left approximately 10,000 people dead, but which left the stadiums unscathed. FIFA kept faith in the country, and the **Azteca Stadium** went on to become the first venue to host two FIFA World Cup final matches – and Mexico the first country to stage two FIFA World Cups. The Azteca – formally named the "Estadio Guillermo Canedo", after a Mexican football official – was built in 1960 using 100,000 tonnes of concrete, four times as much as was needed for the old Wembley.

ARCHITECTS' PREROGATIVE

Distinctive and creative elements were added to the stadiums built especially for the 2010 FIFA World Cup in South Africa, including the giraffe-shaped towers at **Nelspruit's Mbombela stadium**, the 350-metre-long arch with its mobile viewing platform soaring above **Durban's main arena**, and the white "petals" shrouding the Nelson Mandela Bay stadium in Port Elizabeth.

UNSUCCESSFUL HOSTING BIDS

1930	Hungary, Italy, Netherlands, Spain, Sweden
1934	Sweden
1938	Argentina, Germany
1950	None
1954	None
1958	None
1962	Argentina, West Germany
1966	Spain, West Germany
1970	Argentina
1974	Spain
1978	Mexico
1982	West Germany
1986	Colombia*, Canada, USA
1990	England, Greece, USSR
1994	Brazil, Morocco
1998	Morocco, Switzerland
2002	Mexico
2006	Brazil, England, Morocco, South Africa
2010	Egypt, Libya/Tunisia, Morocco
2014	None
2018	England, Netherlands/Belgium, Spain/Portugal
2022	Australia, Japan, South Korea, USA

* Colombia won hosting rights for 1986 but later withdrew.

MORE MARACANA

No other stadium than the **Maracana** in Rio de Janeiro was considered for even a moment when it came to choosing the host venue for the 2014 FIFA World Cup in Brazil. On 13 July it duly became the second venue, after the Estadio Azteca in Mexico City, to host the FIFA World Cup final for the second time. Although the official attendance is now given as 173,850, it is thought that anything up to 210,000 may have jammed the Maracana for the 1950 final group match between Brazil and Uruguay. Several redevelopments saw capacity reduced to an all-seater capacity of around 75,000 by the time of the 2014 showpiece between Germany and Argentina. The latest facelift for Maracana, which is owned by the Rio de Janeiro state government, cost an estimated $500m. As one of the first stadiums to be ready, it hosted the final of the 2013 Confederations Cup "rehearsal" tournament. The Maracana will also stage the Opening and Closing Ceremonies of the Rio de Janeiro 2016 Olympic Games.

RATIONAL IN RUSSIA

Organizers of the 2018 FIFA World Cup in Russia plan to return to the "clusters" system of adjacent city venues to ease travel, accommodation and logistical problems, thus reducing the costs for fans. Unlike Brazil 2014, one city – Moscow – will have two venues: the **Luzhniki** Olympic Stadium and Spartak Moscow's new home. The "clusters" concept was last used in the United States in 1994. Michel Platini, president of the France 1998 organizing committee, scrapped the idea to spread the top teams all around the country. FIFA wanted to reinstate the system for the 2014 finals in Brazil but local organizers refused.

HOSTS WITH THE MOST

No other single-hosted FIFA World Cup has used as many venues as the 14 spread across Spain in 1982. The 2002 tournament was played at 20 different venues, but ten of these were in Japan and ten in co-host country South Korea.

FIFA WORLD CUP PENALTIES

FIFA WORLD CUP PENALTY SHOOT-OUTS

Year	Round	120-minute Score	Winners	Shoot-out Score
1982	Semi-final	West Germany 3 France 3	West Germany	5-4
1986	Quarter-final	West Germany 0 Mexico 0	West Germany	4-1
1986	Quarter-final	France 1 Brazil 1	France	4-3
1986	Quarter-final	Belgium 1 Spain 1	Belgium	5-4
1990	Second round	Republic of Ireland 0 Romania 0	Republic of Ireland	5-4
1990	Quarter-final	Argentina 0 Yugoslavia 0	Argentina	3-2
1990	Semi-final	Argentina 1 Italy 1	Argentina	4-3
1990	Semi-final	West Germany 1 England 1	West Germany	4-3
1994	Second round	Bulgaria 1 Mexico 1	Bulgaria	3-1
1994	Quarter-final	Sweden 2 Romania 2	Sweden	5-4
1994	Final	Brazil 0 Italy 0	Brazil	3-2
1998	Second round	Argentina 2 England 2	Argentina	4-3
1998	Quarter-final	France 0 Italy 0	France	4-3
1998	Semi-final	Brazil 1 Netherlands 1	Brazil	4-2
2002	Second round	Spain 1 Republic of Ireland 1	Spain	3-2
2002	Quarter-final	South Korea 0 Spain 0	South Korea	5-3
2006	Second round	Ukraine 0 Switzerland 0	Ukraine	3-0
2006	Quarter-final	Germany 1 Argentina 1	Germany	4-2
2006	Quarter-final	Portugal 0 England 0	Portugal	3-1
2006	Final	Italy 1 France 1	Italy	5-3
2010	Second round	Paraguay 0 Japan 0	Paraguay	5-3
2010	Quarter-final	Uruguay 1 Ghana 1	Uruguay	4-2
2014	Second round	Brazil 1 Chile 1	Brazil	3-2
2014	Second round	Costa Rica 1 Greece 1	Costa Rica	5-3
2014	Quarter-final	Netherlands 0 Costa Rica 0	Netherlands	4-3
2014	Semi-final	Argentina 0 Netherlands 0	Argentina	4-2

BAGGIO OF DISHONOUR

Pity poor **Roberto Baggio**: the Italian maestro stepped up in three FIFA World Cup penalty shoot-outs, more than any other player – and has been a loser in every one. Most painfully, it was his shot over the bar that gifted Brazil the trophy at the end of the 1994 Final. But he had also ended on the losing side against Argentina in a 1990 semi-final and would do so again, against France in a 1998 quarter-final. At least, in 1990 and 1998, his own attempts were successful.

FIRST IS BETTER

Nine penalty shoot-outs in a row were won by the team taking the first kick. The run started with South Korea's quarter-final defeat of Spain in the 2002 FIFA World Cup and ended after Costa Rica's second round win over Greece in 2014. The Netherlands went second and still beat Costa Rica in the 2014 quarter-finals and then went first when losing the semi-final to Argentina.

WOE FOR ASAMOAH

Ghana striker **Asamoah Gyan** is the only player to have missed two penalties during match-time at FIFA World Cups. He hit the post with a spot-kick against the Czech Republic during a group game at the 2006 tournament, then struck a shot against the bar with the final kick of extra-time in Ghana's 2010 quarter-final versus Uruguay. Had he scored then, Gyan would have given Ghana a 2–1 win – following Luis Suarez's goal-stopping handball on the goal-line – and a first African place in a FIFA World Cup semi-final. Despite such a traumatic miss, Gyan did then step up to take Ghana's first penalty in the shoot-out, again striking it high – but this time into the back of the net. His team still lost, though, 4–2 on penalties.

FRENCH KICKS

The first penalty shoot-out at a FIFA World Cup finals came in the 1982 semi-final in Seville between West Germany and France, when French takers Didier Six and **Maxime Bossis** were the unfortunate players to miss. The same two countries met in the semi-finals four years later – and West Germany again won, though in normal time, 2-0. The record for most shoot-outs is shared by the 1990 and 2006 tournaments, with four apiece. Both semi-finals in 1990 went to penalties, while the 2006 final was the second to be settled that manner – Italy beating France 5-3 after David Trezeguet struck the crossbar.

COSTA RICA'S KRUL FATE

Costa Rica enjoyed a thrilling ride at the 2014 FIFA World Cup. Los Ticos started by topping a first round "Group of Death", featuring three former world champions in Uruguay, Italy and England. Coach Jorge Luis Pinto then saw his men draw 1-1 with Greece in the second round and win the shoot-out 5-3 to reach the quarter-finals for the first time ever. Heroes were goalkeeper Keylor Navas, in saving from Teo Gekas, and last-shot defender Michael Umana. History appeared to be repeating itself when Costa Rica held Netherlands goalless to earn another shoot-out. But this time they were foiled by Dutch coach Louis Van Gaal. He sent on reserve goalkeeper **Tim Krul** as substitute for Jasper Cillessen in the last minute of extra time, as Van Gaal explained, "because he has a longer reach." Krul duly saved kicks from Bryan Ruiz and Umana and the Dutch won the shoot-out 4-3. Costa Rica were still welcomed home as heroes.

THREE IN ONE

Argentina's stand-in goalkeeper Sergio Goycochea set a tournament record by saving four shoot-out penalties in 1990 – though West Germany's Harald Schumacher managed as many, across the 1982 and 1986 tournaments. Portugal's Ricardo achieved an unprecedented feat by keeping out three attempts in a single shoot-out, becoming an instant hero in his side's quarter-final win over England in 2006.

PENALTY SHOOT-OUTS BY COUNTRY

5	Argentina (4 wins, 1 defeat)	1	Belgium (1 win)
4	Germany/West Germany (4 wins)	1	Bulgaria (1 win)
		1	Paraguay (1 win)
4	Brazil (3 wins, 1 defeat)	1	Portugal (1 win)
4	France (2 wins, 2 defeats)	1	South Korea (1 win)
4	Italy (1 win, 3 defeats)	1	Sweden (1 win)
3	Netherlands (1 win, 2 defeats)	1	Ukraine (1 win)
		1	Uruguay (1 win)
3	Spain (1 win, 2 defeats)	1	Yugoslavia (1 win)
3	England (3 defeats)	1	Chile (1 defeat)
2	Costa Rica (1 win, 1 defeat)	1	Ghana (1 defeat)
2	Republic of Ireland (1 win, 1 defeat)	1	Greece (1 defeat)
		1	Japan (1 defeat)
2	Mexico (2 defeats)	1	Switzerland (1 defeat)
2	Romania (2 defeats)		

GERMAN EFFICIENCY

Germany, or West Germany, have won all four of their FIFA World Cup penalty shoot-outs, more than any other team. Argentina also have four wins, but they have lost one – to Germany in the 2006 quarter-final. The German run began with a semi-final victory over France in 1982, when goalkeeper Harald Schumacher was the matchwinner, despite being lucky to stay on the pitch for a vicious extra-time foul on France's Patrick Battiston. West Germany also reached the 1990 final thanks to their shoot-out expertise, this time proving superior to England – as they similarly did in the 1996 European Championships semi-final. In that 2006 quarter-final, Germany's goalkeeper Jens Lehmann consulted a note predicting the direction the Argentine players were likely to shoot towards. The vital information was scribbled on a scrap of hotel notepaper by Germany's chief scout Urs Siegenthaler. The only German national team to lose a major tournament penalty shoot-out were the West Germans, who contested the 1976 UEFA European Championships final against Czechoslovakia – their first shoot-out experience, and clearly an effective lesson, because they have not lost a shoot-out since.

THE PLAYERS WHO MISSED IN SHOOT-OUTS

Argentina: Diego Maradona (1990), Pedro Troglio (1990), Hernan Crespo (1998), Roberto Ayala (2006), Esteban Cambiasso (2006)
Brazil: Socrates (1986), Julio Cesar (1986), Marcio Santos (1994), Willian (2014), Hulk (2014)
Bulgaria: Krassimir Balakov (1994)
Chile: Mauricio Pinilla (2014), Alexis Sanchez (2014), Gonzalo Jara (2014)
Costa Rica: Bryan Ruiz (2014), Michael Umana (2014)
England: Stuart Pearce (1990), Chris Waddle (1990), Paul Ince (1998), David Batty (1998), Frank Lampard (2006), Steven Gerrard (2006), Jamie Carragher (2006)
France: Didier Six (1982), Maxime Bossis (1982), Michel Platini (1986), Bixente Lizarazu (1998), David Trezeguet (2006)
Germany/West Germany: Uli Stielike (1982)
Ghana: John Mensah (2010), Dominic Adiyiah (2010)
Greece: Theofanis Gekas (2014)
Italy: Roberto Donadoni (1990), Aldo Serena (1990), Franco Baresi (1994), Daniele Massaro (1994), Roberto Baggio (1994), Demetrio Albertini (1998), Luigi Di Biagio (1998)

Japan: Yuichi Komano (2010)
Mexico: Fernando Quirarte (1986), Raul Servin (1986), Alberto Garcia Aspe (1994), Marcelino Bernal (1994), Jorge Rodriguez (1994)
Netherlands: Phillip Cocu (1998), Ronald de Boer (1998), Ron Vlaar (2014), Wesley Sneijder (2014)
Portugal: Hugo Viana (2006), Petit (2006)
Republic of Ireland: Matt Holland (2002), David Connolly (2002), Kevin Kilbane (2002)
Romania: Daniel Timofte (1990), Dan Petrescu (1994), Miodrag Belodedici (1994)
Spain: Eloy (1986), Juanfran (2002), Juan Carlos Valeron (2002), Joaquin (2002)
Sweden: Hakan Mild (1994)
Switzerland: Marco Streller (2006), Tranquillo Barnetta (2006), Ricardo Cabanas (2006)
Ukraine: Andriy Shevchenko (2006)
Uruguay: Maximiliano Pereira (2010)
Yugoslavia: Dragan Stojkovic (1990), Dragoljub Brnovic (1990), Faruk Hadzibegic (1990)

PART 3: UEFA EUROPEAN CHAMPIONSHIP

THE UEFA European Championship finals have gone from being a four-team curiosity, snubbed by major nations, to perhaps the third-biggest sporting event on earth, behind only the FIFA World Cup and the Summer Olympic Games. UEFA, the European football confederation, was founded during the 1954 FIFA World Cup in Switzerland and initially set itself the task of creating a championship for national teams. Many major European nations – such as Italy, West Germany and England – refused to take part in the initial competition, launched in 1958, because their national associations feared fixture congestion. So the first finals, featuring four nations, were staged in France and saw the Soviet Union end up as first winners after defeating Yugoslavia in the final in Paris's original Parc des Princes.

Now the map of Europe has changed so remarkably that, while UEFA's membership has more than doubled, the Soviet Union and Yugoslavia no longer exist. The Soviets also reached the second finals in 1964 but lost their crown in the final against their Spanish hosts in the Estadio Bernabeu in Madrid. Spain's playmaker Luis Suarez, from Italy's Internazionale, thus became the first player to win the European Championship and the European Cup in the same season.

In the tournament's early years, qualifying was based on a simple two-legged knockout system, but this was amended to a group-based format and then, in 1980, the finals were expanded to eight nations. That year saw West Germany win for a second time, having previously triumphed in 1972. The next expansion, to 16 teams in England in 1996, saw unified Germany win their record third title, defeat the Czech Republic (once half of Czechoslovakia) with an extra-time golden goal.

In 2000 France won the first finals with co-hosts – Belgium and the Netherlands. Greece shocked hosts Portugal in 2004, while Spain won back-to-back championships in co-hosted finals in 2008 and 2012, first in Austria and Switzerland then in Poland and Ukraine. Euro 2016 featured, for the first time, 24 teams. Portugal beat the hosts France in the final. In 2020, London's Wembley stadium will stage the semi-finals and final, but 13 cities in 13 different nations will host games.

> Captain Cristiano Ronaldo went off injured after 25 minutes of the 2016 UEFA European Championship final against hosts France, but was given back the armband to collect Portugal's first major trophy after their 1-0 extra-time victory.

The UEFA European Championship qualifying competition is now a huge event in its own right. For Euro 2016, 53 countries battled through a group stage to join hosts France, who qualified automatically. Times had changed since the 1960 competition when only 17 nations entered and were winnowed down by a two-leg knockout tournament. The 1968 tournament was the first for which a group stage was introduced with seven groups of four and one group of three. By 2014 UEFA had 54 members so the qualifying competition has had to grow to match that expansion. For Euro 2016 the top two in all nine groups and the third-placed team with the best record all qualified automatically. The remaining four spots were decided by two-legged play-offs between the eight other third-placed teams.

QUICK TURNOVER

Germany's **Joachim Low** was the only manager from the eight Euro 2008 quarter-finalists still in his job for the 2016 finals. Low guided Germany to the final that year in Austria and Switzerland and then to the semi-finals in Poland and Ukraine in 2012. Two years later, he further enhanced his reputation when Germany defeated Argentina in Rio de Janeiro's Maracana to win the 2014 FIFA World Cup in Brazil.

IRISH VICTORY NOT ENOUGH

West Germany's 1-0 defeat by Northern Ireland in Hamburg on 11 November 1983 was their first-ever home loss in the qualifying competition, but their 2-1 win over Albania in Saarbrucken four days later enabled them to pip Northern Ireland on goal difference for a place in the 1984 finals.

FONTAINE MAKES HISTORY JUST SO

Just Fontaine of France scored the first hat-trick in Euro history in the inaugural 1958-60 tournament. Fontaine, top scorer at the 1958 FIFA World Cup, hit three goals in France's 5-2 second-round win over Austria in Paris on 13 December 1959. France won the return 4-2 for a 9-4 aggregate win and went on to host the finals, at which they finished fourth.

ROCKING UP

Gibraltar became the most recent European Championship qualifying competition debutants when they played Poland in September 2014. UEFA had tightened their rules for admission to the federation, but the Gibraltar Football Association appealed to the Court of Arbitration for Sport and their 16-year legal battle ended in 2013, when the CAS asserted their right to join Europe's football family. UEFA decided, diplomatically, that Spain and Gibraltar would be kept apart in competition draws. There was no dream home competitive debut for the "Rock", as they suffered a 7-0 defeat by Poland in a match played in Faro in neighbouring Portugal. Tormentor-in-chief was Robert Lewandowski, who scored four times. Things got no easier for Gibraltar in their remaining matches as, despite scoring two goals, they conceded 57 in all, including another eight to Poland and seven more to both Germany and the Republic of Ireland.

GERMANS RUN UP 13

Germany's 13-0 win in San Marino on 6 September 2006 was the biggest victory margin in qualifying history. **Lukas Podolski** (4), Miroslav Klose (2), Bastian Schweinsteiger (2), Thomas Hitzlsperger (2), Michael Ballack, Manuel Friedrich and Bernd Schneider scored the goals. The previous biggest win was Spain's 12-1 rout of Malta in 1983.

GERMANY'S WEMBLEY WONDER NIGHT

West Germany's greatest-ever team announced their arrival at Wembley on 29 April 1972, when they beat England 3-1 in the first leg of the UEFA European Championship quarter-finals. Uli Hoeness, Gunter Netzer and Gerd Muller scored the goals. West Germany went on to win the trophy, beating the Soviet Union 3-0 in the final. Their team at Wembley was: Sepp Maier; Horst Hottges, Georg Schwarzenbeck, Franz Beckenbauer, Paul Breitner; Jurgen Grabowski, Herbert Wimmer, Gunter Netzer, Uli Hoeness; Sigi Held, Gerd Muller. Eight of them played in West Germany's 1974 FIFA World Cup final win over the Netherlands.

APPEARANCES IN THE FINALS TOURNAMENT

12	West Germany/Germany
11	Soviet Union/CIS/Russia
10	Spain
9	Czechoslovakia/Czech Republic
	England
	France
	Italy
	Netherlands
8	Denmark
7	Portugal
6	Sweden
5	Belgium
	Croatia
	Romania
	Yugoslavia
4	Greece
	Switzerland
	Turkey
3	Hungary
	Poland
	Republic of Ireland
2	Austria
	Bulgaria
	Scotland
	Ukraine
1	Albania
	Iceland
	Latvia
	Northern Ireland
	Norway
	Slovakia
	Slovenia
	Wales

Includes appearances as hosts/co-hosts.

LEWANDOWSKI ON TERMS WITH HEALY

Poland's **Robert Lewandowski** was leading marksman in the UEFA Euro 2016 qualifying competition with 13 goals – to equal the mark set by Northern Ireland's **David Healy** in the Euro 2008 preliminaries. The difference was that, unlike the luckless Healy, Lewandowski's goals shot his team to the finals and extended a proud record. After being the Polish league's top scorer with Lech Poznan, he reached 100 goals in the German Bundesliga quicker than any non-German-born player, achieving the feat for Borussia Dortmund and then Bayern Munich. Lewandowski's qualifying goals saw him rise up to fifth in Poland's all-time scoring charts.

HOSTS ARE PLACED IN EURO 2016 QUALIFYING GROUP

France, as hosts, qualified automatically for the 2016 UEFA European Championship finals. However, they were included in the qualifying competition draw and were placed in Group I. They did not play competitive matches, but had friendlies against the team not in action during each round of games. France thus had home and away friendlies against the five Group I teams, Albania, Armenia, Denmark, Portugal and Serbia.

PANCEV FORCED TO MISS OUT

Yugoslavia's **Darko Pancev** (born in Skopje on 7 September 1965) was top scorer in the qualifiers for Euro 1992 with ten goals. Yugoslavia topped qualifying Group Four, but they were banned from the finals because of their country's war in Bosnia, so Pancev never had the chance to shine. After the break-up of the Yugoslav federation, he went on to become the star player for the new nation of Macedonia.

ANDORRA, SAN MARINO STRUGGLE

Minnows Andorra and San Marino each have yet to win a European Championship qualifier. Andorra have lost all of their 50 games, with a goal difference of 11-149. San Marino, whose first-ever point came in a November 2014 0-0 draw with Estonia, have lost their other 65 matches. San Marino's goal difference is 7-289 and their -55 goal difference in 2008 qualifying is the worst ever.

DUTCH EDGE FIRST PLAY-OFF

The first-ever group qualifying play-off was held on 13 December 1995 at Liverpool's Anfield stadium when the Netherlands beat the Republic of Ireland 2-0 to clinch the final place at Euro 96. Patrick Kluivert scored both Dutch goals.

EURO 2016 REVIEW

The 15th European Championship was held in June and July 2016 on the competition's regular four-year cycle that has run ever since 1960. For the third time the finals were staged in France, with matches in 10 cities spread across the length and breadth of the country. As well as the hosts, 23 further nations took part including other former winners in Czech Republic (previously Czechoslovakia), Germany (the unified West and East Germany), Italy, Russia (previously Soviet Union) and Spain.

DYNAMIC DUO

Portugal's victory brought double delight for central defender **Pepe** and striker **Cristiano Ronaldo**. Both had also won the UEFA Champions League six weeks earlier when Real Madrid defeated neighbours Atletico in a penalty shoot-out in Milan. They were the eighth and ninth players to collect both winners' medals in the same season after Luis Suarez (Internazionale and Spain in 1964), Hans Van Breukelen, Ronald Koeman, Barry Van Aerle and Gerald Vanenburg (Netherlands and PSV Eindhoven in 1988), as well as Fernando Torres and Juan Mata (Spain and Chelsea) in 2012.

HISTORY LESSON FROM BALE BOYS

Euro 2016 was the first major tournament since the 1986 World Cup to feature at least three of the four British home nations. Wales, inspired by Real Madrid forward **Gareth Bale**, wrote their own place into the history books by reaching the semi-finals. They beat Northern Ireland in the second round, which also marked the end of the line for the Irish Republic at the hands of France. England's much-vaunted attack managed only two goals from open play in their four matches: their two other goals came from an Eric Dier free-kick against Russia and a Wayne Rooney penalty against Iceland.

PORTUGAL'S FAIRY TALE FANTASY COMES TRUE

Portugal won the first major trophy in their history when they defeated hosts France 1-0 after extra time in the final of the Euro 2016 at the Stade de France in Saint-Denis. They did so with animal instincts, according to manager Fernando Santos. After the match he said: "We were as simple as doves and as wise as serpents." He also described match-winner Eder as "an ugly duckling" who turned into a swan. Eder had made no impact at Swansea in the English Premier League at the start of the season, but then moved to French club Lille to regain the confidence that was rewarded with his 109th-minute winning goal. This was the first European final to remain goalless in the regulation 90 minutes; four others had ended at 1-1 before the extra period, while West Germany and Czechoslovakia shared four goals in 1976, the only final to be decided in a penalty shoot-out – the Czechs winning 5-3.

PLAY IT AGAIN, GABOR

Hungary made a bright cherry-red return on their first appearance in the finals since finishing fourth in 1972. Stars of the Magyars' show included tracksuit-trousers-wearing goalkeeper **Gabor Kiraly**, who became the oldest player ever to appear in the finals at 40 years 86 days.

GERMAN TRIO LEAVE THEIR MARK

Consolation to Germany, beaten by France in the semi-finals, was to see three of their players named in UEFA's official Team of the Tournament. Defender Jerome Boateng and midfielder Toni Kroos had been World Cup-winners in 2014 but Bayern Munich right-back Joshua Kimmich was a big-stage newcomer. Sir Alex Ferguson, former Manchester United manager, was among the panel who chose the team: The Team of the Tournament, as chosen by UEFA's technical observers, was: Rui Patricio (Portugal) – Joshua Kimmich (Germany), Jerome Boateng (Germany), Pepe (Portugal), Raphael Guerrero (Portugal) – Toni Kroos (Germany), Joe Allen (Wales) – Antoine Griezmann (France), Aaron Ramsey (Wales), Dmitri Payet (France) – Cristiano Ronaldo (Portugal).

THE FINALS RECKONING

1960 Soviet Union 2, Yugoslavia 1
after extra time (Paris)
1964 Spain 2, Soviet Union 1 (Madrid)
1968 Italy 1, Yugoslavia 1
after extra time (Rome)
Replay: Italy 2, Yugoslavia 0 (Rome)
1972 West Germany 3, Soviet Union 0
(Brussels)
1976 Czechoslovakia 2, West Germany 2
after extra time
Czechoslovakia 5-3 on pens (Belgrade)
1980 West Germany 2, Belgium 1 (Rome)
1984 France 2, Spain 0 (Paris)
1988 Netherlands 2 Soviet Union 0 (Munich)
1992 Denmark 2, Germany 0 (Gothenburg)
1996 Germany 2, Czech Republic 1
golden goal, after extra time (Wembley)
2000 France 2 Italy 1
golden goal, after extra time (Rotterdam)
2004 Greece 1, Portugal 0 (Lisbon)
2008 Spain 1, Germany 0 (Vienna)
2012 Spain 4 Italy 0 (Kyiv)
2016 Portugal 1, France 0 after extra time
(Saint-Denis)

ZLATAN FADE–OUT

Sweden striker **Zlatan Ibrahimovic** said his goodbyes to both his national team and to French football after his country's first-round exit. Ibrahimovic, about to quit Paris Saint-Germain for Manchester United, did not manage to mark his farewell to national team football with a goal.

THE ICEMEN COMETH ... IN GLORY

Iceland made a massive impression at the Euro 2016 finals not only through their remarkable debut tournament run to the quarter-finals, but also thanks to the "Huh" chant of their fans. At one stage it was estimated that eight per cent of the population of 330,000 were in France, including newly elected Prime Minister Sigurdur Ingi Johannsson. The players flew home as heroes, especially Hannes Halldorsson who recorded 27 saves, more than any other goalkeeper at the finals, midfielder Gylfi Sigurdsson and the goalscorers in the historic second-round win over England, Ragnar Sigurdsson and Kolbeinn Sigthorsson.

'NEW COLUNA' LIVES UP TO HIS PRICE

Renato Sanches was voted Young Player of the Tournament at Euro 2016, ahead of France's Kingsley Coman and Portugal team-mate Raphael Guerreiro. The 18-year-old was an influential substitute in Portugal's first four matches in France to earn his first international start in the quarter-final against Poland – when he scored his first international goal. Two games later, aged 18 years and 328 days against France, he became the youngest-ever player in the final and youngest winner. Sanches, compared with old hero Mario Coluna by manager Fernando Santos, thus justified the €35 million fee Bayern Munich had just paid to Benfica.

UEFA EUROPEAN CHAMPIONSHIP TEAM RECORDS

FANCY SEEING YOU AGAIN

When Spain and Italy met in the 2012 final it was the fourth time UEFA European Championship opponents had faced each other twice in the same tournament. Each time, it followed a first-round encounter. The Netherlands lost to the Soviet Union, then beat them in the final in 1988; Germany beat the Czech Republic twice at Euro 96, including the final; and Greece did the same to Portugal in 2004. Spain and Italy drew in Euro 2012's Group C, with Cesc Fabregas replying to Antonio Di Natale's opener for Italy. Their second showdown was rather less even.

THREE OFF AS CZECHS ADVANCE

Czechoslovakia's 3-1 semi-final win over the Netherlands in Zagreb, on 16 June 1976, featured a record three red cards. The Czechs' Jaroslav Pollak was dismissed for a second yellow card – a foul on Johan Neeskens – after an hour. Neeskens followed in the 76th minute for kicking Zdenek Nehoda. Wim van Hanegem became the second Dutchman dismissed, for dissent, after Nehoda scored the Czechs' second goal with six minutes of extra-time left.

DENMARK'S UNEXPECTED TRIUMPH

Denmark were unlikely winners of UEFA Euro 1992. They had not even expected to take part after finishing behind Yugoslavia in their qualifying group, but they were invited to complete the final eight when Yugoslavia were barred for security fears following the country's collapse. Goalkeeper **Peter Schmeichel** was their hero – in the semi-final shoot-out win over the Netherlands and again in the final against Germany, when goals by John Jensen and Kim Vilfort earned Denmark a 2-0 win.

SWEET UEFA

In 56 years, the UEFA European Championship has grown to become arguably the most important international football tournament after the FIFA World Cup. Only 17 teams entered the first four-team tournament, won by the Soviet Union in 1960 – yet 53 took part in qualifying for the right to join hosts France in a newly expanded 24-team event in 2016. Germany (formerly West Germany) and Spain have each won the competition three times, though the Germans have played and won most matches (49 and 26, respectively), as well as scoring and conceding more goals (72 and 48) than any other nation. Defender Berti Vogts is the only man to win the tournament as a player (1972) and coach (1996), both with the Germans. Portugal's 2016 triumph, in their 35th UEFA European Championship finals match, means England have now played most tournament games (31) without ever managing to lift the trophy.

DOMENGHINI RESCUES ITALY

The most controversial goal in the history of the final came on 8 June 1968. Hosts Italy were trailing 1-0 to Yugoslavia with ten minutes left. The Yugoslavs seemed still to be organizing their wall when Angelo Domenghini curled a free-kick past goalkeeper Ilja Pantelic for the equalizer. Yugoslavia protested but the goal was allowed to stand. Italy won the only replay in finals history 2-0, two days later, with goals from Gigi Riva and Pietro Anastasi.

FRANCE BOAST PERFECT RECORD

France, on home soil in 1984, are the only side to win all their matches since the finals expanded beyond four teams. They won them without any shoot-outs, too, beating Denmark 1-0, Belgium 5-0 and Yugoslavia 3-2 in their group, Portugal 3-2 after extra-time in the semi-finals and Spain 2-0 in the final.

CZECHS WIN MOST EFFICIENT SHOOT-OUT

The most efficient penalty shoot-out in the finals was the third-place play-off between hosts Italy and Czechoslovakia, in Naples on 21 June 1980. The Czechs won 9-8, following a 1-1 draw. After eight successful spot-kicks each, Czech goalkeeper **Jaroslav Netolicka** saved Fulvio Collovati's kick. In 2016, there were also 18 penalties when Germany won their quarter-final against Italy, 6-5 at Bordeaux, with the last of Italy's four misses being by Matteo Darmian.

FRANCE STRIKE, WITHOUT STRIKERS

France still hold the record for the most goals scored by one team in a finals tournament, 14 in 1984. Yet only one of those goals was netted by a recognized striker – Bruno Bellone, who hit the second in their 2-0 final win over Spain. France's inspirational captain, Michel Platini, supplied most of the French firepower, scoring an incredible nine goals in five appearances. He hit hat-tricks against Belgium and Denmark and a last-gasp winner in the semi-final against Portugal. Midfielders Alain Giresse and Luis Fernandez chipped in with goals in the 5-0 win over Belgium. Defender Jean-Francois Domergue gave France the lead against Portugal in the semi-finals, and added another in extra-time after Jordao had put Portugal 2-1 ahead.

SAME OLD SPAIN

Spain not only cruised their way to the largest winning margin of any UEFA European Championship final by trouncing Italy 4-0 in the climax to 2012 – they also became the first country to successfully defend the title. David Silva, **Jordi Alba** – with his first international goal – and substitutes Fernando Torres and Juan Mata got the goals in Kiev's Olympic Stadium on 1 July. Spain thus landed their third major trophy in a row, having won Euro 2008 and the 2010 FIFA World Cup.

TOP TEAM SCORERS IN THE FINALS

1960	Yugoslavia	6
1964	Spain, Soviet Union, Hungary	4
1968	Italy	4
1972	West Germany	5
1976	West Germany	6
1980	West Germany	6
1984	France	14
1988	Netherlands	8
1992	Germany	7
1996	Germany	10
2000	France, Netherlands	13
2004	Czech Republic	9
2008	Spain	12
2012	Spain	12
2016	France	13

BIGGEST WINS IN THE FINALS

Netherlands 6, Yugoslavia 1, 2000
France 5, Belgium 0, 1984
Denmark 5, Yugoslavia 0, 1984
Sweden 5, Bulgaria 0, 2004

SPAIN REFUSE TO MEET SOVIETS

Political rivalries wrecked the planned clash between Spain and the Soviet Union in the 1960 quarter-finals. The fascist Spanish leader, General Francisco Franco, refused to allow Spain to go to the communist Soviet Union – and banned the Soviets from entering Spain. The Soviet Union were handed a walkover on the grounds that Spain had refused to play. Franco relented four years later, allowing the Soviets to come to Spain for the finals. He was spared the embarrassment of presenting the trophy to them, however, as Spain beat the Soviet Union 2-1 in the final.

UEFA EUROPEAN CHAMPIONSHIP WINNERS

3	West Germany/Germany (1972, 1980, 1996)
	Spain (1964, 2008, 2012)
2	France (1984, 2000)
1	Soviet Union (1960)
	Italy (1968)
	Czechoslovakia (1976)
	Netherlands (1988)
	Denmark (1992)
	Greece (2004)
	Portugal (2016)

DELLAS TIMES IT RIGHT FOR GREECE

Greece scored the only "silver goal" victory in Euro history in a 2004 semi-final. (The silver goal rule meant that a team leading after the first period of extra-time won the match.) **Traianos Dellas** headed Greece's winner seconds before the end of the first period of extra-time against the Czech Republic in Porto on 1 July. Both golden goals and silver goals were abandoned for UEFA Euro 2008, and drawn knockout ties reverted to being decided over the full 30 minutes of extra-time, and penalties if necessary.

TOSS FAVOURS HOSTS ITALY

Italy reached the 1968 final on home soil thanks to the toss of a coin. It was the only game in finals history decided in such fashion. Italy drew 0-0 against the Soviet Union after extra-time in Naples on 5 June 1968. The Soviet captain, Albert Shesternev, made the wrong call at the toss – so Italy reached the final where they beat Yugoslavia.

PLAYER RECORDS

SHEARER TALLY BOOSTS ENGLAND

Alan Shearer is the only Englishman to top the finals scoring chart. Shearer led the scorers with five goals as England lost on penalties to Germany in the Euro 96 semi-final at Wembley. He netted against Switzerland, Scotland and the Netherlands (two) in the group and gave England a third-minute lead against the Germans. He added two more goals at Euro 2000 and now is behind only Michel Platini and Cristiano Ronaldo in the all-time list.

ILYIN GOAL MAKES HISTORY

Anatoly Ilyin of the Soviet Union scored the first goal in UEFA European Championship history when he netted after four minutes against Hungary on 29 September 1958. A crowd of 100,572 watched the Soviets win 3-1 in the Lenin Stadium, Moscow. The Soviet Union went on to win the first final, in 1960.

GOLDEN ONE-TOUCH

Spain striker Fernando Torres claimed the Golden Boot, despite scoring the same number of goals – three – as Italy's Mario Balotelli, Russia's Alan Dzagoev, Germany's Mario Gomez, Croatia's Mario Mandzukic and Portugal's Cristiano Ronaldo. The decision came down to number of assists – with Torres and Gomez level on one apiece – then amount of time played. The 92 minutes spent on the pitch by Torres, compared to Gomez, meant his contributions were deemed better value for the prize.

VONLANTHEN BEATS ROONEY RECORD

The youngest scorer in finals history was Switzerland midfielder **Johan Vonlanthen.** He was 18 years 141 days when he netted in their 3-1 defeat by France on 21 June 2004. He beat the record set by England forward Wayne Rooney four days earlier. Rooney was 18 years 229 days when he scored the first goal in England's 3-0 win over the Swiss. Vonlanthen retired from football at the age of 26 in May 2012 due to a knee injury.

TREBLE TROUBLE

There has been no UEFA European Championship hat-trick since David Villa, for Spain v Russia in 2008 – only the tournament's eighth ever. The first came from West Germany substitute Dieter Muller, v Yugoslavia, in 1976. There were seven doubles in 2016: Antoine Griezmann (two), France, v Republic of Ireland and v Germany; Alvaro Morata, Spain, v Turkey; Romelu Lukaku, Belgium, v Republic of Ireland; Balazs Dzsudzsak, Hungary, v Portugal; Cristiano Ronaldo, Portugal, v Hungary; and Olivier Giroud, France, v Iceland.

KIRICHENKO NETS QUICKEST GOAL

The fastest goal in the history of the finals was scored by Russia forward **Dmitri Kirichenko**. He netted after just 67 seconds to give his side the lead against Greece on 20 June 2004. Russia won 2-1, but Greece still qualified for the quarter-finals – and went on to become shock winners. The fastest goal in the final was Spain midfielder Jesus Pereda's sixth-minute strike in 1964, when Spain beat the Soviet Union 2-1. The latest opening goal was Eder's 109th-minute winner for Portugal against France in the 2016 final.

TOP SCORERS IN FINALS HISTORY

1 Michel Platini (France) 9
= Cristiano Ronaldo (Portugal)
3 Alan Shearer (England) 7
4 Nuno Gomes (Portugal) 6
= Antoine Griezmann (France)
= Thierry Henry (France)
= Zlatan Ibrahimovic (Sweden)
= Patrick Kluivert (Netherlands)
= Wayne Rooney (England)
= Ruud van Nistelrooy (Netherlands)

BIERHOFF NETS FIRST "GOLDEN GOAL"

Germany's **Oliver Bierhoff** scored the first golden  goal in the history of the tournament when he hit the winner against the Czech Republic in the Euro 96 final at Wembley on 30 June. (The golden goal rule meant the first team to score in extra-time won the match.) Bierhoff netted in the fifth minute of extra-time. His shot from 20 yards deflected off defender Michal Hornak and slipped through goalkeeper Petr Kouba's fingers.

PONEDELNIK'S MONDAY MORNING FEELING

Striker Viktor Ponedelnik headed the Soviet Union's extra-time winner to beat Yugoslavia 2-1 in the first final on 10 July 1960 – and sparked some famous headlines in the Soviet media. The game in Paris kicked off at 10pm Moscow time on Sunday, so it was Monday morning when Ponedelnik – whose name means "Monday" in Russian – scored. He said: "When I scored, all the journalists wrote the headline 'Ponedelnik zabivayet v Ponedelnik' – 'Monday scores on Monday'." This goal, in the 113th minute, remains the latest ever in a European Championship/Nations Cup final.

MARCHING ORDERS

Only one man has been sent off in a UEFA European Championship final: France defender Yvon Le Roux, who received a second yellow card with five minutes remaining of his team's 2-0 triumph over Spain in 1984. The most red cards were shown at Euro 2000, when the ten dismissals included Romania's Gheorghe Hagi, Portugal's **Nuno Gomes**, Italy's Gianluca Zambrotta and the Czech Republic's Radoslav Latal who, having been sent off at Euro 96, is the only man to be dismissed in two tournaments. At Euro 2016, there were only three red cards.

VASTIC THE OLDEST

The oldest scorer in finals history is Austria's Ivica Vastic. He was 38 years and 257 days old when he equalized in the 1-1 draw with Poland at UEFA Euro 2008.

TOP SCORERS IN THE FINALS

Year	Player	
1960	Francois Heutte (France)	2
	Milan Galic (Yugoslavia)	
	Valentin Ivanov (Soviet Union)	
	Drazan Jerkovic (Yugoslavia)	
	Slava Metreveli (Soviet Union)	
	Viktor Ponedelnik (Soviet Union)	
1964	Ferenc Bene (Hungary)	2
	Dezso Novak (Hungary)	
	Jesus Pereda (Spain)	
1968	Dragan Dzajic (Yugoslavia)	2
1972	Gerd Muller (West Germany)	4
1976	Dieter Muller (West Germany)	4
1980	Klaus Allofs (West Germany)	3
1984	Michel Platini (France)	9
1988	Marco van Basten (Netherlands)	5
1992	Dennis Bergkamp (Netherlands)	3
	Tomas Brolin (Sweden)	
	Henrik Larsen (Denmark)	
	Karlheinz Riedle (Germany)	
1996	Alan Shearer (England)	5
2000	Patrick Kluivert (Netherlands)	5
	Savo Milosevic (Yugoslavia)	
2004	Milan Baros (Czech Republic)	5
2008	David Villa (Spain)	4
2012	Mario Balotelli (Italy)	3
	Alan Dzagoev (Russia)	
	Mario Gomez (Germany)	
	Mario Mandzukic (Croatia)	
	Cristiano Ronaldo (Portugal)	
	Fernando Torres (Spain)	
2016	Antoine Griezmann (France)	6

LOW CONQUERS ALMOST ALL

Germany coach Joachim Low holds the record for most UEFA European Championship matches and victories in charge. His side's shoot-out victory over Italy in a Euro 2016 quarter-final took him to 11 victories, before their 2-0 defeat to France in the semi-finals put him on 17 games across the 2008, 2012 and 2016 competitions.

NAMES ON THEIR SHIRTS

Players wore their names as well as their numbers on the back of their shirts for the first time at Euro 92. They had previously been identified only by numbers.

TAKE CLATT

In 2012, Pedro Proenca from Portugal achieved the double feat of refereeing the UEFA Champions League final between Chelsea and Bayern Munich and that summer's UEFA European Championship final between Spain and Italy. English referee Mark Clattenburg went one better in 2016: he did his homeland's FA Cup final between Manchester United and Crystal Palace in May, June's UEFA Champions League final between Real Madrid and Atletico Madrid and the UEFA European Championship final between France and Portugal in July.

GREEKS HAND ALBANIA WALKOVER

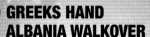

When Greece were drawn against Albania in the first round of the 1964 tournament, the Greeks immediately withdrew, handing Albania a 3-0 walkover win. The countries had technically been at war since 1940. The Greek government did not formally lift the state of war until 1987, although diplomatic relations were re-established in 1971.

RECORD EURO GOAL DROUGHT

Between **Xabi Alonso**'s added-time penalty in Spain's 2-0 quarter-final defeat of France and Mario Balotelli's 20th-minute semi-final strike for Italy in their 2-1 victory against Germany, Euro 2012's goalless spell lasted 260 minutes – a UEFA European Championship record.

DOUBLING UP

The 2016 UEFA European Championship final between hosts France and eventual champions Portugal was the sixth to go to extra-time but the first to be goalless after 90 minutes, before Eder's 109th-minute winner – the latest opening goal in any Euros final.

ELLIS BLOWS THE WHISTLE

English referee **Arthur Ellis** took charge of the first UEFA European Championship final between the Soviet Union and Yugoslavia in 1960. Ellis had also refereed the first-ever European Cup final, between Real Madrid and Reims, four years earlier. After he retired from football, he became the "referee" on the British version of the Europe-wide game show *It's a Knock-out*.

FINALS HOSTS

1960	France
1964	Spain
1968	Italy
1972	Belgium
1976	Yugoslavia
1980	Italy
1984	France
1988	West Germany
1992	Sweden
1996	England
2000	Netherlands and Belgium
2004	Portugal
2008	Austria and Switzerland
2012	Poland and Ukraine
2016	France

HOSTS WITH (ALMOST) THE MOST

In 2000, Belgium and the Netherlands began the trend for dual hosting the UEFA European Championship finals – it was the first time the tournament was staged in more than one country. The opening game was Belgium's 2-1 win over Sweden in Brussels on 10 June, with the final in Rotterdam. Austria and Switzerland co-hosted Euro 2008, starting in Basel and climaxing in Vienna, before Poland and Ukraine teamed up in 2012. Warsaw staged the opening match and Kiev was the host city for the final.

SHARE AND SHARE ALIKE

Ten venues across France were used for the 2016 UEFA European Championship. This equalled the record set by Portugal in 2004, and was two more than the eight stadia which were used in the three shared tournaments (four in each country): Belgium and the Netherlands in 2000; Austria and Switzerland in 2008; and Poland and Ukraine in 2012. It will be all change for the finals in 2020, however, as, for the first time, the first round group stage and first two knock-out rounds will be played across 13 cities in 13 different countries. England has the honour of hosting both semi-finals and the final, with all three to be played at London's Wembley Stadium.

PEAKING EARLY

Just as at the 2012 UEFA European Championship, where the first-round game between England and Sweden in Kyiv attracted the tournament's highest official attendance (64,640), the Euro 2016 final between France and Portugal could not claim the event's biggest crowd. Instead, that honour went to the French hosts' 5-2 victory over Iceland in the quarter-finals, watched in the Stade de France by 76,833 spectators.

UEFA EUROPEAN CHAMPIONSHIP FINAL REFEREES

1960	Arthur Ellis (England)
1964	Arthur Holland (England)
1968	Gottfried Dienst (Switzerland)
	Replay: Jose Maria Ortiz de Mendibil (Spain)
1972	Ferdinand Marschall (Austria)
1976	Sergio Gonella (Italy)
1980	Nicolae Rainea (Romania)
1984	Vojtech Christov (Czechoslovakia)
1988	Michel Vautrot (France)
1992	Bruno Galler (Switzerland)
1996	Pierluigi Pairetto (Italy)
2000	Anders Frisk (Sweden)
2004	Markus Merk (Germany)
2008	Roberto Rosetti (Italy)
2012	Pedro Proenca (Portugal)
2016	Mark Clattenburg (England)

THE "ITALIAN JOB"

The 1968 finals in Italy were used as the backdrop to a famous English-language film – *The Italian Job*, starring Michael Caine – about a British gang who use the cover of the finals to stage a daring gold robbery in Turin. The film was released in England on 2 June 1969.

GOALS AREN'T EVERYTHING

The expanded, 24-team UEFA European Championship may have boasted more goals than any previous Euros – 108 in all. But these came at a rate of just 2.12 per game – the lowest since the 1996 UEFA European Championship's 2.06. Euro 2016's three own goals was another competition record – the unlucky players putting into their own nets were the Republic of Ireland's Ciaran Clark, Northern Ireland's Gareth McAuley and Iceland's Birkir Mar Saevarsson.

KEEPING IT CLEAN

Only three red cards were shown during Euro 2016 – to Albania captain **Lorik Cana**, Aleksandar Dragovic of Austria and the Republic of Ireland's Shane Duffy – which was the same tally as at each of the 2008 and 2012 UEFA European Championships. In contrast, twice as many players were sent off at the 2004 tournament. The final, however, saw ten yellow cards shown, the most ever shown in any UEFA European Championship match.

THE WORLD'S OLDEST surviving international championship finds its rich history repeating itself even in a modern football world otherwise unrecognizable since the days when Uruguay won the inaugural South American Championship in 1916 – a time when much of the rest of the world was embroiled in the First World War.

Travel was an awkward, costly and time-consuming business for the first competitive nations of South America. The possibility of flying to Europe and back for even a single game was beyond officials' imagination. Hence the need for South America to organize itself and create its own early competitions.

The founding members of world federation FIFA, in 1904, had all been European. South American nations such as Brazil, Argentina and Uruguay were not slow in signing up but the opportunities for inter-continental competition were minimal.

The South Americans decided to organize their own international competitions, which led to the creation, in 1916, of the South American Championship. Four countries contested that opening tournament, hosts Argentina, Brazil, Chile and Uruguay, who were the inaugural winners. Fast forward 99 years, and 12 months after staging a spectacular FIFA World Cup in Brazil, South America was the venue for another high-class football extravaganza in the form of the 2015 Copa America.

Once again, the old masters of Brazil and Argentina missed out on the top prize as the hosts Chile, after 99 years of trying, landed the trophy for the first time in their history. Argentina lost on penalties, the same fate suffered by Brazil in the quarter-finals. The next "ordinary" Copa America is scheduled for Brazil in 2019, but a special Centenario celebration event was staged in 2016 – outside the continent, in the United States – in 2016. The event provided a sense of *déjà vu*, as Chile defeated Argentina on penalties for the second year running.

> **Chile's race to celebrate with Francisco Silva after he had scored the winning penalty of the shoot-out against Argentina in the final of the 2016 Copa America Centenario.**

COPA AMERICA 2016 REVIEW

The 45th Copa America was held in June 2016, just 12 months after the 44th. This one was, however, a special one-off Copa America Centenario, staged to mark the 100th anniversary of the inaugural tournament. For the first time, it was played outside South America – instead, in ten cities across the United States. As well as the ten CONMEBOL nations, six other countries – all from the CONCACAF region – took part: the US hosts, Mexico, 2014 Copa Centroamericana holders Costa Rica, 2014 Caribbean Cup champions Jamaica and play-off winners Haiti and Panama.

RAIN STOPPED PLAY

Chile and Colombia endured an agonizing wait to complete their 2016 Copa America Centenario semi-final. Chile led 2-0 going in at half-time, but a torrential downpour and storm at Chicago's Soldier Field stadium meant the second half was delayed for two-and-a-half hours. Colombia had never recovered from a two-goal half-time deficit to win a Copa America game and that record remained intact when the players finally returned to the field, and played out the rest of the match. The half-time scoreline didn't change and it ended 2-0.

CHILE, SLIGHT RETURN

After waiting 99 years for their first Copa America title, Chile made it two in two years as they retained their 2015 trophy in the following year's special Copa America Centenario. They again beat Argentina in the June 2016 final, though this time they were managed by Argentina-born former Spain international Juan Antonio Pizzi, who had succeeded Jorge Sampaoli five months earlier. After a goalless draw, the Chileans prevailed 4-2 on penalties in New Jersey's MetLife Stadium – with the final, decisive spot-kick struck home by defensive midfielder Francisco Silva. **The trophy** handed over was a special new design, solely for the Copa America Centenario.

CHANGING CHANGES

The Copa America Centenario was the first international tournament to implement new Laws of the Game introduced for 2016–17 by the International Football Association Board. These included allowing teams to bring on a fourth substitute in extra-time of the final – although neither Chile nor Argentina opted to do so.

BACCA OF THE NET

Colombia's AC Milan striker **Carlos Bacca** scored the only goal of the 2016 Copa America Centenario's third-place play-off against the USA in Glendale, Arizona – giving his country their best Copa America finish since lifting the trophy for the only time 15 years earlier. It was a happier end to the tournament for Bacca than in the previous year's Copa America, when he was sent off moments after the final whistle against Brazil for pushing Neymar and given a two-game ban.

WISDOM OF SALOMON

Venezuela striker **Salomon Rondon** became the first Venezuelan to score at three different Copa Americas in a 1-0 first-round win at the 2016 Copa America Centenario that put his side through to the knock-out stages and eliminated opponents Uruguay. He added another in the quarter-finals, but could not prevent Venezuela losing 4-1 to Argentina. Rondon previously scored against eventual champions Paraguay at the 2011 tournament, when his country achieved a best-ever fourth-place finish and again in 2015, against Colombia, before they went out in the first round.

TEAM OF THE TOURNAMENT

Goalkeeper:	Claudio Bravo	(Chile)
Defenders:	Mauricio Isla	(Chile)
	Nicolas Otamendi	(Argentina)
	Gary Medel	(Chile)
	Jean Beausejour	(Chile)
Midfielders:	Javier Mascherano	(Argentina)
	Arturo Vidal	(Chile)
	Charles Aranguiz	(Chile)
Forwards:	Lionel Messi	(Argentina)
	Eduardo Vargas	(Chile)
	Alexis Sanchez	(Chile)

FIRED UP FOR FOURTH

The United States, first-time Copa America hosts in 2016, equalled their best finish in the tournament by matching the fourth-place they previously gained in Argentina in 1995. In 1993 and 2007, when invited to compete, they had failed to progress past the first round. They also set an unwanted standard in 2016, however, as no team was shown more than their three red cards – to DeAndre Yedlin, Jermaine Jones and Michael Orozco. Yedlin was dismissed in the last group match against Paraguay – a 1-0 US victory – after receiving two yellow cards in a minute early in the second half.

HITTING THE WRONG NOTE

Uruguay not only endured a disappointing start to their Copa America Centenario campaign with a 3-1 defeat to Mexico on 5 June, but also disappointment even before kick-off when the Chilean national anthem was played as well as theirs. Tournament organizers later issued a "sincere" apology. The following day, Bolivia's national flag was displayed upside-down on video screens ahead of their game in Orlando against Panama – and, to add insult to injury, they suffered a 2-1 defeat.

BRAVO, BRAVO

Chile goalkeeper and captain **Claudio Bravo** was named man of the match in the final to go with his second Copa America winner's medal and the honour of again lifting the trophy. He was also awarded the Golden Glove prize for being the tournament's best goalkeeper, while there were also individual prizes for two team-mates: Eduardo Vargas claimed the Golden Boot as top scorer, with six goals, while Alexis Sanchez took the Golden Ball as the best player. In March 2016 Bravo had become the first Chilean international to reach a century of caps, in a 2-1 defeat to Argentina in the qualification campaign for the 2018 FIFA World Cup.

HAVING A BALL

What looked like it could be the last football kicked in international football by **Lionel Messi** was captured and taken home as a souvenir by a Chile fan celebrating his side's final triumph over Messi's Argentina. Pedro Vasquez grabbed the ball as Messi's shoot-out penalty soared into the stands of the MetLife Stadium in New Jersey and took it all the way home to his Chilean city of Antofagasta. It was only the next day he heard how Messi was now retiring from international football. Mr Vasquez vowed to pass it on to his grandson, saying: "It's historical and I'll keep it with me. I'm not going to sell it even if it could be auctioned for millions."

COPA AMERICA TEAM RECORDS

LITTLE NAPOLEON

In 1942, Ecuador and their goalkeeper Napoleon Medina conceded more goals in one tournament than any other team, when they let in 31 goals across six games – and six defeats. Three years later he and his team-mates finally managed to keep a clean sheet, in a goalless draw against Bolivia – but still managed to let in another 27 goals in their five other matches.

LUCK OF THE DRAW

Paraguay reached the 2011 final despite not winning a single game in normal play. Instead, they drew all three matches in the first-round group stage, then needed penalties to win their quarter-final against Brazil and semi-final versus Venezuela after both games ended goalless. Perhaps not surprisingly, their captain **Justo Villar** was voted the tournament's best goalkeeper.

COPA AMERICA WINNERS

1916	Uruguay (league format)
1917	Uruguay (league format)
1919	Brazil 1 Uruguay 0
1920	Uruguay (league format)
1921	Argentina (league format)
1922	Brazil 3 Paraguay 1
1923	Uruguay (league format)
1924	Uruguay (league format)
1925	Argentina (league format)
1926	Uruguay (league format)
1927	Argentina (league format)
1929	Argentina (league format)
1935	Uruguay (league format)
1937	Argentina 2 Brazil 0
1939	Peru (league format)
1941	Argentina (league format)
1942	Uruguay (league format)
1945	Argentina (league format)
1946	Argentina (league format)
1947	Argentina (league format)
1949	Brazil 7 Paraguay 0
1953	Paraguay 3 Brazil 2
1955	Argentina (league format)
1956	Uruguay (league format)
1957	Argentina (league format)
1959	Argentina (league format)
1959	Uruguay (league format)
1963	Bolivia (league format)
1967	Uruguay (league format)
1975	Peru 4 Colombia 1 (on aggregate, after three games)
1979	Paraguay 3 Chile 1 (on aggregate, after three games)
1983	Uruguay 3 Brazil 1 (on aggregate, after two games)
1987	Uruguay 1 Chile 0
1989	Brazil (league format)
1991	Argentina (league format)
1993	Argentina 2 Mexico 1
1995	Uruguay 1 Brazil 1 (Uruguay won 5-3 on penalties)
1997	Brazil 3 Bolivia 1
1999	Brazil 3 Uruguay 0
2001	Colombia 1 Mexico 0
2004	Brazil 2 Argentina 2 (Brazil won 4-2 on penalties)
2007	Brazil 3 Argentina 0
2011	Uruguay 3 Paraguay 0
2015	Chile 0 Argentina 0 (Chile won 4-1 on penalties)
2016	Chile 0 Argentina 0 (Chile won 4-2 on penalties)

HOSTING RIGHTS BY COUNTRY

Country		
Argentina	9	(1916, 1921, 1925, 1929, 1937, 1946, 1959, 1987, 2011)
Chile	7	(1920, 1926, 1941, 1945, 1955, 1991, 2015)
Uruguay	7	(1917, 1923, 1924, 1942, 1956, 1967, 1995)
Peru	6	(1927, 1935, 1939, 1953, 1957, 2004)
Brazil	4	(1919, 1922, 1949, 1989)
Ecuador	3	(1947, 1959, 1993)
Bolivia	2	(1963, 1997)
Paraguay	1	(1999)
Colombia	1	(2001)
Venezuela	1	(2007)
USA	1	(2016)

EXTRA TIME

The longest match in the history of the Copa America was the 1919 final between Brazil and Uruguay. It lasted 150 minutes, 90 minutes of regular time plus two extra-time periods of 30 minutes each.

HOW IT STARTED

The first South American "Championship of Nations", as it was then known, was held in Argentina from 2–17 July 1916, during the country's independence centenary commemorations. The tournament was won by Uruguay, who drew with Argentina in the last match of the tournament. It was an inauspicious beginning. The 16 July encounter had to be abandoned at 0-0 when fans invaded the pitch and set the wooden stands on fire. The match was continued at a different stadium the following day and still ended goalless ... but Uruguay ended up topping the mini-league table and were hailed the first champions. **Isabelino Gradin** was the inaugural tournament's top scorer. The event also saw the foundation of the South American federation CONMEBOL, which took place a week into the competition on 9 July 1916. From that point on the tournament was held every two years, though some tournaments are now considered to have been unofficial. There was, a three-year gap between the 2004 and 2007 tournaments, and the competition is now staged every four years instead.

SUB-STANDARD

During the 1953 Copa America, Peru were awarded a walkover win when Paraguay tried to make one more substitution than they were allowed. Would-be substitute Milner Ayala was so incensed, he kicked English referee Richard Maddison and was banned from football for three years. Yet Paraguay remained in the tournament and went on to beat Brazil in the final – minus, of course, the disgraced Ayala.

TARGET PRACTICE

Despite ending the 2016 Copa America Centenario as runners-up again, Argentina extended their records for most Copa America matches won, 111, and goals scored, 422 – the last two of which were two of which were struck by Gonzalo Higuain in a 4-0 victory over the USA in the 2016 Copa America Centenario semi-final in Houston. Argentina have also now lost more Copa America shoot-outs than any other side, five.

HISTORY MEN

The Copa America is the world's oldest surviving international football tournament, having been launched in 1916 when four nations entered: Argentina, Brazil, Chile and Uruguay. Bolivia, Colombia, Ecuador, Paraguay, Peru and Venezuela had all joined by 1967. In 1910, an unofficial South American championship was won by Argentina, who beat Uruguay 4-1 in the decider – though the final match had been delayed a day after rioting fans burnt down a stand at the Gimnasia stadium in Buenos Aires.

FALLEN ANGELS

Argentina's 1957 Copa America-winning forward trio of Humberto Maschio, Omar Sivori and Antonio Valentin Angelillo became known by the nickname "the angels with dirty faces". At least one of them scored in each of the side's six matches – Maschio finished with nine, Angelillo eight and Sivori three. Argentina's most convincing performance was an opening 8-2 win over Colombia, in which Argentina had scored four goals and missed a penalty within the first 25 minutes. The dazzling displays made Argentina, not eventual winners Brazil, favourites for the following year's FIFA World Cup. Before then, however, Maschio, Sivori and Angelillo had all been lured away to Europe by Italian clubs and the Argentine federation subsequently refused to pick them for the trip to Sweden for the FIFA World Cup. Sivori and Maschio ultimately made it to the FIFA World Cup, in 1962. However, to fury back home, they did so wearing not the light blue-and-white stripes of Argentina, but the Azzurri blue of their newly adopted Italy.

CONSISTENT COLOMBIANS

In 2001, Colombia, who went on to win the trophy for the first and only time in their history, became the only country to go through an entire Copa America campaign without conceding a single goal. They scored 11 themselves, more than half of them from six-goal tournament top scorer **Victor Aristazabal**. Keeping the clean sheets was goalkeeper Oscar Cordoba, who had previously spent much of his international career as back-up to the eccentric Rene Higuita. Just a month earlier, Cordoba had won the South American club championship, the Copa Libertadores, with Argentine side Boca Juniors.

TRIUMPHS BY COUNTRY

Uruguay 15 (1916, 1917, 1920, 1923, 1924, 1926, 1935, 1942, 1956, 1959, 1967, 1983, 1987, 1995, 2011)
Argentina 14 (1921, 1925, 1927, 1929, 1937, 1941, 1945, 1946, 1947, 1955, 1957, 1959, 1991, 1993)
Brazil 8 (1919, 1922, 1949, 1989, 1997, 1999, 2004, 2007)
Peru 2 (1939, 1975)
Paraguay 2 (1953, 1979)
Chile 2 (2015, 2016)
Bolivia 1 (1963)
Colombia 1 (2001)

MORE FROM MORENO

Argentina were not only responsible for the Copa America's biggest win, but also the tournament's highest-scoring game, when they put 12 past Ecuador in 1942 – to no reply. Jose Manuel Moreno's five strikes in that game included the 500th goal in the competition's history. Moreno, born in Buenos Aires on 3 August 1916, ended that tournament as joint top scorer with team-mate Herminio Masantonio – hitting seven goals. Both men ended their international careers with 19 goals for their country, though Moreno did so in 34 appearances – compared to Masantonio's 21. Masantonio scored four in the Ecuador thrashing.

JAMAICA STILL WAITING

To date, four teams have appeared in only one Copa America: Japan (1999), Honduras (2001), and Haiti and Panama (both 2016). Jamaica played in the Copa America for the second time in 2016, having played a year earlier too, but they are still to avoid defeat. They lost 1-0 to each of Uruguay, Paraguay and Argentina in 2015, and in 2016 lost 1-0 to Venezuela, 2-0 to Mexico and 3-0 to Uruguay. Their side included Wes Morgan, who had won a shock English Premier League title with Leiceser City, and skipper Adrian Mariappa, who had ended the season as an FA Cup runner-up for Crystal Palace. Mariappa was born in London to a Fijiian father and a mother with Jamaican parents.

COPA AMERICA PLAYER RECORDS

FROG PRINCE

Chilean goalkeeper Sergio Livingstone holds the record for most Copa America appearances, with 34 games, across the 1941, 1942, 1945, 1947, 1949 and 1953 tournaments. Livingstone, nicknamed "The Frog", was voted player of the tournament in 1941 – becoming the first goalkeeper to win the award – and might have played even more Copa America matches had he not missed out on the 1946 competition. Livingstone, born in Santiago on 26 March 1920, spent almost his entire career in his home country – save for a season with Argentina's Racing Club in 1943–44. Overall, he made 52 appearances for Chile between 1941 and 1954, before retiring and becoming a popular TV journalist and commentator.

CHILE'S ILL FORTUNE

The first Copa America own goal was scored by Chile's Luis Garcia, giving Argentina a 1-0 win in 1917, in the second edition of the tournament. Even more unfortunately for Chile, Garcia's strike was the only goal by one of their players throughout the tournament – making Chile the first team to fail to score a single goal in a Copa America competition.

MOST GAMES PLAYED

1	Sergio Livingstone (Chile)	34
2	Zizinho (Brazil)	33
3	Leonel Alvarez (Colombia)	27
4	Carlos Valderrama (Colombia)	27
5	Javier Mascherano (Argentina)	26
6	Alex Aguinaga (Ecuador)	25
=	Claudio Taffarel (Brazil)	25
8	Teodoro Fernandez (Peru)	24
9	Angel Romano (Uruguay)	23
10	Djalma Santos (Brazil)	22
=	Claudio Suarez (Mexico)	22

OVERALL TOP SCORERS

1	Norberto Mendez (Argentina)	17
=	Zizinho (Brazil)	17
3	Teodoro Fernandez (Peru)	15
=	Severino Varela (Uruguay)	15
5	Ademir (Brazil)	13
=	Jair da Rosa Pinto (Brazil)	13
=	Gabriel Batistuta (Argentina)	13
=	Jose Manuel Moreno (Argentina)	13
=	Hector Scarone (Uruguay)	13
10	Paolo Guerrero (Peru)	11
=	Herminio Masantonio (Argentina)	11
=	Victor Agustin Ugarte (Bolivia)	11
=	Eduardo Vargas (Chile)	11

REPEATING THE FEAT

Gabriel Batistuta is the only Argentinian to win the award twice as leading marksman at the Copa America. He made his *Albiceleste* debut only days before the 1991 event in which his six goals – including a crucial strike in the concluding match (it was a mini group as opposed to a final) victory over Colombia – earned a transfer from Boca Juniors to Fiorentina. Nicknamed "Batigol" in Italy, he was joint top scorer in 1995, with four goals, along with Mexico's Luis Garcia.

LIKE GRANDFATHER, LIKE FATHER, LIKE SON

Diego Forlan's two goals in the 2011 Copa America final helped Uruguay to a 3-0 victory over Paraguay and their record 15th South American championship. They also ensured he followed in family footsteps in lifting the trophy – his father **Pablo** was part of the Uruguay side who won in 1967, when his grandfather Juan Carlos Corazzo was the triumphant coach. Corazzo had previously managed Uruguay's winning team in 1959. The brace against Paraguay put the youngest Forlan level with Hector Scarone as Uruguay's all-time leading scorer, with 31 goals. Yet it was Forlan's strike partner Luis Suarez – opening goal-scorer in the final – who was voted best player of the 2011 tournament.

MAGIC ALEX

When Alex Aguinaga lined up for Ecuador against Uruguay in his country's opening game at the 2004 event, he became only the second man to take part in eight different Copa Americas – joining legendary Uruguayan goalscorer Angel Romano. Aguinaga, a midfielder born in Ibarra on 9 July 1969, played a total of 109 times for his country – 25 of them in the Copa America, a competition that yielded four of his 23 international goals. His Copa America career certainly began well: Ecuador went undefeated for his first four appearances, at the 1987 and 1989 events, but his luck had ran out by the time his Ecuador career was coming to an end: he lost his final seven Copa America matches.

START TO FINISH

Colombia playmaker Carlos Valderrama and defensive midfielder **Leonel Alvarez** played in all 27 of their country's Copa America matches between 1987 and 1995, winning ten, drawing ten and losing seven – including third-place finishes in 1987, 1993 and 1995. Valderrama's two Copa America goals came in his first and final appearances in the competition – in a 2-0 victory over Bolivia in 1987 and a 4-1 thrashing of the United States eight years later.

ED BOY

Two players have monopolized the Golden Boot prizes for top marksmen at recent Copa America tournaments. **Eduardo Vargas** ended the 2016 Copa America Centenario not only as a champion for the second successive year, but this time adding the Golden Boot to his own personal collection of honours – he won the same prize in 2015, albeit jointly with Peru's Paulo Guerrero who had himself clinched the Golden Boot outright at the previous tournament in 2011. Four of Vargas's six goals in 2016 came in Chile's 7-0 quarter-final trouncing of Mexico, making him only the 13th man to score at least four in one Copa America match. Vargas's other achievements for Chile include scoring in six consecutive internationals (nine goals) during 2013, beating the previous record of five shared by Carlos Caszely and Marcelo Salas.

FANTASTIC FIVES

Four players have scored five goals in one Copa America game: Hector Scarone in Uruguay's 6-0 win over Bolivia in 1926; Juan Marvezzi in Argentina's 6-1 win over Ecuador in 1941; Jose Manuel Moreno in Argentina's 12-0 win over Ecuador in 1942; and Evaristo de Macedo in Brazil's 9-0 win over Colombia in 1957.

LOW–KEY JOSE

The first-ever Copa America goal, in 1916, was scored by Jose Piendibene – setting Uruguay on the way to a 4-0 triumph over Chile. But he is not thought to have marked the moment with any great extravagance – Piendibene, renowned for his sense of fair play, made a point of not celebrating goals, to avoid offending his opponents.

PELE'S INSPIRATION

Brazilian forward **Zizinho** jointly holds the all-time goalscoring record for the Copa America, along with Argentina's Norberto Mendez. Both men struck 17 goals, Zizinho across six tournaments and Mendez three – including the 1945 and 1946 tournaments, which featured both men. Mendez was top scorer once and runner-up twice and won championship medals on all three occasions, while Zizinho's goals helped Brazil take the title only once, in 1949. Zizinho, Pele's footballing idol, would emerge from the 1950 FIFA World Cup as Brazil's top scorer and was also voted the tournament's best player – but was forever traumatized by the hosts' surprise defeat to Uruguay that cost Brazil the title.

COPA AMERICA OTHER RECORDS

OPEN ARMS

Only four men have coached a country other than their native one to Copa America glory. The first was Englishman Jack Greenwell, with Peru in 1939. Brazilian Danilo Alvim was the second, with Bolivia in 1963 – against Brazil. History repeated itself in 2015 and 2016, when Argentina-born Jorge Sampaoli and then Juan Antonio Pizzi took Chile to Copa glory, both times beating Argentina in final penalty shoot-outs.

HOME COMFORTS

Uruguay have a unique record in remaining unbeaten in 38 Copa America games on home turf, all played in the country's capital Montevideo – comprising 31 wins, seven draws. The last tournament match they hosted was both a draw and a win – 1-1 against Brazil in 1995, with Uruguay emerging as champions, 5-3 on penalties after Fernando Alvez saved Tulio's penalty.

INVITED GUESTS

1993	Mexico (runners-up), United States
1995	Mexico, United States (fourth)
1997	Costa Rica, Mexico (third)
1999	Japan, Mexico (third)
2001	Costa Rica, Honduras (third), Mexico (runners-up)
2004	Costa Rica, Mexico
2007	Mexico (third), United States
2011	Costa Rica, Mexico
2015	Jamaica, Mexico
2016	Costa Rica, Haiti, Jamaica, Mexico, Panama, United States (hosts, fourth)

WRONG JUAN

It took 21 years, but Uruguay's Juan Emilio Piriz became the first Copa America player sent off, against Chile in 1937 – the first of 186 dismissals in the Copa (15 players and Ecuador coach Gustave Quienteros saw red in 2016). Some 142 disgraced players have been shown red cards since FIFA introduced the card system in 1970.

MULTI–TASKING

Argentina's **Guillermo Stabile** not only holds the record for most Copa America triumphs as coach – he trounces all opposition. He led his country to the title on no fewer than six occasions – in 1941, 1945, 1946, 1947, 1955 and 1957. No other coach has lifted the trophy more than twice. Stabile coached Argentina from 1939 to 1960, having been appointed at the age of just 34. He lasted for 123 games in charge, winning 83 of them – and still managed to coach three clubs on the side at different times throughout his reign. He remained as Red Star Paris manager during his first year in the Argentina role, then led Argentine club Huracan for the next nine years – before leading domestic rivals Racing Club from 1949 to 1960. Stabile's Argentina may have, unusually, missed out on Copa America success in 1949, but that year brought the first of three Argentina league championships in a row for Stabile's Racing Club.

CAPTAIN CONSISTENT

Uruguay's 1930 World Cup-winning captain **Jose Nasazzi** is the only footballer to be voted player of the tournament at two different Copa America tournaments. Even more impressively, he achieved the feat 12 years apart – first taking the prize in 1923, then again in 1935. He was a Cup winner in 1923, 1924, 1926 and 1935. Nasazzi also captained Uruguay to victory in the 1924 and 1928 Olympic Games and in the 1930 World Cup.

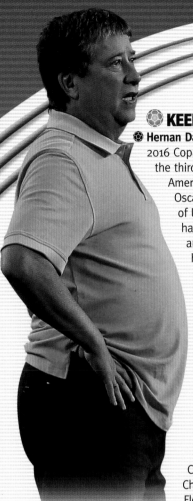

KEEP COMING BACK

Hernan Dario Gomez coached Panama at the 2016 Copa American Centenario, making him only the third man to manage at six different Copa America tournaments. Close behind him is Oscar Washington Tabarez, who took charge of Uruguay at a fifth Copa America in 2016, having been in charge in 1989, 2007, 2011 and 2015. Dario Gomez previously led his native Colombia in 1995, 1997 and 2011, and Ecuador in 2001 and 2004. He is now level on tournaments with Guillermo Stabile, Argentina boss in 1941, 1945, 1946, 1947, 1955 and 1957, and Francisco Maturana who took Colombia to the finals in 1987, 1989, 1993 and 2001 and Ecuador in 1995 and 1997. Dario Gomez had been Maturana's assistant both at Colombian club Atletico Nacional and taking Colombia to third place at the 1987 Copa America. Stabile solely holds the record for managing most Copa America matches (44), followed by Chile's Luis Tirado (35), Paraguay's Manuel Fleitas Solich (33), Maturana (27), Tabarez (26) and Dario Gomez (23).

TROPHY—WINNING COACHES

6 Guillermo Stabile (Argentina 1941, 1945, 1946, 1947, 1955, 1957)

2 Alfio Basile (Argentina 1991, 1993)
Juan Carlos Corazzo (Uruguay 1959, 1967)
Ernesto Figoli (Uruguay 1920, 1926)

1 Jorge Pacheco and Alfredo Foglino (Uruguay 1916)
Ramon Platero (Uruguay 1917)
Pedro Calomino (Argentina 1921)
Lais (Brazil 1922)
Leonardo De Lucca (Uruguay 1923)
Ernesto Meliante (Uruguay 1924)
Americo Tesoriere (Argentina 1925)
Jose Lago Millon (Argentina 1927)
Francisco Olazar (Argentina 1929)
Raul V Blanco (Uruguay 1935)
Manuel Seoane (Argentina 1937)
Jack Greenwell (Peru 1939)
Pedro Cea (Uruguay 1942)
Flavio Costa (Brazil 1949)
Manuel Fleitas Solich (Paraguay 1953)
Hugo Bagnulo (Uruguay 1956)
Victorio Spinetto (Argentina 1959)
Danilo Alvim (Bolivia 1963)
Marcos Calderon (Peru 1975)
Ranulfo Miranda (Paraguay 1979)
Omar Borras (Uruguay 1983)
Roberto Fleitas (Uruguay 1987)
Sebastiao Lazaroni (Brazil 1989)
Hector Nunez (Uruguay 1995)
Mario Zagallo (Brazil 1997)
Wanderlei Luxemburgo (Brazil 1999)
Francisco Maturana (Colombia 2001)
Carlos Alberto Parreira (Brazil 2004)
Dunga (Brazil 2007)
Oscar Washington Tabarez (Uruguay 2011)
Jorge Sampaoli (Chile 2015)
Juan Antonio Pizzi (Chile 2016)

GOALS AT A PREMIUM

In terms of goals per game, the 2011 Copa America was the second tightest of all time – with only 54 strikes hitting the back of the net in 26 matches, an average of 2.08 per game. The 1922 tournament, in Brazil, saw fewer – 22 goals in 11 games, an average of two. Both competitions were a far cry from the prolific 1927 event in Peru, where 37 goals across six games averaged out at 6.17. The 91 goals in 2016 came at an average of 2.84 per match.

SEEING RED

Brazil may have the worst FIFA World Cup disciplinary record, but neighbours Uruguay assume that unenviable position in the Copa America. Uruguayan players have been sent off 32 times – the latest being **Matias Vecino** against Mexico in 2016 – followed by Peru and Argentina on 24 dismissals apiece, Brazil and Venezuela (20 each), Chile (18), Paraguay (14), Bolivia (13), Colombia and Ecuador (11 apiece), Mexico (ten), the United States (three), Costa Rica (two), and Honduras, Jamaica, Japan and Panama (one each).

MARKARIAN MAKES HIS MARK

The 2011 Copa America was not only a Uruguayan success story for the eventual champions, but also third-placed Peru's Uruguayan coach Sergio Markarian. Uruguay's winning manager Oscar Washington Tabarez had Markarian as his club coach at Bella Vista in the 1970s. Markarian could also claim some credit for Paraguay's runners-up finish, having been a successful and influential coach in that country during the 1980s, 1990s and early 21st century.

PART 5:
AFRICA CUP OF NATIONS

THE AFRICAN governing football confederation – Confederation Africaine de Football (or CAF) – is three years younger than UEFA, yet their cross-continental tournament, the Africa Cup of Nations, kicked off before the first European Championship. Formed on 8 February 1957, the CAF announced the first championship just three days later.

Egypt's ultimate triumph in that inaugural tournament set an appropriate pattern – the "Pharaohs" have won a record number of championships overall (seven) – but the competition has changed, and progressed, plenty since then.

Only three teams entered in 1957, but 51 nations vied for 15 qualification spots at the last event, in 2015, alongside already-qualified hosts Equaltorial Guinea who were replacing original choice Morocco. The global prominence of the Africa Cup of Nations has also grown, especially as the spotlight falls on major African stars taking time off from European club duties every other January. There have been mounting calls for the competition to be moved to the middle of the year, to avoid disrupting European league seasons, but these have been rejected for climatic and seasonal reasons.

Whatever the place in the calendar, the trophy – now in its third physical incarnation – will always be contested with vivacious skills and fierce local pride. More different countries have won the ACN than any other continental championship, with glory being shared among 14 separate nations – including Africa's largest three countries Sudan, Algeria and Congo DR, as well as mid-sized entrants such as Cameroon, Morocco, the Ivory Coast, winners in 2015, and early standard-setters Ghana, plus surprise 2012 champions Zambia.

Unusually, ACN 2010's preliminary rounds gained extra importance as they were integrated into Africa's FIFA World Cup 2010 qualification competition.

Kolo Toure shows off the Africa Cup of Nations on the Ivory Coast's lap of honour after the team had won the trophy for the second time in 2015 – both have come after beating Ghana in the final

TEST OF ENDURANCE

The Ivory Coast have won the two highest-scoring penalty shoot-outs in full international history – they defeated Ghana 11-10 over 24 penalties in the 1992 Africa Cup of Nations final, and Cameroon 12-11, over the same number of kicks, in the quarter-finals of the 2006 Africa Cup of Nations.

GHANA AGAIN

Ghana's "Black Stars" became the first country to reach the final of four consecutive Africa Cup of Nations, lifting the trophy in 1963 and 1965 and finishing runners-up in 1968 and 1970. They have now reached eight finals in all – a tally matched only by Egypt. The two countries have also staged the tournament four times apiece.

FROM TRAGEDY TO TRIUMPH

Zambia's unexpected glory at the 2012 African Cup of Nations was both fitting and poignant as the setting for their glory was just a few hundred metres from the scene of earlier calamity. The 2012 players spent the day before the final against **Ivory Coast** laying flowers in the sea in tribute to the 30 people killed when a plane crashed off the coast of Gabonese city Libreville on 27 April 1993. Victims that day included 18 Zambian internationals flying to Senegal for a FIFA World Cup qualifier. French coach Herve Renard dedicated the 2012 victory to the dead, after watching his side beat Ivory Coast 8-7 on penalties following a goalless draw after extra-time. Centre-back Stoppila Sunzu struck the decisive spot-kick, after Ivory Coast's Kolo Toure had his penalty saved by Kennedy Mweene and Gervinho blazed his over the bar. Both teams were competing in their third African Cup of Nations final, Ivory Coast having won in 1992 and lost in 2006, while Zambia had finished runners-up in 1974 and 1994. Zambia's success was the climactic surprise of a tournament that produced shocks when traditional powerhouses Egypt, Cameroon, Nigeria and South Africa all failed to even make the finals – then Senegal, Angola and Morocco were knocked out in the first round.

REIGNING PHARAOHS

Egypt dominate the Africa Cup of Nations records. They won the first tournament, in 1957, having been helped by a bye to the final when semi-final opponents South Africa were disqualified, and have emerged as champions another six times since – more than any other country. Their victories in the last three tournaments – 2006, 2008 and 2010 – make them the only country to lift the trophy three times in a row. They have also appeared a record 22 tournaments, playing 90 matches – one more than Ghana (who have appeared in two fewer finals) and three more than the Ivory Coast. Egypt have won 51 matches in all, followed by Ghana on 50, Nigeria on 46, Ivory Coast on 39 and Cameroon on 37.

BAFANA BRILLIANCE

The Africa Cup of Nations has been won by its hosts on 11 separate occasions – including three times by Egypt and twice by Ghana. But perhaps the most surprising host-country triumph was South Africa's in 1996. The country had returned to international football only four years earlier, post-apartheid, when an 82nd-minute penalty by Theophilus "Doctor" Khumalo gave them a win over Cameroon on 7 July 1992. In February 1996, substitute Mark Williams scored both goals against Tunisia as South Africa won the Africa Cup of Nations trophy – lifted by white captain **Neil Tovey**, and handed over by the country's president Nelson Mandela, in Johannesburg's Soccer City stadium. South Africa were not even meant to be hosts, but stepped in for original choice Kenya who were stripped of staging rights after falling behind on new stadium-building.

GIMME GUINEA GIMME

Guinea equalled the record for biggest ever win at an African Cup of Nations when they beat Botswana 6-1 in a first-round match in 2012 – though both teams failed to make it out of Group D. Guinea were also only the third team to score six times in one match at a finals, following Egypt's 6-3 win over Nigeria in 1963 and Ivory Coast's 6-1 defeat of Ethiopia seven years later. The only other game to match the record-winning margin saw Guinea not as the victors but the victims, going down 5-0 to Ivory Coast in 2008.

EQUATORIAL DEBUTANTS

Equatorial Guinea took part in an Africa Cup of Nations finals for the first time in 2012, thanks to co-hosting the tournament with Gabon. Equatorial Guinea had never managed to qualify before while Gabon had reached the finals only four times previously. Botswana and Niger were the 2012 competition's other first-timers. The opening match of the 2012 competition was staged in Equatorial Guinea, in Bata, while the final was played in Gabonese city Libreville. The 2012 event was only the second to be shared between two host nations, after Ghana and Nigeria shared duties in 2000. Libya was awarded the right to host the Africa Cup of Nations, for a second time, in 2013, but turmoil in the country meant it was switched to South Africa, despite Nigeria initially being nominated as first reserve. Equatorial Guinea stepped in as solo hosts in 2015, replacing original choice Morocco. Libya withdrew as 2017 hosts, Gabon taking on the honour instead.

FOUR SHAME

Hosts **Angola** were responsible for perhaps the most dramatic collapse in Africa Cup of Nations history, when they threw away a four-goal lead in the opening match of the 2010 tournament. Even more embarrassingly, they were leading 4-0 against Mali with just 11 minutes left, in the capital Luanda's Estadio 11 de Novembro. Mali's final two goals, by Barcelona's Seydou Keita and Boulogne's Mustapha Yatabare, were scored deep into stoppage-time. Mali failed to make it through the first round, while Angola went out in the quarter-finals.

TOURNAMENT TRIUMPHS

- 7 Egypt (1957, 1959, 1986, 1998, 2006, 2008, 2010)
- 4 Cameroon (1984, 1988, 2000, 2002)
  Ghana (1963, 1965, 1978, 1982)
- 3 Nigeria (1980, 1994, 2013)
- 2 Ivory Coast (1992, 2015)
  Zaire/Congo DR (1968, 1974)
- 1 Algeria (1990)
  Congo (1972)
  Ethiopia (1962)
  Morocco (1976)
  South Africa (1996)
  Sudan (1970)
  Tunisia (2004)
  Zambia (2012)

TOURNAMENT APPEARANCES

- 22 Egypt
- 21 Ivory Coast
- 20 Ghana
- 17 Cameroon, Nigeria, Zaire/DR Congo, Tunisia, Zambia
- 16 Algeria
- 15 Morocco
- 13 Senegal
- 11 Guinea
- 10 Burkina Faso, Ethiopia
- 9 Mali, South Africa
- 8 Sudan
- 7 Angola, Congo, Togo
- 6 Gabon
- 5 Kenya, Uganda
- 4 Mozambique
- 3 Benin, Libya
- 2 Cape Verde, Equatorial Guinea, Liberia, Malawi, Namibia, Niger, Sierra Leone, Zimbabwe
- 1 Botswana, Mauritius, Rwanda, Tanzania

THE WAITING IS THE HARDEST PART

There are 16 countries still waiting to make their debut at an Africa Cup of Nations tournament: Burundi, Central African Republic, Chad, Comoros, Djibouti, Eritrea, Gambia, Guinea-Bissau, Lesotho, Madagascar, Mauritania, Sao Tome and Principe, Seychelles, Somalia, South Sudan and Swaziland – although South Sudan only entered qualifying for the first time in 2015. Burundi did come close to making the 1994 event, only to lose a play-off to Guinea on penalties. The two sides had finished on equal points, goal difference and goals scored in their qualifying group, before drawing 0-0 – Guinea, spearheaded by former Marseille and Liverpool striker **Titi Camara**, then inched through 5-4 in the shoot-out.

YO, YOBO

Nigeria's **Joseph Yobo** – formerly of Marseille in France and Everton in England – was brought on to acclaim in the closing moments of Nigeria's victory over Burkina Faso in the 2013 final, his sixth Africa Cup of Nations. He then had the honour of lifting the trophy as skipper. Ivory Coast's 2015 champions included Boubacar Barry and Kolo Toure, both playing in their seventh tournament to match the tally of Egypt's Hossam Hassan and Cameroon's Geremi Nijtap. But the record for most Africa Cup of Nations tournaments remains shared by Cameroon's Rigobert Song and Eygpt's Ahmed Hassan, both of whom played in 1996, 1998, 2000, 2002, 2004, 2006, 2008 and 2010. Song's run included an unprecedented 35 games in a row.

REVOLUTION #9

No player has scored more goals in one Africa Cup of Nations than Zaire's Ndaye Mulamba's nine during the 1974 tournament. Three months later he was sent off at the FIFA World Cup in West Germany, as his team crashed to a 9-0 defeat against Yugoslavia.

STAR STRUCK

Gabon's Chiva Star Nzigou became the Africa Cup of Nations' youngest-ever player when he took the field against South Africa in January 2000, aged 16 years and 91 days. Gabon lost the game 3-1 and finished bottom of Group B without a win from three games.

PROLIFIC POKOU

Ivory Coast striker Laurent Pokou scored a record five goals in one Africa Cup of Nations match, as his side trounced Ethiopia 6-1 in the first round of the 1968 tournament. He finished top scorer at that tournament, and the following one – though ended both without a winners' medal. Only modern-day Cameroon star Samuel Eto'o has overtaken his overall Africa Cup of Nations tally of 14 goals.

OPENING GOAL

The first Africa Cup of Nations goal was a penalty scored by Egypt's Raafat Ateya in the 21st minute of their 2-1 semi-final win over Sudan in 1957. But his team-mate Mohamed Diab El-Attar would soon take over – he not only scored Egypt's second goal that day, but all four goals in the final against Ethiopia.

TOURNAMENT TOP SCORERS

Year	Player	Goals
1957	Mohamed Diab El-Attar (Egypt)	5
1959	Mahmoud Al-Gohari (Egypt)	3
1962	Abdelfatah Badawi (Egypt) Mengistu Worku (Ethiopia)	3
1963	Hassan El-Shazly (Egypt)	6
1965	Ben Acheampong (Ghana) Kofi Osei (Ghana) Eustache Mangle (Ivory Coast)	3
1968	Laurent Pokou (Ivory Coast)	6
1970	Laurent Pokou (Ivory Coast)	8
1972	Salif Keita (Mali)	5
1974	Ndaye Mulamba (Zaire)	9
1976	Keita Aliou Mamadou 'N'Jo Lea' (Guinea)	4
1978	Opoku Afriyie (Ghana) Segun Odegbami (Nigeria) Philip Omondi (Uganda)	3
1980	Khaled Al Abyad Labied (Morocco) Segun Odegbami (Nigeria)	3
1982	George Alhassan (Ghana)	4
1984	Taher Abouzaid (Egypt)	4
1986	Roger Milla (Cameroon)	4
1988	Gamal Abdelhamid (Egypt) Lakhdar Belloumi (Algeria) Roger Milla (Cameroon) Abdoulaye Traore (Ivory Coast)	2
1990	Djamel Menad (Algeria)	4
1992	Rashidi Yekini (Nigeria)	4
1994	Rashidi Yekini (Nigeria)	5
1996	Kalusha Bwalya (Zambia)	5
1998	Hossam Hassan (Egypt) Benni McCarthy (South Africa)	7
2000	Shaun Bartlett (South Africa)	5
2002	Julius Aghahowa (Nigeria) Patrick Mboma (Cameroon) Rene Salomon Olembe (Cameroon)	5
2004	Francileudo Santos (Tunisia) Frederic Kanoute (Mali) Patrick Mboma (Cameroon) Youssef Mokhtari (Morocco) Jay-Jay Okocha (Nigeria)	4
2006	Samuel Eto'o (Cameroon)	5
2008	Samuel Eto'o (Cameroon)	5
2010	Mohamed **Nagy 'Gedo'** (Egypt)	5
2012	Pierre-Emerick Aubameyang (Gabon) Cheick Diabate (Mali) Didier Drogba (Ivory Coast) Christopher Katongo (Zambia) Houssine Kharja (Morocco) Manucho (Tunisia) Emmanuel Mayuka (Zambia)	3
2013	Emmanuel Emenike (Nigeria) Mubarak Wakaso (Ghana)	4
2015	Ahmed Akaichi (Tunisia) Andre Ayew (Ghana) Javier Balboa (Equatorial Guinea) Thievy Bifouma (Congo) Dieumerci Mbokani (DR Congo)	3

SIBLING HARMONY

Both teams in the final of the 2015 Africa Cup of Nations called upon a pair of brothers. Runners-up Ghana included Jordan and Andre Ayew, while Ivory Coast's champions were spearheaded by captain **Yaya Toure** and his centre-back brother Kolo. All four brothers took penalties in the 2015 final and scored, unlike in 2012, when the Ivory Coast were beaten in another penalty shoot-out, this time against Ghana. Yaya had been substituted in extra time, but Kolo missed in the 8-7 loss. Zambia's triumphant captain in 2012, player of the tournament Christian Katongo, had among his team-mates brother Felix – he came off the bench – and they both scored in that shoot-out. There is a history of siblings enjoying victory in the Africa Cup of Nations. In 1962, when Ethiopia won the trophy, denying Egypt a third title, they were captained by Luciano Vassalo, whose brother Italo scored the goal that gave Ethiopia a 3-2 extra-time lead in the final – they eventually won 4-2. In 1988 Francois Omam-Biyik and brother Andre Kana-Biyik helped Cameroon to win the tournament, though Francois was injured in the opening match.

SAM THE MAN

Cameroon's Samuel Eto'o, who made his full international debut – away to Costa Rica on 9 March 1997 – one day short of his 16th birthday, is the Africa Cup of Nations' all-time leading goalscorer. He was part of Cameroon's victorious teams in 2000 and 2002, but had to wait until 2008 to pass Laurent Pokou's 14-goal Africa Cup of Nations record. That year's competition took his overall tally to 16 goals – only for the former Real Madrid and Barcelona striker, now with Italy's Internazionale, to add another two in 2010. In 2005, Eto'o became the first player to be named African Footballer of the Year three years running. He has also won an Olympic Games gold medal with Cameroon in 2000 and the UEFA Champions League three times, with Barcelona in 2006 and 2009 – scoring in both finals – and Inter in 2010.

CHIK KING

Tunisia midfielder **Yassine Chikhaoui** hit the first hat-trick of the qualification campaign for the 2017 Africa Cup of Nations. He opened the scoring against Djibouti on 12 June 2015 with a ninth-minute penalty and had completed his treble within the first 23 minutes. His team went on to win 8-1, equalling Tunisia's biggest ever margin of victory – matching a pair of 7-0 triumphs, over Togo in January 2000 and Malawi in March 2005.

AFRICA CUP OF NATIONS ALL-TIME TOP SCORERS

1	Samuel Eto'o (Cameroon)	18
2	Laurent Pokou (Ivory Coast)	14
3	Rashidi Yekini (Nigeria)	13
4	Hassan El-Shazly (Egypt)	12
5	Didier Drogba (Ivory Coast)	11
=	Hossam Hassan (Egypt)	11
=	Patrick Mboma (Cameroon)	11
8	Kalusha Bwalya (Zambia)	10
=	Ndaye Mulamba (Zaire)	10
=	Francileudo Santos (Tunisia)	10
=	Joel Tiehi (Ivory Coast)	10
=	Mengistu Worku (Ethiopia)	10

NO HASSLE FOR HASSAN

Egypt's **Ahmed Hassan** not only became the first footballer to play in the final of four different Africa Cup of Nations in 2010 – he also became the first to collect his fourth winners' medal. Earlier in the same tournament, his appearance in the quarter-final against Cameroon gave him his 170th cap – a new Egyptian record. Hassan marked the game with three goals – one in his own net and two past Cameroon goalkeeper Carlos Kameni – although one appeared not to cross the line.

AFRICA CUP OF NATIONS: FINALS

1957	(Host country: Sudan) Egypt 4 Ethiopia 0
1959	(Egypt) Egypt 2 Sudan 1
1962	(Ethiopia) Ethiopia 4 Egypt 2 (aet)
1963	(Ghana) Ghana 3 Sudan 0
1965	(Tunisia) Ghana 3 Tunisia 2 (aet)
1968	(Ethiopia) Zaire/Congo DR 1 Ghana 0
1970	(Sudan) Sudan 1 Ghana 0
1972	(Cameroon) Congo 3 Mali 2
1974	(Egypt) Zaire/Congo DR 2 Zambia 2
	Replay: Zaire/Congo DR 2 Zambia 0
1976	(Ethiopia) Morocco 1 Guinea 1 (Morocco win mini-league system)
1978	(Ghana) Ghana 2 Uganda 0
1980	(Nigeria) Nigeria 3 Algeria 0
1982	(Libya) Ghana 1 Libya 1 (aet; Ghana win 7-6 on penalties)
1984	(Ivory Coast) Cameroon 3 Nigeria 1
1986	(Egypt) Egypt 0 Cameroon 0 (aet; Egypt win 5-4 on penalties)
1988	(Morocco) Cameroon 1 Nigeria 0
1990	(Algeria) Algeria 1 Nigeria 0
1992	(Senegal) Ivory Coast 0 Ghana 0 (aet; Ivory Coast win 11-10 on penalties)
1994	(Tunisia) Nigeria 2 Zambia 1
1996	(South Africa) South Africa 2 Tunisia 0
1998	(Burkina Faso) Egypt 2 South Africa 0
2000	(Ghana & Nigeria) Cameroon 2 Nigeria 2 (aet; Cameroon win 4-3 on penalties)
2002	(Mali) Cameroon 0 Senegal 0 (aet; Cameroon win 3-2 on penalties)
2004	(Tunisia) Tunisia 2 Morocco 1
2006	(Egypt) Egypt 0 Ivory Coast 0 (aet; Egypt win 4-2 on penalties)
2008	(Ghana) Egypt 1 Cameroon 0
2010	(Angola) Egypt 1 Ghana 0
2012	(Gabon & Equatrorial Guinea) Zambia 0 Ivory Coast 0 (aet; Zambia 8-7 on pens)
2013	(South Africa) Nigeria 1 Burkina Faso 0
2015	(Equatrorial Guinea) Ivory Coast 0 Ghana 0 (aet; Ivory Coast 9-8 on pens)

GEDO BLASTER

Egypt's hero in 2010 was Mohamed Nagy, better known by his nickname "Gedo" – Egyptian Arabic for "Grandpa". He scored the only goal of the final, against Ghana, his fifth of the tournament, giving him the Golden Boot. Yet he did all this without starting a single game. He had to settle for coming on as a substitute in all six of Egypt's matches, playing a total of 135 minutes in all. Gedo – born in Damanhur on 3 October 1984 – made his international debut only two months earlier, and had played just two friendlies for Egypt before the tournament proper.

TOGO'S TRAGIC FATE

Togo were the victims of tragedy shortly before the 2010 Africa Cup of Nations kicked off – followed by expulsion from the event. The team's bus was fired on by Angolan militants three days before their first scheduled match, killing three people: the team's assistant coach, press officer and bus driver. The team returned home to Togo for three days of national mourning, and were then thrown out of the competition by the CAF as punishment for missing their opening game against Ghana. Togo were later expelled from the 2012 and 2014 competitions, but this sanction was overturned on appeal in May 2010.

RENARD REDEEMED

In 2015, Frenchman **Herve Renard** became the first coach to win the Africa Cup of Nations with two different countries. This time he was in charge of Ivory Coast as they defeated Ghana on penalties. Three years earlier, Renard's Zambia had defeated the Ivorians, also on spot-kicks, in what was his second spell as national coach. He had resigned in 2010 to become Angola's coach, and his return was not universally welcomed in Zambia. All was forgiven when his team won their first Africa Cup of Nations. Renard's celebrations included carrying on to the pitch injured defender Joseph Musonda, who had limped off after ten minutes of the final. He also handed his winner's medal to Kalusha Bwalya, probably Zambia's greatest ever player. Bwalya later coached Zambia but, by the time of the 2012 final, he was president of the country's football association.

UNFINISHED BUSINESS

Beware – if you go to see Nigeria play Tunisia, you may not get the full 90 minutes. Nigeria were awarded third place at the 1978 Africa Cup of Nations after the Tunisian team walked off after 42 minutes of their play-off, with the score at 1-1. They were protesting about refereeing decisions, but thus granted Nigeria a 2-0 victory by default. Oddly enough, it had been Nigeria walking off when the two teams met in the second leg of a qualifier for the 1962 tournament. Their action came when Tunisia equalized after 65 minutes. The punishment was a 2-0 win in Tunisia's favour – putting them 3-2 ahead on aggregate.

MAURITANIA MANIA

Mauritania made unwanted Africa Cup of Nations history by having five players sent off during a qualifier away to Cape Verde in June 2003, forcing the match to be abandoned. The hosts were leading 3-0 at the time and that stood as the final result.

MEET THE NEW (BIG) BOSS, SAME AS THE OLD (BIG) BOSS

Stephen Keshi – known to admiring fans as "Big Boss" – became only the second man to win the Africa Cup of Nations as both player and manager, when leading Nigeria to the title in 2013. He previously lifted the trophy as captain in 1994. The Nigerian football association, for so long mired in corruption and mismanagement claims, had their grudging faith in Keshi vindicated in summer 2013 – though he was their 19th manager in 19 years. Before Keshi, the only man to win the tournament both as a player and manager was Egypt's Mahmoud Al-Gohary – top scorer in 1959 and in charge 39 years later. Hassan Shehata, striker when Egypt finished third in 1970, then won a record-breaking three times as his country's coach.

NO GOAL GLUT

The 2015 event was the second-lowest-scoring Africa Cup of Nations of all-time, with an average of 2.12 goals per game – only the 1.59 in 2002 was lower. The most prolific finals was in 2008, with an average of exactly three goals per match.

ATAK ATTACKS

South Sudan won an international for the first time on 5 September 2015, when midfielder Atak Lual got the only goal of a 2017 Africa Cup of Nations qualifier against Equatorial Guinea. The game was played at South Sudan's national stadium in Juba. South Sudan had initially gained independence as a country in 2011, receiving CAF admission in February 2012 and FIFA status three months later. They drew their first official international, 2-2 against Uganda on 10 July 2012, but their winless run continued with one more draw and ten defeats before that success against Equatorial Guinea.

MISSING THE POINT

The absences of Cameroon, Nigeria and reigning champions Egypt from the 2012 African Cup of Nations were surprising – though each could at least comfort themselves on not missing out in quite such embarrassing circumstances as South Africa. They appeared happy to play out a goalless draw with Sierra Leone in their final qualifier, believing that would be enough to go through – and greeted the final whistle with celebrations on the pitch. But they were mistaken in thinking goal difference would be used to separate teams level on points in their group, with Niger qualifying instead thanks to a better head-to-head record. South Africa's distraught coach Pitso Mosimane admitted misinterpreting the rules and deliberately targeting his side's tactics towards a draw. The South African football association initially appealed against elimination, claiming goal difference should be the decider – but ultimately decided not to pursue the matter.

MISSING A (HAT-)TRICK

The last of the Africa Cup of Nations' 15 hat-tricks was scored back in 2008, by **Soufiane Alloudi** in the opening half-hour of Morocco's 5-1 first-round win over Namibia. Only Egypt's Hassan El-Shazly has hit two trebles: his first came in a 6-3 first-round victory over Nigeria in 1963; he repeated the feat, six years later, in a 3-1 victory over Ivory Coast in the third-place play-off.

RECENT AFRICA CUP OF NATIONS-WINNING COACHES

1988	Claude Le Roy (Cameroon)
1990	Abdelhamid Kermali (Algeria)
1992	Yeo Martial (Ivory Coast)
1994	Clemens Westerhof (Nigeria)
1996	Clive Barker (South Africa)
1998	Mahmoud El-Gohary (Egypt)
2000	Pierre Lechantre (Cameroon)
2002	Winfried Schafer (Cameroon)
2004	Roger Lemerre (Tunisia)
2006	Hassan Shehata (Egypt)
2008	Hassan Shehata (Egypt)
2010	Hassan Shehata (Egypt)
2012	Herve Renard (Zambia)
2013	Stephen Keshi (Nigeria)
2015	Herve Renard (Ivory Coast)

PART 6:
OTHER FIFA TOURNAMENTS

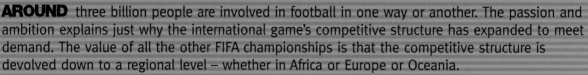

AROUND three billion people are involved in football in one way or another. The passion and ambition explains just why the international game's competitive structure has expanded to meet demand. The value of all the other FIFA championships is that the competitive structure is devolved down to a regional level – whether in Africa or Europe or Oceania.

That brings world competition down to a local level and increasingly imaginative concepts for tournament hosting means that more and more nations enjoy the opportunity to welcome the world. An obvious example was the 2012 FIFA Under-17 Women's World Cup in Azerbaijan – a relatively new member of the world football family. And, in 2015, New Zealand hosted the men's FIFA Under-20 World Cup – a tournament won by Serbia, that nation's first-ever success in a world football competition. Such events encourage and acknowledge the work of enthusiasts at grassroots levels worldwide. Regional confederations organize international championships for players in a wide range of age groups.

In 1977, FIFA extended its worldwide development programme with the launch of the FIFA World Youth Cup. The Soviet Union beat Mexico in the first final, in Tunisia. Eight years later came the FIFA Under-17 World Cup. Simultaneously, the Olympic Games football tournament became an Under-23 event with an exception for teams in the finals to field up to three over-age players. In 2000, FIFA stepped into the senior club sphere with the launch of FIFA Club World Cup. These events, at the top of world football, encouraged regional confederations to create their own tournaments so their teams could take to the world stage and face elite opponents.

Captain Andres Iniesta and his Barcelona team-mates celebrate the Spanish club's 3–0 victory over Argentina's River Plate in the 2015 FIFA Club World Cup final in Yokohama, Japan.

FIFA U-20 WORLD CUP

First staged in 1977 in Tunisia and known as the FIFA Youth World Championship until 2005, the FIFA U-20 World Cup is the world championship for footballers under the age of 20. It has featured some of the game's most notable names. Staged in alternate years, the tournament's most successful team has been Argentina, who have lifted the trophy on six occasions.

SERBIA TAKE HEART

Serbia won their first major FIFA prize defeating favourites Brazil 2-1 after extra time in the final of the 2015 FIFA U-20 World Cup. They were guided to success in Auckland, New Zealand, by the commanding displays of the event's top goalkeeper in captain Predrag Rajkovic and powerful Sergej Milinkovic in midfield. The team lived up to their motto of "one team with one heart". They were taken to extra time in all four knockout matches and beat Brazil with a goal from Nemanja Maksimovic two minutes from the end of extra time. Stanisa Mandic gave Serbia a 70th-minute lead, only for substitute Andreas Pereira to equalize three minutes later. A penalty shoot-out seemed likely until Maksimovic struck in the 118th minute.

SUPER SUB

The Soviet Union became the first winners of the FIFA Under-20 World Cup when they beat hosts Mexico 9-8 on penalties after a 2-2 draw in the 1977 final. Their shoot-out hero was substitute goalkeeper Yuri Sivuha, who had replaced Aleksandre Novikov during extra-time. It remains the only time the Soviet Union won the event, though their striker **Oleg Salenko**, a future 1994 FIFA World Cup Golden Boot winner, took the top scorer award in 1989, with five goals. Two years later, fellow Soviet Sergei Sherbakov also finished top scorer, also with five goals, although his full international career was less successful. He played only twice for Ukraine before injuries suffered in a car accident in 1993 left him in a wheelchair.

DOMINANT DOMINIC

Ghana became the first African country to lift the trophy when they upset Brazil in the 2009 final – despite playing 83 of the 120 minutes with just 10 men, following Daniel Addo's red card. The final finished goalless, one of only two games in which **Dominic Adiyiah** failed to score. He ended the tournament as top scorer with eight goals and also won the Golden Ball prize for best player. Immediately afterwards a further reward was a transfer from Norway's Fredrikstad to Italy's AC Milan. The Silver Ball went to Brazil's Alex Teixeira, even though it was his missed penalty, when the final shoot-out went to sudden death, which handed Ghana victory.

LISBON LIONS

In 1991, **Portugal** became the first hosts to win the tournament with a team that became known as the country's "Golden Generation", featuring Luis Figo, Rui Costa, Joao Pinto, Abel Xavier and Jorge Costa. Portugal's winning squad was coached by Carlos Queiroz, who would later manage the full national side twice, with spells in charge at Real Madrid and as assistant at Manchester United in between. Their penalty shoot-out win over Brazil in the final was played at Benfica's iconic Estadio da Luz in the capital Lisbon. In 2001, Argentina became the second team to lift the trophy on home territory.

SAVIOUR SAVIOLA

Javier Saviola has scored more goals in one FIFA Under-20 World Cup than any other player – he managed 11 in seven games at the 2001 competition, as his side Argentina went on to beat Ghana in the final, with Saviola scoring his team's three unanswered goals. Saviola, born on 11 December 1981 in Buenos Aires, was playing for River Plate at the time but joined Barcelona for £15 million not long afterwards – before later signing for the Spanish side's arch-rivals Real Madrid. When Pele picked his 125 "greatest living footballers" for FIFA in March 2004, 22-year-old Saviola was the youngest player on the list.

OSCAR WINNING

Only one player has scored a hat-trick in the final of a FIFA Under-20 World Cup: Brazilian midfielder Oscar, who hit all his side's goals in their 3-2 triumph over Portugal to claim the latest trophy in August 2011. He was further rewarded by making his senior Brazil debut the following month, against Argentina. They were actually Oscar's first goals of the tournament staged in Colombia, with the Golden Shoe going to his team-mate Henrique for five goals in the preceding six matches – including the 200th goal in FIFA Under-20 World Cup history, in a 3-0 first-round victory over Austria.

CAPTAIN MARVELS

Two men have lifted both the FIFA Under-20 World Cup and the FIFA World Cup as captain: Brazil's Dunga (in 1983 and 1994) and Argentina's Diego Maradona (in 1979 and 1986). Many had expected Maradona to make Argentina's full squad for the 1978 FIFA World Cup but he missed out on selection. He showed his potential by being voted best player at the 1979 youth tournament in Japan.

TOURNAMENT HOSTS AND FINAL RESULTS

1977 (Host: Tunisia) USSR 2 Mexico 2 (aet: USSR win 9-8 on penalties)
1979 (Japan) Argentina 3 USSR 1
1981 (Australia) West Germany 4 Qatar 0
1983 (Mexico) Brazil 1 Argentina 0
1985 (USSR) Brazil 1 Spain 0 (aet)
1987 (Chile) Yugoslavia 1 West Germany 1 (aet: Yugoslavia win 5-4 on penalties)
1989 (Saudi Arabia) Portugal 2 Nigeria 0
1991 (Portugal) Portugal 0 Brazil 0 (aet: Portugal win 4-2 on penalties)
1993 (Australia) Brazil 2 Ghana 1
1995 (Qatar) Argentina 2 Brazil 0
1997 (Malaysia) Argentina 2 Uruguay 1
1999 (Nigeria) Spain 4 Japan 0
2001 (Argentina) Argentina 3 Ghana 0
2003 (United Arab Emirates) Brazil 1 Spain 0
2005 (Holland) Argentina 2 Nigeria 1
2007 (Canada) Argentina 2 Czech Republic 1
2009 (Egypt) Ghana 0 Brazil 0 (aet: Ghana win 4-3 on penalties)
2011 (Colombia) Brazil 3 Portugal 2 (aet)
2013 (Turkey) France 0, Uruguay 0 (aet: France win 4-1 on penalties)
2015 (New Zealand) Serbia 2, Brazil 1 (aet)

WHAT A MESSI

Lionel Messi was the star of the show for Argentina in 2005, and not just for scoring both his country's goals in the final – both from the penalty spot. He achieved a hat-trick by not only winning the Golden Boot for top scorer and Golden Shoe for best player, but also by captaining his side to the title. This feat was emulated two years later by compatriot Sergio Aguero, who scored once in the final against the Czech Republic, before team-mate Mauro Zarate struck a late winner. Four other men have finished as both top scorer and as the tournament's best player (as voted by journalists) – Brazil's Geovani in 1983, Argentina's Javier Saviola in 2001, Dominic Adiyiah of Ghana in 2009 and another Brazilian, Henrique, in 2011.

TOURNAMENT TOP SCORERS

Year	Scorer	Goals
1977	Guina (Brazil)	4
1979	Ramon Diaz (Argentina)	8
1981	Ralf Loose (West Germany), Roland Wohlfarth (West Germany), Taher Amer (Egypt), Mark Koussas (Argentina)	4
1983	Geovani (Brazil)	6
1985	Gerson (Brazil), Balalo (Brazil), Muller (Brazil), Alberto Garcia Aspe (Mexico), Monday Odiaka (Nigeria), Fernando Gomez (Spain), Sebastian Losada (Spain)	3
1987	Marcel Witeczek (West Germany)	7
1989	Oleg Salenko (USSR)	5
1991	Sergei Sherbakov (USSR)	5
1993	Ante Milicic (Australia), Adriano (Brazil), Gian (Brazil), Henry Zambrano (Colombia), Vicente Nieto (Mexico), Chris Faklaris (USA)	3
1995	Joseba Etxeberria (Spain)	7
1997	Adailton Martins Bolzan (Brazil)	10
1999	Mahamadou Dissa (Mali), Pablo (Spain)	5
2001	Javier Saviola (Argentina)	11
2003	Fernando Cavenaghi (Argentina), Dudu (Brazil), Daisuke Sakata (Japan), Eddie Johnson (USA)	4
2005	Lionel Messi (Argentina)	6
2007	Sergio Aguero (Argentina)	7
2009	Dominic Adiyiah (Ghana)	8
2011	Henrique (Brazil)	5
2013	Ebenezer Assifuah (Ghana)	6
2015	Viktor Kovalenko (Ukraine), Bence Mervo (Hungary)	5 5

BRIGHT BLUES

France won the FIFA U-20 crown for the first time when they beat Uruguay 4-1 on penalties after the second goalless draw in the final in three tournaments. Les Bleus won despite finishing only second to favourites Spain in Group A. They then gained in confidence from a 4-1 thrashing of hosts Turkey in the second round. In Juventus midfielder Paul Pogba, France also boasted the tournament's best player, while their goalkeeper Alphonse Areola, with two spot-kick saves, was decisive in the final shoot-out.

FIFA U-17 WORLD CUP

First staged in China in 1985, when it was known as the FIFA Under-16 World Championship, the age limit was adjusted from 16 to 17 in 1991 and the tournament has been labelled the FIFA U-17 World Cup ever since 2007. The 2015 finals were staged in Chile when reigning champions Nigeria ran out again as deserved winners for a record-extending fifth time. They have also been runners-up on three occasions.

GOLDEN BOYS

Nigeria extended their command of world youth football in 2015 when the Golden Eaglets won their fifth title by beating Mali 2-0 in Santiago. The winning margin could have been greater: Nigeria's Osinachi Ebere missed a penalty in only the third minute. **Victor Osimhen** opened the scoring with his 10th goal in the tournament, and he became the single-event highest scorer. In reaching the final Nigeria scored 21 goals in six games including victories over hosts Chile by 5-1, Brazil by 3-0 and Mexico by 4-2 in semi-finals.

TAKING WING

Nigeria's youth side, the "Golden Eaglets", became the first African nation to win a FIFA tournament when they triumphed at the inaugural Under-16 FIFA World Cup in 1985 (it became an Under-17 event in 1991). Their opening goal in the final against West Germany was scored by striker Jonathan Akpoborie, who would go on to play for German clubs Stuttgart and Wolfsburg.

GOALS FLO

The first player to win both the Golden Ball and the Golden Shoe at the FIFA U-17 World Cup was French striker **Florent Sinama-Pongolle**. His nine goals in 2001 set a tournament record for one player. His tally included two hat-tricks in the opening round. Unlike Cesc Fabregas, two years later, Sinama-Pongolle ended the final on the winning side. The team goalscoring record is held by Spain, who struck 22 times on their way to third place in 1997. Sinama-Pongolle's scoring record was equalled in 2011 by Ivory Coast striker Souleymane Coulibaly. While Sinama-Pongolle needed six matches, the young Ivorian managed his in just four games but his team only reached the second round – though he earned a transfer from Italy's Siena to English Premier League club Tottenham Hotspur not long afterwards.

SEOUL SURVIVOR

The final of the 2007 tournament was the first to be hosted by a former FIFA World Cup venue – the 68,476-capacity Seoul FIFA World Cup Stadium in South Korea's capital, which had been built for the 2002 FIFA World Cup. The game was watched by a crowd of 36,125, a tournament record. The 2007 event was the first to feature 24 teams instead of 16, and was won by Nigeria – after Spain missed all three of their spot-kicks in a penalty shoot-out.

GOOD AND BAD BOY BOJAN

Barcelona star **Bojan Krkic** quickly went from hero to villain in the final moments of Spain's semi-final victory over Ghana in 2007 – he scored his team's winner with four minutes of extra-time remaining, but was then sent off for a second yellow-card offence just before the final whistle. His expulsion meant he was suspended for the final, which Spain lost on penalties to Nigeria.

GOLDEN HAUL

West Germany's Marcel Witeczek is the only person to finish top scorer at both a FIFA Under-16 World Championship and the Under-20 version of the event. The Polish-born striker hit eight goals at the 1985 Under-16 tournament, followed by seven more at the Under-20 championship two years later. Brazil's Adriano – a different Adriano to the one who later played for the senior side and Serie A club Internazionale – came closest to equalling the feat: he won the Golden Shoe, for top scorer, after scoring four goals at the 1991 FIFA Under-17 World Cup, then the Golden Ball, for best player, at the Under-20 event in 1993.

LITTLE ITALY

The 1991 tournament was originally scheduled to take place in Ecuador, but a cholera outbreak in the country meant it was switched to Italy instead – though played in much smaller venues than those that had been used for the previous year's senior FIFA World Cup in the country. The 1991 tournament was the first to be open to Under-17s – the first three had been known as the FIFA U-16 World Cup.

TOURNAMENT TOP SCORERS

Year	Player	Goals
1985	Marcel Witeczek (West Germany)	8
1987	Moussa Traore (Ivory Coast)	5
	Yuri Nikiforov (USSR)	5
1989	Khaled Jasem (Bahrain)	3
	Fode Camara (Guinea)	3
	Gil (Portugal)	3
	Tulipa (Portugal)	3
	Khalid Al Roaihi (Saudi Arabia)	3
1991	Adriano (Brazil)	4
1993	Wilson Oruma (Nigeria)	6
1995	Daniel Allsopp (Australia)	5
	Mohamed Al Kathiri (Oman)	5
1997	David (Spain)	7
1999	Ishmael Addo (Ghana)	7
2001	Florent Sinama-Pongolle (France)	9
2003	Carlos Hidalgo (Colombia)	5
	Manuel Curto (Portugal)	5
	Cesc Fabregas (Spain)	5
2005	Carlos Vela (Mexico)	5
2007	Macauley Chrisantus (Nigeria)	7
2009	Borja (Spain)	5
	Sani Emmanuel (Nigeria)	5
	Sebastian Gallegos (Uruguay)	5
	Haris Seferovic (Switzerland)	5
2011	Souleymane Coulibaly (Ivory Coast)	9
2013	**Valmir Berisha** (Sweden)	7
2015	Victor Osimhen (Nigeria)	10

HIGH–FLYING EAGLETS

In 2013, remarkably, the teams that finished first, second and third, respectively in Group F, ended the tournament in that order. Nigeria's Golden Eaglets won in fine style to complete a memorable year in which the seniors won the African Cup of Nations and qualified for the FIFA World Cup finals. The unbeaten juniors crushed Mexico 3-0 in the final. In addition star forward Kelechi Iheanacho was named best player and Dele Alampasu top goalkeeper. Sweden, thanks in part to top-scorer Valmir Berisha (seven goals), finished third in their first-ever appearance in the finals.

GOMEZ AT HOME

Mexico became the first host country to lift the FIFA U-17 World Cup trophy on home soil, when they beat Uruguay 2-0 in the final in the Azteca Stadium in Mexico City in July 2011. The Golden Ball award for the tournament's best player went to Mexican winger **Julio Gomez,** whose brace against Germany in the semi-final including a spectacular bicycle-kick for the last-minute winner – though he played only ten minutes of the final, as a substitute, after picking up an injury in the previous game.

FAB FABREGAS

Spain's Cesc Fabregas joined Florent Sinama-Pongolle as only two players to win both the Golden Shoe, for top scorer, and the Golden Ball, for best player, at a FIFA Under-17 World Cup. He took both prizes after scoring five goals at the 2003 tournament, despite losing the final to Brazil. He and team-mate David Silva would later be part of the senior Spanish team who won the 2008 and 2012 European Championships as well as the 2010 World Cup in South Africa in between. Fabregas, born in Arenys de Mar on 4 May 1987, left Barcelona for Arsenal a month after the 2003 tournament before returning home and then heading back to London with Chelsea in 2014.

HOSTS AND FINAL RESULTS

(Host country)

1985	(China) Nigeria 2 West Germany 0
1987	(Canada) USSR 1 Nigeria 1 (aet: USSR win 4-2 on penalties)
1989	(Scotland) Saudi Arabia 2 Scotland 2 (aet: Saudi Arabia win 5-4 on penalties)
1991	(Italy) Ghana 1 Spain 0
1993	(Japan) Nigeria 2 Ghana 1
1995	(Ecuador) Ghana 3 Brazil 2
1997	(Egypt) Brazil 2 Ghana 1
1999	(New Zealand) Brazil 0 Australia 0 (aet: Brazil win 8-7 on penalties)
2001	(Trinidad & Tobago) France 3 Nigeria 0
2003	(Finland) Brazil 1 Spain 0
2005	(Peru) Mexico 3 Brazil 0
2007	(South Korea) Nigeria 0 Spain 0 (aet: Nigeria win 3-0 on penalties)
2009	(Nigeria) Switzerland 1 Nigeria 0
2011	(Mexico) Mexico 2 Uruguay 0
2013	(United Arab Emirates) Nigeria 3 Mexico 0
2015	(Chile) Nigeria 2 Mali 0

FIFA CONFEDERATIONS CUP

The FIFA Confederations Cup has assumed numerous guises over the years. In 1992 and 1995 it was played in Saudi Arabia and featured a collection of continental champions. From 1997 to 2003 FIFA staged a tournament every two years. The tournament was played in its current format for the first time in Germany in 2005. It is now celebrated throughout the football world as the Championship of Champions.

OVERALL TOP SCORERS

1	Cuauhtemoc Blanco (Mexico)	9
=	Ronaldinho (Brazil)	9
3	Fernando Torres (Spain)	8
4	Romario (Brazil)	7
=	Adriano (Brazil)	7
6	Marzouk Al-Otaibi (Saudi Arabia)	6
7	Alex (Brazil)	5
=	John Aloisi (Australia)	5
=	Luis Fabiano (Brazil)	5
=	Fred (Brazil)	5
=	Vladimir Smicer (Czech Rep.)	5
=	Robert Pires (France)	5

FAB'S FIVE

Brazil's victory over the United States in the 2009 final made them the first country to complete a hat-trick of FIFA Confederations Cup triumphs, following success in 1997 and 2005. But they did it the hard way, needing to come back from two goals down at half-time before winning 3–2 – thanks to a late goal from captain and centre-back Lucio. **Luis Fabiano**, who ended as tournament top scorer with five goals overall, struck the other two goals. His team-mate Kaka was voted best player, with Luis Fabiano second and America's Clint Dempsey third.

TOURNAMENT TOP SCORERS

1992	Gabriel Batistuta (Argentina), Bruce Murray (USA) 2
1995	Luis Garcia (Mexico) 3
1997	Romario (Brazil) 7
1999	Ronaldinho (Brazil), Cuauhtemoc Blanco (Mexico), Marzouq Al-Otaibi (Saudi Arabia) 6
2001	Shaun Murphy (Australia), Eric Carriere (France), Robert Pires (France), Patrick Vieira (France), Sylvain Wiltord (France), Takayuki Suzuki (Japan), Hwang Sun-Hong (South Korea) 2
2003	Thierry Henry (France) 4
2005	Adriano (Brazil) 5
2009	Luis Fabiano (Brazil) 5
2013	Fernando Torres (Spain) 5 Fred (Brazil) 5

FIT FOR A KING

Before being rebranded as the FIFA Confederations Cup, a tournament bringing together the continental champions of the world was known as the King Fahd Cup and was hosted in Saudi Arabia. Copa America holders Argentina reached both finals, beating their hosts in the first in 1992 thanks to goals by Leonardo Rodriguez, Claudio Caniggia and Diego Simeone. Only four teams took part in the 1992 event, with the United States and the Ivory Coast also represented, but world champions Germany and European champions Holland did not participate. In 1995, a six-team version was won by European champions Denmark. The current eight-team format, with two groups and knockout semi-finals, was adopted in 2005.

TON-UP SUPERSTARS

Andrea Pirlo and Diego Forlan both celebrated their 100th international appearance at the 2013 Confederations Cup. Italy playmaker Pirlo scored the *Azzurri*'s first goal in their opening 2-1 win over Mexico in Maracana. Forlan marked his own achievement (becoming the first Uruguayan to reach 100 caps) by hitting a brilliant left-footed drive which proved the decisive goal in a 2-1 victory over Nigeria.

NO STOPPING NEYMAR

The 2013 Confederations Cup crowned a memorable six months for Brazilian striker Neymar. In January he had been voted South American Footballer of the Year for the second successive year and in June he agreed to leave Santos and take up a five-year contract with Spanish champions Barcelona. In one of his farewell appearances in Brazil, Neymar da Silva Santos Junior struck the first goal of the Confederations Cup in only the third minute of the tournament's opening match against Japan. Neymar scored in each of Brazil's group matches and then again in the defeat of Spain in the final.

HIGH-TECH INSURANCE

Goal-line technology was used at the Confederations Cup for the first time in Brazil. GoalControl, a German company, won a tender to install its system in all six venues. In fact, it was never needed to decide a goal-scoring issue, but FIFA was satisfied it functioned effectively. Howard Webb, lone English referee at the competition, hailed "the reassurance the system gives us".

BURSTING A SOUTH SEA BUBBLE

Minnows Tahiti suffered the heaviest defeat in Confederations Cup history when they crashed 10-0 to Spain in the 2013 tournament in Brazil. The South Pacific part-timers – including an accountant, a carpenter and a teacher – were not too upset, however. None of them had ever even dreamed of playing in the legendary Maracana or against the world and European champions and now they had done both in one match. The Oceania champions also conceded a cup record 24 goals in their three games, with Jonathan Tehau scoring their historic single goal, against Nigeria, in return. The defeat by Spain equalled the Cup's largest single-match aggregate: in 1999, Brazil thrashed Saudi Arabia 8-2.

BRILLIANT BRAZIL

Brazil's 3-0 demolition of world and European champions Spain in the 2013 final in Maracana enhanced their historical command of the Confederations Cup. Their 12th consecutive win in the competition saw Luiz Felipe Scolari's men become the first nation to land the Cup three times in a row. They scored at least three goals in each of their title match victories and are the competition's only four-times champions. Brazil set a standard off the pitch as well: record ticket sales generated a 16-match aggregate attendance of 804,659 for an average of 50,291 per game. The 68 goals averaged out at 4.25 per match, the most prolific marksmanship over the last six competitions.

SHARED SADNESS

The 2003 FIFA Confederations Cup was overshadowed by the tragic death of Cameroon's 28-year-old midfielder **Marc-Vivien Foe**, who collapsed on the Lyon pitch after suffering a heart attack 73 minutes into his country's semi-final win against Colombia. After Thierry Henry scored France's golden-goal winner against Cameroon in the final, he dedicated his goal to Foe, who played much of his club career in the French championship. When the trophy was presented at the Stade de France in Paris, it was jointly lifted by the captains of both teams – Marcel Desailly for France and Rigobert Song for Cameroon.

CLINT MAKES AMERICA'S DAY

The United States' surprise run to the 2009 final included a shock semi-final win over Spain that ended the European champions' long unbeaten run. Heading into the match, Spain had won a record 15 international matches in a row – and gone 35 successive games unbeaten, a tally shared with Brazil. But their hopes of extending their run to 36 matches were ruined by goals from US striker Jozy Altidore and winger **Clint Dempsey**. The result put the Americans into the final of a FIFA men's senior competition for the first time.

FIFA CONFEDERATIONS CUP HOSTS AND FINAL RESULTS

1997	(Host country: Saudi Arabia) Brazil 6 Argentina 0
1999	(Mexico) Mexico 4 Brazil 3
2001	(South Korea and Japan) France 1 Japan 0
2003	(France) France 1 Cameroon 0
	(aet: France win on golden goal)
2005	(Germany) Brazil 4 Argentina 1
2009	(South Africa) Brazil 3 United States 2
2013	(Brazil) Brazil 3 Spain 0

FIFA CLUB WORLD CUP

As is the case with the FIFA Confederations Cup, the FIFA Club World Cup has been played in several different formats since 1960, when Real Madrid defeated Penarol. In its current guise, the competition pits the champion clubs from all six continents against each other. It has been staged on an annual basis, mostly in Japan from 2005, apart from two hostings in Abu Dhabi and in 2013 and 2014 in Morocco.

CORINTHIAN SPIRIT

Brazilian club Corinthians not only succeeded Barcelona as FIFA Club World Cup champions in 2012 but also equalled the Spanish side's record as two-time winners and with a record of six matches won overall. Peruvian striker Paolo Guerrero scored the only goal of their semi-final victory over Egypt's Al-Ahly, and repeated the feat in the final against England's Chelsea. The Corinthians line-up included goalkeeper and player-of-the-tournament **Cassio**, as well as Danilo and Fabio Santos, a pair who had both won the tournament with Sao Paulo seven years earlier. Defeat for the European champions also prevented newly-appointed Chelsea manager Rafael Benitez from equalling former Barcelona boss Pep Guardiola in winning the tournament twice. Benitez previously lifted the trophy as Internazionale coach in 2010.

WINNERS BY COUNTRY*

10 Brazil
9 Argentina, Italy
7 Spain
6 Uruguay
4 Germany
3 Netherlands
2 Portugal, England
1 Paraguay, Yugoslavia

*Includes Intercontinental Cup

MOROCCO GO–AHEAD

Morocco staged the December 2014 tournament for a second successive year, despite having just withdrawn from hosting the following month's Africa Cup of Nations because of fears of the spread of the ebola virus. Organizers were happy to go ahead with the FIFA competition because none of the clubs taking part came from nations struggling to contain the disease.

THE REIGN OF SPAIN

Spain has commanded the honours at the FIFA Club World Cup over the past six years. Between them Barcelona and Real Madrid have won four of the last seven finals. Real Madrid defeated San Lorenzo in 2014 and Barcelona scored a triumph of their own against Argentinian opponents, this time River Plate, in 2015. One goal from Lionel Messi and two from **Luis Suarez** secured a 3-0 victory to provide Barcelona with their fifth trophy of the year after the Spanish league and cup, UEFA Champions league and UEFA Super Cup. Suarez, with five goals in two matches, won the golden boot as top scorer and golden ball as best player.

SIX APPEAL

Barcelona's triumph in 2009 made them the first club to lift six different major trophies in one calendar year: the FIFA Club World Cup, the UEFA Champions League, the UEFA European Super Cup, and a Spanish hat-trick of La Liga, Copa del Rey and Super Cup. This made their trophy cabinet one cup heavier than Liverpool's in 2001, when Gerard Houllier's men won the FA Cup, League Cup and Charity Shield in England and the UEFA Cup and Super Cup in Europe.

VETERAN IVAN

New Zealand's Auckland City were one of the surprises of the 2014 FIFA Club World Cup, spearheaded by 38-year-old **Ivan Vacelich** who won the bronze award for third best player at the tournament. Only Real Madrid's Sergio Ramos and Cristiano Ronaldo finished ahead of him. Auckland City finished third, the highest finish for a club from Oceania. They beat Cruz Azul on penalties, after a 1-1 draw in the third-place play-off.

SWITCHING SYSTEMS

From 1960 until 1968, the Intercontinental Cup was settled, not on aggregate scores, but by using a system of two points for a win and one for a draw. This meant a third, deciding match was needed in 1961, 1963, 1964 and 1967. No team that had not been worse off on aggregate after the first two legs had gone on to win the third match, though before losing their play-off 1-0 to Argentina's Racing Club in 1967, Celtic would have won the two-legged tie if aggregate scores and away goals counted. The Scottish side won their home leg 1-0, before losing 2-1 away. From 1980 until 2004, the annual event was a one-off match staged in Japan.

FIGURE OF EIGHT

Manchester United's 5-3 win over Gamba Osaka in the semi-final of the FIFA Club World Cup in 2008 was the highest-scoring single game in the history of the competition in all its forms – bettering the 5-2 victory over Benfica by a Santos team featuring Pele in 1962. Even more amazingly, all but two of the goals in the Manchester United–Gamba game were scored in the final 16 minutes, plus stoppage-time. United were leading 2-0 with 74 minutes gone, before a burst of goals – including two by substitute Wayne Rooney – at both ends. Manchester United became the first team to score five goals in the FIFA Club World Cup's revised format.

LONG-DISTANCE, LONG-RUNNING RIVALRY

The precursor to the modern FIFA Club World Cup was the Intercontinental Cup, also known informally as the World Club Cup and/or the Europe–South America Cup, which pitted the champions of Europe and South America against each other. Representatives of UEFA and CONMEBOL contested the event from 1960 to 2004, but now all continental federations send at least one club to an expanded Club World Cup organized and endorsed by the world federation, FIFA. The original final, in 1960, was between Spain's Real Madrid and Uruguay's Penarol. After a goalless draw in the rain in Montevideo, Real triumphed 5-1 at their own stadium in Madrid – including three goals scored in the first eight minutes, two of them by Ferenc Puskas. The two clubs are among five sharing the record for Intercontinental Cup triumphs, with three victories apiece – the others being Argentina's Boca Juniors, Uruguay's Nacional and AC Milan of Italy. Milan are the only one of these clubs to have added a FIFA Club World Cup to their tally, as the championship was first contested in 2000 (in Brazil) before it was swallowed up by the Intercontinental Cup and was instituted on an annual basis.

SUCCESS IN PHASES

Since FIFA introduced its own, expanded Club World Cup in 2000, with representatives from all the world's continental football federations, Brazilian sides have the best overall record – with Corinthians the first winners. Carlo Ancelotti's AC Milan finally broke the Brazilian stranglehold in 2007, when the trophy was lifted by club captain Paolo Maldini, who had appeared for Milan – alongside Alessandro Costacurta – in five Intercontinental Cup showdowns between 1989 and 2003.

AFRICAN DOUBLE

In 2010, for the first time in Intercontinental Cup or official FIFA Club World Cup history, an African team contested the final. TP Mazembe from the Democratic Republic of Congo, defeated South American champions Internacional, from Brazil, 2-0 in their semi-final. Internacional, winners in 2006, were the first former FIFA Club World Cup champions to compete for a second time. Mazembe achieved the surprise victory despite missing their star striker and captain Tresor Mputu, who was serving a one-year ban for furiously chasing a referee after a match in May 2010. Raja Casablanca, from host nation Morocco, became the second African finalists when they finished, also runners-up, to Bayern Munich in 2013.

FIFA CLUB WORLD CUP FINALS (2000–15)

2000	Corinthians (Brazil) 0	
	Vasco da Gama (Brazil) 0	
	(aet: Corinthians win 4-3 on penalties)	
2005	Sao Paulo (Brazil) 1 Liverpool (England) 0	
2006	Internacional (Brazil) 1 Barcelona (Spain) 0	
2007	AC Milan (Italy) 4	
	Boca Juniors (Argentina) 2	
2008	Manchester United (England) 1	
	LDU Quito (Ecuador) 0	
2009	Barcelona (Spain) 2	
	Estudiantes (Argentina) 1 (aet)	
2010	Internazionale (Italy) 3	
	TP Mazembe (DR Congo) 0	
2011	Barcelona (Spain) 4 Santos (Brazil) 0	
2012	Corinthians (Brazil) 1 Chelsea (England) 0	
2013	Bayern Munich (Germany) 2	
	Raja Casablanca (Morocco) 0	
2014	Real Madrid (Spain) 2	
	San Lorenzo (Argentina) 0	
2015	Barcelona (Spain) 3	
	River Plate (Argentina) 0	

OVERALL WORLD CLUB CHAMPIONS (1960–2015*)

4 wins: Real Madrid, Spain (1960, 1998, 2002, 2014); AC Milan, Italy (1969, 1989, 1990, 2007)

3 wins: Penarol, Uruguay (1961, 1966, 1982); Internazionale, Italy (1964, 1965, 2010); Nacional, Uruguay (1971, 1980, 1988); Bayern Munich, West Germany/Germany (1976, 2001, 2013); Boca Juniors, Argentina (1977, 2000, 2003); Sao Paulo, Brazil (1992, 1993, 2005); Barcelona, Spain (2009, 2011, 2015)

2 wins: Santos, Brazil (1962, 1963); Ajax, Netherlands (1972, 1995); Independiente, Argentina (1973, 1984); Juventus, Italy (1985, 1996); Porto, Portugal (1987, 2004); Manchester United, England (1999, 2008); Corinthians, Brazil (2000, 2012)

1 win: Racing Club, Argentina (1967); Estudiantes, Argentina (1968); Feyenoord, Netherlands (1970); Atletico de Madrid, Spain (1974); Olimpia Asuncion, Paraguay (1979); Flamengo, Brazil (1981); Gremio, Brazil (1983); River Plate, Argentina (1986); Red Star Belgrade, Yugoslavia (1991); Velez Sarsfield, Argentina (1994); Borussia Dortmund, Germany (1997); Internacional, Brazil (2006)

* = not contested in 1975 and 1978

MEN'S OLYMPIC FOOTBALL TOURNAMENT

First played at the 1900 Olympic Games in Paris, although not recognized by FIFA as an official tournament until London 1908, the men's Olympic football tournament was played in strict accordance with the Games' strong amateur tradition until 1984, when pros were allowed to play. The competition is now an Under-23 event – with allowance for three over-age players – to give rising stars the chance of major tournament experience. Since World War 2, however, no Olympic champions have won the FIFA World Cup within 10 years.

CZECH OUT

The climax of the 1920 Olympic Games tournament is the only time a major international football final has been abandoned. Czechoslovakia's players walked off the pitch minutes before half-time, in protest at the decisions made by 65-year-old English referee John Lewis – including the dismissal of Czech player Karel Steiner. Belgium, who were 2-0 up at the time, were awarded the victory, before Spain beat Holland 3-1 in a play-off for silver.

MEN'S OLYMPIC FOOTBALL FINALS

1896 Not played
1900 (Paris, France)
Gold: Upton Park FC (GB) Silver: USFSA XI (France) Bronze: Universite Libre de Bruxelles (Belgium) (only two exhibition matches played)
1904 (St Louis, US)
Gold: Galt FC (Canada) Silver: Christian Brothers College (US) Bronze: St Rose Parish (US) (only five exhibition matches played)
1908 (London, England)
Great Britain 2 Denmark 0 (Bronze: Holland)
1912 (Stockholm, Sweden)
Great Britain 4 Denmark 2 (Bronze: Holland)
1916 Not played
1920 (Antwerp, Belgium) Belgium 2 Czechoslovakia 0
(Gold: Belgium, Silver: Spain, Bronze: Holland)
1924 (Paris, France)
Uruguay 3 Switzerland 0 (Bronze: Sweden)
1928 (Amsterdam, Netherlands)
Uruguay 1 Argentina 1; Uruguay 2 Argentina 1 (Bronze: Italy)
1932 Not played
1936 (Berlin, Germany) Italy 2 Austria 1 (aet) (Bronze: Norway)
1940 Not played
1944 Not played
1948 (London, England) Sweden 3 Yugoslavia 1 (Bronze: Denmark)
1952 (Helsinki, Finland) Hungary 2 Yugoslavia 0 (Bronze: Sweden)
1956 (Melbourne, Australia) USSR 1 Yugoslavia 0 (Bronze: Bulgaria)
1960 (Rome, Italy) Yugoslavia 3 Denmark 1 (Bronze: Hungary)
1964 (Tokyo, Japan) Hungary 2 Czechoslovakia 1 (Bronze: Germany)
1968 (Mexico City, Mexico) Hungary 4 Bulgaria 1 (Bronze: Japan)
1972 (Munich, West Germany) Poland 2 Hungary 1 (Bronze: USSR/East Germany)
1976 (Montreal, Canada) East Germany 3 Poland 1 (Bronze: USSR)
1980 (Moscow, USSR) Czechoslovakia 1 East Germany 0 (Bronze: USSR)
1984 (Los Angeles, USA) France 2 Brazil 0 (Bronze: Yugoslavia)
1988 (Seoul, South Korea) USSR 2 Brazil 1 (Bronze: West Germany)
1992 (Barcelona, Spain) Spain 3 Poland 2 (Bronze: Ghana)
1996 (Atlanta, USA) Nigeria 3 Argentina 2 (Bronze: Brazil)
2000 (Sydney, Australia) **Cameroon** 2 Spain 2
(Cameroon win 5-3 on penalties) (Bronze: Chile)
2004 (Athens, Greece) Argentina 1 Paraguay 0 (Bronze: Italy)
2008 (Beijing, China) **Argentina 1** Nigeria 0 (Bronze: Brazil)
2012 (London, England) Mexico 2 Brazil 1 (Bronze: South Korea)

BARCELONA BOUND

Future Barcelona team-mates Samuel Eto'o and Xavi scored penalties for opposing sides in 2000, when Cameroon and Spain contested the first Olympic final to be settled by a shoot-out. Ivan Amaya was the only player to miss, handing Cameroon gold.

RETROSPECTIVE MEDALS

Football was not played at the very first modern Summer Olympics, in Athens in 1896, and the football tournaments played at the 1900 and 1904 events are not officially recognized by FIFA. Medals were not handed out to the winning teams at the time – with Great Britain represented in 1900 by the Upton Park club from East London – though the International Olympic Committee has since allocated first, second and third place to the countries taking part.

BLOC PARTY

Eastern European countries dominated the Olympic Games football competitions from 1948 to 1980, when professional players were officially banned from taking part. Teams comprising so-called "state amateurs" from the Eastern Bloc took 23 of the 27 medals available during those years. Only Sweden, in 1948, brought gold medals west of the Iron Curtain. Sweden also collected bronze four years later, before Denmark claimed silver in 1960 and Japan bronze in 1968.

LAPPING IT UP

Until London 2012, Uruguay had a perfect Olympic football record. They won gold on the first two occasions they took part (1924 and 1928). Those Games were seen as a world championship and helped prompt FIFA into organizing the first World Cup in 1930 – also won by Uruguay, who included 1924 and 1928 gold medallists Jose Nasazzi, Jose Andrade and **Hector Scarone** (right) in their squad. Uruguay's 1924 champions are thought to have pioneered the lap of honour.

LONDON CALLING

Mexico were the unexpected winners when **Wembley Stadium** became the first venue to stage two men's Olympic Games football finals as part of London 2012. The stadium hosted the showpiece game when England's capital held the Olympics in 1948 and London is also now the only city to stage three separate summer Olympics, though the football final back in 1908 was played at White City. **Oribe Peralta** scored both goals as Mexico – managed by Luis Tena, assistant coach to the senior team – defeated Brazil 2-1 in the 2012 final. A late reply by Hulk was little consolation for the highly-fancied South Americans - though Brazil's Leandro Damiao did end the summer as six-goal top scorer. London 2012 matches were shared with cities away from the English capital, including Hampden Park in Glasgow, Old Trafford in Manchester, St James' Park in Newcastle and the City of Coventry Stadium. A united British team competed in the Olympic finals for the first time since 1960, featuring English Premier League stars such as Ryan Giggs and Craig Bellamy.

AFRICAN AMBITION

Ghana became the first African country to win an Olympic football medal, picking up bronze in 1992, but Nigeria went even better four years later by claiming the continent's first Olympic football gold medal – thanks to Emmanuel Amunike's stoppage-time winner against Argentina. Nigeria's triumph came as a huge surprise to many – especially as their rival teams included such future world stars as Brazil's Ronaldo and Roberto Carlos, Argentina's Hernan Crespo and Roberto Ayala, Italy's Fabio Cannavaro and Gianluigi Buffon, and France's Robert Pires and Patrick Vieira. Future FIFA World Cup or UEFA European Championship winners to have played at Summer Olympics include France's Michel Platini and Patrick Battiston (at the Montreal Games in 1976); West Germany's Andreas Brehme and Brazil's Dunga (Los Angeles, 1984); Brazil's Taffarel, Bebeto and Romario and West Germany's Jurgen Klinsmann (Seoul, 1988); France's Vieira, Pires and Sylvain Wiltord, Italy's Cannavaro, Buffon and Alessandro Nesta, and Brazil's Roberto Carlos, Rivaldo and Ronaldo (Atlanta, 1996); Italy's Gianluca Zambrotta and Spain's Xavi, Carles Puyol and Joan Capdevila (Sydney, 2000); and Italy's Daniele De Rossi, Andrea Pirlo and Alberto Gilardino (Athens, 2004).

BLUE STARS FIFA YOUTH CUP

Staged on an annual basis by Zurich club FC Blue Stars since 1939, and granted FIFA's patronage since 1991, the Blue Stars/FIFA Youth Cup tournament has become football's premier youth event and features many teams from around the globe. Several of the game's greatest names – from Bobby Charlton to David Beckham – had their first taste of international football competition at the event.

GRASSHOPPERS LEAP TO SEVENTH TITLE

Grasshoppers won their seventh FIFA Blue Stars trophy after a 2-0 win against West Ham United in the 2016 final. Goals from Sherko Kareem Gubari and Nikola Mijatovic capped off a memorable competition for the Swiss side, and Kareem Gubari received the Adidas Golden Ball for his standout performances during the competition. Third and fourth place went to Anderlecht from Belgium and St Pauli from Germany respectively, while last year's champions FC Luzern had to settle for sixth place. Grasshoppers are now two wins clear of fellow Swiss side FC Zurich in titles, but 11 behind 18-time winners Manchester United.

BRAVO, GUSTAVO

Two weeks before the 2014 FIFA World Cup kicked off, Brazilians were celebrating – not back home but in Switzerland where Atletico Paranaense marked their Blue Stars debut by lifting the trophy. Samba musicians and dancers brought a carnival atmosphere to the occasion even before the start of the final against Portugal's Benfica, watched by 15,000 spectators including FIFA president Sepp Blatter. The game was settled in the end by a single goal by Atletico playmaker Gustavo. He was also awarded the Golden Ball for player of the tournament, while team-mate Macanhan was acclaimed as best goalkeeper. The bronze medal match was an all-Swiss affair, with Grasshoppers beating FC Zurich on penalties.

RAISING THE BARÇA

No Spanish side took part until Barcelona's involvement in 1988, with a team featuring midfielder **Josep Guardiola** and right-back Albert Ferrer, both of whom would help the club to their first European Cup triumph in 1992.

HEART OF THE BLATTER

Long before he was elected FIFA president in 1998, Sepp Blatter was a keen amateur footballer who played centre-forward for Swiss club FC Sierre in the Blue Stars tournament in the early 1950s. He is now an honorary member of FC Blue Stars.

BRAZIL FORTUNE

It took until 1999 for the tournament to be won by a non-European club when Sao Paulo of Brazil edged FC Zurich on penalties. With Kaka in their squad, they won again in 2000 and Argentina's Boca Juniors became the third South American winners in 2010.

BLUE STARS CHAMPIONSHIPS

Manchester United 18
(1954, 1957, 1959, 1960, 1961, 1962, 1965, 1966, 1968, 1969, 1975, 1976, 1978, 1979, 1981, 1982, 2004, 2005)
Grasshoppers 7
(1939, 1956, 1971, 1987, 1998, 2006, 2016)
FC Zurich 5
(1946, 1949, 2008, 2012, 2013)
Barcelona 3
(1993, 1994, 1995)
FC Young Fellows 3
(1941, 1942, 1953)
AC Milan 2
(1958, 1977)
Arsenal 2
(1963, 1964)
AS Roma 2
(1980, 2003)
FK Austria Vienna 2
(1947, 1948)
Sao Paulo 2
(1999, 2000)
Spartak Moscow 2
(1991, 1992)
Atletico Paranaense 1
(2014)
FC Basel 1
(2009)
Boca Juniors 1
(2010)
FC Luzern 1
(2015)
FC Porto 1
(2011)

FIFA FUTSAL WORLD CUP

Developed in South America in the 1930s, Futsal – a variant of five-a-side indoor football – has enjoyed a huge surge in popularity, and participation numbers, in recent years. The first FIFA Futsal World Cup was staged in Holland in 1989 and has been contested on a four-yearly basis since 1992. Two teams have dominated the event: Spain (with two wins) and, above all, Brazil (five wins).

THE FIRST MANOEL

Brazilian Manoel Tobias can claim to be the FIFA Futsal World Cup's most prolific goalscorer, with 43 in 32 appearances. Tobias, born in Salgueiro on 19 April 1971, represented his country in the 1992, 1996, 2000 and 2004 tournaments – only once ending up on the losing side within normal time. He ended both the 1996 and 2000 competitions with the prizes for both best player and top scorer.

CUBAN EMBARGO

Cuba hold the record for the fewest goals scored in a single tournament. They managed only one goal in their three games at the 2000 FIFA Futsal World Cup, while conceding 20 in defeats to Iran, Argentina and eventual champions Spain.

SAMBA SUPREMACY

Predictably for a game relying heavily on swift, deft passing and nimble footwork, Brazil have excelled at Futsal. Since FIFA inaugurated its Futsal World Cup in 1989, Brazil have won the trophy five times out of a possible seven – finishing runners-up to Spain in 2000 and third behind Spain and Italy four years later. Brazil have ended every tournament as the top-scoring team, hitting the back of the net a record 78 times during eight games in 2000 – at a rate of 9.3 goals per match. Their largest FIFA Futsal World Cup win was a 29-2 trouncing of Guatemala in 2000 – though their best-ever scoreline, an overall record for Futsal, came when they beat East Timor 76-0 in October 2006. Strangely, their first-ever FIFA Futsal World Cup match, in the first-round group stage in 1989, ended in a 3-2 loss to Hungary.

BACK OF THE NETO

The 2012 FIFA Futsal World Cup was the largest yet, with 24 countries taking part in Thailand – four more than the 2008 tournament. Yet it was a familiar story at the climax, with Brazil and Spain contesting the final for the fourth time, and the South Americans again emerged victorious, this time with a 3-2 win after extra time. The winning goal, the second of a brace, was scored by the man voted player of the tournament – Brazil's Neto – though Russia's Eder Lima claimed the golden boot thanks to his nine goals across the competition. The tournament also saw **Falcao** score his 337th goal, making him Brazil's all-time leading goalscorer in futsal. He reached the 350-goal mark in December 2013.

FIFA FUTSAL WORLD CUP FINALS (and hosts)

1989 (Hosts: Holland) Brazil 2 Holland 1
1992 (Hong Kong) Brazil 4 United States 1
1996 (Spain) Brazil 6 Spain 4
2000 (Guatemala) Spain 4 Brazil 3
2004 (Chinese Taipei) Spain 2 Italy 1
2008 (Brazil) Brazil 2 Spain 2
   (aet: Brazil win 4-3 on penalties)
2012 (Thailand) **Brazil 3 Spain 2** (aet)

NINE'S ENOUGH

Russia's Pula may have pipped Falcao to the top scorer prize in 2008 (with 16 goals to 15), but the Brazilian, who had already won both the Golden Ball and Golden Shoe awards four years earlier, was voted player of the tournament. Pula's 16 goals across the 2008 event included nine in one game – an all-time FIFA Futsal World Cup record – as the Solomon Islands were thrashed 31-2.

PART 7:
WOMEN'S FOOTBALL

THE 2015 FIFA WOMEN'S WORLD CUP broke all sorts of records in providing further evidence that, in having claimed once that "the future of football is feminine," FIFA president Sepp Blatter was not as far off the mark as his critics suggested.

More than 30 million women are playing football across the globe and social media bubbled over in excitement when United States captain Carli Lloyd completed her hat-trick in the FIFA Women's World Cup final by shooting home from the halfway line against Japan.

The success of the Canada tournament also prompted calls for better investment in the game and for the world's great clubs to sink more money into women's football sections. Such recognition has taken a long time. Women's football was first recorded in England more than a century ago, but it was then banned by the Football Association in 1921. This led to the creation of an independent women's association with a cup competition of its own. Only in the 1980s did the Women's FA come back under the wing of the FA. Women's football developed simultaneously elsewhere and the surge of interest ultimately led, in the early 1980s, to the first formal European Championships and, in 1988, to a FIFA invitational tournament in Chinese Taipei.

FIFA launched an inaugural world championship in 1991, which was won by the United States to establish their claim to primacy in the game. The Americans duly hosted the next FIFA Women's World Cup, which saw a record crowd of 90,185 celebrate their shoot-out victory over China in the final in Pasadena. They underlined their No.1 status by winning the first women's football gold medal at the Olympic Games in 1996, taking silver in 2000 and gold again in 2004, 2008 and 2012.

FIFA set up a world youth championship in 2002, initially for players aged Under-19, later amended to Under-20, and added an Under-17 event to the international calendar in 2008. Women's football, once considered a fleeting sporting fashion, is here to stay.

Trophy time for the United States after their devastating 5-2 victory over Japan in the final of the 2015 FIFA Women's World Cup in Vancouver.

FIFA WOMEN'S WORLD CUP

The first FIFA Women's World Cup finals were held in China in 1991. Twelve teams, divided into three groups of four, took part, with the top two in each group, plus the two "best losers" going through to the knockout quarter-finals. The tournament was expanded in 1999 to include 16 teams in four groups. There was further expansion in 2015, with Canada as hosts, to 24 teams in six groups of four, with the top two plus four best third-placed teams reaching the knockout second round.

HAVELANGE'S DREAM COMES TRUE

The FIFA Women's World Cup was the brainchild of former FIFA president João Havelange. The tournament began as an experimental competition in 1991 and has expanded in size and importance ever since. The success of the 1999 finals in the United States was a turning point for the tournament, which now attracts big crowds and worldwide TV coverage. The USA and Norway – countries in which football (soccer) is one of the most popular girls' sports – dominated the early competitions. The Americans won the inaugural competition and the 1999 tournament. Norway lifted the trophy in 1995. Germany became the dominant force in the new century, winning the trophy in 2003 and retaining it in 2007. The recent emergence of challengers such as Brazil, China and Sweden underlined the worldwide spread and appeal of the women's game.

PITCH PERFECT

There was controversy ahead of the 2015 finals over the decision to play all ties on artificial turf. FIFA and the Canadian organisers justified this on the grounds of climatic challenges and the need for a metaphorical level playing field. Goal-line technology was also employed for the first time.

US CELEBRATE FIRST ACHIEVEMENT

The USA's victory in the inaugural FIFA Women's World Cup in 1991 made them the first USA team to win a world football title. The USA men's best performance came when they reached the semi-finals in 1930, losing 6-1 to Argentina.

ASIA MAJORS

Japan's women became the country's first football side to claim a FIFA world title when they upset the odds to win the 2011 FIFA Women's World Cup, beating favourites USA 3-1 on penalties after a 2-2 draw. Player of the tournament Homare Sawa had levelled the scores with just three minutes of extra-time remaining, before **Saki Kumagai** struck the winning spot-kick in the shoot-out. Japan had failed to win in the two teams' previous 25 meetings, losing 22 and drawing three. The Japanese women's previous best FIFA World Cup performance had been reaching the quarter-finals in 1995. The 2011 generation's triumph was all the more moving, as they dedicated the victory to victims of the devastating tsunami that had struck Japan in March that year.

FIFA WOMEN'S WORLD CUP FINALS

Year	Venue	Winners	Runners-up	Score
1991	Ghuangzhou	USA	Norway	2-1
1995	Stockholm	Norway	Germany	2-0
1999	Los Angeles	USA	China	0-0
USA won 5-4 in penalty shoot-out				
2003	Los Angeles	Germany	Sweden	2-1 (aet)
2007	Shanghai	Germany	Brazil	2-0
2011	Frankfurt	Japan	USA	2-2 (aet)
Japan won 3-1 in penalty shoot-out				
2015	Vancouver	USA	Japan	5-2

THIRD–PLACE PLAY–OFF MATCHES

Year	Venue	Winners	Losers	Score
1991	Guangzhou	Sweden	Germany	4-0
1995	Gavle	USA	China	2-0
1999	Los Angeles	Brazil	Norway	0-0
Brazil won 5-4 in penalty shoot-out				
2003	Los Angeles	USA	Canada	3-1
2007	Shanghai	USA	Norway	4-1
2011	Sinsheim	Sweden	France	2-1
2015	Montreal	England	Germany	1-0

FOUR GAIN DOUBLE MEDALS

Four of the USA's 1991 winners were in the team that beat China on penalties in the 1999 final: **Mia Hamm** (left), Michelle Akers, Kristine Lilly and Julie Foudy.

WINNERS KEEP SQUAD TOGETHER

Six Germany players appeared in their 2003 and 2007 final wins: **Kerstin Stegemann**, Birgit Prinz, Renate Lingor, Ariane Hingst and Kerstin Garefrekes started both games, while Martina Muller came on as a substitute both times.

SPANISH REBELLION

Spain's FIFA Women's World Cup finals debut quickly turned sour. They won only one point from their three group games in Canada in 2015 and were eliminated. On returning home, the players blamed veteran coach Ignacio Quereda, citing insufficient preparation for the cooler climate, lack of warm-up friendlies and poor analysis of opponents. They concluded: "We need a change. We have conveyed this to the coach and his staff."

GERMANS SET DEFENSIVE RECORD

In 2007, Germany became the first team to make a successful defence of the FIFA Women's World Cup. They also set another record. They went through the tournament – six games and 540 minutes – without conceding a single goal. As a result, their goalkeeper Nadine Angerer overhauled Italy keeper Walter Zenga's record of 517 minutes unbeaten in the 1990 men's finals. The last player to score against the Germans had been Sweden's **Hanna Ljungberg** in the 41st minute of the 2003 final. The run ended when Christine Sinclair of Cananda scored after 82 minutes of Germany's opening game in 2011.

CANADA'S RECORD TURNOUT

Canada's enthusiasm for the 2015 FIFA Women's World Cup broke many records. The total attendance of 1,353,506 was the best for any FIFA women's competition, beating the previous Women's World Cup total of 1,194,215, set in the USA in 1999 (albeit from 20 more matches). The 54,027 who watched the hosts play England in the quarter-finals in Vancouver was a Canadian record for a women's game and one of seven matches to top 50,000 fans.

TOP TEAMS

Country	Winners	Runners-up	Third
USA	3	1	3
Germany	2	1	-
Norway	1	1	1
Japan	1	1	-
Brazil	-	1	1
Sweden	-	1	2
China	-	1	-
England	-	-	1

TOP TEAM SCORERS

1991:	USA	25
1995:	Norway	23
1999:	China	19
2003:	Germany	25
2007:	Germany	21
2011:	USA	13
2015:	Germany	20

TOP ALL-TIME TEAM SCORERS

1	USA	112
2	Germany	111
3	Norway	86
4	Brazil	59
=	Sweden	59

THE FIRST GAME

The first-ever game in the FIFA Women's World Cup finals was hosts China's 4-0 win over Norway at Guangzhou on 16 November 1991. A 65,000 crowd watched the game.

THE REGULAR EIGHT

Eight teams have played in all six finals tournaments – Brazil, China, Germany, Japan, Nigeria, Norway, Sweden and the United States.

NORWAY POST LONGEST WIN RUN

Norway, winners in 1995, hold the record for the most consecutive matchtime wins in the finals – ten. Their run started with an 8-0 win over Nigeria on 6 June 1995 and continued until 30 June 1999 when they beat Sweden 3-1 in the quarter-finals. It ended when they lost 5-0 to China in the semi-finals on 4 July.

UNBEATEN CHINA SENT HOME

In 1999, China became the only team to go through the finals without losing a match, yet go home empty-handed. The Chinese won their group games, 2-1 against Sweden, 7-0 against Ghana and 3-1 against Australia. They beat Russia 2-0 in the quarter-finals and Norway 5-0 in the semi-finals, but they lost on penalties to the USA in the final after a 0-0 draw. In 2011, Japan became the first team to lift the trophy despite losing a match in the first-round – as had runners-up the USA.

FIFTEEN ON TARGET FOR NORWAY

Norway hold the record for scoring in the most consecutive games – 15. They began their sequence with a 4-0 win over New Zealand on 19 November 1991 and ended it with a 3-1 win over Sweden in the quarter-finals on 30 June 1999.

THE LOWEST CROWD...

The lowest attendance for any match at the finals came on 8 June 1995, when only 250 spectators watched the 3-3 draw between Canada and Nigeria at Helsingborg.

HAT-TRICKS AT THE DOUBLE

Germany are the only team to have twice scored double figures in a game at the finals. The first time was an 11-0 thrashing of Argentina in Shanghai in the 2007 finals, when Birgit Prinz and Sandra Smisek both scored hat-tricks. Then, in Canada in 2015, the Germans crushed Ivory Coast 10-0 in the first round with trebles for strikers Celia Sasic and Anja Mittag.

AMERICANS BANK ON LLOYD

Carli Lloyd was the runaway winner of the Golden Ball as star player of the 2015 World Cup finals. She crowned a decade of international football by scoring a hat-trick in the 5-2 defeat of Japan in the final. Best of all was the hat-trick goal which Lloyd struck from the halfway line. Amazingly, this goal was the United States' fourth of the final and the match was only 16 minutes old. Previously she had helped the US finish third and runners-up at the 2007 and 2011 Women's World Cups respectively. The 33-year-old had also scored the gold medal-winning goals in the finals of both the 2008 and 2012 Olympic Games.

QUICKEST RED AND YELLOW

The record for the fastest red card is held by Australia's Alicia Ferguson, who was sent off in the second minute of their 3-1 defeat by China in New York on 26 June 1999. North Korea's Ri Hyang Ok received the quickest yellow card, in the first minute of their 2-1 defeat by Nigeria in Los Angeles on 20 June 1999.

THE FASTEST GOAL

Lena Videkull of Sweden netted the fastest goal in finals history when she scored after 30 seconds in their 8-0 win over Japan at Foshan on 19 November 1991. Canada's **Melissa Tancredi** struck the second-fastest goal – after 37 seconds – in their 2-2 draw with Australia in Chengdu on 20 September 2007.

PRINZ SEIZES FINALS CHANCE

In 2007, Birgit Prinz became the first player to appear in three FIFA Women's World Cup finals. She was also the youngest player to appear in a FIFA Women's World Cup final. The Germany forward was 17 years 336 days when she started in the 2-0 defeat by Norway in 1995. Team-mate Sandra Smisek was just 14 days older. The oldest finalist was Sweden's Kristin Bengtsson, who was 33 years 273 days when her side lost to Germany in the 2003 final.

HOT SHOT AKERS SETS THE STANDARD

US forward Michelle Akers (born in Santa Clara on 1 February 1966) hold the record for the most goals scored in a single finals tournament – ten in 1991. She also set a record for the most goals scored in one match, with five in the USA's 7-0 quarter-final win over Taiwan at Foshan on 24 November 1991. Akers grabbed both goals in the USA's 2-1 victory in the final, including their 78th-minute winner. Judges voted her as FIFA's Women's Player of the 20th Century.

THE FASTEST SUBSTITUTIONS

The fastest substitutions in finals history were both timed at six minutes. Taiwan's defender Liu Hsiu Mei was subbed by reserve goalkeeper Li Chyn Hong in their 2-0 win over Nigeria in Jiangmen on 21 November 1991. Li replaced No. 1 keeper Lin Hui Fang, who had been sent off. Therese Lundin subbed for the injured Hanna Ljungberg, also after six minutes, in Sweden's 2-0 win over Ghana at Chicago on 26 June 1999.

DANILOVA THE YOUNGEST SCORER

The youngest scorer at the finals was Russia's Elena Danilova. She was 16 years 96 days when she scored her country's only goal in the 2003 quarter-final against Germany at Portland on 2 October. The Germans scored seven in reply.

MORACE HITS FIRST HAT–TRICK

Carolina Morace of Italy scored the first hat-trick in finals history when she netted the last three goals in Italy's 5-0 win over Taiwan at Jiangmen on 17 November 1991.

ENGLAND'S GLORY IN CANADA

England flew home from Canada after finishing third in their most successful Women's World Cup. Coach Mark Sampson, who replaced Hope Powell after a disappointing 2013 European Championship, saw his team stutter in their opening game, losing 1-0 to France. They recovered to beat Mexico and Colombia, both times 2-1, to finish group runners-up and reach the knockout stage. That 2-1 scoreline remained the theme as England beat Norway and then hosts Canada by that score to reach their first-ever FIFA Women's World Cup semi-final, **Lucy Bronze** scoring the decisive second goal in both games. But the semi-final ended tearfully in a 2-1 extra-time defeat by holders Japan. Laura Bassett settled it inadvertently with an own goal two minutes into added time at the end of the second half. England recovered morale magnificently to beat European champions Germany 1-0 for third place with a Fara Williams penalty in the second period of extra-time deciding the bronze medal. Sampson compared his team with the World Cup-winning men of 1966, saying: "Moments from 1966 like the Hurst hat-trick, the Moore tackle – these players will be remembered forever for this tournament. I really hope, in 50 or 60 years, people mark this team as legends of the country."

FIFA WOMEN'S WORLD CUP
PLAYER OF THE TOURNAMENT

Year	Venue	Winner
1991	China	Carin Jennings (USA)
1995	Sweden	Hege Riise (Norway)
1999	USA	Sun Wen (China)
2003	USA	Birgit Prinz (Germany)
2007	China	Marta (Brazil)
2011	Germany	Homare Sawa (Japan)
2015	Canada	Carli Lloyd (USA)

FIFA WOMEN'S WORLD CUP FINALS TOP SCORER

1991	Michelle Akers (USA)	10
1995	Ann-Kristin Aarones (Norway)	6
1999	Sissi (Brazil)	7
2003	Birgit Prinz (Germany)	7
2007	Marta (Brazil)	7
2011	Homare Sawa (Japan)	5
2015	Celia Sasic (Germany)	6
	Carli Llloyd (USA)	6

ALL–TIME TOP SCORERS

1	Marta (Brazil)	15
2	Birgit Prinz (Germany)	14
=	Abby Wambach (USA)	14
4	Michelle Akers (USA)	12
5	Sun Wen (China)	11
=	Bettina Wiegmann (Germany)	11
7	Ann-Kristin Aarones (Norway)	10
=	Heidi Mohr (Germany)	10
9	Linda Medalen (Norway)	9
=	Hege Riise (Norway)	9
=	Christine Sinclair	9

FIFA WOMEN'S WORLD CUP WINNING CAPTAINS

1991	April Heinrichs (USA)
1995	Heidi Store (Norway)
1999	Carla Overbeck (USA)
2003	Bettina Wiegmann (Germany)
2007	Birgit Prinz (Germany)
2011	Homare Sawa (Japan)
2015	Christie Rampone (USA)

MOST FINALS APPEARANCES (BY GAMES)

1	Kristine Lilly (USA)	30
2	Abby Wambach (USA)	25
3	Formiga (Brazil)	24
=	Julie Foudy (USA)	24
=	Birgit Prinz (Germany)	24
=	Homare Sawa (Japan)	24
7	Joy Fawcett (USA)	23
=	Mia Hamm (USA)	23
9	Bente Nordby (Norway)	22
=	Hege Riise (Norway)	22
=	Bettina Wiegmann (Germany)	22

TEAM PLAYERS

Only six players have been named in the tournament all-star teams at two separate FIFA Women's World Cups: China's Wang Liping, Germany's Bettina Wiegmann, Brazil's Marta, Japan's Aya Miyama and the USA's Shannon Boxx and Hope Solo. In both 2007 and 2011, all-star squads were chosen, but FIFA reverted to 11 players in 2015.

US RECORD AUDIENCE

The United States' FIFA Women's World Cup 2015 defeat of Japan was the most-watched football match – men or women – in US history. Fox Sports registered almost 23 million viewers, an increase of 77 percent compared with the 2011 final between the same teams. Telemundo recorded its Spanish-language audience at 1.27 million viewers.

LAST-DITCH FIRST

Japan's 2011 success was bittersweet at the last for defender **Azuza Iwashimizu**, whose red card in stoppage-time of extra-time against the USA made her the first player to be sent off in a FIFA Women's World Cup final. Her punishment was for a foul on American attacker Alex Morgan, just minutes after Japan had equalised at 2-2.

THE FIRST SENDING OFF

Taiwan goalkeeper Lin Hui Fang was the first player to be sent off in finals history. She was red-carded after six minutes of Taiwan's 2-0 win over Nigeria in Jiangmen on 21 November 1991.

SUN RATTLES THE MEN

In 1999, Shanghai-born **Sun Wen** became the first woman player ever to be nominated for the Asian Footballer of the Year award, following her performances in China's run to the 1999 FIFA Women's World Cup final. Three years later, she won the Internet poll for FIFA's Women's Player of the 20th Century.

OTHER WOMEN'S TOURNAMENTS

OLYMPIC RINGING THE CHANGES

Germany forward Birgit Prinz was the only player to score in all of the first four Olympic women's finals tournaments but missed out on London 2012 because her country did not qualify. That allowed Brazil's Cristiane to push ahead as all-time top scorer, adding two to take her tally to 12. Prinz's Olympic haul of ten goals was also equalled in 2012 by Canada's Christine Sinclair.

WOMEN'S OLYMPIC FINALS

Year	Venue	Winners	Runners-up	Score
1996	Atlanta	USA	China	2-1
2000	Sydney	Norway	USA	3-2
	Norway won with a golden goal			
2004	Athens	USA	Brazil	2-1 (aet)
2008	Beijing	USA	Brazil	1-0 (aet)
2012	London	USA	Japan	2-1

THIRD-PLACE PLAY-OFFS

Year	Venue	Winners	Losers	Score
1996	Atlanta	Norway	Brazil	2-0
2000	Sydney	Germany	Brazil	2-0
2004	Athens	Germany	Sweden	1-0
2008	Beijing	Germany	Japan	2-0
2012	London	Canada	France	1-0

MEDALLISTS

Country	Gold	Silver	Bronze
USA	4	1	-
Norway	1	-	1
Brazil	-	2	-
China	-	1	-
Japan	-	1	-
Germany	-	-	3
Canada	-	-	1

WOMEN'S OLYMPIC TEAM TOP SCORERS

1996:	Norway	12
2000:	USA	9
2004:	Brazil	15
2008:	USA	12
2012:	USA	16

WOMEN'S OLYMPIC INDIVIDUAL TOP SCORERS

1996:	Ann-Kristin Aarones (Norway)	
	Linda Medalen (Norway)	
	Pretinha (Brazil)	4
2000:	Sun Wen (China)	4
2004:	Cristiane (Brazil)	
	Birgit Prinz (Germany)	5
2008:	Cristiane (Brazil)	5
2012:	Christine Sinclair (Canada)	6

CRISTIANE'S TREBLE DOUBLE

Brazil striker **Cristiane** is the only player to score two hat-tricks in FIFA Olympic history. She netted three in a 7-0 win over hosts Greece in 2004 and added another treble in a 3-1 win over Nigeria in Beijing four years later. Birgit Prinz is the only other hat-trick scorer, with four goals against China in 2004.

GERMANS CHALK UP BIGGEST WIN

Germany hold the record for the biggest win in the Olympic finals. They beat China 8-0 at Patras on 11 August 2004, with Birgit Prinz scoring four times. The Germans' other goals came from Pia Wunderlich, Renate Lingor, Conny Pohlers and Martina Muller. Yet, in a major surprise, Germany failed to qualify for the women's football tournament at the 2012 Olympic Games in London. The 2011 FIFA Women's World Cup was used as UEFA's qualifiers, meaning beaten quarter-finalists Germany fell short. Semi-finalists Sweden – including their most-capped player Therese Sjogran – and France, whose stars include midfielder Louisa Necib, went through to the 2012 event instead.

HOSTS WITH THE MOST

The FIFA Under-20 Women's World Cup is held every two years, in contrast to the four-yearly senior contest. Since 2010, the younger players' event has been staged by the same nation one year before they host the FIFA Women's World Cup. In 2014, Canada became the first country to host the Under-20 tournament twice, having previously done so in 2002 – while Germany emerged as the second three-times champions, emulating the USA. **Lena Petermann's** (No. 18) 98th-minute goal broke the extra-time deadlock in the final against Nigeria in Montreal on 24 August 2014. The runners-up could at least claim the competition's best player, and top scorer, seven-goal Asisat Oshoala – whose haul included four in Nigeria's 6-2 semi-final victory over North Korea. France finished third after beating North Korea 3-2 in the third-place playoff.

LATE STARTS, LATE FINISHING

Carli Lloyd scored the winning goal for the USA, against Brazil, to clinch Olympic gold in 2008 – then struck the decisive brace in the London 2012 final, as her team beat Japan 2-1. Other memorable moments of the women's football tournament at London 2012 included Alex Morgan's winner for the USA against Canada in the semi-final – she made it 4-3 three minutes into stoppage-time at the end of extra-time, the latest goal in Olympic history. Hosts Great Britain fielded a team for the first time and although they finished top of their first round group with a perfect three wins from three, without conceding a goal, they were beaten 2-0 by Canada in the quarter-final and missed out on a medal.

JAPAN'S DOUBLE JOY

Japan clinched the AFC Asian Women's Cup title for the first time in 2014, when the tournament was staged in Vietnam. Defender **Azusa Iwashimizu** not only scored the winner in extra-time stoppage-time in the semi-final against China, but also struck the only goal of the final against Australia – some solace for her red card in the 2011 FIFA Women's World Cup final. Also in 2014, Japan won the FIFA Under-17 Women's World Cup for the first time, beating Spain 2-0 in the final in Costa Rica and seeing five-goal Hina Sugita voted best player. North Korea beat the USA 2-1 in the inaugural final in New Zealand in 2008, before South Korea beat Japan on penalties following a 3-3 draw in the climax to the tournament in Trinidad and Tobago two years later. France goalkeeper Romane Bruneau was the heroine of another shoot-out in the 2012 final in Azerbaijan, decisively saving two spot-kicks after a 1-1 draw with North Korea.

US DOMINATE OLYMPIC GOLDS

The USA have dominated the Olympic football tournament since it was introduced at the 1996 Games in Atlanta. They have won four gold medals and finished runners-up in the other final. Norway and China were the Americans' early challengers, with Brazil, FIFA Women's World Cup holders Germany and Japan proving their toughest rivals in the past three Olympics (2004, 2008 and 2012). The tournament has rapidly grown in popularity, attracting record crowds at the 2008 Olympic Games in Beijing. FIFA have added two worldwide competitions for younger teams, too. The FIFA U-20 Women's World Cup was staged for the first time in 2000 and the first edition of the Under-17 event followed in 2008. Once more, the USA have been prominent, though they have faced a strong challenge from North Korea in recent years.

FIFA U-20 WOMEN'S WORLD CUP
FINALS

Year	Venue	Winner	Runners-up	Score
2002	Edmonton	USA	Canada	1-0 (aet)
2004	Bangkok	Germany	Chile	2-0
2006	Moscow	North Korea	China	5-0
2008	Santiago	USA	North Korea	2-1
2010	Bielefeld	Germany	Nigeria	2-0
2012	Tokyo	USA	Germany	1-0
2014	Montreal	Germany	Nigeria	1-0 (aet)

TOP SCORERS

Year	Scorer	Goals
2002	Christine Sinclair (Canada)	10
2004	Brittany Timko (Canada)	7
2006	Ma Xiaoxu (China), Kim Song Hui (North Korea)	5
2008	Sydney Leroux (USA)	5
2010	Alexandra Popp (Germany)	10
2012	Kim Un-Hwa (Japan)	7
2014	Asisat Oshoala (Nigeria)	7

FIFA U-17 WOMEN'S WORLD CUP
FINALS

Year	Venue	Winner	Runners-up	Score
2008	Auckland	North Korea	USA	2-1 (aet)
2010	Port of Spain	South Korea	Japan	3-3 (aet)
	(South Korea won 5-4 on penalties)			
2012	Baku	France	North Korea	1-1 (aet)
	(France won 7-6 on penalties)			
2014	San Jose (CR)	Japan	Spain	2-0

TOP SCORERS

Year	Scorer	Goals
2008	Dzsenifer Marozsan (Germany)	6
2010	Yeo Min-Ji (South Korea)	8
2012	Ri Un-Sim (North Korea)	8
2014	Deyna Castellanos (Venezuela)	6
	Gabriela Garcia (Venezuela)	6

LOOK BACK IN ANGERER

Germany's 59-match unbeaten run in the UEFA Women's European Championship was ended by Norway in September 2013, who won 1-0 in a first-round group game. The Germans avenged the loss in the final, also 1-0, Anja Mittag the goalscorer, and two penalty saves by Nadine Angerer, later voted player of the tournament. This was Germany's sixth straight European title, a run dating back to 1995. France captain Sandrine Soubeyrand, aged 39 years and 340 days, made her 198th international appearance and became the oldest ever woman to play in the finals.

SINCLAIR HITS FIVE

Christine Sinclair of Canada and Alexandra Popp of Germany share the record for most goals scored in a single FIFA Under-20 Women's World Cup. Each struck 10, Sinclair in 2002 and Popp eight years later. Sinclair also holds the record for the most goals in one game. She netted five in Canada's 6-2 quarter-final win over England at Edmonton on 25 August 2002. But Popp is the only player to score in all of her country's six games at a tournament. Only Sinclair and Popp have won both the Golden Ball for best player and Golden Shoe for top scorer. Sinclair finished the 2012 Olympics as six-goal top-scorer in the women's football tournament. Her tally included a hat-trick – in vain – in Canada's 4-3 semi-final defeat to the US.

KIM GRABS ONLY HAT-TRICK

North Korea's **Kim Song-Hi** netted the only hat-trick in any final of the FIFA Under-20 Women's World Cup. It came in their 5-0 win over China on 3 September 2006.

APPENDIX 1: FIFA AWARDS

AT THE START of each new year, world football swaps match kit for formal party gear to hail a range of achievements and achievers from the previous 12 months as FIFA hosts its annual gala in the game's international capital which is the Swiss city of Zurich. The 2015 Gala – staged in January 2016 – was no exception, despite the turbulence which had assailed the world governing body over the previous nine months.

One of the strengths of football even as a game of 11-a-side is that, when it comes to appreciation and celebration, both teams and individuals can be hailed and rewarded.

Footballer of the Year awards have contributed to the fabric of football history. One of the earliest, in England, was created in the late 1940s, while the Paris magazine *France Football* followed up with its now-discontinued European Footballer of the Year award in the mid-1950s. First winner of both awards was Sir Stanley Matthews, the original "Wizard of Dribble", in England in 1948 and in Europe in 1956.

The FIFA awards, celebrating their 25th year, also embrace the *France Football* organization whose *Ballon d'Or* had been merged into the world event in 2010. Hence the headline award remains that for the leading player of the past 12 months. National team coaches and captains and journalists from around the world granted overwhelming approval to Argentina and Barcelona's Lionel Messi. The women's player award went to United States midfielder Carli Lloyd.

A "perfect mix" of team and player recognition has also been achieved through the World XI chosen annually now in partnership with FIFPro, the international players' union.

The FIFA/FIFPro Team of the Year take to the stage in Zurich at the FIFA Ballon d'Or Gala after having been selected by their fellow professionals from all around the world in the annual ballot.

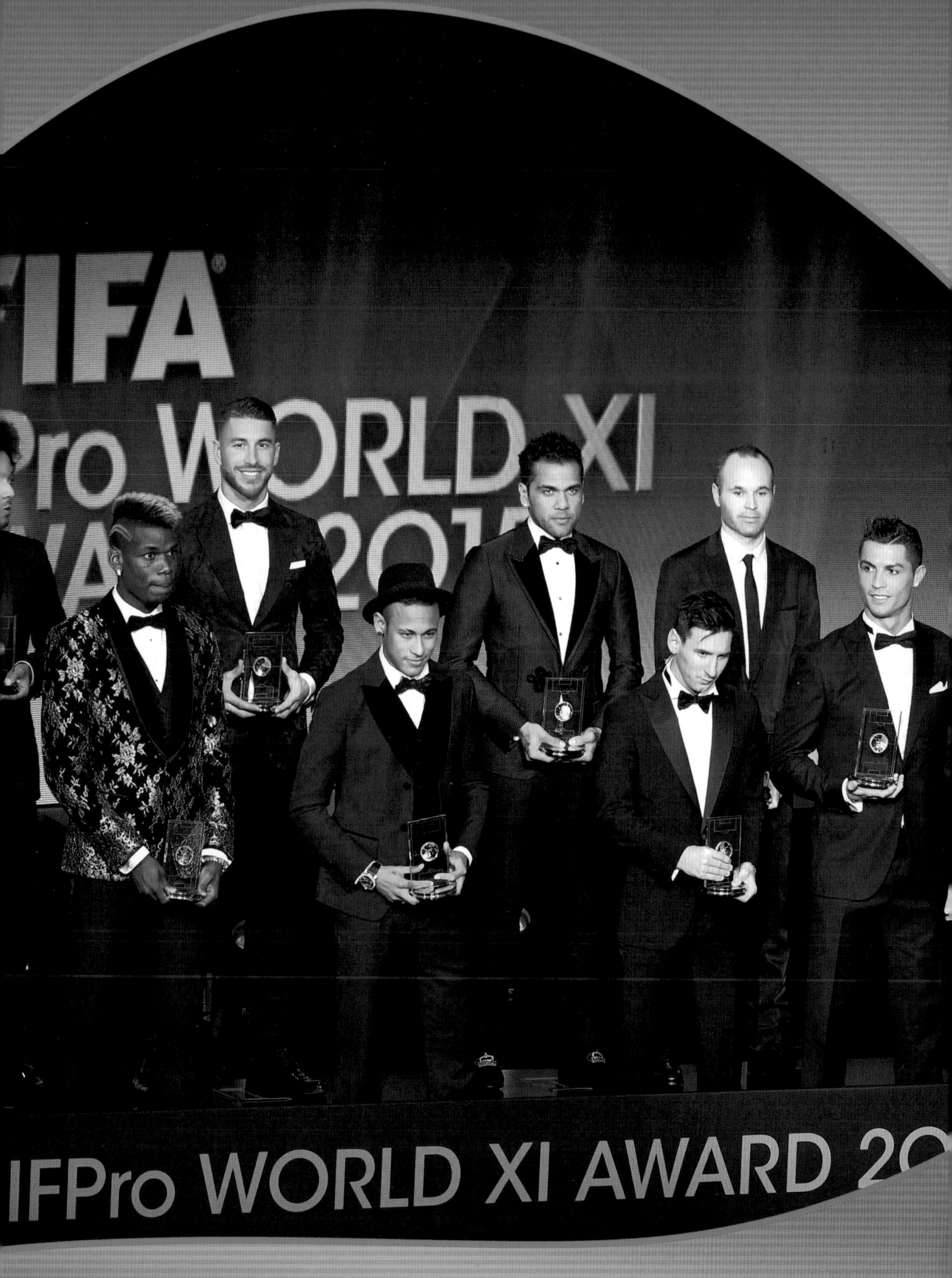
FIFA
Pro WORLD XI
IFPro WORLD XI AWARD 20

FIFA PLAYER OF THE YEAR 2015

LIONEL MESSI

Lionel Messi was crowned FIFA World Player of the Year for a record fifth time at the annual FIFA Gala in Zurich in January 2016. The 28-year-old Argentinian collected 41.33 percent of the vote with Portugal and Real Madrid's Cristiano Ronaldo second on 27.76 percent and Barcelona's Brazilian Neymar third on 7.86 percent.

Ronaldo had won for the previous two years. Between them, he and Messi have won the past eight awards to underline how their personal rivalry has commanded so many of the world game's most prestigious events.

Messi had a remarkable year even by his own astonishing standards with five major club trophies, 52 goals and 26 assists in 61 games – meaning one goal every 101 minutes and one assist every 202 minutes. He also accumulated the best minutes-per-goal rate – 80 – of anyone scoring a minimum of 10 goals across Europe's top five leagues during 2015.

Messi was directly involved in 49 Barcelona goals in the Spanish league (34 scored and 15 assists), equal with Ronaldo. He also scored in all six club tournaments in 2015 from which Barcelona emerged winning five, including the FIFA Club World Cup only a matter of weeks before the awards ceremony. Neymar, Messi's 23-year-old Barcelona club-mate, was the first Brazilian to finish in the top three since Kaka won the 2007 award. Their voting "constituency" comprised 165 national team coaches, 162 national team captains and 171 journalists.

Messi said: "It's a very special moment for me to be back here on this stage, winning another Ballon d'Or again after having seen Cristiano win it for the past two years. It's incredible that it's my fifth. Much more than anything I would have dreamed of as a kid."

PREVIOUS WINNERS

1991 Lothar Matthaus **(Germany)**
1992 Marco van Basten **(Netherlands)**
1993 Roberto Baggio **(Italy)**
1994 Romario **(Brazil)**
1995 George Weah **(Liberia)**
1996 Ronaldo **(Brazil)**
1997 Ronaldo **(Brazil)**
1998 Zinedine Zidane **(France)**
1999 Rivaldo **(Brazil)**
2000 Zinedine Zidane **(France)**
2001 Luis Figo **(Portugal)**
2002 Ronaldo **(Brazil)**
2003 Zinedine Zidane **(France)**
2004 Ronaldinho **(Brazil)**
2005 Ronaldinho **(Brazil)**
2006 Fabio Cannavaro **(Italy)**
2007 Kaka **(Brazil)**
2008 Cristiano Ronaldo **(Portugal)**
2009 Lionel Messi **(Argentina)**
2010 Lionel Messi **(Argentina)**
2011 Lionel Messi **(Argentina)**
2012 Lionel Messi **(Argentina)**
2013 Cristiano Ronaldo **(Portugal)**
2014 Cristiano Ronaldo **(Portugal)**

FIFA WOMEN'S PLAYER OF THE YEAR 2015

CARLI LLOYD

Carli Lloyd was always a solid favourite to win the FIFA Women's Player of the Year prize after she climaxed her remarkable career with her achievements during the United States' World Cup-winning achievement in Canada in 2015.

The 33-year-old midfielder was not only an influential captain of the US team but also inspired her team-mates with performances which included a hat-trick in the final against Japan. Lloyd, whose goals included a sensational strike from the halfway line, had already earned the Golden Ball as best player in the tournament.

Former Germany striker Celia Sasic finished second in the FIFA awards roster despite having retired halfway through 2015 at the age of 27. However in the first half of the year she had been top scorer in the FIFA Women's World Cup with six goals and also won the UEFA Champions League with Frankfurt. Placed third was Japan midfielder Aya Miyama who had captained her country to the FIFA Women's World Cup final, where they lost to the US.

Votes were cast by 136 national team coaches, 135 national team captains and 106 journalists. Lloyd collected a decisive 35.28 percent of all votes, ahead of Sasic (12.60 percent) and Miyama (9.88 percent). Lloyd had been one of three US players on the original award shortlist, more than any other nation, along with goalkeeper Hope Solo and winger Megan Rapinoe. She said: "It has been a dream ever since I started with the national team. Keep your dreams and just go after them."

A second German nomination, along with Sasic, was for 2013 winner Nadine Angerer after what had been her final year of international football. For the first time since the early 2000s there was no place in the shortlist for Brazilian women's superstar and five-time winner Marta.

PREVIOUS WINNERS

2001	Mia Hamm	**(United States)**
2002	Mia Hamm	**(United States)**
2003	Birgit Prinz	**(Germany)**
2004	Birgit Prinz	**(Germany)**
2005	Birgit Prinz	**(Germany)**
2006	Marta	**(Brazil)**
2007	Marta	**(Brazil)**
2008	Marta	**(Brazil)**
2009	Marta	**(Brazil)**
2010	Marta	**(Brazil)**
2011	Homare Sawa	**(Japan)**
2012	Abby Wambach	**(United States)**
2013	Nadine Angerer	**(Germany)**
2014	Nadine Kessler	**(Germany)**

Luis Enrique achieved a remarkable double for Spanish club Barcelona at the annual awards gala staged by international governing body FIFA. Not only was he hailed as World Coach of the Year but his club's superstar forward Lionel Messi carried off the prize as Player of the Year. Jill Ellis, coach of the United States team who won the Women's World Cup, took the women's coach award.

Enrique and Ellis were selected for top honours by the coaches and captains of the world's national teams as well as by an international media jury and received their awards during the 90-minute show at Zurich's Kongresshaus hosted by Northern Irish actor James Nesbitt and British journalist Kate Abdo.

Enrique, a former Spain international midfielder, was honoured after a remarkable first season in charge of Barcelona which saw the club win five of the six competitions for which they challenged.

One of the prizes which always attracts not only worldwide attention but fans' participation is the Puskas Award for the best goal of the year, named in honour of the late Honved and Hungary, Real Madrid and Spain hero. More than 1.6 million fans cast their votes via social media with the winner being Brazilian Wendell Lira from Goianesia, who topped the poll with 46.7 percent of the votes for his goal against Atletico Goianiense. He finished ahead of Barcelona's Lionel Messi (33.3 percent) and Alessandro Florenzi of AS Roma (7.1 percent).

A poll organized by international players' union FIFPro among 26,478 professional players from around the world selected the annual FIFA FIFPro World XI. The 2015 team, in 4–3–3 formation, was: Manuel Neuer; Dani Alves, Sergio Ramos, Thiago Silva, Marcelo; Andres Iniesta, Luka Modric, Paul Pogba; Cristiano Ronaldo, Lionel Messi, Neymar.

The celebrated FIFA Fair Play Award was presented to all the football organisations and clubs around the world that are working to support refugees.

Former German international **Gerald Asamoah**, who campaigns for the welfare of refugees, received the award from former South African icon Lucas Radebe on behalf of all the awardees. The conflict in Syria and ensuing refugee crisis had seen football respond in many imaginative ways to help address refugees' plight.

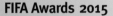

FIFA Awards 2015

Men's Player of the Year: Lionel Messi (Argentina, Barcelona)

Women's Player of the Year: Carli Lloyd (United States)

Men's Football Coach of the Year: Luis Enrique (Spain, Barcelona)

Women's Football Coach of the Year: Jill Ellis (United States)

FIFA Ferenc Puskas Award (Outstanding goal): Wendell Lira (Brazil), Goianesia v Atletico Goianiense

Fair Play Award: All football organizations working to support refugees

FIFA/FIFPro Team of the Year: Manuel Neuer (Germany, Bayern Munich); Dani Alves (Brazil, Barcelona), Sergio Ramos (Spain, Real Madrid), Thiago Silva (Brazil, Paris Saint-Germain), Marcelo (Brazil, Real Madrid); Andres Iniesta (Spain, Barcelona), Luka Modric (Croatia, Real Madrid), Paul Pogba (France, Juventus); Cristiano Ronaldo (Portugal, Real Madrid), Lionel Messi (Argentina, Barcelona), Neymar (Brazil, Barcelona).

1991
Fair Play award: Real Federacion Espanola de Futbol (Spanish FA), Jorginho (Brazil)

1992
Fair Play award: Union Royale Belge des Societes de Football Association

1993
Fair Play award: Nandor Hidgekuti (Hungary)*, Football Association of Zambia
Top Team of the Year: Germany
Best Mover of the Year: Colombia
award presented posthumously

1994
Top Team of the Year: Brazil
Best Mover of the Year: Croatia

1995
Fair Play award: Jacques Glassmann (France)
Top Team of the Year: Brazil
Best Mover of the Year: Jamaica

1996
Fair Play award: George Weah (Liberia)
Top Team of the Year: Brazil
Best Mover of the Year: South Africa

1997
Fair Play award: Irish spectators at the FIFA World Cup preliminary match versus Belgium, Jozef Zovinec (Slovak amateur player), Julie Foudy (United States)
Top Team of the Year: Brazil
Best Mover of the Year: Yugoslavia

1998
Fair Play award: National associations of Iran, the United States and Northern Ireland
Top Team of the Year: Brazil
Best Mover of the Year: Croatia

1999
Fair Play award: New Zealand football community
Top Team of the Year: Brazil
Best Mover of the Year: Slovenia

2000
Fair Play award: Lucas Radebe (South Africa)
Top Team of the Year: Holland
Best Mover of the Year: Nigeria

2001
Presidential award Marvin Lee (Trinidad)*
Fair Play award: Paolo Di Canio (Italy)
Top Team of the Year: Honduras
Best Mover of the Year: Costa Rica
award presented posthumously

2002
Presidential award: Parminder Nagra (England)
Fair Play award: Football communities of Japan and Korea Republic
Top Team of the Year: Brazil
Best Mover of the Year: Senegal

2003
Presidential award: Iraqi football community
Fair Play award: Fans of Celtic FC (Scotland)
Top Team of the Year: Brazil
Best Mover of the Year: Bahrain

2004
Presidential award: Haiti
Fair Play award: Confederacao Brasileira de Futebol
Top Team of the Year: Brazil
Best Mover of the Year: China PR
Interactive World Player: Thiago Carrico de Azevedo (Brazil)

2005
Presidential award: Anders Frisk (Sweden)
Fair Play award: Football community of Iquitos (Peru)
Top Team of the Year: Brazil
Best Mover of the Year: Ghana
Interactive World Player: Chris Bullard (England)

2006
Presidential award: Giacinto Facchetti (Italy)*
Fair Play award: Fans of the 2006 FIFA World Cup

Top Team of the Year: Brazil
Best Mover of the Year: Italy
Interactive World Player: Andries Smit (Holland)
award presented posthumously

2007
Presidential award: Pele (Brazil)
Fair Play award: FC Barcelona (Spain)
Top Team of the Year: Argentina
Best Mover of the Year: Mozambique

2008
Presidential award: Women's football (presented to the United States women's team)
Fair Play award: Armenia, Turkey
Development award: Palestine
Interactive World Player: Alfonso Ramos (Spain)
Top Team of the Year: Spain
Best Mover of the Year: Spain

2009
Presidential award: Queen Rania Al Abdullah of Jordan [co-chair of 1Goal: Education for All]
Fair Play Award: Sir Bobby Robson (England)*
Development prize: Chinese Football Association
Interactive World Player: Bruce Grannec (France)
Top Team of the Year: Spain
FIFA Ferenc Puskas Award (outstanding goal): Cristiano Ronaldo, Manchester United v FC Porto
award presented posthumously

2010
Coach of the Year (men): Jose Mourinho (Internazionale, then Real Madrid)
Coach of the Year (women): Silvia Neid (Germany women)
FIFA Ferenc Puskas Award (outstanding goal): Hamit Altintop, Turkey v Kazakhstan
Presidential award: Archbishop Desmond Tutu, South Africa
Fair Play Award: Haiti Under-17 women's team

2011
Coach of the Year (men): Pep Guardiola (Barcelona)
Coach of the Year (women): Norio Sasaki (Japan women)
FIFA Ferenc Puskas Award (outstanding goal): Neymar, Santos v Flamengo
Presidential award: Sir Alex Ferguson, Manchester United
Fair Play award: Japan Football Association

2012
Coach of the Year (men): Vicente Del Bosque (Spain)
Coach of the Year (women): Pia Sundhage (Sweden)
FIFA Ferenc Puskas Award (outstanding goal): Miroslav Stoch, Fenerbahce v Genclerbirligi
Presidential: Franz Beckenbauer (Germany)
Fair Play award: Uzbekistan Football Federation

2013
Coach of the Year (men): Jupp Heynckes (Bayern Munich)
Coach of the Year (women): Silvia Neid (Germany)
FIFA Ferenc Puskas Award (outstanding goal): Zlatan Ibrahimovic, Sweden v England
Presidential: Jacques Rogge (Honorary President, IOC)
Fair Play award: Afghanistan Football Federation

2014
Coach of the Year (men): Joachim Low (Germany)
Coach of the Year (women): Ralf Kellerman (Germany, Wolfsburg)
FIFA Ferenc Puskas Award (outstanding goal): James Rodriguez, Colombia v Uruguay
Presidential: Hiroshi Kagawa (Japanese journalist)
Fair Play Award: FIFA World Cup volunteers

APPENDIX 2: FIFA/COCA-COLA WORLD RANKINGS

Germany were No.1 when FIFA's world rankings system was first calculated and published in December 1992. They returned there in July 2014 after winning the FIFA World Cup in Brazil but were toppled from top spot, a year later, by 2015 Copa America finalists Argentina. Lionel Messi and company held on at the top after finishing runners-up in the both the Copa America, then the 2016 Copa America Centenario. The ranking system provides a monthly statistical insight into the rise and fall of the fortunes of both traditional powers and aspiring minnows. Placings are computed on results in international A games and consider match status, goals scored, strength of opposition and regional balance, all based on games played over a rolling four-year phase.

Argentina may have lost out to Chile in the final of the 2016 Copa America Centenario (on penalties), but they still retained their status as the top-ranked nation in world football.

FIFA MEN'S WORLD RANKINGS 2016

Despite losing to Chile in the final of the Copa America Centenario, Argentina retained their No.1 spot in the FIFA world rankings, while Chile remained at No.5. Newly crowned European champions Portugal rose two places to No.6, but the big climbers from Euro 2016 were runners-up France (up 10 places to No.7) and semi-finalists Wales (up 15 places to No.11). The July 2016 rankings saw no fewer than 31 teams climb by more than 10 positions, including Venezuela (46th, up 31), Guinea-Bissau (75th, up 40), Kenya (86th, up 43), New Zealand (93rd, up 54) and Puerto Rico (112th, up 46).

Dimitri Payet scored three times for France at Euro 2016. The hosts had to settle for the runners-up spot, but still rose 10 places (to 7th) in the FIFA World Rankings.

RANKINGS (as at July 2016)

Pos.	Country	Pts	(+/-)
1	Argentina	1585	(-)
2	Belgium	1401	(-)
3	Colombia	1331	(-)
4	Germany	1319	(-)
5	Chile	1316	(-)
6	Portugal	1266	(+2)
7	France	1189	(+10)
8	Spain	1165	(-2)
9	Brazil	1156	(-2)
10	Italy	1155	(+2)
11	Wales	1137	(+15)
12	Uruguay	1130	(-3)
13	England	1107	(-2)
14	Mexico	1044	(+2)
15	Croatia	1022	(+12)
16	Poland	1011	(+11)
17	Ecuador	1002	(-4)
18	Switzerland	957	(-3)
19	Turkey	915	(-1)
19	Hungary	915	(+1)
21	Austria	875	(-11)
22	Iceland	871	(+12)
23	Slovakia	867	(+1)
24	Romania	856	(-2)
25	USA	855	(+6)
26	Netherlands	848	(-12)
27	Costa Rica	840	(-4)
28	Northern Ireland	822	(-3)
29	Bosnia and Herzegovina	813	(-9)
30	Ukraine	801	(-11)
31	Republic of Ireland	800	(+2)
32	Algeria	781	(-)
33	Czech Republic	768	(-3)
34	Peru	765	(+14)
35	Côte d'Ivoire	751	(+1)
36	Ghana	749	(+1)
37	Albania	739	(+5)
38	Russia	728	(-9)
39	Iran	674	(-)
40	Sweden	656	(-5)
41	Senegal	651	(-)
42	Paraguay	636	(+2)
43	Egypt	632	(+2)
44	Denmark	630	(-6)
45	Tunisia	627	(+2)
46	Venezuela	621	(+31)
47	Serbia	612	(+7)
48	Korea Republic	592	(+2)
49	Norway	588	(+2)
50	Scotland	584	(-7)
51	Panama	580	(+5)
52	Greece	579	(-12)
53	Cameroon	575	(+5)
54	Morocco	574	(+8)
55	Jamaica	573	(-9)
56	Uzbekistan	569	(+10)
57	Japan	564	(-4)
58	Trinidad and Tobago	558	(+6)
59	Australia	555	(-)
59	Congo DR	555	(-7)
61	Mali	546	(+2)
62	Cape Verde Islands	545	(-13)
63	Guinea	544	(-8)
64	Slovenia	542	(-7)
65	Saudi Arabia	540	(-)
65	Finland	540	(+2)
67	South Africa	530	(+1)
68	Benin	525	(+7)
69	Uganda	522	(+3)
70	Congo	514	(-10)
70	Nigeria	514	(-9)
72	Belarus	507	(+6)
73	Burkina Faso	487	(-)
74	United Arab Emirates	484	(-4)
75	Guinea-Bissau	482	(+40)
76	Israel	471	(-5)
77	Bulgaria	446	(-8)
78	Jordan	438	(+2)
79	Qatar	425	(+5)
80	St. Kitts and Nevis	423	(+12)
81	China PR	422	(-)
82	Honduras	398	(+4)
83	Antigua and Barbuda	393	(-)
84	Equatorial Guinea	389	(-8)
85	Cyprus	387	(-1)
86	Central African Republic	386	(+10)
86	Kenya	386	(+43)
88	Zambia	385	(-9)
89	Botswana	378	(-2)
90	Sierra Leone	376	(+18)
90	Guatemala	376	(+1)
92	Liberia	370	(+31)
93	Libya	366	(+29)
93	New Zealand	366	(+54)
95	Montenegro	365	(-5)
96	Mozambique	362	(+1)
97	Kazakhstan	359	(+15)
98	Gabon	355	(-10)
99	Iraq	354	(+3)
100	Canada	350	(-7)
100	Haiti	350	(-26)
102	Armenia	348	(+8)
103	Swaziland	344	(+14)
104	Syria	341	(-3)
104	Kyrgyzstan	341	(+7)
106	Nicaragua	340	(-1)
106	Oman	340	(-6)
108	Togo	339	(-13)

Chris Coleman has masterminded Wales' staggering rise in recent times, leading the Welsh to the semi-finals at Euro 2016 and up to 11th place in the FIFA World Rankings.

109	Bolivia	338	(-27)	145	Tajikistan	220	(+19)	180	Cambodia	95	(+4)
109	Latvia	338	(-5)	146	Luxembourg	219	(-)	181	Solomon Islands	92	(-5)
111	Rwanda	334	(-8)	147	Aruba	216	(-4)	182	Liechtenstein	88	(-14)
112	Zimbabwe	332	(+3)	148	Hong Kong	213	(-5)	183	Chinese Taipei	85	(+8)
112	Puerto Rico	332	(+46)	149	Lebanon	208	(+2)	183	Bangladesh	85	(-2)
114	Chad	326	(-8)	150	Afghanistan	206	(+6)	185	Timor-Leste	84	(-8)
114	Palestine	326	(-1)	151	Lesotho	204	(+4)	185	Seychelles	84	(-5)
116	Estonia	323	(-22)	152	India	200	(+11)	187	Fiji	82	(-1)
117	Korea DPR	320	(-19)	153	South Sudan	197	(+4)	188	Bermuda	77	(-21)
118	Georgia	318	(+19)	153	São Tomé e Príncipe	197	(-1)	188	Nepal	77	(-6)
119	Mauritania	317	(+2)	155	Comoros	191	(+7)	190	Kosovo	66	(-)
120	Turkmenistan	312	(+14)	156	Barbados	182	(-16)	191	Indonesia	65	(-4)
121	Cuba	305	(+5)	156	St Vincent and the Grenadines	182	(-8)	192	Bhutan	64	(-4)
121	Thailand	305	(-4)					193	Sri Lanka	58	(-4)
123	Tanzania	300	(+13)	158	Singapore	175	(-9)	194	Pakistan	54	(-2)
124	Namibia	298	(+11)	159	Grenada	171	(-9)	195	Macau	50	(+1)
125	El Salvador	297	(-26)	160	Myanmar	167	(+1)	196	US Virgin Islands	44	(-2)
125	Burundi	297	(+7)	161	New Caledonia	162	(+22)	196	Montserrat	44	(-2)
127	Lithuania	293	(-)	162	Yemen	160	(+16)	198	Brunei Darussalam	33	(-1)
128	Bahrain	289	(+2)	163	Gambia	154	(+2)	199	Cayman Islands	21	(-)
129	Guyana	280	(+1)	164	Papua New Guinea	152	(+29)	200	San Marino	20	(-)
130	Niger	277	(-13)	164	Belize	152	(-50)	200	Turks and Caicos Islands	20	(-2)
131	Madagascar	273	(-23)	166	Moldova	151	(-7)	202	Mongolia	13	(+1)
132	Ethiopia	270	(-7)	167	Malaysia	149	(+6)	203	Andorra	12	(-1)
133	Malawi	269	(-26)	168	American Samoa	128	(-)	204	British Virgin Islands	11	(-3)
134	Curaçao	261	(+20)	168	Cook Islands	128	(-)	205	Anguilla	0	(-1)
135	Philippines	256	(-15)	170	Suriname	123	(+20)	205	Bahamas	0	(-1)
136	Faroe Islands	254	(-47)	171	St Lucia	121	(-26)	205	Djibouti	0	(-1)
137	Azerbaijan	253	(+1)	172	Guam	120	(-12)	205	Eritrea	0	(-1)
137	Angola	253	(-14)	173	Dominica	117	(-1)	205	Somalia	0	(-1)
139	Dominican Republic	243	(+14)	174	Maldives	115	(-)	205	Tonga	0	(-1)
139	FYR Macedonia	243	(-)	175	Tahiti	114	(+4)				
139	Vietnam	243	(-6)	176	Malta	109	(-10)				
142	Sudan	229	(-14)	177	Laos	107	(-3)				
142	Mauritius	229	(-)	178	Samoa	106	(-10)				
144	Kuwait	223	(-3)	179	Vanuatu	103	(+6)				

FIFA WOMEN'S WORLD RANKINGS 2016

The latest FIFA Women's World Rankings, released in July 2016, revealed no changes in the top 10, with 2015 Women's FIFA World Cup winners United States retaining top spot, followed by Germany, France, England and Australia. The most notable movement was that of Bulgaria, which rose 68 places to 69th. Argentina and Guam were among 48 nations which had not played a match in the previous 18 months and, as a result, were considered inactive and thus no longer ranked. These countries' points totals were the last ones before they became unranked.

United States co-captain **Becky Sauerbrunn** helped her team to remain at the top of the FIFA World Rankings in 2015 following their success in the FIFA Women's World Cup.

RANKINGS (as at July 2016)

Pos.	Country	Pts	(+/-)
1	USA	2168	(-)
2	Germany	2115	(-)
3	France	2064	(-)
4	England	2021	(-)
5	Australia	2011	(-)
6	Sweden	2002	(-)
7	Japan	1991	(-)
8	Brazil	1982	(-)
9	Korea DPR	1952	(-)
10	Canada	1938	(-)
11	Norway	1923	(-)
12	China PR	1914	(-)
13	Netherlands	1902	(-)
14	Spain	1861	(+1)
15	Switzerland	1850	(+4)
16	Iceland	1849	(+4)
17	New Zealand	1848	(-1)
18	Italy	1847	(-4)
19	Korea Republic	1843	(-2)
20	Denmark	1838	(-2)
21	Scotland	1778	(-)
22	Russia	1762	(-)
23	Ukraine	1756	(-)
24	Colombia	1748	(-)
25	Austria	1747	(-)
26	Belgium	1737	(+2)
27	Mexico	1732	(-1)
28	Finland	1726	(-1)
29	Costa Rica	1658	(+1)
30	Thailand	1643	(+2)
31	Republic of Ireland	1639	(+2)
32	Czech Republic	1638	(-1)
33	Poland	1636	(-4)
34	Vietnam	1620	(+1)
35	Wales	1607	(+1)
36	Romania	1593	(+3)
37	Nigeria	1592	(-)
38	Chinese Taipei	1590	(-)
39	Hungary	1566	(+1)
40	Portugal	1565	(+1)
41	Slovakia	1541	(+2)
42	Uzbekistan	1540	(-)
43	Serbia	1529	(+2)
44	Myanmar	1527	(-)
45	Trinidad and Tobago	1494	(+2)
46	Ghana	1487	(+2)
47	Cameroon	1484	(-1)
48	Papua New Guinea	1473	(+1)
49	Belarus	1456	(+1)
50	Ecuador	1451	(+2)
51	Equatorial Guinea	1446	(-)
52	South Africa	1442	(+2)
53	Croatia	1427	(-)
54	Jordan	1423	(+1)
55	Iran	1418	(+2)
56	Israel	1414	(-1)
57	India	1412	(+1)
58	Turkey	1409	(+2)
59	Slovenia	1405	(-)
60	Bosnia and Herzegovina	1404	(+2)
61	Northern Ireland	1388	(+1)
62	Côte d'Ivoire	1386	(-2)
63	Greece	1378	(+2)
63	Venezuela	1378	(+1)
65	Haiti	1372	(+1)
66	Kazakhstan	1355	(+1)
67	Jamaica	1352	(+1)
68	Hong Kong	1347	(+1)
69	Bulgaria	1344	(+68)
70	Indonesia	1321	(+2)
71	Tunisia	1313	(-)
72	Philippines	1312	(+1)
73	United Arab Emirates	1309	(-3)
74	Morocco	1299	(+1)
75	Guatemala	1297	(+2)
76	Fiji	1292	(+2)
76	Albania	1292	(-)
78	Bahrain	1288	(+1)
79	Egypt	1287	(+4)
80	Faroe Islands	1286	(+2)
81	Algeria	1283	(-7)
82	Guyana	1274	(+2)
83	Laos	1273	(+2)
83	Estonia	1273	(-3)
85	Malaysia	1260	(+1)
86	Tonga	1258	(+1)
87	New Caledonia	1252	(+1)
88	Senegal	1248	(+1)
89	Lithuania	1226	(+2)
90	Montenegro	1225	(-1)
91	Mali	1222	(+2)
92	Cuba	1217	(-)
93	Zimbabwe	1208	(+2)
94	Congo	1206	(-)
95	Palestine	1192	(+1)
96	Dominican Republic	1191	(+1)
97	El Salvador	1188	(+1)
98	Cook Islands	1185	(+1)
99	Moldova	1174	(+1)
100	Latvia	1171	(+1)

Defender **Saskia Bartusiak** has been an integral part of the Germany side since 2007. She took over the captaincy of the world's second-ranked team in 2015.

100	Malta	1171	(+1)
102	Singapore	1166	(+1)
103	Puerto Rico	1156	(+1)
104	Ethiopia	1155	(+1)
105	Solomon Islands	1144	(+1)
106	Georgia	1141	(+4)
107	Samoa	1138	(-)
108	Luxembourg	1134	(-)
108	Kyrgyzstan	1134	(-)
110	Cyprus	1124	(+1)
111	Nepal	1120	(+1)
112	Nicaragua	1083	(+1)
113	Guinea	1077	(+1)
114	FYR Macedonia	1069	(-)
115	Burkina Faso	1060	(+1)
116	Gabon	1052	(+1)
117	Namibia	1026	(+2)
118	Zambia	1021	(-)
119	St. Lucia	989	(+1)
120	Bangladesh	987	(+1)
121	Sri Lanka	978	(+1)
122	Lebanon	949	(+1)
123	Maldives	948	(+1)
124	Tanzania	947	(+1)
125	St Kitts and Nevis	942	(+1)
126	Grenada	914	(+2)
127	Dominica	900	(+2)
128	Malawi	838	(+3)
129	Swaziland	836	(+3)
130	Kenya	822	(+3)
131	Aruba	745	(+4)
132	Botswana	732	(+4)

Argentina *	1621	(-99)
Chile *	1559	(+4)
Paraguay *	1459	(+4)
Peru *	1412	(+4)
Panama *	1363	(+4)
Uruguay *	1361	(+4)
Azerbaijan *	1341	(+4)
Guam *	1287	(-53)
Tahiti *	1238	(+4)
Bolivia *	1217	(+4)
Benin *	1187	(+4)
Suriname *	1152	(+4)
Honduras *	1152	(+4)
Vanuatu *	1139	(+4)
Angola *	1134	(+4)
Congo DR *	1132	(+4)
Sierra Leone *	1132	(+4)
Armenia *	1104	(+4)
American Samoa *	1075	(+4)
Eritrea *	1060	(+4)
St Vincent and the Grenadines *	1000	(+4)
Rwanda *	996	(+4)
Barbados *	979	(+4)
Uganda *	965	(+4)
Bermuda *	943	(+4)
Syria *	927	(+4)
Guinea-Bissau *	927	(+4)
Pakistan *	926	(-6)
Macau *	922	(+4)
Afghanistan *	889	(-3)
Libya *	883	(+4)
Iraq *	882	(+4)
Liberia *	877	(+4)

Mozambique *	873	(+4)
Kuwait *	870	(+4)
British Virgin Islands *	867	(+4)
Qatar *	864	(+4)
US Virgin Islands *	852	(+4)
Cayman Islands *	849	(+4)
Lesotho *	836	(+4)
Curaçao *	831	(+4)
Belize *	825	(+4)
Bhutan *	778	(+1)
Antigua and Barbuda *	767	(+4)
Andorra *	763	(+4)
Comoros *	761	(+4)
Madagascar *	714	(+4)
Turks and Caicos Islands *	704	(+4)
Mauritius **	335	(+4)

* Inactive for more than 18 months and therefore not ranked.

** Provisionally listed, but not ranked as they have not played more than five matches against officially ranked teams.

INDEX

PICTURE CREDITS

The publishers would like to thank the following sources for their kind permission to reproduce the pictures in this book. The page numbers for each of the photographs are listed below, giving the page on which they appear in the book and any location indicator (C-centre, T-top, B-bottom, L-left, R-right).

Getty Images: 159TL; /2010 Qatar 2022: 182R; /AFP: 53C, 108B, 117TL, 117BL, 127B, 161BR, 169L, 194BR, 206BL, 208L; /Suhaimi Abdullah: 133R; /Luis Acosta/AFP: 18BR; /Nelson Almeida/AFP: 183L; /Anadolu Agency: 100BL, 176BL; /Odd Andersen/AFP: 33R, 166TR; /Rodrigo Arangua/AFP: 110TR, 112TR, 156TL; /The Asashi Shimbun: 174C; /Matthew Ashton/Corbis: 95BL, 151TL; /Evren Atalay/Anadolu Agency: 249TL; /Anthony Au-Yeung/LatinContent: 154TL; /Brian Bahr: 148BR; /Scott Barbour: 130BL; /Steve Bardens: 40L; /Dennis Barnard/Fox Photos: 105TL; /Lars Baron: 28TL, 58BL, 105B, 152-153, 188-189, 193BL, 226BR, 231BR, 236BR; /Michel Barrault/Michel Piquemal/Onze/Icon Sport: 78B; /Juan Barreto/AFP: 114T; /Farouk Batiche/AFP: 122TL, 159B; /Robyn Beck/AFP: 179TR; /Sandra Behne/Bongarts: 134BL; /Fethi Belaid/AFP: 121BR, 213BR, 215R; /Bentley Archive/Popperfoto: 76C, 77BL, 167BR; /Gunnar Berning/Bongarts: 175BL; /Manuel Blondeau/Icon Sport: 193T; /Lionel Bonaventure/AFP: 4-5B; /Bongarts: 36L, 165BL; /Shaun Botterill: 20T, 59BL, 126TR, 176C, 178BR, 185TR, 186R, 196BR; /Cris Bouroncle/AFP: 220T; /Gabriel Bouys/AFP: 42TR, 42B; /Chris Brunskill: 16BL, 89BR, 96C, 160TC, 164TR, 168BR, 246-247; /Clive Brunskill: 111R; /Simon Bruty: 17TR, 114BR; /Rodrigo Buendia/AFP: 101BL; /Martin Bureau/AFP: 199; /Eric Cabanis/AFP: 156R; /Jose Cabezas/AFP: 154TR; /Giuseppe Cacace/AFP: 35T, 183B; /David Cannon: 18L, 39R, 53BR, 72BR, 104TR; /Jean Catuffe: 19BR, 47TL, 125B, 160TR, 170BL; /Central Press: 75BL; /Central Press/Hulton Archive: 60BR; /Andre Chaco/FotoArena/LatinContent: 181BL; /Graham Chadwick: 72TR; /Stanley Chou: 239L; /Steve Christo/Corbis: 140BR; /Chung Sung-Jun: 135TR, 159TR; /Robert Cianflone: 79T, 81L; /Shaun Clark: 5T; /Timothy A Clary/AFP: 151BR; /Tim Clayton/Corbis: 5B, 200-201; /Thomas Coex/AFP: 163R; /Fabrice Coffrini/AFP: 31R, 52TR, 59T, 154BR, 174BL, 178BL, 240-241; /Chris Cole: 107BR, 176TR; /Phil Cole: 55BR, 84C, 146BL; /Vinicius Costa: 120TR; /Charlie Crowhurst: 150L; /Jonathan Daniel: 102R; /Anesh Debiky/Gallo Images: 217TL; /Stephane de Sakutin/AFP: 185L; /Carl de Souza/AFP: 118-119, 171TR, 210-211; /Adrian Dennis/AFP: 175TR, 196TR; /Philippe Desmazes/AFP: 184TR; /Khaled Desouki/AFP: 215TL, 215BL, 217C; /Dimitar Dilkoff/AFP: 50B; /Kevork Djansezian: 149C; /Denis Doyle: 43BR, 46L; /Stephen Dunn: 124BR; /Josh Edelson/AFP: 144-145; /Paul Ellis/AFP: 27C; /Don Emmert/AFP: 203BL; /Darren England: 156BL, 156BR; /Francisco Estrada/LatinContent: 136BR; /Evening Standard: 132; /Jonathan Ferrey: 55TR; /Franck Fife/AFP: 21BR, 23TR, 123TR, 198TR, 212TC, 232-233; /Julian Finney: 35BL, 49TR, 114L; /Stu Forster: 90BL, 91BL, 103TL, 181TR, 249TR; /Foto Olimpik/NurPhoto: 4-5T, 69BR, 193BR; /Stuart Franklin: 59R, 172TL, 242BR, 243TL, 245; /Romeo Gacad/AFP: 56C; /Lluis Gene/AFP: 37TR; /Paul Gilham: 7, 43TR, 93BR, 126C; /Georges Gobet/AFP: 57BR; /Alex Goodlett/LatinContent: 113T; /Sergio Goya/AFP: 204C; /Mark Graham/AFP: 136L; /Otto Greule Jr: 148TR; /Laurence Griffiths: 8-9, 29TL, 34B, 54L, 74TR, 77C, 162T, 168L, 192TR; /Alex Grimm: 47BR, 67TR, 222C, 223R, 238BR; /Jeff Gross: 47BL, 134TR, 150BR; /Gianluigi Guercia/AFP: 186BL, 214B; /Jack Guez/AFP: 158BR; /Valery Hache/AFP: 66L, 120C, 175C; /Norman Hall/LatinContent: 209BR; /Matthias Hangst: 192L; /Ronny Hartmann/AFP: 86TR, 190B; /Ferdi Hartung/ullstein bild: 29BL; /Alexander Hassenstein: 4C, 26T; /Alexander Hassenstein/Bongarts: 22TR, 29R, 190T; /Haynes Archive/Popperfoto: 61BR, 158TR, 205BL; /Richard Heathcote: 125R; /Scott Heavey: 89C, 91T; /Alexander Heimann/Bongarts: 151BL; /Thearon W Henderson: 5C; /Patrick Hertzog/AFP: 41BR, 88TR; /Mike Hewitt: 16L, 22R, 63BR, 66B, 91BR, 109BL, 112B, 226L, 229L, 236TL, 243BR, 244; /Hagen Hopkins: 142TR; /Boris Horvat/AFP: 38BL, 197T; /Harry How: 147L; /Hulton Archive: 166BL, 174BR; /isifa: 81BR; /Catherine Ivill: 19TR; /Karim Jaafar/AFP: 134L, 141TR; /Alain Jocard/AFP: 10-11; /Jose Jordan/AFP: 46BR; /Jasper Juinen: 14C, 44C, 45TL; /Gorm Kallestad/AFP: 64L; /Nicholas Kamm/AFP: 98-99, 115T, 203T; /Cuneyt Karadag/Anadolu Agency: 71C; /Keystone: 18TR, 60BL, 75BR; /Keystone/Hulton Archive: 31BL, 45BL, 69BL; /Saeed Khan/AFP: 137R, 154BL; /Rob Kim: 143BR; /Ian Kington/AFP: 16TR; /Ross Kinnaird: 170TR; /Pedro Kirilos/LatinContent: 185R; /Glyn Kirk/AFP: 229BR; /Attila Kisbenedek/AFP: 60L; /Toshifumi Kitamura/AFP: 157C, 226TR; /Joe Klamar/AFP: 55L, 65TR; /Christof Koepsel: 225C; /Mark Kolbe: 128-129, 131TL, 131C; /Patrick Kovarik/AFP: 95C; /Kirill Kudryavtsev/AFP: 74B, 185B; /Lukasz Laskowski/PressFocus/MB Media: 23BR; /Nolwenn Le Gouic/Icon Sport: 63C, 86L; /David Leah: 173TL; /David Leah/Mexsport: 146TR; /Christopher Lee: 80TR; /Bryn Lennon: 70TR; /Francisco Leong/AFP: 24TR, 75C; /Matthew Lewis: 66TR, 169B; /Alex Livesey: 56TR, 63TR, 83TL, 85C, 90C, 137BR, 155TR, 167R, 221BR, 224L; /Juan Mabromata/AFP: 111TL; /Ian MacNicol: 57TL, 71BL, 191BR; /Pierre-Philippe Marcou/AFP: 44TL, 124TL, 168TR; /Francois-Xavier Marit/AFP: 179TL; /Clive Mason: 26L, 87BL, 117TR, 125TL, 163BL; /Masterpress: 218-219; /Jamie McDonald: 38T, 54BR, 60TR, 70C, 82TR, 103B, 140TL, 187, 223BL; /Chris McGrath: 101TR; /Marty Melville/AFP: 143T; /Alex Menendez/LatinContent: 106BL; /Craig Mercer/CameraSport: 49BR; /Philippe Merle/AFP: 117R; /Aris Messinis/AFP: 196L; /Daniel Mihailescu/AFP: 73B; /Douglas Miller/Keystone: 12BL; /Jason Miller: 251TL; /Teaukura Moetaua: 143L; /Sandra Montanez: 237T; /Dean Mouhtaropoulos: 4T, 44B, 52BL, 131TR, 165TR; /Peter Muhly/AFP: 70BR, 94B, 191L; /Dan Mullan: 68B; /Hoang Dinh Nam/AFP: 138BL, 148C; /Mark Nolan: 131BR; /Adam Nurkiewicz: 20B; /Kiyoshi Ota: 133BL; /Cem Ozdel/Anadolu Agency: 105TR; /Jeff Pachoud/AFP: 195C; /Doug Pensinger: 14BR; /Christian Petersen: 202BR; /Ryan Pierse: 92BL, 172B; /Jan Pitman/Bongarts: 180TR; /Hrvoje Polan/AFP: 50C, 52C; /Joern Pollex: 28R, 123C; /Popperfoto: 13C, 15TL, 25L, 26BR, 28BL, 31C, 51BR, 62BL, 72C, 82C, 108L, 111BL, 127L, 135L, 138R, 139T, 141B, 149BL, 157BR, 165BR, 167L, 172C, 194BL, 198B, 207BL, 208BR, 228BL; /Mike Powell: 182L; /Savo Prelevic/AFP: 97B; /Craig Prentis: 147TR; /Adam Pretty: 107TR; /Gary M Prior: 108TR; /Manuel Queimadelos Alonso: 242TL; /Ben Radford: 109C, 133T, 173BR; /Aizar Raldes/AFP: 116TL; /Michael Regan: 12TR, 13T, 13BR, 88B; /Kyle Rivas: 149TR; /Rafa Rivas/AFP: 45R; /Miguel Rojo/AFP: 102TL; /Rolls Press/Popperfoto: 15B, 33B, 106TR; /Quinn Rooney: 239BC; /Clive Rose: 79BL, 89BL, 104BL, 147BR, 161TR, 166TL, 177BL, 178TL, 180BL; /Martin Rose: 21C, 25TR; /Martin Rose/Bongarts: 87TR, 92BR; /Mark Runnacles: 76L; /STR/AFP: 136TR; /Jewel Samad/AFP: 69TR; /Issouf Sanogo/AFP: 122BL, 126L, 127TR; /Genia Savilov/AFP: 67L; /Philipp Schmidli: 230L; /Roberto Schmidt/AFP: 162BL; /Rich Schultz: 209TL; /Antonio Scorza/AFP: 113BL; /Abdelhak Senna/AFP: 216, 217BR; /Lefty Shivambu/Gallo Images: 212TR, 215C; /Raul Sifuentes/LatinContent: 115BR; /Torsten Silz/AFP: 169TR; /Javier Soriano/AFP: 161L, 195B, 197BR; /Jamie Squire: 120BR, 121TL; /Michael Steele: 51T, 82BL, 97TR, 178TR; /Srdjan Stevanovic: 79R, 251TR; /Graham Stuart/AFP: 76TR; /Chris Szagola/LatinContent: 207TR; /Henri Szwarc/Bongarts: 33TL; /Trond Tandberg: 65BL; /Bob Thomas: 27R, 30TR, 32TL, 32BL, 32BR, 37B, 38BR, 48TR, 57R, 62TR, 63BL, 67BR, 68TR, 70BL, 75TL, 83C, 90TR, 90BR, 92C, 102BR, 103C, 104BR, 109TR, 110BL, 113BR, 121TR, 135BR, 180C, 184B, 186BR, 191TR; /Bob Thomas/Popperfoto: 46TR, 96BL, 155B; /Mark Thompson: 64TR, 212BR; /John Thys/AFP: 95R; /Miguel Tovar/LatinContent: 116B; /Pedro Ugarte/AFP: 171BR; /ullstein bild: 61TR, 78C; /Pius Utomi Ekpei/AFP: 213TR; /VCG: 227; /VI Images: 24B, 37TL, 40B, 41T, 74C; /Robert van den Brugge/AFP: 48BL; /Manus van Dyk/Gallo Images: 214L; /Claudio Villa: 96BR; /Claudio Villa/Grazia Neri: 34TR; /Hector Vivas/LatinContent: 202L, 203BR; /Friedemann Vogel: 87BR, 234C; /Ian Walton: 14TL, 39BL, 81TR, 150TR; /Lakruwan Wanniarachchi/AFP: 139B; /Koji Watanabe: 228TR; /Dave Winter/Icon Sport: 4B, 54T; /Mustafa Yalcin/Anadolu Agency: 2

PA Images: 78TR, 206BR, 229TR; /ABACA Press: 163TL; /AP: 164BL; /Matthew Ashton: 39TL, 107C, 130C, 142B; /Greg Baker/AP: 235BL; /Jon Buckle: 237BR; /Roberto Candia/AP: 235TL; /Barry Coombs: 58TR; /Malcolm Croft: 157TL; /Claudio Cruz/AP: 224C; /DPA: 22L, 27TL, 130TR, 160BL; /Adam Davy: 234B; /Sean Dempsey: 25BR; /Paulo Duarte/AP: 68C; /Denis Farrell/AP: 182B; /Dominic Favre/AP: 84B; /Gouhier-Hahn-Orban/ABACA: 84TR; /Michel Gouverneur/Reporter: 222BL; /Intime Sports/AP: 58C; /Julie Jacobson/AP: 239BR; /Lee Jin-Man/AP: 236TR; /Ross Kinnaird: 207C; /Tony Marshall: 34L, 86B, 106TL, 165TL, 205TR, 221TL, 224TR, 225TR, 230TR; /Cathal McNaughton: 12C; /Phil O'Brien: 30BL; /Panoramic: 222R; /Eraldo Peres/AP: 231BL; /Natacha Pisarenko/AP: 208C; /Nick Potts: 19BL; /Peter Robinson: 35BR, 36TR, 62C, 76BR, 80BL, 100L, 177TR, 220BL, 220BR; /S&G and Barratts: 15TR, 17B, 71BR, 174TR; /SMG: 77TR; /Scanpix Norway: 65BR; /Ariel Schalit/AP: 122R; /Murad Sezer/AP: 23C; /Sven Simon: 106BR; /Neal Simpson: 51BL, 73TR, 85BR, 206T; /Michael Sohn/AP: 238TR; /Jon Super/AP: 235TR; /Topham Picturepoint: 83BL, 94TL, 100BR; /John Walton: 93TR, 103TR; /Witters: 179B

Wikimedia Commons: 204BR

Every effort has been made to acknowledge correctly and contact the source and/or copyright holder of each picture and Carlton Books Limited apologises for any unintentional errors or omissions that will be corrected in future editions of this book.

ABOUT THE AUTHOR

Keir Radnedge has been covering football for more than 40 years. He has written countless books on the subject, from tournament guides to comprehensive encyclopedias, aimed at all ages. His journalism career included the *Daily Mail* for 20 years, as well as the *Guardian* and other national newspapers and magazines in the UK and abroad. He is a former editor of *World Soccer*, generally recognized as the premier English-language magazine on global football. In addition to his writing, Keir has been a regular analyst for BBC radio and television, Sky Sports and the American cable news channel CNN. He also edited a tournament newspaper at the FIFA World Cup tournaments of 1982, 1986 and 1990. He has also scripted video reviews of numerous international football tournaments. He is also the London-based editor of SportsFeatures.com, the football and Olympic news website.

ACKNOWLEDGEMENTS

Special thanks to Aidan Radnedge for support and assistance and an incomparable insight into the most intriguing corners of the world game.